PRE-ISLAMIC

This book delves into the political and cultural developments of pre-Islamic Arabia, focusing on the religious attitudes of the inhabitants of the Arabian Peninsula and its northern extension into the Syrian desert. Between the third and the seventh century, Arabia was on the edge of three great empires (Iran, Rome and Aksūm) and at the centre of a lucrative network of trade routes. Valentina A. Grasso offers an interpretative framework which contextualizes the choice of Arabian elites to become Jewish sympathisers and/or convert to Christianity and Islam by probing the mobilization of faith in the shaping of Arabian identities. For the first time the Arabians of the period are granted autonomy from marginalizing (mostly Western) narratives framing them as 'barbarians' inhabiting the fringes of Rome and Iran and/or deterministic analyses in which they are depicted retrospectively as exemplified by the Muslims' definition of the period as *Jāhilīyah,* 'ignorance'.

VALENTINA A. GRASSO is an Assistant Professor at the Catholic University of America. She was previously Visiting Assistant Professor at New York University's Institute for the Study of the Ancient World, and an affiliate member of the ERC project 'The Qur'an as a Source for Late Antiquity'.

PRE-ISLAMIC ARABIA

Societies, Politics, Cults and Identities during Late Antiquity

VALENTINA A. GRASSO

The Catholic University of America

CAMBRIDGE
UNIVERSITY PRESS

CAMBRIDGE
UNIVERSITY PRESS

Shaftesbury Road, Cambridge CB2 8EA, United Kingdom

One Liberty Plaza, 20th Floor, New York, NY 10006, USA

477 Williamstown Road, Port Melbourne, VIC 3207, Australia

314–321, 3rd Floor, Plot 3, Splendor Forum, Jasola District Centre, New Delhi – 110025, India

103 Penang Road, #05–06/07, Visioncrest Commercial, Singapore 238467

Cambridge University Press is part of Cambridge University Press & Assessment, a department of the University of Cambridge.

We share the University's mission to contribute to society through the pursuit of education, learning and research at the highest international levels of excellence.

www.cambridge.org
Information on this title: www.cambridge.org/9781009253000

DOI: 10.1017/9781009252997

First published 2023
First paperback edition 2025

A catalogue record for this publication is available from the British Library

Library of Congress Cataloging-in-Publication data
NAMES: Grasso, Valentina A., 1993– author.
TITLE: Pre-islamic Arabia : societies, politics, cults and identities during late antiquity / Valentina A. Grasso, Institute for the Study of the Ancient World, New York University.
DESCRIPTION: Cambridge, United Kingdom ; New York, NY : Cambridge University Press, 2023. | Includes bibliographical references and index.
IDENTIFIERS: LCCN 2022034947 | ISBN 9781009252966 (hardback) | ISBN 9781009252997 (ebook)
SUBJECTS: LCSH: Arabian Peninsula – History – To 622.
CLASSIFICATION: LCC DS231 .G73 2023 | DDC 939.49–dc23/eng/20220726
LC record available at https://lccn.loc.gov/2022034947

ISBN 978-1-009-25296-6 Hardback
ISBN 978-1-009-25300-0 Paperback

In memory of Manuela Russo

Contents

List of Tables *page* viii
Acknowledgements ix
Note on Abbreviations xi

1 An Introduction to the Study of Pre-Islamic Arabia 1

2 North Arabia between the Late Third and the Fifth Century: Borders and Conversions 39

3 A Late Antique Kingdom's Conversion: Jews and Sympathizers in South Arabia 70

4 The Shape of the Sixth Century I: The South 92

5 The Shape of the Sixth Century II: The North 132

6 The Ḥijāzī Islam: Narratives and Frameworks Re-Examined 172

7 Conclusion 208

Appendix 221
Bibliography 225
Index 264

Tables

1.1 ʿ*rb(n)* and ʾʿ*rb* in South Arabian inscriptions *page* 32
A.1 Mention of the ʿ*rb*/ʿ*rbn* 221
A.2 Mention of the ʾʿ*rb* 222
A.3 The South Arabian rulers' titles (375–565) 223
A.4 Joint Epigraphic attestation of ʿ*rb* and ʾʿ*rb* 224
A.5 The Jafnids' epigraphic corpus 224

Acknowledgements

Firstly, I would like to thank my PhD supervisor, Garth Fowden, whose expertise was invaluable in writing this work and sharpening my thinking. I am forever indebted to you for your patient support and advice and for all the opportunities I was given to further my research. You epitomize the kind of scholar I hope to become in the years to come. I would also like to thank Elizabeth Fowden for her encouragement and support during my PhD, and all the people involved in the Cambridge Late Antique and Medieval Middle East Seminar for our stimulating discussions. I would like to single out Andrew Marsham for his comments on my first-year examination report, *Journal of Late Antiquity* article and dissertation, and Ralph Lee for introducing me to Gəʿəz. My last 'Cambridge acknowledgement' goes to the Arts and Humanities Research Council, the Cambridge Trust, the Faculty of Divinity and St Edmund's College Without their funding, this work would not have been possible. During the last year of my Ph.D., I received funding from Duke University as the recipient of the Joseph Shatzmiller Fellowship at the Jewish Studies Seminar. Right before my Ph.D. defense, I also received a generous grant from the American Society of Overseas Research for working for the Southern Red Sea Archaeological Histories Project under the supervision of Michael Harrower. Those were great opportunities that widely enriched my knowledge of the ancient world. During the last four academic years, I have attended or organized fifty conferences and often received funding for attending these gatherings. I would like to express my gratitude to the British Association of Near Eastern Archaeology. The BANEA meeting in 2018 was the first-ever academic conference where I presented a paper, and I was awarded a student bursary from the association to participate in the meeting.

I am incredibly grateful to my BA and MA supervisors, respectively, Marco Moriggi at the University of Catania (the *alma mater* of one of the 'founders' of Late Antiquity, the Sicilian historian Santo Mazzarino) and Roberto Tottoli at the University of Naples 'L'Orientale' for their valuable guidance before my 'PhD journey'. I want to also thank Jack Tannous (Princeton University) for his continual support after meeting in Princeton in 2018 and 2019. During the same stays in Princeton, I had the pleasure to meet Glen Bowersock and Peter Brown, who have been an endless source of inspiration. I would also like to give my special regards to the organizers of the Fourth Hiob Ludolf Centre Summer School in Ethiopian and Eritrean Manuscript Studies (particularly Alessandro Bausi) and all the people who made the Hill Museum & Manuscript Library/Dumbarton Oaks Syriac Program possible. I would also like to acknowledge my colleagues from my excavations in Jordan, Sicily and Iraqi Kurdistan for their outstanding collaboration.

A special thank you also goes to my PhD examiners, Peter Sarris at the University of Cambridge and Prof. Christian Sahner at the University of Oxford, for their thoughtful comments during my viva examination in early June 2021. Similarly, I would like to thank the two anonymous reviewers and editors of Cambridge University Press (in particular Michael Sharp) who were enthusiastic about this manuscript and to whom I am grateful for their concise and precious comments. Several conversations at the Institute for the Study of the Ancient World (and especially during the "Indian Ocean Figures that Sailed Away" seminar, in the process of becoming an edited volume co-edited with Divya Kumar-Dumas) and with the members of the European Research Council project QaSLA, 'The Qur'an as a Source for Late Antiquity', have profoundly impacted my research, and I am looking forward to making use of our stimulating discussions in my next monograph.

Finally, I would like to express my deepest gratitude to my family (in all its extended forms) and my two oldest-standing friends, Alexa Richetti and Roberto Catra. Our jamming sessions of post-punk music and shopping for Emily the Strange clothing will always be my most cherished memories of our tumultuous teenage years. You were here when I published my Bildungsroman at nineteen, and you are here ten years later, while I am wrapping this book at the ripe old age of twenty-nine (we never thought we'd make it this far!). A massive thank you to my Cambridge friends, in particular Zou Tangsheng (thank you for reading this, I owe you – another – one!), Luis Fernando Rivera, Tom Brady, Dan Fodor, Esteban Garcia, Zuheir bin Zaidon, Gurashish Singh, Arastu Sharma, Andre Cruz, and, last but not least, Manuel Giardino. You are always there for me. I could not have completed this book without the help of Amanda Mary Cooney, who sat down with me to proofread every single word. Last but not least, my gratitude extends to my husband Antonio Patrick D'Amico for our stimulating discussions in Cambridge, the algid Italian Alps and the arid Sicilian seashore during my PhD days pre- and post-pandemic, and later in the surroundings of Yale University and New York University while waiting for this book's publication. You are my *scoglio*.

Note on Abbreviations

All contractions of classical authors are derived from the *Oxford Classical Dictionary*, and all mentioned inscriptions can be found in the bibliography. The footnotes and bibliography follow the *Chicago Manual of Style*. For the transliteration of Arabic and Syriac I used the American Library Association – Library of Congress Romanization Tables. For Gəʿəz I adopted the *Encyclopaedia Aethiopica* translitteration system.

CHAPTER 1

An Introduction to the Study of Pre-Islamic Arabia

1.1 Premise

Pre-Islamic Arabia is a rarely explored subject. Yet first-millennium Arabia is a particularly fertile ground for a historical enquiry into ethnicity, human conflict and the transition from polytheism to monotheism. This book, based on my dissertation submitted for the degree of doctor of philosophy at the University of Cambridge in early April 2021,[1] is the first extended study by a single author on the late antique history of the Arabian Peninsula and its northern extension (the Syrian Desert). A particular focus is on religious attitudes, with a view to shedding light on cultural developments and events between the end of the third and the beginning of the seventh centuries. This was a period of significant change culminating in the rise of Islam. Accordingly, the temporal boundaries of this enquiry are roughly delineated by the epitaph of Imru' al-Qays, one of the earliest and most famous kings 'of the Arabs', dated to 328, and by the death of Muḥammad, prophet of the new Muslim community (*Ummah*), in 632.[2] However, establishing the geographical limits of a region that was never unified by a single political entity is a complex task. Arabia was either fragmented as it is today or incorporated into a broader entity as in Muslim times. The absence of a unified political structure in this region allows for writing the 'history of Arabia' without falling into the anachronistic fallacy of referring to a modern concept such as the 'nation'.[3]

1 Submitted 7 April 2021, defended 4 June 2021, approved 29 July 2021.

2 This book is titled 'Pre-Islamic Arabia' but could have also been titled 'Late Antique Arabia'. I chose the first option and inserted a clarifying 'Late Antiquity' only in the subtitle, as I do not expect all my readers to be familiar with the debated boundaries of Late Antiquity. 'Ancient Arabia' would have sounded too vague, while 'Arabia (300–700 CE)' or 'Arabia (328–632)' would have been too rigid. As this book aims to write the history of the Arabian Peninsula before the rise of Islam, I concluded that a pragmatic and widely accessible title and subtitle would have been the present ones.

3 Discursive constructions such as the 'history of Italy' to refer to the period before the establishment of the modern Italian state in 1861 are indeed problematic.

On the other hand, it becomes necessary to clarify where exactly the Arabian Peninsula 'ends'. Moreover, if Arabia is understood as the 'land of the Arabs', it is also imperative to clearly define this group.

Recent enquiries into the history of pre-Islamic Arabia have adopted the 200 mm/year isohyet (rainfall line) as the northernmost border of the Arabian Peninsula,[4] corresponding to the 'absolute limit of rain-fed agriculture'.[5] Yet this approach is problematic because it does not consider social mobility and dynamic cultural interactions between nomads (dependent on cities for bare subsistence and utensils) and sedentary groups (who relied on nomads for tasks ranging from simple warfare to the escorting of trading goods). Sedentary Arabians supported themselves through agriculture and pastoralism. Yet they were also active traders, as testified by a wide array of inscriptions pointing to a symbiosis between settled populations and nomads in the Ḥawrān in the first four centuries of the first millennium.[6] Michael Macdonald, one of the foremost scholars to adopt the 200 mm/year isohyet as a border,[7] has recently pointed out that 'the traditional antithesis of the "Desert and the Sown" hinders, rather than helps, our understanding'.[8]

Moreover, while it is common to delineate geographical boundaries on the basis of scripts and/or languages, the use of *one language* to define *one space* is also inherently problematic for pre-Islamic Arabia. Scholars have claimed that language provided both a sense of cultural cohesion for Arabs and, at the same time, a feeling of distinction from non-Arabs,[9] and that the pre-Islamic *'rb* were 'people of Arabic language'.[10] There is, however, much uncertainty regarding the extent to which language was a bonding force for the inhabitants of the Arabian Peninsula before the appearance of the Qur'ān, the first Arabic document on parchment. While fewer than twenty inscriptions are universally accepted to be in 'Old Arabic', several

[4] R. G. Hoyland, *Arabia and the Arabs from the Bronze Age to the Coming of Islam* (London: Routledge, 2001), 3.

[5] D. J. Murphy, *People, Plants and Genes: The Story of Crops and Humanity* (Oxford: Oxford University Press, 2007), 27.

[6] M. C. A. Macdonald, 'Romans Go Home? Rome and Other "Outsiders" as Viewed from the Syro-Arabian Desert', in *Inside and Out: Interactions between Rome and the Peoples on the Arabian and Egyptian Frontiers in Late Antiquity*, ed. J. H. F. Dijkstra and G. Fisher (Leuven: Peeters, 2014), 145–64.

[7] G. Fisher (ed.), *Arabs and Empires before Islam* (Oxford: Oxford University Press, 2015).

[8] M. C. A. Macdonald, 'Graffiti and Complexity: Ways-of-Life and Languages in the 343 Hellenistic and Roman Harrah', in *Landscapes of Survival: The Archaeology and Epigraphy of Jordan's North-Eastern Desert and Beyond*, ed. P. M. M. G. Akkermans (Leiden: Brill, 2020), 343–54.

[9] Hoyland, *Arabia and the Arabs*, 230.

[10] C. J. Robin, 'La pénétration des Arabes nomades au Yémen', *Revue du monde musulman et de la méditerranée* 61 (1991), 71–88, at p. 71.

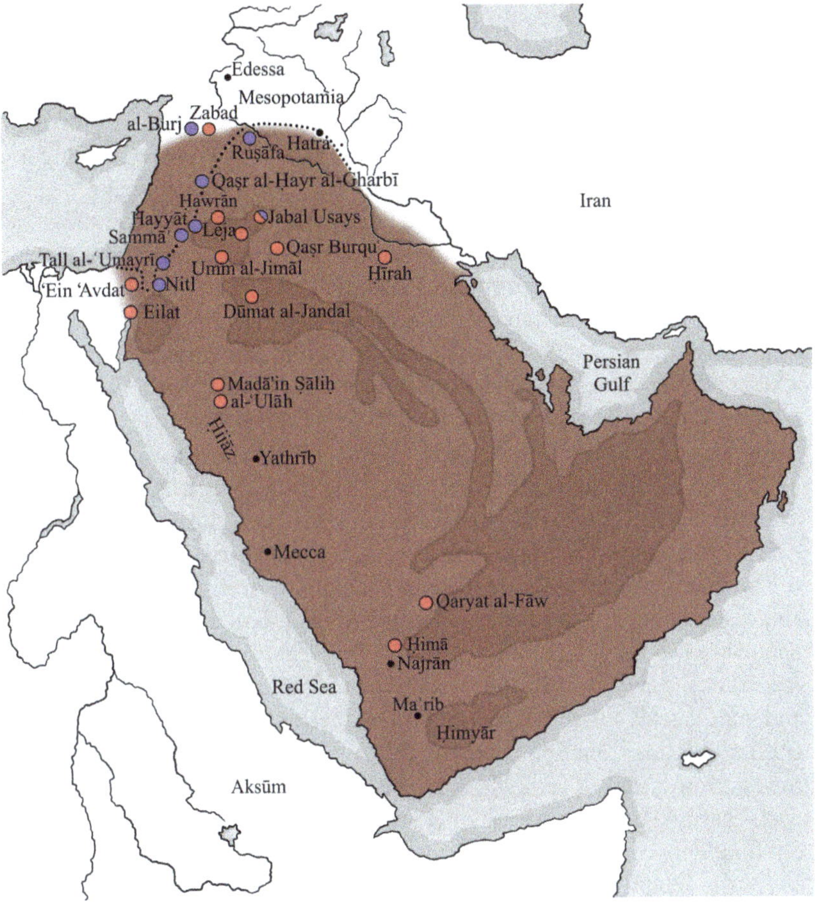

1.1 Map of the Arabian Peninsula.
Grasso and D'Amico (2021). The map was adapted from Hoyland (2001), p. 4 (who adapted his map from Macdonald (2000), p. 39). The dotted line corresponds to the 200 mm (8 inches) of rainfall per year (Hoyland and Macdonald). The red dots mark where Nabateo-Arabic, and Old Arabic inscriptions have been found (Grasso). In contrast, the blue dots correspond to the sites where Jafnid inscriptions have been discovered (Grasso). Several new inscriptions were discovered in the summer of 2021 by the Ṭāʾif-Mecca Epigraphic Survey Project, funded by the King Faisal Center for Research and Islamic Studies. The inscriptions are not featured in this map as they are unpublished at the time of writing this book.

languages and scripts were recorded in the peninsula during pre-Islamic times. Alongside the Ancient North and South Arabian corpora, the 'Nabateo-Arabic' (or 'Transitional') and 'Old Arabic' inscriptions constitute a valuable tool to uncover the history of pre-Islamic Arabia (see Figure 1.1).[11] Although the Nabatean Kingdom, established between Negev and Ḥijāz (the geographical location of modern-day Medina and Mecca), was incorporated into Rome's Arabian Province by Trajan in 106,[12] the evolving Nabatean script continued the Nabateans' legacy, as it spread throughout Arabia and eventually replaced the Ancient North Arabian script.[13]

Whereas recreating the history of the Arabs before the formation of an Arab consciousness and an Arabian unified collectivity has generated anachronistic approaches in the past, the spread throughout the peninsula of Old Arabic lends weight to the notion of the existence of a certain degree of cultural uniformity in the region. The epigraphic fusion of southern and northern Arabian local features (e.g., theonyms) further supports a global vision of pre-Islamic Arabia. The geographical boundaries of this book are thus defined as being both linguistic and political. While we can consider the most southern 'border' to be the Arabian Sea, we can define the northern border as being a linguistic barrier, passing through Zabad (Syria), where the northernmost Old Arabic inscription was found. This area includes the Syrian Desert, as most of the graffiti in Ancient North Arabian was found there. Finally, the western and eastern boundaries correspond to the Arabian borders of the Roman and Sasanian empires and, more precisely, to the *limites* of their Arabian allies' federations, that is, the Tanūkh, Salīḥids and Jafnids for the Roman Empire, and the Naṣrids for the Sasanian Empire.[14] Thus, the western limit of this enquiry is a line stretching from ʿAqaba to Zabad (roughly corresponding to the 200 mm/year isohyet), where all the inscriptions of the Jafnids, the main sixth-century Arabian partners of Rome, were discovered. Likewise, the eastern boundary corresponds to the borders of the Arabian Naṣrids.

At the dawn of Islam, the Arabian Peninsula was fringed with great empires (Iran, Rome and Aksūm) and was at the centre of a lucrative network of trade routes. Therefore, this book aims to pull together all the strands of the composite cultural and political milieu of the region, placing its history in the context of the broader environment of Late Antiquity. Although the

11 L. Nehmé, 'Aramaic or Arabic? The Nabataeo-Arabic Script and the Language of the Inscriptions Written in This Script', in *Arabic in Context*, ed. A. al-Jallad (Leiden: Brill, 2017), 75–98; L. Nehmé, 'A Glimpse of the Development of the Nabatean Script into Arabic Based on Old and New Epigraphic Material', in *The Development of Arabic as a Written Language*, ed. M. C. A. Macdonald (Oxford: Oxford University Press, 2010), 47–88.

12 G. W. Bowersock, 'A Report on Arabia Provincia', *Journal of Roman Studies* 61 (1971), 219–42.

13 For an introduction to Nabatean, see G. Garbini, *Introduzione all'epigrafia* semitica (Brescia: Paideia, 2006), 209.

14 Jafnids and Naṣrids are also respectively known as the tribe of Ghassān/Ghassanids and tribe of Lakhm/Lakhmids. The use of Jafnids and Naṣrids indicates no single tribal units but federations. This use is preferable as it defines the leaders of these groups and not the group itself, which is rarely mentioned in the sources.

kingdoms of South Arabia and Aksūm were transterritorial and multiethnic (or at least composed of one ethnic group dominating over people perceived as 'other'), I use the word 'kingdom' to define these polities as they were made up of several territories and peoples only for a short period during Late Antiquity (i.e., Aksūm's invasion of South Arabia and the following establishment of a satellite polity ca. 530–5, and South Arabia's conquests in Central Arabia ca. 535–65). The use of the word 'empire' requires that 'different peoples within the polity will be governed differently',[15] but we have minimal information to assess how South Arabia and Aksūm dealt with the people they conquered. Moreover, I use the word 'Iran' or 'Sasanian' to refer to the empire of the Sasanians (224–651) and the term 'Rome' to refer to the Roman Empire (both Western and Eastern). The rationale behind this motivation is simple. The lexeme *ērān* is attested as a political entity on the first Sasanian ruler Ardashīr I's investiture relief at Naqsh-e Rostam in Fārs and on his coins.[16] Ardashīr's 'idea of *Ērānšahr*, 'the kingdom of Iran', persisted through time by Shāpūr I (who expanded the rulers' title to 'King of Kings of Iran and Non-Iran'), Narseh and Shāpūr III, who adopted the lexeme.[17] The use of this endonym is preferable to the name of the south-western province of 'Persia' or to the exonym 'Persian', used by Greek historians from the fifth century BCE, while the Achaemenid Empire (550–330 BCE) referred to itself as 'The Empire' (*Khshassa*).[18] The same considerations apply to the use of the word 'Rome'. Anthony Kaldellis has recently demonstrated that the so-called 'Byzantines' considered themselves Roman and called their polity *Romanía*.[19] Scholars have condemned Kaldellis' label of this entity as a 'nation state' instead of an empire, but it remains undeniable that the 'Byzantines' of Late Antiquity defined themselves as Romans.[20] To avoid

15 J. Burbank and F. Cooper, *Empires in World History: Power and the Politics of Difference* (Princeton: Princeton University Press, 2010), 8.

16 The term is also attested in the Avesta but not as a political concept. For the first attestation on Ardashīr's relief see G. Herrmann (ed.), *The Sasanian Rock Reliefs at Naqsh-i Rustam* (Berlin: Reimer, 1989).

17 M. P. Canepa, 'Iran under the Parthian and Sasanian Dynasties', in *The Oxford World History of Empire*, Vol. 2, *The History of Empires*, ed. C. A. Bayly, P. Bang and W. Scheidel (Oxford: Oxford University Press, 2020), 290–324, at p. 296.

18 A. S. Shahbazi, 'The Achamenid Persian Empire (550–330 BCE)', in *The Oxford Handbook of Iranian History*, ed. T. Daryaee (Oxford: Oxford University Press, 2011), 120–41, at p. 131.

19 A. Kaldellis, *Romanland: Ethnicity and Empire in Byzantium* (Cambridge, MA: Harvard University Press, 2019).

20 According to Kaldellis, 'Byzantium sometimes veered close to being a homogeneous national state, with a vast majority of Romans and small ethnic minorities in the provinces (e.g., in 930 ad), whereas at other times, after a phase of conquests, it veered nearer to being a true empire, the hegemony of Romans over many non-Romans (e.g., by 1050)'. See Kaldellis, *Romanland*, xiv. For an opposing view see A. Cameron, 'Bitter Furies of Complexity', *Times Literary Supplement* (20 September 2019), 28–9.

privileging an (often 'external') perspective over another, I use endonyms to refer to the political entities mentioned in this work. The use of 'Aksūm/Aksūmite Empire' is preferred to 'Ethiopia/Ethiopian Empire', as a large portion of ancient Aksūm included Eritrean territories.

As recently highlighted, 'it is an incontestable fact that the suffocating majority of attention falls on the same small part of the world'.[21] The study of geographical areas such as Arabia is still vastly underrepresented in any academic debate concerning medieval history. Any such debate has often become synonymous with the sole study of western Europe. It is imperative to widen the geographic focus of contemporary enquiries in Late Antiquity to understand this period better, counterbalancing the Eurocentric views of the past that have long dominated and shaped our comprehension of the broader medieval world. Such a shift in direction and focus may well be considered challenging and slightly intimidating because of historical reasons and the need for knowledge of somewhat 'obscure' languages from the regions which are the focus of this neglected (geographical) area of study. However, the few steps taken so far in this direction to expand the academic 'common' geographical area of enquiry have dramatically contributed to our understanding of this world. Reflecting on the past of regions that have been pushed into the historical shadows and the interactions of these regions with what was the *oikumene* of past Western scholarship (notoriously centred around Rome) will deepen our understanding of the fluid relations of past and contemporary societies. As stated by Robert Hoyland in his discussion of early Islam, the problem 'is not so much lack of the right materials, but of the right perspective'.[22] By exploiting an eclectic array of archaeological sources and literary accounts, primarily composed in Greek, Syriac and Arabic, I hope to offer an original perspective on the cultural milieu of late antique Arabia. The structure of contemporary universities usually compels scholars to look at these disciplines in a compartmentalized way. This approach has led Semitic philologists to work on Qur'ānic lexicon and rhetoric, while classicists focus on the Jafnids and archaeologists study the testimonies of South Arabia. Interactions between these disciplines are sporadic and often superficial. My attempt is to pull the interactions of cultures in pre-Islamic Arabia together, investigating the cultural milieu where the inhabitants of the peninsula lived and connecting the neglected

[21] P. Frankopan, 'Why We Need to Think about the Global Middle Ages', *Journal of Medieval Worlds* 1 (2019), 5–10.

[22] R. G. Hoyland, *The Late Antique World of Early Islam: Muslims among Christians and Jews in the East Mediterranean* (Princeton: Princeton University Press, 2015), 559.

sociopolitical, religious and economic history of Arabia with its surroundings to construct a coherent historical narrative out of our fragmentary sources and fill a gap in the studies of Late Antiquity.

This first chapter is divided into three sections. First, I present a brief survey of previous scholarship concerning the history of late antique Arabia, the genesis of the Qur'ān and early Islam. I then discuss the sources available for historical research into pre-Islamic Arabia and explore the meaning of the lexemes 'Arabia' and 'Arabians/Arabs' from Antiquity to the rise of Islam, examining what these terms meant in various periods. In Chapter 2, I move on to an analysis of the political context of North Arabia (from the Syrian Desert to the Najd) between the third and the fifth centuries and the religious attitudes of the inhabitants of this region after Constantine's conversion to Christianity. The Arabians allied with Iran will receive less space than their Roman counterparts for two reasons. First, there are fewer Iranian sources than Roman sources, so any description of these groups remains highly speculative. Second, Iran had no claims of cultural monopoly. Zoroastrians did not proselytize as much as Christians, and they were not crucial actors in an inquiry into the history of pre-Islamic Arabia. Moreover, while 'Christian culture' was largely heterogenous, I am going to use 'Christianity' over 'Christianities' for the sake of clarity. Chapter 3 focuses on the rise of Judaism in the South Arabian kingdom of Ḥimyar during the same period, offering an interpretative late antique framework for the monotheism of fourth- and fifth-century Ḥimyar and contextualizing the choice made by South Arabian elites to become Jewish sympathizers. Chapter 4 is a chronological continuation of Chapter 3, shifting in focus to the arrival of Christianity in the region and positing economic factors as the leading cause for the massacre of Najrān and the shaping of sixth-century South Arabia while comparing this region with Aksūm. Chapter 5 mirrors Chapter 4, shedding light on the two federations of North Arabia – the kingdoms of Jafnids and Naṣrids – focusing on the impact of Christianity and providing a sociopolitical framework for the relationship between these kingdoms and Rome and Iran through a comparison with the Germans and the Türks.

The history of pre-Islamic Arabia needs to be analysed by taking into account the entire Arabian Peninsula, not only parts of it. Similarly, Islam cannot be understood in isolation from the political and cultural milieux of the surrounding regions. At the same time, this book aims to write the history of pre-Islamic Arabia rather than the origins of Islam. Therefore, only Chapter 6 addresses the Ḥijāz directly, looking at the religious communities in the region at the time of Muḥammad. After evaluating the decline of polytheism in pre-Islamic Arabia and making a case for the existence of henotheistic beliefs, I compare and contrast Muḥammad's prophetic career with that of the other Arabian prophets, offering some reflections on the Qur'ān itself. My analysis focuses on the sociopolitical exploitation of cults as a mechanism for establishing identities from the end of the third to the beginning of the seventh century. This is not to say that every conversion and religious attitude were subordinated to economic interests and political power in the period, but rather that elites' conversion and their religious rhetorics had a profound impact on the shaping of the world of Late Antiquity and that the rhetoric of faith became a valuable weapon to be used in economic warfare in the period. Chapter 7 concludes by pulling these various strands together and answers one final question: what made the Arabian milieu capable of producing Scripture of such universal appeal as the Qur'ān? As highlighted by Michael Schmauder in an analysis of the interactions between Rome and the steppe empires in south-eastern Europe, 'the model of marginal cultures striving for integration into the cultural and political structure of the dominant civilisation' needs to be revised.[23]

In summary, this book delves into the political and cultural developments of pre-Islamic late antique Arabia. It offers an interpretative framework that contextualizes the choice of Arabian elites to become Jewish sympathizers and/or convert to Christianity and Islam by pursuing a line of enquiry probing a sociopolitical exploitation of cults in the shaping of Arabian identities. I argue that the Arabian rulers' cautious conversion follows a broad late antique trend which aimed to ease the transition for their subjects and/or to assume a neutral position towards the developments of the surrounding empires. While adopting and internalizing the culture of their powerful trading partners, the Arabians retained a degree of cultural autonomy as testified by the widespread adoption of Judaism, Miaphysitism,[24] East Syrian Christianity[25] and local henotheistic cults. Late antique political entities operating in Arabia exploited these systems of belief as the *casus belli* of expeditions pursuing trade monopolies. The

[23] M. Schmauder, 'Huns, Avars, Hungarians: Reflections on the Interaction between Steppe Empires in Southeast Europe and the Late Roman to Early Byzantine Empires', in *Complexity of Interaction along the Eurasian Steppe Zone in the First Millennium* CE, ed. J. Bemmann and M. Schmauder (Bonn: Rheinische Friedrich-Wilhems Universität, 2015), 671–92, at p. 682.

[24] The Miaphysites believe that Christ has a single nature (*mia-physis*) in which humanity and divinity are united. They are often referred to as 'non-Chalcedonian', as they did not accept the Chalcedonian definition which maintained the 'two natures' (*dyo-physis*) of Christ.

[25] The Iranian bishops referred to the Christian Church of Iran as 'that of the East' in the documents of their first council (410). They accepted the belief in the dual nature Christology proposed by the Patriarch of Constantinople, Nestorius (d. 451), whose Christology was rejected in 431 at the First Council of Ephesus.

conjunction of faith and commerce (exemplified by the emergence of 'pilgrimage nodes') shaped Arabia's urban landscape and paved the way for the rise of Islam.

Throughout the first millennium, rulers' importation of foreign 'religions' was often aimed at overcoming internal divisions in a wide array of places such as Rome, South Arabia and Central Asia. Nonetheless, the systems of belief that local Arabian dynasties sponsored by exhibiting monumental inscriptions and funding the construction of religious buildings probably failed to take hold among the lower classes and the more geographically isolated peoples of the region. The political fragmentation of Arabia was further exacerbated by the Christological controversies seeping through Arabia's social strata due to the preaching of exiled monks. It was only after the fall of local political entities such as that of Ḥimyar and the kingdoms of North Arabia that the conditions for the political and religious unification of Arabia materialized, and a prophet from inner Arabia succeeded in vanquishing factional segregation and converging political, economic and religious interests and attitudes (e.g., scriptural with pagan and henotheist) through the founding of an autochthonous and universalistic (and thus easily exportable in sharp contrast to Zoroastrianism) belief system articulated in the newly formed local *lingua franca* and script. Islam leveraged the dissatisfaction with current political rule and emerged in its Arabian milieu to gain economic advantages, eliminate Iran's hegemony over the region and settle tribal divisions. At the same time, it provided a faith-based process for establishing identities and overcoming competing tendencies characteristic of the broader late antique world. In the second half of the seventh century, the adoption of kingly conduct by the Umayyad caliphs, more akin to that of Roman and Iranian rulers and of the Arabian Ḥimyarites and Jafnids than that of Muḥammad, signalled the completion of a process based on the belief in an extramundane dimension.[26]

Muslim accounts emphasize the barbarism of Romans and pre-Islamic Arabians in similar terms. However, while Islam inherited the ideological portrayal of pre-Islamic Arabians as barbarians and in antithesis to *ʿilm* ('knowledge'), the 'rupture' between 'pre-Islamic' and 'Islamic' ought to be reconceptualized as a process of transformation. No historical framing of the emergence of Islam can be traced without pre-Islamic Arabia. Hence, by focusing on the different degrees of participation and mediation as well

[26] A. Marsham, *Rituals of Islamic Monarchy: Accession and Succession in the First Muslim Empire* (Edinburgh: Edinburgh University Press, 2009).

as on buffer zone policies, this book aims to be the first extended study on this subject which positions the Arabians and the 'peripheries' of the late antique empires at the centre. My goal is to liberate and grant autonomy to the Arabians from marginalizing (mostly Western-produced) narratives framing the Arabians as 'barbarians' inhabiting the fringes of Rome and Iran and/or deterministic analyses in which they are similarly depicted retrospectively as exemplified by the Muslims' definition of the period as *Jāhilīyah*, 'ignorance'.[27] The recent exhibition *Roads of Arabia*, organized by the Saudi Commission for Tourism and Antiquities, showcased artefacts dated from the early lower Palaeolithic to the Ottoman period. The exhibition aimed to tell the story of the region's development over millennia but failed to cover the centuries before the emergence of Islam, partly corresponding to the period of Late Antiquity (just a few steps divided a series of frescoes datable to the first centuries CE from the first Islamic inscriptions, but these steps are supposed to cover half a millennium).[28]

While the Sasanians were Rome's greatest enemy in this period, the negative counterparts of the Romans in the literary sources were the 'barbarians'. This Roman label produces a misleading sense of a collective entity conceding with 'an inferior state of human evolution'.[29] Although the Romans perceived a binary division between their 'human and civilized category' and the 'barbarians', the relationship between these two categories was dynamic, and it was possible to cross boundaries by process of 'acculturation'. Unlike other empires' 'labels of otherness', shared blood was not a funding criterion to determine foreign peoples in late antique Rome. In China, for example, unfamiliar people were addressed by using ethnonyms that had no relation to cultural behaviour, as exemplified by Ban Gu's (d. 92) description of the Xiongnu.[30] In both regions of Eurasia, the rise of Buddhism and Christianity slowly caused the disintegration of the 'barbarians' collective identity', as people inhabiting the borders of the Roman and Chinese *oecumene* embraced monotheism. In the second half of the first millennium, the rise of the third 'universal' monotheistic

[27] For an example of a Eurocentric use of the word in modern scholarship, see N. Lenski's introduction to the monumental *The Cambridge Companion to the Age of Constantine* at p. 2: 'His deployment of barbarian military officers and auxiliary troops enabled the ongoing vitality of the late Roman army.'

[28] For this exhibition, see A. I. Al-Ghabban et al. (eds), *Roads of Arabia* (Paris: Musée du Louvre, 2010).

[29] Y. Dauge, *Le Barbare: Recherches sur la conception romaine de la barbarie et de la civilization* (Bruxelles: Latomus, 1981), 19–20.

[30] Ban Gu, *Han shu*, 94.b; Randolph B. Ford, *Rome, China, and the Barbarians: Ethnographic Traditions and the Transformation of Empires* (Cambridge: Cambridge University Press, 2020), esp. 96–129.

religion, Islam, reinforced fears of otherness and led to new mental frontiers based on faith. The emergence of Islam, the fast Muslim conquests and the consequent creation of the Muslim Commonwealth smashed physical borders. Still, it created new mental challenges, exacerbating existing cultural divisions and creating new *sine qua non* to mark otherness.[31]

1.2 A Brief Survey of Previous Research

The modern debate on the genesis of Islam started in 1833. In that year, the father of Reform Judaism, Abraham Geiger, published a book titled *Was hat Mohammed aus dem Judenthume aufgenommen?*, making an early contribution to the formation of Qur'ānic studies by analysing all Islamic references to biblical figures and underlining the rabbinic influences on the Qur'ānic material.[32] This publication rapidly encouraged scholars to evaluate the development of early Islam through a comparative analysis of the Old and/or New Testaments and the Qur'ān. The discrepancy between these preliminary results was striking. On the one hand, scholars such as Hartwig Hirschfeld,[33] Josef Horovitz,[34] Heinrich Speyer[35] and Charles Torrey[36] strongly emphasized the intertextuality between the Jewish corpus and the Qur'ān. On the contrary, others, such as Richard Bell[37] and Tor Andræ[38] repeatedly highlighted the Qur'ān's Christian background. In 1860, another seminal book was published, namely *Geschichte des Qorans* by Theodor Nöldeke.[39] The latter did not get involved in the contentious debate about Judeo-Christian influences on the Qur'ān but instead offered a deep analysis of the Qur'ānic *suwar* (chapters), proposing an authoritative chronology of the internal structure of the Muslim Holy Book. This work was shortly followed by Julius Wellhausen's enquiry into the pagan cults of Arabia (upholding Christian influence on the Qur'ān),[40] and by

31 I adopt Garth Fowden's definition of 'commonwealth' as 'a group of politically discrete but related polities collectively distinguishable from other polities or commonwealths by a shared culture and history'. See G. Fowden, *Empire to Commonwealth: Consequences of Monotheism in Late Antiquity* (Princeton: Princeton University Press, 1993).

32 A. Geiger, *Was hat Mohammed aus dem Judenthume Aufgenommen?* (Bonn: F. Baaden, 1883).

33 H. Hirschfeld, *Beitrage Zur Erklärung des Koran* (Leipzig: O. Schulze, 1886).

34 J. Horovitz, *Koranische Untersuchungen* (Berlin: De Gruyter, 1926).

35 H. Speyer, *Die Biblischen Erzaehlungen Im Qoran* (Leipzig: G. Olms, 1931).

36 C. C. Torrey, *Jewish Foundation of Islam* (New York: KTAV, 1967).

37 R. Bell, *The Origin of Islam in Its Christian Environment* (Edinburgh: Edinburgh University Press, 1925).

38 T. Andræ, *Der Ursprung des Islams und das Christentum* (Uppsala: Almqvist & Wiksells, 1926).

39 T. Nöldeke, *Geschichte des Qorans* (Göttingen: Dieterichschen Buchhandlung, 1860).

40 J. Wellhausen, *Reste arabischen Heidentums* (Berlin: De Gruyer, 1961).

Ignác Goldziher's studies on the *aḥādīth* (accounts about Muḥammad)[41] and *tafāsīr* (Qur'ānic exegesis).[42]

In 1936, an original article by Johann Fück outstripped much of the preceding scholarship grounded in biblical studies, marking a change of interest in Qur'ānic research away from the comparative approach focused on the biblical tradition.[43] Instead, it foregrounded the study of Muḥammad's biography, as did the famous books by William Montgomery Watt, published in the mid-1950s.[44] Gonzague Ryckmans' work on pre-Islamic idolatry also appeared during the same years.[45] A renewed interest in the composite milieu on the eve of Islam was later shown in the 1970s by the provocative works of the so-called 'revisionist school of Islamic studies'. John Wansbrough, one of its significant exponents, argued that the Qur'ān went through a long period of oral transmission within various independent sectarian communities familiar with Judaic-Christian preaching. He also claimed that the Qur'ān had been redacted in Mesopotamia during the eighth century.[46] The same year, Patricia Crone and Michael Cook published a controversial thesis claiming that Islam emerged from the preaching of a Jewish messianic movement called 'Hagarism'.[47] While Wansbrough and Crone vastly overstated these cases, Gerald Hawting confirmed that the emergence of Islam owed more to debates and disputes among monotheists than to arguments with idolaters.[48] Crone also published a groundbreaking reassessment of the Meccan trade, which had the merit of engaging many scholars in further debates,[49] as exemplified by her verbal crossfire with Robert Serjeant.[50] While the works of the revisionist school had considerable value, many of them are now considered

41 I. Goldziher, *Muhammedanische Studien* (Halle: Max Niemeyer, 1889–90).

42 I. Goldziher, *Die Richtungen der Islamischen Koranauslegung* (Leiden: Brill, 1920).

43 J. Fück, 'Die Originalität des Arabischen Propheten', *Zeitschrift der Deutschen Morgenländischen Gesellschaft* 90 (1936), 509–25.

44 W. M. Watt, *Muḥammad at Mecca* (Oxford: Oxford University Press, 1953); W. M. Watt, *Muḥammad at Medina* (Oxford: Oxford University Press, 1956).

45 G. Ryckmans, *Les religions arabes préislamiques* (Louvain: Universitaires, 1951).

46 J. Wansbrough, *Qur'ānic Studies: Sources and Methods of Scriptural Interpretation* (Oxford: Oxford University Press, 1977); J. Wansbrough, *The Sectarian Milieu* (Oxford: Oxford University Press, 1978).

47 P. Crone and M. Cook, *Hagarism: The Making of the Islamic World* (Cambridge: Cambridge University Press, 1977).

48 G. H. Hawting, *The Idea of Idolatry and the Emergence of Islam* (Cambridge: Cambridge University Press, 1999).

49 P. Crone, *Meccan Trade and the Rise of Islam* (Princeton: Princeton University Press, 1987).

50 R. B. Serjeant, 'Meccan Trade and the Rise of Islam: Misconceptions and Flawed Polemics', *Journal of the American Oriental Society* 110 (1990), 472–86; P. Crone, 'Serjeant and Meccan Trade', *Arabica* 39 (1992), 216–40.

outdated. The discovery of the Ṣanʿāʾ palimpsest and, more recently, that of the Qurʾānic manuscript in Birmingham, carbon-dated with 95.4 per cent accuracy to between 568 and 645 CE, rendered many of their theories obsolete.[51]

At the end of the twentieth century, an interest in pre-Islamic Arabia was reignited, mainly thanks to Toufic Fahd's enquiry.[52] The beginning of the new century also saw the creation of the *Encyclopaedia of the Qurʾān*[53] and Andrew Rippin's work on the *tafāsīr* (Qurʾānic exegesis),[54] composed on the lines of Goldziher's previous studies. At the same time, the revolutionary research of Christoph Luxenberg was released, which proposed an eccentric Syro-Aramaic reading of the Qurʾān as if it were a Christian oeuvre.[55] The book sparked a resurgence of research focused on interactions between the scriptural communities and their impact on the formation of Islam, particularly for those inclined to read Judeo-Christian influence in the Qurʾān. In the same period, a surge of interest among classicists in Rome's neighbours led to numerous attempts to include the Arabian Peninsula in studies on the Eastern Roman Empire. However, the focus of these enquiries remained steadily centred on Rome.

From 1984 to 1995, Irfan Shahid published a series of volumes titled *Byzantium and the Arabs*, which aimed to explore the relations between the Roman Empire and the 'Arabs' from the fourth to the sixth centuries and, in so doing, provide 'a background for answering the largest question in Arab–Roman relations, namely, why the Arabs were able in the seventh century to bring about the annihilation of the Roman imperial army at the decisive battle of the Yarmūk on 20 August, A.D.636'.[56] Although bogged down by tangential excursuses and repetitions,[57] Shahid's publication had many merits, especially in regard to its exhaustive bibliography. Literary sources in Syriac, Arabic, Latin and Greek were extensively explored. However, Shahid's works had two major methodological problems. First,

51 G. S. Reynolds, 'Variant Readings: The Birmingham Qur'an in the Context of Debate on Islamic Origins', *Times Literary Supplement* (7 August 2015), 14–15.

52 T. Fahd, *Arabie préislamique et son environnement historique et culturel* (Leiden: Brill, 1989).

53 J. D. McAuliffe (ed.), *Encyclopaedia of the Qurʾān* (Leiden: Brill, 2001–6).

54 A. Rippin, *The Qurʾān and Its Interpretative Tradition* (Aldershot: Ashgate, 2001).

55 C. Luxenberg, *Die Syro-Aramäische Lesart des Koran* (Berlin: Das Arabische Buch, 2000).

56 I. Shahid, *Rome and the Arabs: A Prolegomenon to the Study of Byzantium and the Arabs* (Washington, DC: Dumbarton Oaks, 1984), ix. See also I. Shahid, *Byzantium and the Arabs in the Fourth Century* (Washington, DC: Dumbarton Oaks, 1984); I. Shahid, *Byzantium and the Arabs in the Fifth Century* (Washington, DC: Dumbarton Oaks, 1989) and I. Shahid, *Byzantium and the Arabs in the Sixth Century* (Washington, DC: Dumbarton Oaks, 1995).

57 E.g., the discussion on Ibn al-Kalbī in Shahid, *Byzantium and the Arabs in the Fourth Century*, 349 ff.

he used the term 'Arab' as an *ethnicon*, though there was a lack of clarity regarding the meaning of this lexeme. The volumes' title is misleading as Shahid dealt only with 'the groups that are termed *foederati*, the allies of Byzantium'.[58] Second, he portrayed the 'Arabs' as a pious Christian group, overstating the importance of Christianity to define the late antique Roman–'Arab' relationship.[59] Maximal interpretations of biased and fragmentary material serve this agenda.[60] The result is a series very much focused on Rome and Christianity and only secondary to (one group of) the 'Arabs', even if Roman sources such as Procopius are accused of employing 'the technique of *suppressio veri* and *suggestio falsi*'.[61]

Shahid's monumental series was preceded by *The Roman Empire and Its Neighbours* (1967) by Fergus Millar, who returned to 'Rome's Arab Allies' multiple times before passing away in 2019.[62] Shahid's and Millar's works converge on various points, as testified by Shahid's glowing review of Millar's *The Roman Near East, 31 BC–AD 337* (1993). Shahid concurs on the fact that 'their [the "Arabs"] Arabness was much diluted by the forces of Hellenization and Romanization', though he complains against Millar's portrayal 'of the Arabs as those nomads of the steppe who appear as a threat to the Roman-controlled Near East'.[63] Millar had argued for the existence of a Near Eastern public culture dominated by Greco-Roman culture under the effect of 'Romanization', discussing whether to place the Roman Near East as part of the 'Orient' or the Greco-Roman world.[64] Millar focused on what he defines as 'distinctive pockets of "Romanness"', giving large space to the role played by the Greek language.[65] As shown in

58 Shahid, *Byzantium and the Arabs in the Fourth Century*, xvi.

59 Consider for example Shahid's considerations on the existence of Christian Arabic liturgies and pre-Islamic Bible translations in *Byzantium and the Arabs in the Fourth Century*, 435 ff.

60 E.g., the argument on Theodore's construction of churches in *Byzantium and the Arabs in the Sixth Century*, Vol. 2, 182.

61 Shahid, *Byzantium and the Arabs in the Sixth Century*, Vol. 1, 22.

62 F. Millar, *The Roman Empire and Its Neighbours* (London: Weidenfeld and Nicolson, 1967); F. Millar, *The Roman Near East, 31 BC–AD 337* (Cambridge, MA: Harvard University Press, 1993); F. Millar, 'Ethnic Identity in the Roman Near East, 325–450: Language, Religion, and Culture', *Mediterranean Archaeology* 11 (1998), 159–76; F. Millar, *Rome, the Greek World and the East* (Chapel Hill: University of North Carolina Press, 2002–6); F. Millar, 'Christian Monasticism in Roman Arabia at the Birth of Mahomet', *Semitica et Classica* 2 (2009), 97–115; F. Millar, 'Rome's Arab Allies in Late Antiquity: Conceptions and Representations from within the Frontiers of the Empire', in *Commutatio et Contentio: Studies in the Late Roman, Sasanian, and Early Islamic Near East* (Düsseldorf: Wellem, 2010), 199–226; F. Millar, *Empire, Church and Society in the Late Roman Near East: Greeks, Jews, Syrians and Saracens* (Leuven: Peeters, 2015).

63 I. Shahid, 'The Roman Near East, 31 BC–AD 337 by Fergus Millar (review)', *The Catholic Historical Review*, 81 (1995), 251–52, at p. 252.

64 Millar, *The Roman Near East.*

65 Millar, *Rome, the Greek World and the East*, Vol. 3, 380.

Chapter 5, Greek is documented in a few monumental inscriptions written by elites in Arabia. The thousands of examples of Safaitic graffiti, which can potentially shed light on the 'common people', are entirely omitted from the narrative. As Shahid, Millar reserved in recent times large space to the 'Arab or Saracen allies (*foederati*)', arguing that they constituted the only case in which 'local territorial political formations' were 'other than Greek cities'.[66] This Romano-centric vision is what I would like to counterbalance with this work.[67]

Another prolific scholar addressing the relationship between Rome and Arabia in the 1980s was Glen W. Bowersock in *Roman Arabia* (1983).[68] Millar defined the book as an 'intelligible narrative and administrative framework for more ambitious future studies'.[69] *Roman Arabia* was followed by *Late Antiquity: A Guide to the Postclassical World*, edited by Bowersock, Peter Brown and Oleg Grabar (1999),[70] a pioneering collaborative work that succeeded Peter Brown's seminal book *The World of Late Antiquity*, today considered as a sort of manifesto of late antique studies.[71] In 1936, the thought-provoking thesis of the then twenty-year-old Santo Mazzarino had anticipated Brown's attempt to grant autonomy to the 'history of the later Roman Empire' after being uniquely conceived as an 'imperial "storia della decadenza"'.[72] Although the concept of Late Antiquity was also identifiable in the preceding works of the art historians Alois Riegl (who coined the term *Spätantike*) and Josef Strzygowski,[73] Brown is today considered the 'inventor of late antiquity' in popular culture.[74] As he advocated in its pages, *The World of Late Antiquity* brought 'the average reader a sense

[66] Millar, *Rome, the Greek World and the East*, Vol. 3, 381.

[67] For an exemplary early work addressing and contrasting the concept of Romanization, see G. Woolf, *Becoming Roman: The Origins of Provincial Civilization in Gaul* (Cambridge: Cambridge University Press, 1998).

[68] G. W. Bowersock, *Roman Arabia* (Cambridge, MA: Harvard University Press, 1983).

[69] F. Millar, 'Roman Arabia by Glen W. Bowersock', *The Journal of Interdisciplinary History* 16 (1985), 125.

[70] G. W. Bowersock, P. Brown and O. Grabar (eds), *Late Antiquity: A Guide to the Postclassical World* (Cambridge, MA: Harvard University Press, 1999).

[71] P. Brown, *The World of Late Antiquity* (London: Thames and Hudson, 1971). The following edition (New York, 1989) contained some important bibliographical additions.

[72] The thesis was published as S. Mazzarino, *Stilicone: La crisi imperial dopo Teodosio* (Rome: A. Signorelli, 1942). See also S. Mazzarino, *Aspetti sociali del IV secolo: ricerche di storia tardo-romana* (Rome: L'Erma di Bretschneider, 1951).

[73] For an overview of the two authors, see J. Elsner, 'The Birth of late Antiquity: Riegl and Strzygowski in 1901', *Art History* 25 (2002), 361–70; and M. Ghilardi, 'Alle origini del dibattito sulla nascita dell'arte tardoantico', *Mediterraneo antico* 5 (2002), 117–46.

[74] See for example R. Shao, 'Peter Brown: Inventor of Late Antiquity', *The Daily Princetonian* (20 April 2017).

of the richness and excitement of a once-neglected period'.[75] However, a widely accepted interpretation of Late Antiquity is impossible to find.[76]

At least from Edward Gibbon's *The History of the Decline and Fall of the Roman Empire*, historians have often turned to the wide Eurasian world for their studies (frequently to contextualize European history).[77] In the first publication in the series *Studies in Late Antiquity and Early Islam*, appearing in 1992, Lawrence Conrad and Averil Cameron argued for the joint study of Late Antiquity and Early Islam (potentially into the 'Abbasid revolution').[78] A recent advocate for what we could name the 'elongation' and 'enlargement' of Late Antiquity has also been Garth Fowden, first in his *Empire to Commonwealth: Consequences of Monotheism in Late Antiquity*, and later in his study of the first-millennium world titled *Before and after Muḥammad*.[79] Other works have recently explored the Roman frontier and the rise of Islam within the broader framework of Late Antiquity by integrating it into the philosophical, artistic and legislative framework of the period, for example, Bowersock's latest publication, *The Crucible of Islam*.[80] A series of significant collaborative volumes on the period have also appeared.[81] Hence, this is not the first attempt to expand Late Antiquity, either temporally or geographically. This is also not the first time Arabia has been studied in relation to surrounding empires.[82] However, this is the first time pre-Islamic Arabia in its entirety is the protagonist of a monograph that is dedicated to the study of the late antique world in its political and cultural kaleidoscopic facets. Here I aim to situate the history of pre-Islamic Arabia in this wide interconnected

75 Brown, *The World of Late Antiquity*, 209.

76 L. Cracco Ruggini, 'II Tardoantico: per una tipologia dei punti critici', *Storia di Roma*, 3/1 (Torino: Einaudi, 1993), xxxvii.

77 E. Gibbon, *The History of the Decline and Fall of the Roman Empire* (London, 1776).

78 L. I. Conrad and A. Cameron (ed.), *The Byzantine and Early Islamic Near East I: Problems in the Literary Source Material* (Princeton: Princeton University Press, 1992). See also A. Cameron (ed.), *Late Antiquity on the Eve of Islam* (Abington: Routledge, 2013).

79 Fowden, *Empire to Commonwealth*; G. Fowden, *Before and after Muḥammad: The First Millennium Refocused* (Princeton: Princeton University Press, 2014).

80 G. W. Bowersock, *The Crucible of Islam* (Cambridge, MA: Harvard University Press, 2017). For my thoughts on this work see V. A. Grasso and G. Fowden, 'Review of G. Fisher (ed.), "Arabs and Empires before Islam". Oxford: Oxford University Press, 2015 – G. W. Bowersock, "The Crucible of Islam". Cambridge, MA: Harvard University Press, 2017', *Journal of Roman Studies* 108 (2018), 317–20.

81 To only name three, S. F. Johnson (ed.), *The Oxford Handbook of Late Antiquity* (Oxford: Oxford University Press, 2012); P. Rousseau (ed.), *A Companion to Late Antiquity* (Chichester: John Wiley & Sons, 2012); O. Nicholson (ed.), *The Oxford Dictionary of Late Antiquity* (Oxford: Oxford University Press, 2018).

82 See the publications by Irfan Shahid mentioned earlier.

world, which was not the direct product of a declining classical world, but an actor of new developments, changes and ideas in its rights. A long and a (though still less familiar) 'large' Late Antiquity have been often advanced. Arabia is crucial to the narrative of this enlarged geographical and temporal space not only for its role in Islam's *Mutterland* but for its strategic position between belligerent empires and its central role in what we could define as the Arabian 'Silk Roads', given that silk was only one of the good of any trade route of the time and that there was no single east–west 'road'.[83] Arabia's dramatic landscape also encouraged the ascetic practices of itinerant holy men and fleeing 'heretics', making it a perfect intersection of scriptural traditions. Late Antiquity is not a period of decay but active creation and new developments. For one thing, it is when Christianity spread and Islam rose. The rise of the latter, largely indebted to the spread of the first, took place in inner Arabia, and it is thus mandatory to look at this region for understanding the following shaping of the medieval world. Indeed, the Qur'ān is a product of the world of Late Antiquity but needs to be approached as a monument of ancient Arabia too.

Similarly to works dealing with Central Asia that have characterized the region as a 'crossroads' (i.e., as 'a junction between real cultural entities'),[84] historians of the ancient world often have brought Arabia into the picture mostly in relation to Rome and Iran. On the other side, in recent years, scholars of Islam have undertaken investigations of the Qur'ānic material and the origin of Islam through the study of the Judeo-Christian *Kutub* (books), especially of the Christian tradition composed in Syriac. The Qur'ān has been accordingly interpreted as a composite text extensively rewriting the *Ṣuḥuf Mūsā* ('the Scrolls of Moses').[85] However, this approach tends to neglect the religious attitudes of the different communities who lived

[83] I share Susan Whitfield's suggestion to adopt a more inclusive definition of 'Silk Road' which includes all inland and maritime trade routes and polities throughout Afro-Eurasia to avoid political agendas and the misunderstanding that trade of silk or any other Afro-Eurasian good happened in isolation. The expression also attributes a timeless and ahistorical quality to trade in the region. If needed, it would be preferable to use of the plural word 'roads' than 'road', which convey the sense of a single east–west route. See S. Whitfield, 'Was There a Silk Road?', *Asian Medicine* 3 (2007), 201–13. For the romanticization of this expression, see also K. Rezakhani, 'The Road That Never Was: The Silk Road and Trans-Eurasian Exchange', *Comparative Studies of South Asia, Africa, & the Middle East* 30/3 (2010), 420–33; E. De la Vaissière, 'Trans-Asian Trade, or the Silk Road Deconstructed (Antiquity, Middle Ages)', in *The Cambridge History of Capitalism*, Vol. 1, *The Rise of Capitalism: From Ancient Origins to 1848*, ed. J. G. Williamson and L. Neal (Cambridge: Cambridge University Press, 2014), 101–24.

[84] L. Morris, 'Central Asian Empires', in *Handbook of Ancient Afro-Eurasian Economies*, Vol. 1, *Contexts*, ed. S. von Reden (Berlin: De Gruyter, 2019), 53–94, at p. 57.

[85] Q. 53.36–7. All primary sources translations are mine unless stated otherwise.

at the time of Muḥammad and specifically the Arabian milieu. Although discussion of Qurʾānic origins is nowadays seen within a broader context, the contemporary debate often still focuses on whether the Qurʾān should be seen as entirely dependent on the Judeo-Christian Scriptures in the line of Geiger,[86] or as an original and autochthonous product of Arabia. The latter is the view of Angelika Neuwirth, director of the *Corpus Coranicum*, a German project working towards a critical edition of the Qurʾān.[87] Neuwirth has proposed to read the Qurʾān as the final product of a complex dialogue that engages with its composite late antique context.[88] In the last few years, Jacqueline Chabbi,[89] Reinhard Schulze,[90] and Aziz Al-Azmeh have also offered excellent in-depth analysis on the origins of Islam.[91] From these initiatives, we have realized the full benefits of 'studying early Christianity and Islam comparatively but not a-historically, in other words within a firm sociohistorical framework', by joining together all the sources and disciplines which concern the pre-Islamic and early Islamic milieu.[92] Assuming this remark as a postulate, I now illustrate the different sources that can be used to draw a timeline of the history of pre-Islamic Arabia.[93]

1.3 Reflections on the Sources

In a recently published paper on the pre-Islamic *talbiyāt* (invocations of Allāh made during the pilgrimage to Mecca), Tilman Seidensticker claimed that 'our knowledge of the religious history of [pre-Islamic Arabia] is considerably poorer than it appeared to be as recently as a generation ago'.[94] In the same article, he argued that the most relevant testimonies for a study of the period are the Islamic sources. However, both statements are factual only if we isolate the Ḥijāz from its surroundings. Although 'it is impossible to transfer information from other regions and centuries' to

86 G. S. Reynolds, *The Qurʾān and Its Biblical Subtext* (London: Routledge, 2010).

87 A. Neuwirth, *Der Koran als Text der Spätantike: Ein Europäischer Zugang* (Berlin: Verlag der Weltreligionen, 2010).

88 A. Neuwirth, 'The Qurʾān and Its Biblical Subtext by Gabriel S. Reynolds', *Journal of Qurʾānic Studies* 14 (2012), 131–8.

89 J. Chabbi, *Le seigneur des tribus: l'islam de Mahomet* (Paris: CNRS Éditions, 2013).

90 R. Schulze, *Der Koran und die Genealogie des Islam* (Basel: Schwabe Verlag, 2015).

91 A. al-Azmeh, *The Emergence of Islam in Late Antiquity: Allāh and His People* (Cambridge: Cambridge University Press, 2017).

92 Fowden, *Before and after Muḥammad*, 48.

93 A large part of the next section appeared as V. A. Grasso, 'The Gods of the Qurʾān: The Rise of Ḥijāzī Henotheism during Late Antiquity', in The Study of Islamic Origins: New Perspectives and Contexts, ed. M. B. Mortensen, G. Dye, T. Tesei and I. Oliver (Berlin: De Gruyter, 2021), 297–324.

94 T. Seidensticker, 'Sources for the History of pre-Islamic Religion', in *The Qurʾān in Context*, ed. A. Neuwirth, N. Sinai and M. Marx (Leiden: Brill, 2010), 293–321, at p. 293.

the area where Muḥammad lived, it is equally impossible to imagine this area as isolated from the remaining parts of the Arabian Peninsula. With this section, I offer some reflections on the sources for the religious history of Arabia between the fourth and the sixth centuries CE. In contrast with Seidensticker, I demonstrate that evidence for pre-Islamic Arabia has never been so abundant, illustrating how this material can expand our knowledge of this region in the late antique period.

There is virtually no independent historical information for the Ḥijāz during Late Antiquity. The Qur'ān imparts little information regarding its immediate religious context. In addition to biblical figures (e.g., Abraham and Jesus), the only names that appear are those of three Arab prophets (Hūd, Ṣāliḥ and Shuʿayb), Muḥammad and a certain Abū Lahab. Four religious communities (Jews, Christians, Magians and the Sabians) and only two peoples (the Romans and the Arab Quraysh) are mentioned. Overall, we should hardly consider Scriptures as historical sources, and we should treat the Qur'ān, with its self-presentation as the speech of God, in a similar fashion. The remaining Muslim sources, which date to at least 200 years after the events they describe, are similarly unreliable. Gustav Weil[95] and Goldziher asserted that the *aḥādīth* (sing. *ḥadīth*) were later fabrications by the end of the nineteenth century.[96] The works of these scholars also led to a widespread scepticism towards the historical use of the first Islamic *tawārīkh* (histories), the *tafāsīr* (sing. *tafsīr*) and the *Sīrat Rasūl Allāh* (biography of the Messenger of God). The prejudice towards the Muslim sources grew even further with the works of Crone, who labelled the whole Islamic tradition 'tendentious' as composed in a later cultural environment,[97] and chose to give prominence instead to non-Muslim literary accounts. Although this approach was not universally accepted and the types of sources Crone used were defined as 'a discrete collection of literary stereotypes composed by alien and mostly hostile observers',[98] others adopted an approach similar to Crone's though in a more measured way,[99] recognizing that the Muslim tradition had at least some merit for the period after the Muslim conquests.[100]

95 G. Weil, *Geschichte der Chalifen* (Mannheim: F. Bassermann, 1846–1862).
96 Goldziher, *Muhammedanische Studien*.
97 Crone, *Meccan Trade*, 230.
98 J. Wansbrough, 'Reviewed Work – Hagarism: The Making of the Islamic World by Patricia Crone, Michael Cook', *Bulletin of the School of Oriental and African Studies* 41 (1978), 155–6, at p. 156.
99 R. G. Hoyland, *Seeing Islam as Others Saw It: A Survey and Evaluation of Christian, Jewish and Zoroastrian Writings on Early Islam* (Princeton: Princeton University Press, 1997).
100 R. G. Hoyland, 'Writing the Biography of the Prophet Muḥammad: Problems and Solutions', *History Compass* 5 (2007), 581–602, at p. 591.

The scholarly consensus up to that point was that the traditional Muslim sources were not contemporary to the events they portray but were instead the result of a literary process carried out by the early Islamic community. As such, they were likely inspired by exegetical impulses and/or composed under the influence of later debates, emphasizing the supremacy of Muḥammad's revelation at a time when the *querelle* among the scriptural communities was vivid. Nevertheless, some literary sources, such as the traditions on the life of the Prophet, have been demonstrated to be consistent and 'have an authentic kernel'.[101] Traces of early discussions about the trustworthiness of these testimonies can still be found. Some recently published works have attempted to verify the historicity of the Muslim sources. This has been done by analysing the accounts that negatively portray Muḥammad and are unlikely to have been invented later and by examining their *asānīd* (lists of authorities who transmitted a report). These publications have successfully shed some light on the redactional process of this material. Indeed, like the non-Muslim literary accounts, which, despite their evident apologetic intents, have the merit of being contemporary to the events narrated, the Muslim literary sources constitute a valuable instrument of enquiry. Even if not considered historical documents, these works reflect some of the tendencies of the early Islamic community. Hence, although there are still some attempts to contextualize the Qur'ān using only non-Muslim literature while denying the trustworthiness of Muslim literary sources, other scholars at least esteem the latter's usefulness as 'evidence for the [Islamic] history of ideas'.[102] Collaborative works uniting contributions by specialists in Muslim and non-Muslim materials aim to produce a more balanced perspective, but they are still in their infancy.[103]

The use of pre-Islamic poetry for reconstructing the history of Arabia is also controversial. In 2001, Hoyland labelled this corpus an 'insider' source since it was composed by the inhabitants of Arabia when the events therein were depicted.[104] Nevertheless, many scholars believe that a large portion of the so-called pre-Islamic poems is not pre-Islamic but instead represent a group of later elaborations produced to support the idea which sees the Qur'ān as born in a savage polytheistic milieu. Two of the most provocative

[101] A. Görke, 'Prospects and Limits in the Study of the Historical Muḥammad', in *Transmission and Dynamics of the Textual Sources of Islam*, ed. N. Boekho-van der Voort, K. Versteegh and J. Wagemakers (Leiden: Brill, 2011), 137–51, at p. 141.

[102] C. F. Robinson, *Islamic Historiography* (Cambridge: Cambridge University Press, 2003), 12.

[103] E.g., A. Neuwirth, N. Sinai and M. Marx (eds), *The Qur'ān in Context: Historical and Literary Investigations into the Qur'ānic Milieu* (Leiden: Brill, 2009). For pre-Islamic Arabia, Fisher, *Arabs and Empires before Islam.*

[104] Hoyland, *Arabia and the Arabs*, 8–10.

texts published in this regard were written in the 1920s,[105] largely inspired by the preceding works of Nöldeke[106] and Wilhelm Ahlwardt.[107] After the publication of Milman Parry's work on the Homeric poems,[108] James Monroe convincingly demonstrated that pre-Islamic poetry originated orally and was written down only some centuries after its composition.[109] The use of writing was then no more than auxiliary, and it was only during the Umayyad period (661–750) that the corpus was systematically written down. This view was rejected by Gregor Schoeler, who claimed that 'poets and *ruwāt* (transmitters) possessed written notes and even substantial collections'.[110] If we accept that pre-Islamic poetry was written down after a long period of oral transmission, many problems regarding the authenticity of this corpus become negligible.[111] Muḥammad himself was sometimes mistaken for a poet,[112] and an inscription found in the Negev, containing two lines of poetic Arabic, suggests the existence of poetry in pre-Islamic times.[113] However, although a later reshaping of the texts can explain the standardized Arabic *koinè* of the poems, it does not alter the striking contrast between the libertine context of pre-Islamic poetry and the inspired preaching of the Qurʾān, a text that also teems with literary motifs and strands of narratives, but of a very different nature.[114] Although libertinism and piety could have coexisted (as they did in later Abbasid times), some scepticism towards using this material is reasonable. Because of its controversial dating and irrelevant subject matter, which rarely sheds light on the issues investigated in this work, pre-Islamic poetry will be only marginally examined in this monograph.

Nowadays, we are often lucky enough to integrate the study of literary materials with a range of archaeological finds, rapidly expanding our

105 Ṭ. Ḥusayn, *Fī al-shiʿr al-jāhilī* (Cairo, 1926); D. S. Margoliouth, 'The Origins of Arabic Poetry', *Journal of the Royal Asiatic Society* 57 (1925), 417–49.

106 T. Nöldeke, *Neue Beiträge zur Kenntnis der Poesie der Alten Araber* (Hannover: C. Rümpler, 1864).

107 W. Ahlwardt, *Bemerkungen über die Echtheit der Alten Arabischen Gedichte* (Greifswald: L. Bamberg, 1872).

108 M. Parry, *L'Épithète Traditionnelle dans Homère* (Paris: Les belles lettres, 1928).

109 J. T. Monroe, 'Oral Composition in pre-Islamic Poetry', *Journal of Arabic Literature* 3 (1972), 1–53.

110 G. Schoeler, *The Oral and the Written in Early Islam* (London: Routledge, 2006), 67.

111 An early confutation of Margoliouth's and Ḥusayn's works is in A. J. Arberry, *The Seven Odes: The First Chapter in Arabic Literature* (London: G. Allen & Unwin, 1957), 228–54.

112 Beside the *sūrat al-Shuʿarāʾ* ('The Poets'), see Q. 21.5; 36.69; 52.30; 69.41. Q. 69.42 establishes a separation between poet (*shāʿir*) and soothsayer (*kāhin*).

113 A. Negev, 'Nabatean Inscriptions from ʿAvdat (Oboda)', *Israel Exploration Journal* 13 (1963), 113–24; J. A. Bellamy, 'Arabic Verses from the First/Second Century: The Inscription of ʿEn ʿAvdat', *Journal of Semitic Studies* 35 (1990), 73–9.

114 See N. Jamil, *Ethics and Poetry in Sixth-Century Arabia* (Cambridge: Cambridge University Press, 2017).

understanding of the pre-Islamic milieu and the political structures of the Middle East. Although the archaeology of the Roman Near East has received consideration from early times, studies on the religion of pre-Islamic Arabia are still in their infancy.[115] The digital archives CSAI (Corpus of South Arabian Inscriptions) and OCIANA (Online Corpus of the Inscriptions of Ancient North Arabia) now help scholars to uncover the material culture of ancient civilizations and deliver emerging insights into the history of this much neglected geographical area. The present work is a first attempt to interpret these inscriptions and the available literary sources as a unitary data set. This material offers a corrective reading to the literary accounts and has made obsolete the scanty literature on the cults of Arabia before Islam which was produced in the last century. Indeed, works such as those of Jacques Ryckmans[116] and Joseph Chelhod,[117] produced between the 1940 and the 1960s, are nowadays outdated in many aspects. Studies on literacy in pre-Islamic times and the medieval Middle East are also still in their infancy.[118] It is unclear to what extent Arabians participated consciously in 'acts of authorship', as in the case of other ancient peoples.[119] Nonetheless, the high number of Arabian graffiti appears to offer some information on the 'common people' of Arabia who had only limited connections with the southern Syrian urban centres.[120]

The Arabian origin of this material and its direct witness to the events it attests makes it a more valuable testimony to pre-Islamic Arabian developments than literary sources composed in another time and/or space. Nonetheless, writing the history of Arabia exclusively through studying its epigraphic documents is as dangerous as attempting to do so only using literary sources.[121] Material culture must be integrated *aliorsum* from literary sources. Archaeology is just one of the tools we possess to confirm or disprove the historical accuracy of the Qurʾān, itself a monument, and to illuminate its complex genesis. Similarly, an uncritical reliance on Classical

[115] The journal *Arabian Archaeology and Epigraphy* was founded not even thirty years ago.

[116] Ryckmans, *Religions arabes.*

[117] J. Chelhod, *Le sacrifice chez les Arabes: recherches sur l'évolution* (Paris: Presses universitaires de France, 1955).

[118] For pre-Islamic times, see M. C. A. Macdonald, *Literacy and Identity in pre-Islamic Arabia* (Farnham: Ashgate, 2009). For the medieval Middle East, see J. Tannous, *The Making of the Medieval Middle East: Religion, Society, and Simple Believers* (Princeton: Princeton University Press, 2018).

[119] K. Milnor, *Graffiti and the Literary Landscape in Roman Pompeii* (Oxford: Oxford University Press, 2014), 138.

[120] A. al-Jallad, *An Outline of the Grammar of the Safaitic Inscriptions* (Leiden: Brill, 2015), 1.

[121] A good example of this misguided practice is Y. D. Nevo and J. Koren, *Crossroads to Islam* (New York: Prometheus Books, 2003).

Arabic sources is as problematic as its complete dismissal favouring sources composed in the Eastern Roman milieu. These latter consist of various genres (e.g., church histories, hagiographies, hymns) with multiple purposes and agendas. Seeking to present the available data on pre-Islamic Arabia objectively, I give more space to the sources with good reliability and representativeness. For this reason, archaeological material will have priority over literary accounts. Moreover, I adopt a comparative approach that seeks parallelisms and direct correlations while comparing and contrasting empires, societies and cultural developments and milieux.

1.4 Which Arabia and Which Arabs? A Lexicographic Journey from Antiquity to the Rise of Islam

From a geographic perspective, the Arabian Peninsula is broadly divided into four areas: (1) the western highlands between the Red Sea and the basaltic desert known as *Ḥarrat al-Shām*; (2) the deserts of the central *al-Rubʿ al-Khālī* (Empty Quarter) and Syria; (3) the eastern coast by the Persian Gulf; and (4) the mild southern highlands. In the *Oxford English Dictionary*, an 'Arab' is defined as: 'A member of a Semitic people, originally from the Arabian Peninsula and neighbouring territories, inhabiting much of the Middle East and North Africa.'[122] The definition thus takes into account: (1) in-group identification and belonging to the 'Semitic people'; and (2) the geographical boundaries of the Arabian Peninsula.[123] On the grounds that we cannot use current definitions to interpret the past, I now address the problem of identifying Arabia and the 'Arabs' from Antiquity to the rise of Islam by analysing primary sources dated between the first millennium BCE and the sixth century CE. Were there any Arabs in pre-Islamic Arabia? Modern scholarship has recursively translated the Semitic root *ʿ-r-b* as 'nomads' from the publication of a pioneering work by Theodor Nöldeke onwards,[124] and/or has used the term 'Arabs' to refer to the inhabitants of the Arabian Peninsula in pre-Islamic times.[125] Because

[122] https://en.oxforddictionaries.com/definition/arab.

[123] 'A peninsula of south-western Asia, largely desert, lying between the Red Sea and the Persian Gulf and bounded on the north by Jordan and Iraq'. See https://en.oxforddictionaries.com/definition/arabia.

[124] T. Nöldeke, 'Arabia, Arabians', in *Encyclopaedia Biblica I*, ed. T. K. Cheyne (London: Adam and Charles Black, 1899), 272–5, at pp. 272–3.

[125] E.g. Shahid, *Byzantium and the Arabs* (Washington, DC: Dumbarton Oaks, 1984–95); Fisher, *Arabs and Empires*. A notable and authoritative exception is P. Webb, *Imagining the Arabs: Arab Identity and the Rise of Islam* (Edinburgh: Edinburgh University Press, 2016).

of recent archaeological discoveries, we now know that these interpretations must be revised.

1.4.1 Neo-Assyrians

From Shalmanasser III (858–24 BCE) onwards, mentions of Arabia and the *Aribbi* frequently appear in the Neo-Assyrian annals.[126] The following text can be found in the annals of Sargon (722–705 BCE): 'The tribes of Thamūd, Ibadidi, Marsimani and 'Ephah, the distant *Ar-ba-a-a* who inhabit the desert (*rūqūti āshibūt mad-ba-ri*), who know neither high nor low official (governors nor superintendents), and who had not brought their tribute to any king.'[127] The text also mentions 'Pharaoh, king of Egypt, Shamsi, queen of the *A-rib-bi*, Ita'amra, the Sabean'.[128] While it is unclear whether 'the distant *Ar-ba-a-a* who inhabit the desert' was an epithet of the four aforementioned Arabian groups, it is plausible that these people inhabited the same geographic area. Although only the North Arabian Thamūd are mentioned in many different sources, including the Qur'ān,[129] we can place the *Ar-ba-a-a* geographically, almost certainly between Palestine and North Arabia.

Conversely, it is uncertain if there was a distinction between *Ar-ba-a-a* and *A-rib-bi*. Although the second lexeme may point to populations with a well-established central government,[130] the phrase *āshibūt mad-ba-ri* (and not just the lexeme *Ar-ba-a-a*/*A-rib-bi*) means that the *Ar-ba-a-a* inhabited the desert. This questions previous etymological explanations (based on Neo-Assyrian texts) that the word 'Arab' was synonymous with 'nomad'.[131] In addition, the term 'Arabia' is entirely missing from Neo-Assyrian records. Hence, the Pharaoh is the king of Egypt, but Shamsi is the queen of the *A-rib-bi*, a clear indicator of the lack of a common Arabian identity. The root *'-r-b* merely hints at different groups living broadly in the same

[126] D. D. Luckenbill, *Ancient Records of Assyria and Babylonia* (Chicago: Chicago University Press, 1926), 1.611. Tiglath-Pileser III (745–27) mentions a tributary 'Zabibe Queen of Arabia' and a queen Shamsi of Arabia (Ibid., 1.772–8 and 1.817).

[127] Sargon's Khorsabad text adapted from ibid., 2.17.

[128] Ibid.

[129] Q. 7.73.

[130] Reiterated in other inscriptions. See Luckenbill, *Ancient Records* 2.55.

[131] An 'Hazael king of the Arabians' was met by Esarhaddon (680–69 BCE) in Nineveh (ibid., 518a., 536, 551) and a Hazael Qedarite king is later described by Assurbanipal (668–26 BCE) (ibid., 861) The first king ruled over Dūmat al-Jandal, and was not a nomad (see W. R. Gallagher, *Sennacherib's Campaign to Judah: New Studies* (Leiden: Brill, 1999), 53). Hazael's successor was a Nabatean ally, see Luckenbill, *Ancient Records*, 2.821, 823.

geographical area between the Syrian Desert and the Ḥijāz and indicates both the scattered tribes of the desert and the kings allied with Assur. Nonetheless, there might also have been a differentiation between *Ar-ba-a-a* and *A-rib-bi* based on these groups' relationship with Assyria.

1.4.2 *Old Testament*

The most interesting mentions of the Arabian Peninsula and its inhabitants in the *Tanakh* are found in the book of Jeremiah, datable to the sixth century BCE.[132] The excerpt from Jeremiah names the nations to whom God sent the 'Weeping Prophet': 'and the kings of the isles which are beyond the sea, Dedan, and Tema, and Buz, and all that are in the utmost corners, and all the kings of *ʿrb*, and all the kings of *h-ʿrb* who dwell in the desert (*hshkym b-mdbr*)'.[133] The words used to indicate the desert are *mdbr* and *ʿrb,* respectively translated as 'wilderness' and 'desert', in the King James version of Isaiah 35.[134] Thus, there is a connection between the *ʿrb* and North Arabia, where Dedan, Tayma and Buz are found.[135] Even though the *ʿrb* 'dwell in the desert' both in the annals of Sargon and the book of Jeremiah, dateable to two centuries later, nothing points to a particular 'Arab' ethnicity or lifestyle. Elsewhere in the Bible, the *ʿrb* are mentioned with different people such as the Ethiopians,[136] as well as in connection with unknown places.[137] Nonetheless, there is general agreement that they were found in North Arabia and 'dwelling in the desert' two centuries after the Neo-Assyrian rulers.

1.4.3 *Classical Sources*

In the fifth century BCE, Herodotus defined Arabia as 'the furthest of inhabited lands (*oikumene*) in the direction of midday' delimited in the south by the 'Erythraean Sea', in the north by Assyria and Palestine, in the west by mountains bordering Egypt and the Arabian Gulf and in the east

132 A. D. Hornkohl, *Ancient Hebrew Periodization and the Language of the Book of Jeremiah* (Leiden: Brill, 2014).

133 Jeremiah 25.24 adapted from the King James version.

134 'The wilderness and the solitary place shall be glad for them; and the desert shall rejoice, and blossom as the rose.' Similarly, Jeremiah 17.6 and Isaiah 35.1.

135 Dedan and Arabia are also found in Isaiah 21.13. Arabia also appears in the book of Ezekiel (also datable to the sixth century BCE) in connection with Qedar, ruling over the oasis of Dedan and Tayma (Ezekial 27.21).

136 2 Chronicles 21.16.

137 E.g., Gurbaal in 2 Chronicles 26.7.

by Iran.[138] Shortly after, Xenophon identified Arabia as the land on the left of the Euphrates where Cyrus' army passed through.[139] Four centuries later, Diodorus Siculus (d. ca. 20 BCE) situated Arabia between Syria and Egypt, specifying that the 'part of Arabia which borders upon the waterless and desert country' is called *Arabia Eudaimon* ('Happy Arabia', *Felix* in Latin).[140] After Trajan's annexation of *Nabataea* to the Roman Empire in 106 CE,[141] and the following creation of the *Provincia Arabia* (or *Arabia Petraea*), Ptolemy (d. ca. 170) delimited *Arabia Felix* on the north by *Arabia Petraea* and *Arabia Deserta*, on the east by the Persian Gulf, on the west by the Arabian Gulf and on the south by the Red Sea.[142]

While Arabia included the entire Arabian Peninsula in the classical sources, the *Arabioi* are, according to Herodotus, only the inhabitants of the seaboard of Arabia, known for respecting pledges, wearing girded up mantles, having ridden on camels in the army of Xerxes and venerating Dionysus and Aphrodite (called Alilat).[143] Diodorus Siculus claimed that the '*Arabioi*, who bear the name of Nabateans' inhabited the deserted eastern parts of the peninsula, while the central part is 'ranged over by a multitude of nomadic *Arabioi*' and 'a multitude of farmers and merchants' was found in the northern part lying towards Syria.[144] Strabo (d. ca. 23),[145] Pliny (d. 79)[146] and Ptolemy (d. ca. 170) described a group named *Scenitae* among the various Arabian peoples,[147] and Ammianus Marcellinus (d. ca. 395) claimed that the *Scenitae* Arabs became known as 'Saracens'.[148] The Saracens are mentioned together with the Thamudians in the *Notitia Dignitatum*,[149] and in the work of the first known Syriac author Bardaiṣān (d. 222), who distinguished them from the *Ṭayyāyē*,[150] a common Syriac term denoting the inhabitants of the Arabian Peninsula.[151] A bilingual

138 Hdt. 3.107.1; 4.39; 3.5; 2.8.1; 4.39. Herodotus has no knowledge of a gulf between Persia and Arabia.

139 Xen. *An.* 1.5.

140 Diod. Sic. 2.48.1; 2.49.45.

141 D. F. Graf, 'The Saracens and the Defence of the Arabian Frontier', *Bulletin of the American Schools of Oriental Research* 229 (1978), 1–26, at p. 6.

142 Ptol. *Geo.* 6.7.

143 Hdt. 2.12; 3.8; 7.69; 7.86; 1.131.

144 Diod. Sic. 2.48.3; 2.54.1–3.

145 Strab. 16.2.11 (North Arabia); 16.4.3–4 (South Arabia).

146 Plin. *HN.* 5.12.

147 Ptol. *Geog.* 6.7.

148 Amm. Marc. 23.6.13.

149 *Not. Dign.* 28.17.

150 Bardaiṣān, *Book of the Laws*, 50–51.11.

151 The term originated from the name of the northern Najd tribe Ṭayyi' and from which derives the Persian *Tājik* or *Tāzī* and consequently the Chinese *Dashi*. See H. Park, *Mapping the Chinese and Islamic Worlds: Cross-cultural Exchange in pre-Modern Asia* (Cambridge: Cambridge University Press, 2012), 203.

inscription (Greek and Nabatean) found in a temple Ruwāfa,[152] roughly dated to 166–9 CE, further attests to an early epigraphic appearance of the lexeme 'Saracens' (Nabatean *shrkt,* from the Semitic root *sh-r-k,* 'to associate'; Greek *ethnos*).[153] *Ethnos* also appears in a southern Syrian inscription to a Roman governor by a group defining themselves as *oi apo ethnous nomadōn*, the *ethnos* of the nomads, perhaps soldiers chosen among the nomads.[154]

In conclusion, after Trajan created *Provincia Arabia*, there were three 'Arabias': *Felix, Petraea* and *Deserta.* In a similar fashion to Neo-Assyrians and the Jewish, the classical authors did not consider the inhabitants of South Arabia to be *Arabioi.* Lexemes such as *Scenitae* and *Saraceni* were later used to indicate different peoples inhabiting the Arabian Peninsula, thus distinguishing between unconquerable Bedouins and the first Roman allies. The Romans identified their neighbours based on ethnographic classifications that rarely correspond to late antique self-identification.[155] Hence, the Arabians were, like the Scythians, 'literary constructions of a Greek cultural other, a mirror into which the Greeks might look to perceive more sharply their own civilization'.[156] Similarly, the Huns (a syncretistic entity merging the world of the steppe and the Chinese Empire)[157] were as unlikely to consider themselves Scythians,[158] as the Franks were to consider themselves Germans or the people inhabiting the Arabian Peninsula to think themselves to be Arabs. There is no direct attestation of a group describing themselves as 'Arabs' in ancient times. Nonetheless, ethnic identities were not without meaning, and it is unlikely that perceptions of identity were utterly absent.[159] The separate mentions of Arabs/Arabians in Neo-Assyrian, Jewish and Graeco-Roman texts, which were highly unlikely to have been derived from each other, make it plausible

[152] The Thamudians probably venerated the god 'Ilāhā inside the temple. See J. T. Milik, 'Inscriptions grecques et nabatéennes de Rawwafah', *Bulletin of the Institute of Archaeology* 10 (1971), 54–8, at p. 58.

[153] Macdonald, *Literacy and Identity*, 11–2. See also M. Macdonald et al., 'Arabs and Empires before the Sixth Century', in *Arabs and Empires*, ed. G. Fisher (Oxford: Oxford University Press, 2015), 11–89, at pp. 76–9.

[154] Wadd 2203. See M. Sartre, *Trois études sur l'Arabie romaine et byzantine* (Bruxelles: Revue d'études latines, 1982), 124.

[155] W. Pohl, 'Migrations, Ethnic Groups, and State Building', in *The Cambridge Companion to the Age of Attila*, ed. M. Maas (Cambridge: Cambridge University Press, 2014), 247–64, at p. 255.

[156] N. Di Cosmo, 'China–Steppe Relations in Historical Perspective', in *Complexity of Interaction in Complexity of Interaction along the Eurasian Steppe Zone in the First Millennium* CE, ed. J. Bemmann and M. Schmauder (Bonn: Rheinische Friedrich-Wilhems Universität, 2015), 49–72, at p. 53.

[157] H. J. Kim, *The Huns, Rome and the Birth of Europe* (Cambridge: Cambridge University Press, 2013).

[158] Pohl, 'Migrations, Ethnic Groups, and State Building', p. 255.

[159] Ibid.

that a group, probably inhabiting the north, were already calling themselves as such. Thus, in Sections 1.4.4 and 1.4.5, I investigate the Arabian inscriptions written by men who called themselves 'king of the *ʿrb*'.

1.4.4 Late Antiquity and the Case of Imru' al-Qays

During Late Antiquity, the Eastern Roman Empire became the most flourishing centre of the Mediterranean world, including parts of Italy and southern Spain at the height of its expansion, as well as the Balkans, the north coast of Africa, the Anatolian plateau and the Levant. The rest of the Middle East was dominated by the Sasanian Empire (224–651), which boasted of ruling over a series of *shahr* (lands), including Arabia.[160] As Christianity gained ground with the Roman emperors, renewed hostilities broke out between Rome and Iran. The outbreak of these hostilities had important repercussions on the Arabian Peninsula, as demonstrated by an inscription dated 328 found at the Roman outpost of Namārah, a semi-permanent water reservoir in southern Syria. Written in Arabic using the 'transitional' script, this inscription is the epitaph of Imru' al-Qays ibn ʿAmr, king of the Iran-allied Naṣrids, who flourished between the fourth century and the beginning of the seventh century in southern Iraq. The epitaph defines Imru' al-Qays as 'king of *ʿrb*' (*mlk al-ʿrb*) but also as leader of the ʾAsd and Madhḥij tribes whom he conquered during a military campaign to Najrān. Both groups inhabited the southern fringes of Central Arabia, roughly corresponding to the territory between the Najd and the South Arabian kingdoms (Saudi Arabia-Yemen border). While the ʾAsd occupied the ʿAsīr region,[161] the Madhḥij were located further south.[162] Both groups were independent until Imru' al-Qays' expedition, as proven by a Sabean inscription providing a political map of third-century Arabia.[163] These people were probably threatening the surrounding empires after perfecting the use of the saddle in the third century.[164]

160 Shāpūr I's inscription at Ka'ba-ye Zartosht, 2–3. See P. Huyse, *Die dreisprachige Inschrift Šabuhrs I. an der Kaba-i Zardust (ŠKZ)* (London: School of Oriental and African Studies, 1999), 1: 19–24.

161 Al-Ṭabarī, *Taʾrīkh*, 1.903. For the epigraphical sources, see A. F. L. Beeston, 'Languages of pre-Islamic Arabia', *Arabica* 28 (1981), 178–86, at pp. 183–4.

162 Al-Qalqashandī, *Ṣubḥ al-ʾAʿshā*, 5.57.

163 J. Schiettecatte and M. Arbach, 'The Political Map of Arabia and the Middle East in the Third Century AD Revealed by a Sabaean Inscription', *Arabian Archaeology and Epigraphy* 27 (2016), 176–96.

164 M. J. Zwettler, 'Maʿadd in Late-Ancient Arabian Epigraphy and Other pre-Islamic Sources', *Wiener Zeitschrift für die Kunde des Morgenlandes* 90 (2000), 223–309, at p. 285.

Although it is curious that the epitaph of a Naṣrid king was found not far from the *Limes Arabicus* of the Roman *Provincia Arabia,* the fourth line of the inscription states that Imru' al-Qays was appointed phylarch by the Romans,[165] hinting at the possibility that Imru' worked for both powers. Contemporarily, the Roman Emperor Constantine 'extended his Empire in the extreme south as far as the Blemmyes [in Nubia] and the Aethiopians',[166] intending to counterbalance the Iranians' swift expansion in Arabia by strengthening Rome's position in the Red Sea.[167] The recruitment of Imru' al-Qays complimented Constantine's expansionist policy, the Roman emperor being fascinated by and desiring to emulate the 'great giants' of the classical period.[168] As suggested by his biographer Eusebius, he also wished to promote Christianity in 'pagan remote lands' (d. ca. 339).[169]

Although Imru's epitaph is an important historical document and a clear testimony of an increasing interest in Arabia on the part of the Roman Empire, it is not the first epigraphic evidence written by a 'king of the *'rb'*. Rulers of *'rb* are mentioned in a group of inscriptions from Edessa (Urfa, Turkey) dated to around 165,[170] and in another dated ca. 180 from Hatra (Iraq),[171] possibly reflecting a hegemonic role gained in the Roman–Iranian wars of 163–6. In this corpus, *'rb* here probably refers to a territory and not a community.[172] Accordingly, as the *'rb* were not the main people these kings ruled over but only subsidiary populations, Imru' al-Qays' inscription appears even more significant. Based on the references in Hatran and Old Syriac inscriptions and some linguistic considerations, Michael Macdonald has proposed that *'rb* in Imru' al-Qays' epitaph refers to 'one or more of the areas in the Jazīra and other parts of northern

165 Much has been written about the translation of the term, *frsw* interpreted either as 'horsemen' or 'Persians'. I lean towards Bellamy's interpretation. See J. A. Bellamy, 'A New Reading of the Namārah Inscription', *Journal of the American Oriental Society* 105 (1985), 31–51.

166 Eusebius, *VC*, 1.8.3.

167 For Christianity in Nubia, see V. A. Grasso, 'Rejoice in God! Five Miaphysite Letters from Sixth Century Alexandria', in *Bishops and Bishoprics in Egypt, Nubia and Ethiopia*, ed. A. Tsakos and R. Seignobos (forthcoming). On the relationship between Nubia and its neighbors, see the commandable G. Hatke, *Aksum and Nubia. Warfare, Commerce, and Political Fictions in Ancient Northeast Africa* (New York: New York University Press, 2013).

168 E. Fowden, 'Constantine and the Peoples of the Eastern Frontier', in *Cambridge Companion to the Age of Constantine*, ed. N. Lenski (Cambridge: Cambridge University Press, 2005), 377–98, at p. 378.

169 Eusebius, *Vit. Const.* 1.8.4.

170 See As36; As47; As49. The only dated one is Drijvers 25.

171 E.g., Aggoula 353.

172 In two inscriptions (H336b; H343) the *htry'* and *'rby'* appear as separate populations ('Shamashbarak administrator and the Hatrans old and young, and all the inhabitants of *'rb* and all who live in Ḥatra' (H343)). In Hatra the title *mlk' d(y) 'rb* ('king of *'rb*') is used on inscriptions, in Edessa only the title *shlyṭ' d-'rb* ('governor of *'rb*') is inscribed. See J. Teixidor, 'Bulletin d'epigraphie semitique', *Syria* 48 (1971), 453–93, at pp. 484–5.

Mesopotamia'.[173] Considering that Imru' al-Qays' inscription was found in southern Syria and that he conquered the ʾAsd and Madhḥij tribes (the former found in the Ḥijāz and the latter on the southern fringes of Central Arabia), it is more likely that the *ʿrb* inhabited the area between modern southern Syria and Yemen.

Other inscriptions, written in Greek and Latin, have been found in Namārah.[174] Imru' al-Qays' epitaph, written on a beautifully carved *tabula ansata*, showed his strong connection with Rome, which gave him prominence in the Arabian political milieu. Before Imru's epitaph, no inscription of this kind had been found in the north and central regions of the Arabian Peninsula. Rome's cultural influence played an important role in shaping the modalities of power in the area, as later shown by the case of the Jafnids (see Chapter 5). Although other *ʿrb* kings preceded Imru' al-Qays, it was only under Rome's cultural wing that Arabians started framing their historical memory in such a grand fashion. At the same time, the existence of independent millennial civilizations in the south of the peninsula significantly contributed to the acceleration of the Arabians' process of self-identification.

1.4.5 The Epigraphic Evidence from South Arabia

Several South Arabian inscriptions mention the *ʾʿrb* and the *ʿrb/ʿrbn* before and after the unification of South Arabia at the end of the third century under the kingdom of Ḥimyar (Tables A.1 and A.2). One century after the region's unification, a conspicuous group of monumental inscriptions attest to the new Ḥimyarite title 'king of *ʾʿrb*'.[175] The most ancient of these inscriptions are attributed to Abīkarib Asʿad (ca 400–45), 'king of Saba', dhu-Raydān, Ḥaḍramawt, Yamanat and his/the *ʾʿrb* of *Ṭwdm* and *Thmt*'.[176] *Thmt* probably indicates the coast of western Arabia between Mecca and Medina (ancient Yathrib), while *Ṭwdm* indicates the Najd.[177]

[173] M. C. A. Macdonald et al., '*Provincia Arabia*: Nabatea, the Emergence of Arabic as a Written Language, and Graeco-Arabica', in *Arabs and Empires*, ed. G. Fisher (Oxford: Oxford University Press, 2015), 373–433, at pp. 406–7.

[174] IGLS 16.1385–1414. Recently examined by M. Sartre, 'Namārah du Ṣafā', *Syria* 93 (2016), 45–66.

[175] The lexeme *ʿrb(n)* never appears in the title.

[176] Ja 516.

[177] C. J. Robin, 'The Peoples beyond the Arabian Frontier in Late Antiquity: Recent Epigraphic Discoveries and Latest Advances', in *Inside and Out: Interactions between Rome and the Peoples on the Arabian and Egyptian Frontiers in Late Antiquity*, ed. J. H. F. Dijkstra and G. Fisher (Leuven: Peeters, 2014), 33–82, at p. 46. *Ṭwdm* and *Thmt* possibly mean 'highland' and 'lowland' (J. Retsö, *The Arabs in Antiquity: Their History from the Assyrians to the Umayyads* (London: Routledge, 2002), 558) or 'montagne' et 'plaine côtière' (Robin, 'La pénétration des Arabes nomades au Yémen', 81).

One of Abīkarib Asʿad's royal inscriptions written with his son celebrates the possession of the land of Maʿadd in Central Arabia with the agreement of 'their ʾʿ*rb* of Kindah, Saʿd, ʿUlah and H[...]', all inhabiting the southern fringes of Central Arabia.[178] At the same time, a 'Ḥujrid son of ʿAmr' styled himself '*mlk* (king) of Kiddat', though Kindah was part of Ḥimyar.[179] A century later, king Maʿdīkarib Yaʿfur (r. 519–22) identified as 'their ʾʿ*rb*' both the tribes of Kindah and Madhḥig in the southern fringes of Central Arabia and the Banū Thaʿlabat and Muḍar, found in the northern edges.[180] After a ten year gap, King Abraha (ca 535–65) readopted the royal title following his return from the land of Maʿadd,[181] where he took possession of regions in North and Central Arabia (Table A.3).[182] In another monumental inscription, Kindah, ʿUlah and Saʿd are described as allies of the Ḥimyarite king.[183]

Overall, the twelve groups identified as ʾʿ*rb* in the corpus inhabited different areas of the Arabian Peninsula, from Palestine to Yemen. An inscription written under ruler Yūsuf mentions 'the tribe of Hamdān and their *hgr* and their ʿ*rb*, and the ʾʿ*rb* of Kindah, Muḍar and Madhḥig' found in Central Arabia.[184] As *Hgr* means 'city',[185] *hgr* and ʿ*rb* seem to be in contrast, meaning 'citizens' and 'nomads'.[186] Furthermore, the lexemes ʾʿ*rb* and ʿ*rb* appear together only in a few South Arabian inscriptions (Table A.4).[187] Jan Retsö has suggested that ʾʿ*rb* refers to a South Arabian group dependent on the Ḥimyarite Kingdom while framing the collective ʿ*rb(n)* as

178 As Abīkarib Asʿad claimed to rule in an inscription over 'their' ʾʿ*rb* and in another over the more generic ʾʿ*rb*, he probably changed the title in around 440. His successors rule over 'their' ʾʿ*rb*. See CIH 540; CIH 45+CIH 44; Dostal 1; Gar framm. 3; Gar Sharahbil A. See also Ry 509.

179 U. Avner, L. Nehmé and C. J. Robin, 'A Rock Inscription Mentioning Thaʿlaba, an Arab King from Ghassān', *Arabian Archaeology and Epigraphy* 24 (2013), 237–56, at p. 251. Significantly, while the Ḥimyarites recognized these political powers as being ʾʿ*rb*, no mention of this lexeme is found in Ḥujrid inscription.

180 As well as the so far unidentified *S¹bʿ*. See Ry 510.

181 Murayghān 3.

182 ʾʿ*rb* of Maʿadd and Ṭayy in Central Arabia; Hagar, Khaṭṭ, in Eastern Arabia; Yathrib, modern Medina in Ḥijāz; and Guzām on the borders of Palestine. See C. J. Robin and S. Tayran, 'Soixante-dix ans avant l'Islam: l'Arabie toute entière dominée par un roi chrétien', *Comptes rendus de l''académie des inscriptions et belles lettres* (2012), 525–53, at p. 546.

183 Ry 506.

184 Ry 508.

185 Ry 520; Wellcome A 103664.

186 An inscription similarly mentions the ʾʿ*rb* of Kindah, Muḍar and Madhḥig and the *hgrn* and ʿ*rbn* within the large South Arabian tribe of Hamdān (Ja 1028), while another clearly distinguishes the ʾs²ʿb ḏ-Hmdn (tribe of Hamdān) from the ʿ*rbn* (Ry 507). Ry 510, written in 481 and found in wādī Maʾsal (215 km west of al-Riyād in the Najd), significantly underlines that the ʿ*rbn* are rebellious (*qs¹dm*).

187 ʿ*rb* is sometimes found next to the title as in the Central Middle Sabean inscription Ja 629.

Table 1.1 *ʿrb(n) and ʾʿrb in South Arabian inscriptions*

Lexeme	Relation with Ḥimyar	Possible meaning	E.g., South Arabian mentions
ʿrb(n)	Independent	Nomads ≠ *hgr(n)* 'sedentary' (lit. 'inhabiting cities')	FB-al-ʿAdān 1: 'the wars and the razzias of the ʿ***rbn*** of the region of the East'
ʾʿrb	Dependent	Allies, appearing in the royal *tituli*	MAFRAY-al-Miʿsāl 4: 'ʾʿ***rb*** who were in the town of Shabwa'

independent political entities living between Najrān and Jawf.[188] In other words, *ʿrb(n)* indicate outsiders who were never conquered by South Arabia, while the *ʾʿrb* are Ḥimyar's allies. Much like the Neo-Assyrian *Ar-ba-a-a* and *A-rib-bi* there could be a semantic distinction between *ʿrb(n)* and *ʾʿrb*. As the lexeme *ʿrb(n)* is in contrast to *hgr*, 'citizens' or 'sedentary',[189] *ʿrb(n)* might have been nomads/Bedouins. And indeed, it is possible that the *ʿrb(n)* were independent entities associated with larger communities.[190] The lexeme indicated people with nomadic ways of life, in contrast with the *ʾʿrb* allies.[191] Significantly, as previously suggested by the classical sources, the South Arabians of *Arabia Felix*, with their millennial civilization, did not view themselves as Arabs/Arabians. At the same time, those who were labelled *ʾʿrb* did not consider themselves to be Arabs either.[192]

1.4.6 Qur'ān

In the Qur'ān, the root *ʿ-r-b* is used to indicate either the language of the Muslim Holy Book[193] or a group of people.[194] The authors of the classical

188 Retsö, *The Arabs in Antiquity*, 563.

189 The word *ʿrb* in the Central Middle Sabean Ja 629 has been translated as 'nomads' by CSAI but nothing strictly points to this identification.

190 E.g., that of Hamdān.

191 Hence, Ry 510 could be translated: 'Mʿdkrb Yʿfr, king of Sabaʾ, ḏu-Raydān, Ḥaḍramawt, Yamanat, and their Arab/Arabian allies (*ʾʿrb*) of Ṭwdm and of Thmt announced and recorded this inscription in Mʾs¹lm Gmḥn during an expedition in the plain of Ktʾ to submit the rebellious Arab/Arabian nomads (*ʿrbn*) to him, when Mdhrm made war with him. He undertook this expedition with his tribes Sabaʾ, Ḥimyar, Rḥbtn, Ḥaḍramawt and Yḥn, with their Arab/Arabian allies (*ʾʿrb*) of Kindah and Mḏḥgm and with the banū Ṯʿlbt, Mḍr et S¹bʿ. In the month of Qyẓn, six hundred thirty-one.'

192 This is exemplified by the case of 'Ḥujr son of ʿAmr' who celebrated himself as '*mlk* of Kiddat', and not of the Arabs/Arabians. See Avner, Nehmé and Robin, 'A Rock Inscription Mentioning Thaʿlaba', 251.

193 Q. 27:195; 12:2; 39:28; 41:3, 44; 43:3; 13:37; 16:103; 20:113; 46:12; 42:7.

194 Q. 9:90, 97–9, 101, 120; 48:11, 16; 49:14.

Tafsīr al-Jalālayn and *Tanwīr al-Miqbās min Tafsīr Ibn ʿAbbās* interpret the *aʿrāb* of Q. 9.99 ('among the *al-aʿrāb,* there are some who believe in Allāh and the Last Day') as the Medinan tribes of Juhayna and Muzayna.[195] In contrast, with regards to Q. 9.101, the *al-aʿrāb* are referred to as *munāfiqūn* ('hypocrites'), that is, according to the first *tafsīr*, the tribes of Ashja', from the Najd tribe Ghaṭafān, and the Ḥijāzī Banū Ghifār and the Ghaṭafān, while they are referred to the Banū Asad in the second *tafsīr*). All these groups inhabited North and Central Arabia during Late Antiquity. While Juhayna and Muzayna quickly embraced Islam, the other groups were hostile towards Muḥammad at the beginning of his career as a prophet. Therefore, the Qur'ānic root *ʿ-r-b* did not point to a homogeneous community but to different peoples who shared the geographical boundaries of Medina, where the *suwar* were first revealed to the prophet.

1.4.7 Notes on Ethnicity and Conclusion

The root *ʿ-r-b* indicates groups of people but also means 'offering a sacrifice' and 'squared stones'.[196] These meanings are attested in all Semitic languages,[197] and Gəʿəz.[198] West, steppe and 'mixed people' are also possible semantic explanations of the lexemes Arabia and Arabs/Arabians, thus suggesting that the word did not originate as self-identification. This is especially evident in the case of 'west' as it implies its use by someone 'at the east' (e.g., Sargon, whose seat was in Dur-Sharrukin in Iraq). I will now offer some brief reflections on the concept of ethnicity before drawing a conclusion on the identification of the 'Arabians' of pre-Islamic Arabia.

In a recently published paper, Ahmad al-Jallad introduced two new Safaitic inscriptions (part of the Ancient North Arabian corpus) containing the lexeme *ʿrb*, claiming that the term was an endonym *ethnicon* broadly referring to the tribes inhabiting the desert region in the Ḥarrah.[199] Nonetheless, as the same author acknowledges, the production of Safaitic inscriptions is the only tangible cultural thread connecting the people of the Ḥarrah.[200] The amount of evidence needed to claim that the lexeme *ʿrb* is an ethnicon is arguably insufficient, so the hypothesis is not entirely

195 *Tafsīr al-Jalālayn.*
196 See Minaic and Qatabanic meanings under "rb' in J. C. Biella, *Dictionary of Old South Arabic Sabaean Dialect* (Chico: Scholars Press, 1982), 382–3.
197 See "rb' in D. J. A. Clines (ed.), *Dictionary of Classical Hebrew* (Sheffield: Phoenix Press, 1993), 548.
198 2 Enoch 1.
199 A. al-Jallad, "Arab, 'Aʿrāb, and Arabic in Ancient North Arabia: The First Attestation of (') ʿrb as a Group Name in Safaitic', *Arabian Archaeology and Epigraphy* 31 (2020), 422–35.
200 Al-Jallad, *Outline*, 9.

convincing. Moreover, the presence of *ʿrb* in various regions in Arabia, and not just in the circumscribed area where these two inscriptions were found, further weakens al-Jallad's position. Certainly, if *ʿrb* were indeed an endonym ethnicon, it is more probable that it referred only to some and not all *ʿrb*.

There are apparent impediments to applying modern categories, such as ethnicity, to Antiquity. Today, ethnicity usually refers to group identity based on shared culture, traditions and customs. As pointed out by Walter Pohl, ethnic identity 'is not an inherent quality' but the consequence of 'acts of identification and distinction'.[201] Consequently, an ethnic group and its symbols must be 'recognized from the outside'.[202] For Herodotus, *ethnos* indicated a group viewed as a geographical, political or cultural entity, while *genos*, from the verb 'to be born', was used to define groups whose members were related by birth.[203] In the Hellenistic Egyptian usage, Hellenes, Persians and Arabs were described as *ethnē,* but so were groups such as beekeepers and prostitutes.[204] During Late Antiquity, identities 'only existed through efforts to make them meaningful'.[205] In this particular historical period, identities needed to become less defined, more blurred and increasingly adaptive to accommodate necessarily fluid loyalties caused by the rapidly changing fortunes of the kings of the time, as exemplified by the case of the Frankish of Visigothic kings.[206] 'Essential religious values' thus linked subjects and rulers, as well as individuals and society.[207]

Although Roman literary sources often tend to frame the pre-Islamic inhabitants of the Arabian Peninsula as one group, the Arabians differed in traditions, languages and customs. Indeed, there is not one easily

201 W. Pohl, 'Ethnicity and Empire in the Western Eurasian Steppes', in *Empires and Exchanges in Eurasian Late Antiquity: Rome, China, Iran, and the Steppe, ca. 250–750*, ed. N. Di Cosmo and M. Maas (Cambridge: Cambridge University Press, 2018), 189–205, at p. 192.

202 Ibid.

203 C. P. Jones, 'ἔθνος and γένος in Herodotus', *The Classical Quarterly* 46 (1996), 315–20.

204 D. J. Thompson, 'Hellenistic Hellenes: The Case of Ptolemaic Egypt', in *Ancient Perceptions of Greek Ethnicity*, ed. I. Malkin (Cambridge, MA: Harvard University Press, 2001), 301–22, at p. 309.

205 W. Pohl, 'Ethnicity, Theory, and Tradition: A Response', in *On Barbarian Identity: Critical Approaches to Ethnicity in the Early Middle Ages*, ed. A. Gillet (Turnhout: Brepols, 2002), 221–41, at p. 238.

206 W. Pohl, 'Telling the Difference: Signs of Ethnic Identity', in *Strategies of Distinction: The Construction of Ethnic Communities 300–800*, ed. W. Pohl and H. Reimitz (Leiden: Brill, 1998), 17–69.

207 S. Esders, '"Faithful Believers": Oaths of Allegiance in Post-Roman Societies as Evidence for Eastern and Western "Visions of Community"', in *Visions of Community in the Post-Roman World: The West, Byzantium and the Islamic World*, ed. W. Pohl, C. Gantner and R. E. Payne (London: Routledge, 2012), 357–74, at p. 359.

distinguishable feature that 'held' the Arabians together and allows us to use the term 'Arabs' when referring to pre-Islamic times. This is, of course, not to say that an ethnic group cannot have a mixed background or that ethnicities are biologically transmitted or immutable, rather that, if ethnicity is a social construct, the 'sociality' of the Arabs only emerged following the rise of Islam, as the various polities of Arabia perceived each other as 'foreign' and 'other' based on lineage and culture, in particular of language and faith. As Rachel Mairs puts it in her recent book on what she defines as the 'Hellenist Far East', 'what is important in the construction of an ethnic group and the maintenance of its boundaries is not that a group have any objective common culture but that groups take aspects of their cultural toolkit and invest these with ethnic significance'.[208] Accordingly, they were simply 'Arabians', bounded by shared geographical space, namely, the Arabian Peninsula. Among these Arabians, multiple 'ethnicities' are distinguishable. As already suggested in 1896,[209] Arabness is a notion that became distinguishable only after the establishment of the Muslim community, when a cultural identity was shared by the fragmented tribal societies of the future world conquerors.[210]

At the end of the last century, Michel Gawlikowski suggested reading the Assyrian *Aribi* as indicating 'un mode de vie', namely that of the nomads.[211] In more recent years, Macdonald has suggested that the term 'Arabs' originated as a 'self-designation based on recognizing an ill-defined complex of linguistic and cultural characteristics'.[212] However, this view does not explain why the Assyrians did not use the existing Assyrian terms meaning 'nomads'.[213] At the same time, it is questionable to claim that shared cultural characteristics existed among all the various groups labelled as 'Arabs'. Jan Retsö has instead suggested that 'Arab' 'designates a community of people with war-like properties, standing under the command of a divine hero, being intimately connected with the use of the domesticated camel',[214] but evidence to support this claim is also scant.

208 R. Mairs, *The Hellenistic Far East: Archaeology, Language, and Identity in Greek Central Asia* (Oakland: University of California Press, 2014), 183.

209 D. H. Müller, 'Arabia', in *Paulys Real-Encyclopädie der Classischen Altertumswissenschaft*, ed. G. Wissowa (Stuttgart: Metzler, 1895), 3.344–59.

210 V. A. Grasso and G. Fowden, 'Review', 317–20, at p. 318.

211 M. Gawlikowski, 'Arabes et Arabies dans l'antiquité', *Topoi: Orient-Occident* 14 (2006), 41–6.

212 M. C. A. Macdonald, 'Arabs, Arabias and Arabic before Late Antiquity', *Topoi: Orient-Occident* 16 (2009), 277–332, at p. 296; Grasso and Fowden, 'Review', 319.

213 Grasso and Fowden, 'Review', 319.

214 Retsö, *Arabs in Antiquity*, 623.

Intending to define more precisely the scope and the horizons of this book, the present section has shown how pre-Islamic sources mention the 'Arabs' as the inhabitants of the northern and central parts of the Arabian Peninsula. A distinction between the *'rb* allied with the southern kingdom of Ḥimyar and the independent Bedouins in the same region demonstrates the difficulty of generically classifying the communities living between the Red Sea and the Persian Gulf as 'Arabs'. These people did not possess a distinguishable culture; they did not share a common lifestyle and did not have a common religious creed until the rise of Islam. Even if they did speak one common language, their 'linguistic label would not determine their ethnic identity', as studies have highlighted in the similar possibly shared linguistic case of the Huns and the Avars.[215]

Although shared ethnicity is arguably apparent in a community characterized by (some degree of) homogeneity of culture and shared territory, ethnicity is a 'system of distinctions that allows defining social groups in relation to each other'.[216] Therefore, ethnic identities can change through time and space as ethnicity, from the ancient Greek *ethnos* 'nation', is mostly a practice in process. Thus, I have argued that the connection between the 'Arabs' found in the sources mentioned earlier is purely geographical. These people dwelled in Central and North Arabia but belonged to different tribes, each of which more than likely had different and distinguishable cultural heritages. Hence, it is preferable to use the geographic term 'Arabians' to the ethnic term 'Arabs' when discussing the inhabitants of pre-Islamic Arabia.[217] Use of words such as 'Saracens', instinctively used by students of Rome and Iran,[218] suggests an approach based on an 'external standpoint' and should be similarly disregarded.

While the multicultural Huns and the Xiongnu established their identities on political rather than ethnic grounds, the Arabians forged their own identity after Muḥammad's prophetic career on the grounds of one faith and the one language of its sacred text. However, as Islam had universalist claims just like Christianity, the term 'Muslim' soon became an *ethnicon* used as a term of self-identification, while 'Arab' was rarely self-applied and emerged only after the military success of the 'Muslims'. According to Amartya Sen, 'religion is not, and cannot be, a person's

215 Pohl, 'Ethnicity and Empire in the Western Eurasian Steppes', 191.
216 Pohl, 'Migrations, Ethnic Groups, and State Building', 256.
217 Similarly in Webb, *Imagining the Arabs*, 96. See also Marsham, *Rituals of Islamic Monarchy*, 16, n.9.
218 E.g., M. Bonner, *The Last Empire of Iran* (Piscataway: Gorgias Press, 2020), 109.

all-encompassing identity'.[219] Nonetheless, it is a fact that 'Arabness' became closely connected to ideas in the Qur'ān and, in particular, to its 'Arabic language' (*lisānan ʿarabīyan*).[220] After the rise of Islam and the creation of the Caliphate, Arabic became the tool to record pre-existing oral poetry and historical narratives, laying the foundations for the 'Arab' and 'Muslim' genealogy. Building on George Ostrogorsky's description of the 'Byzantines',[221] the 'Arabians' became Arab, Arabic-speakers and Muslims simultaneously due to the first Muslim conquests. Yet, as Islam expanded outside of Arabia, the 'Arab' (and 'Arabic-speaker') and 'Muslim' identities became increasingly independent of one another, with the progressive detachment of the Arab ethnicon from its religious component. Similarly to the disjunction of the Roman and Christian identities after the ninth century,[222] the label 'Arab' was gradually abandoned to include the 'other' people of the Caliphate. Indeed, although Muḥammad's movement originated in the Arabian Peninsula, the empire which emerged from it became increasingly defined as 'Muslim' and much less commonly as 'Arab'.[223] This empire, with its several capitals, soon located outside the peninsula and forged its identity by imbibing the eclectic cultures of its subjects, especially the Iranian culture, bestowing 'in exchange' Islamic patronage and citizenship. As ethnicities are not biological entities, in the heyday of the Muslim Commonwealth, one could become an 'Arab' through a process of integration and acculturation by converting to Islam, learning Arabic and adhering to the customs and laws of the Caliphate.

In the early twentieth century, Ostrogorsky defined the 'Byzantines' as simultaneously Roman, Greek and Christian.[224] More recently, Anthony Kaldellis has argued that the Romans of Byzantium were an ethnic group and that the 'core national state' of Romanía was not an empire but had an empire.[225] Disputing the 'monstrously inverted riddle' which saw the Roman Empire as the only empire in history 'about which it was possible to identify ethnic minorities but not the majority',[226] Kaldellis also suggested that before the ninth century, 'Roman' and 'Christian' referred

219 A. K. Sen, *Identity and Violence: The Illusion of Destiny* (London: Allen Lane, 2006), 83. I came to this passage through Kaldellis, *Romanland*, 113.

220 E.g., Q. 46.12.

221 G. Ostrogorsky, *History of the Byzantine State* (New Brunswick: Rutgers, 1969), 27.

222 Kaldellis, *Romanland*, 31.

223 The Umayyads are often called an 'Arab' dynasty to distinguish them from the more Muslim Abbasids.

224 Ostrogorsky, *History of the Byzantine State*, 27.

225 Kaldellis, *Romanland*, 267–8.

226 Ibid., 270.

to 'complementary identities of the same group of people'.[227] It could be argued that as Islam 'created the Arabs' through the spread of the language of the Qur'ān, it also 'overcame the Arabs' after the fall of the Caliphate. Thus, we would never refer to contemporary Malaysian Muslims as 'Arabs' (Islam became the majority religion for the Malays in the fifteenth and sixteenth centuries after the fall of the Caliphate, but Arabic never substituted Malayan as an official language). Of the twenty-two countries which are today part of the Arab League and constitute the 'Arab world', only six are found in the Arabian Peninsula (three more, namely Bahrain, Jordan and Syria, are found in its northern extension). These countries share one official language, Arabic, but much like the tribes of pre-Islamic Arabia, they possess different cultural heritages. The history of Arabia is not the history of Islam or vice versa. Similarly, the history of the Arabs is neither the history of the Arabians nor that of the Muslims. Since the end of the first millennium, when Islam attained 'intellectual and institutional maturation',[228] the great majority of the Arabs viewed themselves as belonging to one community, built around one faith, Islam, and with one language, Arabic. However, this was certainly not the case in pre-Islamic Arabia.

[227] Ibid., 107.
[228] Fowden, *Before and after Muḥammad*, 15.

CHAPTER 2

North Arabia between the Late Third and the Fifth Century
Borders and Conversions

This chapter narrates the history of North Arabia between the late third and fifth centuries. In around 224, the Arsacid dynasty in Iran was defeated by the Sasanians, who immediately embarked on a war against Rome.[1] The renewed animosity between the two superpowers of Late Antiquity had repercussions in the Near East, causing the fall of valuable buffer states such as Palmyra and Hatra and the employment of Arabian allies in areas such as North Ḥijāz, where the Romans could no longer easily exercise direct control. These Arabian allied confederacies did not have fixed geographical boundaries and were also often unstable in their alliances, as exemplified by the case of Imru' al-Qays. After shedding light on the sociopolitical situation of North Arabia, I focus on the impact of Constantine's conversion to Christianity, which had the result of creating a cultural network that has been defined as a commonwealth by Dimitri Obolensky,[2] and by Garth Fowden.[3] The concept has been recently revisited by Christian Raffensperger, who has argued that Rome's culture and political power were influential throughout Europe (including Rus) and that the 'Byzantine commonwealth' included all of Christendom.[4] Philip Wood has recently argued the Miaphysites were 'empowered through the invention of new historical narratives: a Miaphysite commonwealth',[5] and I have elsewhere expanded on this theme.[6] What is relevant for this

[1] The Arsacids are also known as Parthians. 'Arsacid' indicated the dynastic name, while 'Parthia' refers to the home province.

[2] D. Obolensky, *The Byzantine Commonwealth: Eastern Europe 500–1453* (New York: Praeger Publishers, 1971).

[3] Fowden, *Empire to Commonwealth*, 170; Fowden, *Before and after Muhammad*, 105.

[4] C. Raffensperger, 'Revisiting the Idea of the Byzantine Commonwealth', *Byzantinische Forschungen* 28 (2004), 159–74; *Reimagining Europe: Kievan Rus' in the Medieval World* (Cambridge, MA: Harvard University Press, 2012).

[5] P. Wood, '*We Have No King but Christ': Christian Political Thought in Greater Syria on the Eve of the Arab Conquest (c.400–585)* (Oxford: Oxford University Press, 2010), 210.

[6] V. A. Grasso, 'Rejoice in God!'.

discussion is that although it is hard to assess Constantine's vision for a Christian empire (or its propagandistic depiction by Eusebius), his religious affiliation had profound repercussions on the map of Late Antiquity. The 'new universal Christian commonwealth embracing Armenians, Iberians, Arabs, and Aksūmites that Constantine had initiated' survived his death,[7] and was mauled by heated diatribes which lasted for centuries. Indeed, the 'first Byzantine Commonwealth' found its 'most distinctive identity' more than one hundred years after Constantine's death in the aftermath of the Council of Chalcedon (451).[8] The inhabitants of the Arabian Peninsula were not simply caught up in the debate post-Chalcedon. They were active actors, as shown by the Jafnid Ḥārith's role in mediating between members of the Miaphysite movement (Chapter 5).[9]

Past scholarship often accepted the narrative about 'uncivilized Arabs' controlled by surrounding empires. The two most significant publications on North Arabia and Christianity, by John Trimingham,[10] and Irfan Shahid,[11] took diametrically opposite views. While Trimingham claimed that Christianity had a marginal role in Arabia, Shahid overestimated its presence and impact. I argue that Christianity had an instrumental role for the North Arabian urban elites and a more limited role among the poorer classes (and especially the rural ones). While the elites and the upper classes adopted Christianity to advance their careers and wealth, the eclectic mix of pagan and incipient scriptural beliefs led to henotheistic tendencies. Sites such as Umm al-Jimāl in Jordan, where eighth of the fifteen churches have been attributed to private contexts,[12] point to the establishment of Christianity as a mainly urban and elite phenomenon in Arabia. What emerges from a combined study of literary and archaeological material is that Arabia was a critical Roman and Iranian area of interest owing to its inland and maritime trade routes and the need for these two empires

[7] E. Fowden, 'Constantine and the Peoples of the Eastern Frontier', 392.

[8] Fowden, *Empire to Commonwealth*, 100. On its identity, note p. 127: 'The Byzantine Commonwealth's identity was twofold, political and cultural, Roman and Christian. But as it came gradually under the influence of Monophysitism, the commonwealth substituted a more specifically Constantinian and Nicaean persona for generalized identification with Rome and the Church.'

[9] Also, V. A. Grasso, 'On the Jafnid al-Ḥārith, from the Jafnid al-Ḥārith: A Translation and Commentary of Syriac Miaphysite Letters from the Sixth Century' (forthcoming).

[10] J. S. Trimingham, *Christianity among the Arabs in pre-Islamic Times* (London: Longman, 1979).

[11] Shahid, *Byzantium and the Arabs.*

[12] B. De Vries, 'Continuity and Change in the Urban Character of the Southern Hauran from the 5th to the 9th Century: The Archaeological Evidence at Umm al-Jimal', *Journal of Mediterranean Archaeology* 13 (2000), 39–45, at p. 41. Only the cathedral looks like a public church. I am grateful to Darrell Rohl, Elizabeth Ann Osinga and Bert De Vries for giving me a tour of the site in the summer of 2018.

to defend their frontiers. However, negotiations with the Arabians, often characterized by an instrumental use of religious faith, were a distinctive feature of the period. Indeed, the Arabians of the third, fourth and fifth centuries were active participants in shaping the political map of Late Antiquity, and their importance must be impartially assessed. This is precisely the aim of this chapter.

2.1 The Making of Arabian Late Antiquity: The Political Map of North Arabia

In the last decade of the second century, Septimius Severus (r. 193–211) took power. Possibly encouraged by his Syrian wife,[13] he enlarged *Provincia Arabia* towards the north,[14] dividing Syria into *Syria Phoenice* and *Coele-Syria* to contain the control of one provincial commander.[15] Severus also reactivated the old *Via Nova Traiana,* which linked the Red Sea to Buṣrā, protecting it with a legion based at Buṣrā (*III Legio Cyrenaica*) and thus assuring Roman control of the caravan trade.[16] After his death, his son Caracalla became emperor (r. 198–217). In 212, Caracalla issued the *Constitutio Antoniniana* granting Roman citizenship to all free men of the empire.[17] The edict permitted the inhabitants of the provinces of the empire to undertake essential roles in the administration of Rome, allowing Philip the Arab, *Philippus Arabus*, born in *Provincia Arabia*, to become Augustus in 244. Philip rose 'from the humble station, as his father was a noblest commander of brigands (*latronum ductor*)'.[18] Although his reign lasted only five years, it is significant that an Arabian was the highest authority in the empire when Rome celebrated its millennium of existence in the heart of the Roman West in 248.[19] While Philip had signed a peace treaty with the Sasanian Shāpūr I (r. ca. 240–70), tensions grew between the two empires immediately after his death, as exemplified by a famous relief with an inscription found at Naqsh-i Rustam portraying Philip and his successor, Valerian the Elder (r. 253–60), begging for mercy from the

13 Cass. Dio 77.4.2–3.

14 Herodian, *History*, 3.9.3.

15 Millar, *The Roman Near East*, 122.

16 M. Piccirillo, *L'Arabia cristiana: dalla provincia imperiale al primo periodo islamico* (Milan: Jaca Book, 2002), 18.

17 For a recent study see A. Imrie, *The Antonine Constitution: An Edict for the Caracallan Empire* (Leiden: Brill, 2018).

18 *Epit. de Caes.* 28.4.

19 W. Ball, *Rome in the East: The Transformation of an Empire* (London: Routledge, 2000), 417.

Sasanian ruler, riding a horse in front of the *mūbadān mūbad*, the high Zoroastrian priest.[20]

Fergus Millar has argued that this period represents 'the height of overt "Romanisation"' in the Near East.[21] Yet, the rise to power of the new belligerent Sasanian dynasty in Iran significantly affected the political map of the Near East. Hatra fell in around 240 under repeated attacks from the Sasanians,[22] followed by the fall of Dura-Europos in about 255.[23] Other cities in northern Syria, such as Antioch, were taken for the first time in three centuries. At the same time, Shāpūr I gained total control of the 'throng of cities and villages and ships' of the Persian Gulf,[24] assuring Iran's monopoly of the trade routes with India through eastern Arabia. Shāpūr II (r. 309–79) was also remarkably successful in developing Iran's defence in his military deployment of Arabian and Hun allies.[25] Conversely, the Roman Empire experienced an internal political struggle for most of the early late antique period. The answer to this political struggle and the inability to rule from the centre was to divide power between regions, as officially formalized with the creation of the Tetrarchy in 293.

A determining factor in the decline of Rome's control in the East was the revolt of Palmyra, its main Eastern ally. Having long served as a buffer state for the Roman Empire, the city took advantage of the Roman Empire's crisis in the third century, ignited by Sassanid aggressions and Germanic raids. When Zenobia, the queen of Palmyra (r. 268–72), broke the Roman yoke, Postumus (r. 260–9) took advantage of the Germanic invasions in the Roman West to found the short-lived Gallic Empire. Palmyra suffered damage during Aurelian's armies' incursion in 272–3, and the Gallic emperor Tetricus I (r. 271–4) was defeated two years later, delaying the economic collapse of Rome. While after the retaking of Gaul, an official of the Gallic Empire was still allowed to continue their careers (Tetricus was even appointed *corrector Lucaniae*),[26] Palmyra's status was limited and reduced to a modest military and administrative role.[27]

20 For a translation of the inscription see D. N. MacKenzie, 'Kerdir's Inscription', in *Iranica diversa*, ed. C. G. Cereti and L. Paul (Rome: Istituto italiano per l'Africa e l'Oriente, 1999), 217–73. See also P. Gignoux, *Les quatre inscriptions du mage Kirdīr* (Paris: Association pour l'avancement des études iraniennes, 1991).

21 Millar, *Roman Near East*, 155.

22 M. Sartre, *The Middle East under Rome* (Cambridge: Cambridge University Press, 2005), 345–6.

23 D. Macdonald, 'Dating the Fall of Dura-Europos', *Historia: Zeitschrift für Alte Geschichte* 1 (1986), 45–68.

24 Amm. 23.6.10.

25 Bonner, *Last Empire of Iran*, 93.

26 Aurel. Vict. *Caes.* 35.5; Eutr. 9.13.

27 Not. Dig. *Leg I illyricorum.*

Moreover, a recent study on the city's production of funerary portraits has shown that Palmyra's decline coincided with the instability caused by the Arsacid invasion of Dura-Europos and Hatra in 239–40 CE, from which the city never recovered.[28]

Palmyra's fall had significant repercussions on the welfare of the Roman Empire and its relationship with the inhabitants of the Near East. Arabian tribes who had migrated northwards and were previously controlled by the buffer state of Palmyra were now in direct contact with the superpowers of the period. The Arabian Tanūkh, for example, helped Aurelian defeat Zenobia and significantly increased their authority in Syria, taking on the duty of patrolling Rome's Arabian frontier. The Romans employed a similar strategy to what the Han defined as 以夷制夷, *yǐ yí zhì yí*, literally meaning 'using' 'foreign race (barbarian)' 'to stop' '(barbarian)': the 'barbarians' needed to be controlled by other 'barbarians'. The Tanūkh alliance with Rome assured them hegemonic power over the caravan routes in Syria and consequently a special position in the political map of North Arabia at the end of the third century. The changed status of some Arabian allies is demonstrated by the introduction of the term 'phylarch', now a specific title awarded by the Romans.[29]

After a period of peace, the animosity between Rome and Iran was reignited when Iran invaded Armenia, which, together with the Red Sea, was one of the favourite battlegrounds of the first millennium. During the reign of Constantius II (r. 337–61), Shāpūr II repeatedly embarked on campaigns to expand Iran's domains. These constant skirmishes were momentarily ended with the signing of treaties between the two superpowers, the first agreed by Shāpūr II and Jovian (r. 363–4) and the second by Shāpūr III (r. 383–8) and Theodosius I (r. 379–95). These treaties redefined the map of the Near East for the whole of the following century, until the outbreak of the wars Kavādh I (488–531) and Anastasius I (r. 491–518). Allied tribes were increasingly in control of the borders of the Arabian borders of the Roman and Iranian empires, and these treaties allowed both empires to concentrate their forces on combatting Germanic and Hunnic incursions into their respective territories. While South Arabia remained neutral throughout the century (see Chapter 3), North Arabia became a sort of 'experimental war zone' where the two empires repeatedly engaged in battle through their alliances with local Arabian tribes.

[28] R. Raja et al., 'Three Hundred Years of Palmyrene History: Unlocking Archaeological Data for Studying Past Societal Transformations', *PLoS ONE* 16 (2021), 1–33, at p. 24.

[29] A. G. Grouchevoy, 'Trois' niveaux' de phylarques. Étude terminologique sur les relations de Rome et de Byzance avec les Arabes avant l'Islam', *Syria* (1995), 105–31.

From the beginning of the fourth century, a series of defensive projects were undertaken along the Roman *Limes Arabicus*, more of a fortified region than a fortified line from the second century onwards.[30] In the last years of the third century, Diocletian built a fortified road known as the *Strata Diocletiana*, which ran from southern Syria to the Euphrates in the north-east and connected Damascus and Palmyra. This road was built to control caravan traffic but revealed itself to be an effective protection instrument; a series of fortifications were constructed along the route in the fourth century. For instance, a new *castellum* known in an inscription as *Castra Praetorii Mobeni* was built at the military centre of Umm al-Jimāl, now defended by high walls.[31] Several forts, such as those at al-Lajjūn,[32] Dayr al-Kahf[33] and Qaṣr Bshīr, were also constructed at this time,[34] and two of them, Dajaniya and ʾUdhruḥ, figure among the significant late Roman fortifications of the time.[35] The Romans also built forts in the *ḥarrah* in the surroundings of permanent water to control the nomads.[36]

At the same time, on the southern border of Iran, Shāpūr II constructed a defensive system close to Ḥīrah (the seat of the Naṣrids), which later became known as *war tāzīgān* 'wall of the Arabs',[37] with watchtowers and forts proceeding from Hīt to Buṣrā.[38] Sasanian fortifications walled out both north-eastern Arabia and the northern steppe in Central Asia. In the fifth century, the fortifications erected in the Caucasus aimed to protect the region from the raids of the people ('Alans') dwelling north of the Caucasus and to increase agricultural and tax income.[39] Mohammad Chaichian provides a different explanation for constructing the late fifth-century Gorgan Wall; he claims it was not built as a defensive barrier against the Hephthalites' raids into Iran as their incursions proceeded

30 Bowersock, *Roman Arabia*, 103–4.

31 Ibid., 176; B. De Vries, *Umm el-Jimal: A Frontier Town and Its Landscape in Northern Jordan*, Vol. 1, *Fieldwork 1972–1981* (Portsmouth: Journal of Roman Archaeology, 1998), 229.

32 D. Kennedy and D. Riley, *Rome's Desert Frontier from the Air* (London: Batsford, 1990), 173.

33 Ibid., 181.

34 Ibid.; V. A. Clark, 'The Roman Castellum of Qasr Bshir', in *The Roman Frontier in Central Jordan*, ed. S. T. Parker (Oxford: Oxford University Press, 1987), 457–95.

35 B. Dignas and E. Winter, *Rome and Persia in Late Antiquity* (Cambridge: Cambridge University Press, 2007), 164.

36 Macdonald, 'Graffiti and Complexity', 346.

37 H. Mahamedi, 'Wall as a System of Frontier Defence during the Sasanid Period', in *Mēnōg ī Xrad: The Spirit of Wisdom, Essays in Memory of Ahmad Tafazzoli* (2004), 145–59.

38 C. Morley, 'The Arabian Frontier: A Keystone of the Sasanian Empire', in *Sasanian Persia: Between Rome and the Steppes of Eurasia*, ed. E. Sauer (Edinburgh: Edinburgh University Press, 2017), pp. 268–83, at p. 273.

39 K. Alizadeh, 'Borderland Projects of Sasanian Empire', *Journal of Ancient History* 2 (2014), 93–115, at p. 110.

east–west, not north–south.[40] He suggests the wall could have also been used as an irrigation canal and a refuge during the flooding seasons, not just as a defensive barrier against the armies of invading tribes.[41] Rome and Iran sometimes collaborated on constructing defensive walls to defend themselves from the Huns of the southern Caucasus.[42]

There were no static borders; frontier zones instead bounded political entities.[43] These borders aimed at keeping people outside and not inside. Scholars have claimed that these defensive structures were constructed to protect the sedentary populations from the threat of nomads,[44] and were a response to the introduction of a new saddle for camel riders. This new saddle probably contributed to an increase in the threat posed by nomadic raids on settlements during the fourth century.[45] Similarly to the Iranian East,[46] there was a dynamic interplay of nomadic and sedentary groups in Arabia. Nonetheless, doubts have been raised about Ammianus Marcellinus' description of nomadic raids in the fourth century.[47] David Graf, in particular, has argued against 'the hypothesis of pillaging hordes of Arab nomads descending on defenceless frontier settlements',[48] using Pierre Briant's concept of *paranoïa obsidionale* to refer to 'a political-psychological complex which perceives the central or imperial state in a constant struggle with brigands on its borders'.[49]

Defensive systems primarily ensured the maintenance and security of the empire's borders, allowing the Romans to quickly move their military units in case of attacks from nomads and their enemy superpower, but also

[40] M. A. Chaichian, *Empires and Walls: Globalization, Migration, and Colonial Domination* (Leiden: Brill, 2014), 53–89.

[41] Ibid.

[42] Alizadeh, 'Borderland Projects of Sasanian Empire', 108.

[43] Alizadeh, 'Overlapping Social and Political Boundaries: Borders of the Sasanian Empire and the Muslim Caliphate in the Caucasus', in *Archaeology of Medieval Islamic Frontiers*, ed. A. Eger (Louisville: University Press of Colorado, 2019), 139–67, at pp. 139–40.

[44] S. T. Parker, 'The Nature of Rome's Arabian Frontier', in *Roman Frontier Studies 1989: Proceedings of the XVth International Congress of Roman Frontier Studies*, ed. V. A. Maxfield and M. J. Dobson (Exeter: University of Exeter Press, 1991), 498–504; S. T. Parker, 'The Roman Frontier in Jordan: An Overview', in *Limes XVIII: Proceedings of the XVIIIth International Congress of Roman Frontier Studies Held in Amman, Jordan*, ed. P. Freeman, J. Bennett, Z. T. Fiema and B. Hoffmann (Oxford: Oxford University Press, 2002), 77–84.

[45] D. F. Graf, *Rome and the Arabian Frontier: From the Nabataeans to the Saracens* (Aldershot: Ashgate, 1997), 393.

[46] R. E. Payne, 'The Making of Turan: The Fall and Transformation of the Iranian East in Late Antiquity', *Journal of Late Antiquity* 9 (2016), 4–41.

[47] Amm. Marc. 23.3.8; 31.6.4.

[48] Graf, *Rome and the Arabian Frontier*, 400.

[49] P. Briant, *État et pasteurs au moyen-orient ancien* (Cambridge: Cambridge University Press, 1982), 9–56; Graf, *Rome and the Arabian Frontier*, 352.

from settled Arabians. Indeed, the Romans feared rebellion, following in the footsteps of Zenobia's revolt, and in 378, the attack of Queen Mavia revealed this fear to be legitimate. In some cases, the forts were built to protect water supplies or scarce agricultural areas, such as those with fertile volcanic soil, as in the case of Umm al-Jimāl, where it is still possible to see the water reservoir. Any goods moving from Arabia to the Persian Gulf would stop in the city before being trans-shipped to Buṣrā and Syria,[50] and a defensive system was needed to protect these traded goods. There is very little evidence for administrative activities such as tax collection, but this also remains a possible use of the late antique fortresses. Finally, the existence of Christian churches allows for the assumption that these defensive centres also had the ideological objective of gaining control over surrounding neighbours: frontiers were indeed more interactive regions rather than strict lines.

The fifth-century 'reduced military presence' on the Roman side is attributable to the relatively peaceful state of Iranian–Roman relations.[51] If the forts were indeed built as protection from the nomads' raids, it is more than legitimate to ask why the nomadic inhabitants of North Arabia did not continue with their incursions in the period. Plausibly, Romans and Iranians had understood that the most effective way of controlling Arabia was to have Arabians fighting for them instead of against them. Therefore, the raiders of the fourth century had arguably become the Arab allies of the fifth century. The Arabian allies then used the fortifications on the *limes* to police the frontier against not only the concurrent superpower but also the Arabians who were not aligned with the superpowers. On the Roman side, allies were appointed as phylarchs and rendered military service for an *annona*.[52] The Tanūkh continued to be important actors in the Roman–Iranian war until 380, when they revolted against the Romans and were replaced by the Salīḥids, based in southern modern Jordan, who in turn were substituted by Ḥujrids and Jafnids in the sixth century (see Chapter 5).[53] Both literary and epigraphic sources attest to these alliances.

Most of the accounts produced in the Roman Empire classify the Arabian allies as 'Saracens' in this period. Significantly, authors such as Ammianus Marcellinus use this lexeme to indicate the units which swore allegiance

[50] De Vries, *Umm al-Jimal*, 237.
[51] Ibid., 131.
[52] O. Schmitt, 'Rome and the Bedouins of the Near East from 70 bc to 630 ad: 700 Years of Confrontation and Coexistence', in *Shifts and Drifts in Nomad–Sedentary Relations*, ed. S. Leder and B. Streck (Wiesbaden: Dr Ludwig Reichert Verlag, 2005), 270–88, at p. 278.
[53] al-Ya'qūbī, *Ta'rīkh* I, 234–236.

to emperor Julian (r. 361–3),[54] as well as those who fought on the Iranian side.[55] A few names of Arabian leaders during this period are known. The Arabian Queen Mavia, for example, is mentioned as a result of her defeat of the Roman armies of Valens (r. 364–78) as far as Egypt in 377–8.[56] This uprising ended with Mavia's conversion to Christianity and her daughter's marriage to Victor, the Roman *magister militum praesentalis*.[57] The ecclesiastical historian Sozomen (d. ca. 450) states that Mavia was *hypospondos* ('under truce'), a tributary to the Roman Empire,[58] pointing to the fact that the relationship between the Romans and Arabian commanders (who were also ambassador-like figures linking tribes and empire) had already been formalized.

According to the *Notitia Dignitatum* (a fourth-century list of Roman offices),[59] the southern part of the Province of Arabia (Negev) was separated and named *Palaestina Salutaris* (*Palaestina III*) in the fourth century. The *equites Saraceni indigenae* in Phoenicia, the *equites Saraceni Thamudeni* in Egypt and the *equites Thamudeni Illyriciani* in Palestine are also mentioned as cavalry forces of the Romans in the period.[60] An earlier third-century Namārah inscription also testifies to the employment of Arabian entities reading *stratēgos parembolōn nomadōn*, 'general of the nomad fortresses', who were probably other Roman desert patrol armies.[61] As for the Iranian side, a sole inscription offers information on the relationship between the Sasanian Empire and Arab allies. This is a bilingual inscription from Pāikūlī by Narseh (r. 273–93), the son of Shāpūr I, which reports that an allied "Amr king of the Naṣrids' paid his respect to the Sasanian king.[62] 'Amr belonged to the same Arab dynasty of Imru' al-Qays and is also possibly mentioned in a poorly preserved Manichean text in Coptic.[63] The superpowers of Late Antiquity probably also employed at this time the

54 Amm. 23.3.8.

55 Ibid., 25.1.3.

56 U. Roberto, 'Il Magister Victor e l'opposizione ortodossa all'imperatore Valente nella storiografia ecclesiastica e nell'agiografia', *Mediterraneo Antico* 6 (2003), 61–93, at pp. 77–81.

57 Sozom. 6.38. See ibid.

58 Ibid.

59 The western section dates to the 420s, while the eastern section dates to around 395. C. Whately, 'Strategy, Diplomacy and Frontiers: A Bibliographic Essay', in *War and Warfare in Late Antiquity*, ed. A. Sarantis and N. Christie (Leiden: Brill, 2013), 101–52, at pp. 114–15.

60 *Not. Dign.*

61 Littman 752.

62 Paikuli inscription see P. O. Skjærvø, and H. Humbach, *The Sassanian Inscription of Paikuli*, 3, 77–139 (Munich: Wiesbaden, 1983). See also C. G. Cereti and G. Terribili, 'The Middle Persian and Parthian Inscriptions on the Paikuli Tower: New Blocks and Preliminary Studies', *Iranica antiqua* 49 (2014), 347–412.

63 *Acts* codex, pl. 99, 28–33.

Arabian Madhḥij tribe, mentioned in the Namārah inscription, as well as in Sabean inscriptions attesting to the land of Madhḥij (*ʾrḍ Mdhḥgm*),[64] and an autonomous 'king of the north' of this tribe.[65] The ʾAsd in south-west modern Saudi Arabia (also mentioned in the Namārah inscription and five Sabean inscriptions) played a similar role in the late antique conflicts.[66]

A Sabean inscription dated to the end of the third century and found at Jabal Riyām (Yemen) further clarifies the map of the Arabian Peninsula.[67] Relating a diplomatic mission undertaken in the area, the inscription mentions the lands of the ʾAsd, Tanūkh, Nabaṭ, Rūmān (probably the Roman provinces of Arabia, Palaestina and/or Syria-Phoenicia), Lakhm (Naṣrid), Tadmur (Palmyra), the Maʿadd from Najd and Ṭayy. It also refers to the lands of Nizār and Liḥyān in Central Arabia in the surroundings of Mecca, Ghassān and Khaṣāsat in south-west Arabia, thus identifying eighth Central Arabian tribal groups inhabiting the area between Najd and Ḥijāz. It further mentions the kingdoms of Nabatea, Palmyra and the Roman Empire (arguably here only the Arabian provinces), as well as the Naṣrids, allies of Iran, and the Tanūkh, partners of Rome, confirming the geographical divisions found in contemporary literary accounts.

If South Arabian inscriptions often confirm the scattered information found in the literary sources, the Safaitic inscriptions, written by pastoral tribes living in southern Syria, are more problematic. Although these inscriptions mention more than a hundred group names, only a few of them are also attested in literary sources.[68] Around ten Safaitic-Greek inscriptions have been found in the Syro-Jordanian Desert.[69] An analysis of this epigraphic evidence has indicated that their authors chose to acquire Greek through a 'deliberate form of education',[70] more than 'simply out of curiosity'.[71] However, based on the existent testimonies, it is speculative to state that the authors of the Safaitic corpus were 'part of the

[64] Bāfaqīh AF 1.

[65] Namely *ʾl-ḥrth bn Kʿbm* king of *ʾS*^{1}*d* and *Mlkm bn Bd* king of Kindah and Mdhḥgm. CIAS 39.11/o 2 n° 8.

[66] Ja 635; Sh 31.

[67] Schiettecatte and Arbach, 'The Political Map of Arabia'.

[68] Such as the Arabic ones, extensively mentioning the alliances between Arabians and Romans at the time. E.g., on the Qud.āʾa, see al-Masʾūdī, *Murūj* 3.214–15.

[69] al-Jallad, *Outline,* 293–294. Three more were recently published by Ahmad al-Jallad, 'New Epigraphica from Jordan II: Three Safaitic-Greek Partial Bilingual Inscriptions', *Arabian Epigraphic Notes* 2 (2016), 55–66.

[70] al-Jallad, 'New Epigraphica from Jordan II', 61.

[71] M. C. A. Macdonald, 'Ancient Arabia and the Written Word', *Proceedings of the Seminar for Arabian Studies* (2010), 5–27, at p. 15.

Hellenized settled population of the Ḥawrān'.[72] The Romans (*Rm*) or the Roman emperor (*qṣr*) often appear in the Safaitic corpus. Sometimes these inscriptions include the first name of a person, followed by expressions of gratitude to a god for protecting while escaping from the Romans.[73] Other inscriptions mention the struggle between Rome and the Nabateans.[74] Two fascinating Safaitic inscriptions refer to the war between Rome and Iran. The first, found in the region of al-Suwaydā' (Syria), mentions 'the year the Iranians fought the Romans at Buṣrā *qṭrẓ*'.[75] The second, located in the governorate of al-Mafraq (Jordan), states: 'He rebelled against the Romans the year the Iranians came to Buṣrā.'[76] This conflict occurred after the second century when the Nabateans lost Buṣrā, and before the end of the fourth century, *terminus ad quem* of the Safaitic corpus.[77] Thus, this battle may have occurred during Shāpūr I's military campaigns, probably during the Syrian campaign in 252–3 or 260.

The Iranians (*mdh*(*y*)) appear only in three other Safaitic inscriptions,[78] attesting to their more frequent contacts with Rome; the Arabians served the Romans in outposts that were otherwise difficult for them to reach, while the Romans provided the Arabians with goods. The existence of a reciprocally beneficial relationship between these two parties and the supposed nomadism of the Safaitic writers has been called into question by the discovery of a collection of Safaitic graffiti in Pompeii.[79] The collection of eighth inscriptions contains simply the first names of the writers (written in Safaitic) and was found on the plaster of the northern wall corridor behind the small theatre on the site of Pompeii.[80] It is unclear if the Pompeian graffiti writers actively participated in 'acts of authorship',[81] or if they were enslaved people or freedmen (possibly businessmen). However, considering the ubiquitous attestation of Safaitic graffiti in the Near East, the existence of this graffiti lends credence to the idea that at least some of the writers were active traders and not just nomadic herders.

72 Graf, *Rome and the Arabian Frontier*, 371.
73 LP 94; LP 157; ZNam 6; CSNS 424; KhNSJ 6.
74 C 4866.
75 C 4448.
76 SIJ 78.
77 Based, however, on an argumentum *ex silentio* namely the lack of Christian references. See Al-Jallad, *Outline*.
78 al-Mafraq Museum 14; RMSK 1; SIJ 88.
79 Jens C. Gysens, 'Safaitic Graffiti from Pompeii', *Proceedings of the Seminar for Arabian Studies* 20 (1990), 1–7.
80 Ibid.
81 Milnor, *Graffiti and the Literary Landscape*, 138.

As in the case of the Germans who were given patrol duty in the outer-lying parts of Rome and of the southern Huns entrusted with the protection of the Gobi frontier,[82] there was a redefinition of how the surrounding empires interacted with the Arabians in the period from the late third to the fifth centuries. Although Arabian tribes were already allied with Rome and Iran in the third century,[83] only in the fourth and fifth centuries had a substantial role in the Rome–Iran wars[84] and were paid for their services.[85] Thanks to the ruinous internal conditions of Rome and the continuous state of war between the two late antique superpowers, the inhabitants of North Arabia thus managed to gain (part of) the autonomy that they had previously lost with the disappearance of the Nabatean Kingdom at the beginning of the second century. In some cases, they pushed further, rebelling against the superpowers, as in the case of Zenobia and Mavia. In others, they energetically promoted themselves by becoming allies of the two superpowers, thereby regaining possession and control of the caravan trade routes. The Syriac Joshua the Stylite pointed out that the war between Iran and Rome under Anastasius I (491–518) was for the Ṭayyāye on both sides 'a source of much profit and they wrought their will upon both kingdoms'.[86] Despite their interactions with Rome and Iran, the Arabians remained intrinsically independent due to the geographical configuration of their area of influence, as Rome and Iran lacked the means to subject and control Arabia directly. The Arabians' independence is proven by their changeable alliances and their autonomous, though fragmented, cultural identity.

Sociopolitical structures in pre-Islamic North Arabia were influenced by the peninsula's geographical and climatic conditions. The gravitation of tribal structures around oases or the creation of social links with settled people in Arabian cities was a definite feature of this period. Tribal members shared ancestors and lineage, and their leaders were chosen among the elderly members of the tribe.[87] From the fourth century onwards, there was a distinct decrease in epigraphic activity in the northern part of the Arabian Peninsula. This is especially true for the Ancient North Arabian languages such as Safaitic. This decrease in North Arabian epigraphic activity happened roughly as Christianity

[82] Bonner, *Last Empire of Iran*, 76.
[83] *Hist. Aug.* 28.2.
[84] Amm. Marc. 23.5.
[85] *Nov. Just.* 24.2.
[86] Joshua the Stylite, *Chronicle* 79.
[87] M. N. K. K. Khel, 'Political System in pre-Islamic Arabia', *Islamic Studies* 20 (1981), 375–93, at p. 386.

started its spread into the Arabian Peninsula. Simultaneously, any hitherto general reluctance to carve inscriptions in Old Arabic disappeared, and examples of such inscriptions became more frequent. Hoyland points to large-scale migrations as an explanation for the disappearance of Ancient North Arabian graffiti and the appearance of inscriptions in Arabic.[88] But this explanation raises more questions than it answers. 'Pride in the development and use of memory', as posited by Macdonald,[89] could explain why Arabic initially favoured oral rather than written traditions. Still, it does not explain why the Ancient North Arabian inscriptions disappeared so abruptly. A feasible explanation for this is that a cultural revolution took place. Declining paganism and incipient monotheism likely led to the disappearance of the Ancient North Arabian graffiti. Once the gods mentioned in the rocks and populating the Arabians' collective imaginary were purged from Arabia, these scripts simply lost their raison d'être.

2.2 The Reverberation of Constantine's Conversion in Arabia

In the first decades of the third century, Ardashīr I (r. 224–42), the founder of the Sasanian Empire, defined the religious adherence of his reign, depicting himself as a true worshipper of Ahura Mazda.[90] One century later, Constantine's conversion to Christianity had significant repercussions inside and outside the Roman Empire. Ardashīr's religious policy was overtaken by the creation of a Christian empire and a Christian Commonwealth, which looked to Rome for cultural and political leadership.[91] The number of Christians grew exponentially during the first millennium and spread widely, from the Pillars of Hercules to the ancient Chinese capital of Xi'an in north-western China, where Christianity first arrived at the time of the early Tang Empire.[92] Although Constantine was possibly not

[88] Hoyland, *Arabia and the Arabs*, 236.

[89] M. C. A. Macdonald, 'The Decline of the "Epigraphic Habit" in Late Antique Arabia: Some Questions', in *L'Arabie à la veille de l'Islam*, ed. C. Robin and J. Schiettecatte (Paris: De Boccard, 2008), 17–27, at p. 23.

[90] See his inscription in Naqsh-i Rustam. F. Grenet, *La geste d'Ardashir fils de Pâbag* (Paris: Éditions A Die, 2003).

[91] Fowden, *Empire to Commonwealth*.

[92] M. Keevak, *The Story of a Stele: China's Nestorian Monument and Its Reception in the West, 1625–1916* (Hong Kong: Hong Kong University Press, 2008). For a shorter and more recent publication, see S. N.C. Lieu and H. Jin Kim, '"Nestorian" Christians and Manicheans as Links between Rome and China', in *Rome and China. Points of Contact*, ed. H. J. Kim, S. N. C. Lieu and R. McLaughlin (Abingdon: Routledge, 2021), 80–107.

the first Christian emperor,[93] his conversion hugely impacted Christian proselytism. It signalled an end to the persecution of the Christians in the Roman Empire and, therefore, a significant growth in the number of converts. This influenced, at least outwardly, the political map of Late Antiquity. Right after Constantine's conversion, king 'Ezana of Aksūm (r. ca. 320–60), Trdat III of Armenia (r. 287–330) and Mirian III of Kartli (Georgia) (r. 284–361) became Christian, arguably because of their wish to strengthen their alliances with Rome.

According to the panegyric work known as *Vita Constantini* and almost undoubtedly attributable to Eusebius of Caesarea (d. 340),[94] Constantine decided to 'venerate his father's God alone' when considering 'what god to adopt to aid him' during the battle on the Milvian Bridge against his rival Maxentius on 28 October 312.[95] Although the same story is reported by the rhetorician and Christian apologist Lactantius (d. ca. 325),[96] material evidence presents a very different picture. Roman coins depicting Constantine together with the pagan god Apollo were minted long after the battle on the Milvian Bridge. Because of the absence of Christian art, there was probably no choice but to use pagan motifs pragmatically.[97] Although crosses and the chi-rho symbol replaced pagan images under Constantine,[98] the triumphal arch erected by the Senate in Rome to honour Constantine's victory does contain symbols of integrated cults, bearing the inscription *instinctu divinitatis* as well as pagan symbols. The latter symbols can be more specifically connected to the cult of *Sol Invictus*,[99] the central theme of which was the recurrent struggle between light and darkness.[100]

The cult of *Sol Invictus* has sometimes been called 'solar monotheism' due to the absolute predominance given to the sun or 'solar henotheism'

[93] Philip the Arab may have preceded him. See Eusebius, *Hist. Eccl.* 6.34. See 6.41.9 for Philip's positive attitude towards Christians. According to the Gallic monk Vincent of Lérins (d. c. 445), the theologian Origen of Alexandria (c. 184–253) wrote to Philip. See *Commonitorium of Vincentius of Lerins*, 17.43. Nonetheless, an inscription found in a temple at Philippopolis, Philip's hometown, suggests that Philip's father Julius Marinus was deified. See Wadd. 2076, and P. Southern, *The Roman Empire from Severus to Constantine* (London: Routledge, 2001), 71.

[94] A. Cameron and S. G. Hall, *Eusebius: Life of Constantine* (Oxford: Oxford University Press, 1999), 4–9.

[95] Eusebius, *Vit. Const.* 1.27–32.

[96] Lactant., *De mort. pers.* 44.5.

[97] Mark Edwards, *Religions of the Constantinian Empire* (Oxford: Oxford University Press, 2015), 197.

[98] Euseb. *Vit. Const.* 1.30–1.

[99] P. Peirce, 'The Arch of Constantine: Propaganda and Ideology in Late Roman Art', *Art History* 12 (1989), 387–418, at p. 406.

[100] G. H. Halsberghe, *The Cult of Sol Invictus* (Leiden: Brill, 1972), 162.

since other gods were subordinated to the sun in the cult.[101] Frescoes, coins, inscriptions and a statue decorating the new city of Constantinople further imply a connection between Constantine and this cult.[102] It was mainly in vogue among the Roman upper classes under Aurelian (r. 270–5), who supposedly introduced it to Rome after being inspired by a Syrian solar cult.[103] Traces of the cult of the Sun-God are widespread. They are found, for example, in the fourth-century hymns of Ephrem the Syrian (d. 373), which often assimilate Jesus with the sun.[104] The cult reached its peak under Constantine's reign and was fervently opposed by late antique Christian authors.[105] The father of Constantine, Constantius I (ca. 250–306), was also a supporter, as suggested by a Latin panegyric probably delivered at Trier on September 307.[106] This blurred monotheism was to some extent congruous with the Neoplatonic belief in a supreme being shared by relevant figures of Constantine's entourage, such as the philosopher Sopatros (d. 325),[107] thus constituting a drift towards Christianity and a mediation between polytheism and philosophical tendencies rather than a Damascene-like conversion. However, the politically astute Constantine probably recognized Christianity and its universal message as a potentially helpful unifying force to help him rule over a vast empire.

In a milieu where religion and politics were deeply entwined, paganism and monotheism were integrated, blending the sacred and the profane. The similarity between the lexeme for the sun in Greek, *Helios*, and the name of the prophet *Elias* (Elijah), probably helped this fusion in the Roman Near East, as exemplified by an inscription found in a church that had previously been a pagan temple at Izra' (southern Syria).[108] Constantine's adoption of *Sol Invictus* as his protector in 310, a successful tool to reconcile the mindsets of pagans and Christians, was either an inspired one or a very propitious one and paved the way towards his acceptance of the Christian God, which he still perceived as a solar deity.[109] Nonetheless,

101 A. Watson, *Aurelian and the Third Century* (London: Routledge, 2003), 196–8.
102 M. Wallraff, 'Constantine's Devotion to the Sun after 324', *Studia Patristica* 34 (2001), 256–69, at p. 256.
103 Watson, *Aurelian and the Third Century*, 193.
104 E.g., Ephrem the Syrian, *Hymn 73*.
105 E.g., the third-century rhetoric teacher Arnobius of Sicca who after his conversion to Christianity, composed the apologetic *Adversus nationes*. See 5.42; 6.12.
106 *Pan. Lat.* 7.14.3.
107 G. A. Kennedy, *Greek Rhetoric under Christian Emperors* (Princeton: Princeton University Press, 1983), 104–8.
108 Wadd. 2497.
109 J. Bardill, *Constantine, Divine Emperor of the Christian Golden Age* (Cambridge: Cambridge University Press, 2012), 330–1.

paganism was not abruptly abandoned after Constantine's conversion by either the lower class of the Roman Empire or the Roman elites and the same Constantine continued to use the solar iconography after his conversion. As with all emperors after Augustus (27 BCE–14 CE), Constantine still became *divus* at his death.[110] His syncretistic fusion of polytheism and monotheism exemplifies the modality in which most late antique conversions took place, inside and outside the Roman Empire.

Pagan cults were either cleverly merged with scriptural monotheisms or performed only in the private sphere, while Christianity was adopted publicly. The Arabian city of Palmyra offers a good illustration of a similarly syncretistic fourth-century milieu. While its pantheon was dominated by the god Baal,[111] and pagan cults were generally predominant in the Arabian Peninsula at least until the fourth century, buildings for 'the one whose name is blessed forever', 'the Lord of the World' and 'the Merciful One' are commonly found.[112] At the same time, Greek inscriptions dedicated to *Theos Hypsistos* spread throughout Syria as well as in Greece, Egypt and Anatolia. A *Theos Hypsistos* mention is found in Petra,[113] and similar denominations are also attested in the south of the Arabian Peninsula from the fourth century onwards. Although it is not impossible that pagans wrote these inscriptions, it is more realistic to attribute them to Jewish or Christian (or Judeo-Christian sympathizers) groups.[114] According to Stephen Mitchell, the Jewish God was called *Theos Hypsistos* as early as the third century BCE,[115] and Jews were undoubtedly present in Palmyra at least from the end of the third century. A significant number of literary sources even claim that Zenobia herself was Jewish. Still, these materials likely belong to a tradition of Christian invective against Paul of Samosata with whom Zenobia corresponded, as hinted by this tradition's earliest dated source, namely the *Historia Arianorum* by Athanasius of Alexandria (d. ca. 373) ('Zenobia was a Jewess, and a supporter of Paul of Samosata').[116]

110 G. W. Bowersock, 'From Emperor to Bishop: The Self-conscious Transformation of Political Power in the Fourth Century A.D.', *Classical Philology* 81 (1986), 298–307, at p. 299.

111 J. Teixidor, *The Pantheon of Palmyra* (Leiden: Brill, 1979), 1–12.

112 J. Teixidor, *The Pagan God: Popular Religion in the Greco-Roman Near East* (Princeton: Princeton University Press, 1977), 122–43.

113 SEG 36 (1986), 1386.

114 S. Mitchell, 'Further Thoughts on the Cult of Theos Hypsistos', in *One God: Pagan Monotheism in the Roman Empire*, ed. S. Mitchell and P. Van Nuffelen, (Cambridge: Cambridge University Press, 2010), 167–208.

115 S. Mitchell and P. Van Nuffelen, 'Introduction: The Debate about Pagan Monotheism', in *One God: Pagan Monotheism in the Roman Empire*, ed. S. Mitchell and P. Van Nuffelen (Cambridge: Cambridge University Press, 2010), 1–15, at p. 10.

116 Athanasius, *History of the Arians*, 71.1.

Although the Queen of Palmyra also appears in the Jerusalem Talmud,[117] no synagogues have been securely identified in Palmyra.[118] A Jewish inscription,[119] confirming a grant of the right of asylum to a synagogue, attributed to Zenobia and Vaballathus,[120] was instead more probably written by Cleopatra VII and her son.[121] Manichaeism was also widespread in late antique Palmyra. The city was perhaps essential for Mani's mission to gain access to Roman Syria and the areas dominated by the Arabian allies.[122] A Middle Iranian text which refers to Mani's proselytism in the Roman Empire mentions Nafshā, Zenobia's sister, and her conversion to Manichaeism thanks to the preaching of Mār Addā, a disciple of Mani.[123] A Parthian and a Sogdian text similarly recount the missionary activity of Mār Addā and the conversion of Nafshā.[124]

The turning point for a firm establishment of Christianity inside and outside the Arabian Peninsula occurred with the Council of Nicaea. After eliminating his political rivals, Constantine realized the importance of integrating and reconciling the different mindsets inside the Christian world. Hence, in May 325, still unbaptized, he ordered the bishops to assemble at Nicaea to deal with the controversy caused by Arius (d. 336), who had affirmed Christ's finite nature and subordination to God, thereby denying his full divinity. The Nicaean Council decided against Arius (who had already been condemned as a heretic by a synod at Alexandria (ca. 320). It declared the Father and Son's consubstantiality (*homoousion*), thus establishing a creed eventually accepted throughout Christendom. The bishops of six Arabian provinces joined the council: Buṣrā (southern Syria), Philadelphia (modern Amman, called by Eusebius of Caesarea '*urbs Arabiae nobilis*'),[125] Esbus (Ḥisbān, near Madaba in Jordan),[126] Sodom

[117] *Mishnah, Terumot* 8.12. Millar implies in *JRS* 61 (1971): 13 that there are other passages mentioning Zenobia and the Jews in the *Jerusalem Talmud.*

[118] E. E. Intagliata, *Palmyra after Zenobia AD 273–750: An Archaeological and Historical Reappraisal* (Oxford: Oxford University Press, 2018), 64–5.

[119] OGIS 129.

[120] F. Millar, 'Paul of Samosata, Zenobia and Aurelian: The Church, Local Culture and Political Allegiance in Third-Century Syria', *Journal of Roman Studies* 61 (1971), 1–17, at p. 13.

[121] K. J. Rigsby, *Asylia: Territorial Inviolability in the Hellenistic World* (Berkeley: University of California Press, 1996), 571.

[122] S. N. C. Lieu, *Manichaeism in Mesopotamia and the Roman East* (Leiden: Brill, 1994), 30–1.

[123] Also known as Adimantus. M2 I R I 1–33; MM II, 301–2. See J. P. Asmussen, *Manichaean Literature: Representative Texts Chiefly from Middle Persian and Parthian Writings* (Delmar: Scholars' Facsimiles & Reprints, 1975).

[124] MMTKGI, 2.5 (170–87), 26; MMTKGI, 3.3 (441–515), 41–5.

[125] Euseb. *Onomasticon*, 16.15.

[126] I am grateful to Oystein LaBianca for allowing me to take part to the 2018 excavation in Ḥisbān.

(perhaps Tall al-Hammam in Jordan),[127] Betharna (Aere in Batanaea, modern al-Ṣanamayn in Syria) and Dionysias (modern al-Suwaydā' in south-western Syria between Buṣrā and Qanawāt). While a certain Pamphilos Taēnōn, possibly a member of the Tanūkh,[128] is found in a subscription,[129] a bishop of Buṣrā named Bēryllos is mentioned by Eusebius,[130] recounting that Origen settled a Christological dispute over his views and correcting 'what was unorthodox'.[131] Origen's intervention in Arabia, with the objective 'to change the opinions of those who had formerly been deluded', is also elsewhere mentioned.[132]

At the Council of Constantinople, called by Theodosius I in 381, six bishops of the province of Arabia are mentioned among the approximately 150 participants. Two men represented two disputing factions in the city of Buṣrā. The bishops of Dionysias, Adraa, Constantine (Tela) and Neapolis were also present. In the subsequent council, held at Ephesus in 431, three Arabian bishops (Antiochus of Buṣrā, Petronius of Nawa in southern Syria and Zosys of Esbus) appear in a list of fifty-three signatories issued by John of Antioch, as well as in a list found in a letter from John of Antioch's council to the clergy of Hierapolis. Antiochus of Buṣrā is also mentioned in a letter naming the supporters of Nestorius and John of Antioch, who were believers in the two natures of Christ. At the time of the council's dissolution, eleven members of the anti-Cyrillian council, including the bishops of Arabia and Syria, had already left the meeting. At the fifth meeting, the Arabian bishops decided to follow the faction led by the patriarch of Antioch. This led to one of the Arabian bishops, Zosys of Esbus, being excommunicated and another, Antiochus of Buṣrā, barely escaping condemnation as a heretic.[133]

About twenty years later, the Council of Chalcedon, convened by Emperor Marcian (r. 450–7), formulated a statement of Christian faith, cautiously adopting the Dyophysite creed. At the sixth session of the

127 S. Collins, 'Where Is Sodom? The Case for Tall el-Hammam', *Biblical Archaeology Review* 39 (2013), 32–41.

128 Shahid, *Byzantium and the Arabs in the Fourth Century*, 330–4.

129 See E. Honigmann, 'La liste originale des pères de Nicée: a propos de l'évêché de "Sodoma" en Arabie', *Byzantion* 14 (1939), 17–76, at p. 56.

130 A different Bēryllos, bishop of Philadelphia in Arabia, is found in Sokrate, *Ecclesiastical History*, 3.7. Socrates mentions those who attended the synod of Antioch against Paul of Samosata which also met under Jovian: Titus of Buṣrā, Arabion of Adraa (modern Darʿā in south-western Syria) and 'Theotimus of the Arabians' (3.25).

131 Eusebius, *Hist. eccl.* 6.33.

132 Ibid., 6.37.

133 Trimingham, *Christianity among the Arabs*, 83.

council, Constantine of Buṣrā signed on behalf of the bishops of Gerasa, Esbus (the Zosys of Ephesus mentioned earlier), Phaena (modern al-Masmiya in southern Syria), Neila, Zeramena, Neapolis, Aere, Neve, Madaba, Maximianopolis (modern Syrian Shaqqā), Eutime, Constantine and Dionysias.[134] The bishops of Philadelphia, Adraa, Canatha (Qanawāt) and Philippopolis (Shahbā) were also present.[135] At the remaining sessions, a 'John of the Saracens' and a 'Eustathius of the nation of the Saracens' appear in the acts.[136] At the seventh session, Bishop Juvenal and Maximus of Antioch agreed to give Jerusalem authority over three Palestinian provinces, but Phoenicia and Arabia remained under Antioch's sphere of influence.

These signatory lists can help us trace the spread of Christianity in the Arabian Peninsula. While in the fourth century, six Arabian bishops joined the Council of Nicaea and the later Council of Constantinople, seventeen Arabian provinces are mentioned in the signatory lists of the Council of Chalcedon dated to the middle of the fifth century. While it is true that these lists do not necessarily indicate the most critical dioceses of Arabia, they still allow for an understanding of just how fast Christianity was spreading throughout the Arabian Peninsula and the level of sympathy felt by the various dioceses towards the different mindsets lacerating the Christian world (e.g., the dependency of the Arabian bishops on Antioch at the Council of Ephesus). Comparing these signatory lists and archaeological sources can further assess the spread of Christianity in the Arabian Peninsula outside and inside the perimeter of the areas dominated by Rome. The sites of the securely identified dioceses represented at the Council of Nicaea all have remnants of churches built during the late antique period. Whereas Christian archaeological evidence dated to before the late fourth century is primarily found in funerary contexts, ecclesiastical constructions transformed landscapes in the fifth and sixth centuries.[137] The site of Buṣrā presents five churches, while in Philadelphia, seven structures have been securely identified. Both cities are mentioned by Ammianus Marcellinus as the most fortified cities of the province, together with Gerash.[138] Buṣrā was not only the seat of the

134 *Acta conciliorum oecumenicorum*, III. See also R. Price and M. Gaddis, *The Acts of the Council of Chalcedon* (Liverpool: Liverpool University Press, 2005), 232.

135 Price and Gaddis, *Acts*, 235.

136 Ibid., 8–9; 123–8; 210–2; 230; 235. Also, in the first and third sessions, 40; 88; 109; 146; 285; 352; 361.

137 W. Bowden, 'The Early Christian Archaeology of the Balkans', in *The Oxford Handbook of Early Christian Archaeology*, ed. W. R. Caraher, T. W. Davis and D. K. Pettegrew (Oxford: Oxford University Press, 2019), 538–56, at p. 537.

138 Amm. Marc. 14.8.13.

Roman governor of Arabia but also the religious capital of the Arabian province, thus, the bishop participated in oecumenical councils.

Not many churches of Arabia are securely dated to the fourth century. One of the churches conventionally dated to the fourth century, that of Sergius in the village of Hīt, in the Ḥawrān plain, dated to 354 because of an inscription,[139] has been recently redated to the sixth century.[140] The earliest churches of Petra, built in the fourth century 'in the wilderness of Saracens',[141] as well as the cathedral and the Church of St Theodore in Gerash, have now been redated to the fifth century.[142] The earliest pagan building converted into a church in Petra is dated 24 July 446.[143] The Ridge Church, the Blue Chapel and the Virgin Mary Basilica were constructed between the fifth and the sixth centuries.[144] As in the case of the church dated to 446, the nearby fifth-century Aaron complex on Jabal Hāruūn replaced a pagan Nabatean building.[145] A crucial fourth-century church is the Marcionite Church in the village of Lababa at Dayr ʿAlī (southern Syria),[146] dated 318, thanks to an inscription identifying the building as 'the synagogue of the Marcionites in the village of Lababa'.[147] The earliest sanctuary in Moses Memorial on Mount Nebo is instead dated to the late fourth and early fifth centuries.[148]

Alan Walmsley has claimed that over 350 churches and chapels were built between the fifth and sixth century in Palestine and Arabia. Although most of his references relate to the archaeology of the Holy Land,[149] an increase in construction is also attested in fifth-century North Arabia. In modern Jordan, particular attention should be given to the site of Gerash, which flourished after the Roman conquest in 63 BCE. The Church of the

139 Wadd. 2124.

140 E. Fowden, *The Barbarian Plain: Saint Sergius between Rome and Iran* (Berkeley: University of California Press, 1999), 105–7.

141 Euseb. *Commentary on Isaiah*, 42:12.

142 A. Michel, *Les églises d'époque byzantine et ummayyade de la Jordanie – Ve–VIIIe siècle: typologie architecturale et aménagements liturgiques, avec catalogue des monuments* (Turnhout: Brepols, 2001), 96–7 and 226–40.

143 Z. T. Fiema and L. Nehmé, 'Ecclesiastical Architecture in Petra', in *Arabs and Empires before Islam*, ed. G. Fisher (Oxford: Oxford University Press, 2015), 390–2, at p. 391.

144 Ibid.

145 Ibid.

146 Marcion of Sinope's (d. ca. 160) main thesis was the incompatibility of the God of the Old and New Testament which led to his total rejection of the Old Testament.

147 Wadd. 2558.

148 M. Piccirillo, *The Mosaics of Jordan* (Amman: American Center of Oriental Research, 1993), 20.

149 A. Walmsley, 'Byzantine Palestine and Arabia: Urban Prosperity in Late Antiquity', in *Towns in Transition: Urban Evolution in Late Antiquity and the Early Middle Ages*, ed. N. J. Christie and S. T. Loseby (Aldershot: Ashgate, 1996), 126–58, at p. 138.

Prophets, Apostles and Martyrs and that of St Theodore were built in 464–5 and 496,[150] and the chapel at Khirbat al-Maqaṭi' is dated to 482–3.[151] Also in modern Jordan, the site of Umm al-Jimāl presents fifteen churches, making it one of the most interesting archaeological sites for Byzantine studies in the world. Although the early twentieth-century Princeton Expedition survey stated that at least one church, the so-called 'Julianus Church', was built in the fourth century, it is now believed that a late fifth- or even sixth-century date is more plausible.[152] A group of mosaics in Jordanian churches are similarly attributed to the late fifth or early sixth century due to similar stylistic traditions.[153] These include the lower mosaics inside the Chapel of the Priest John at Khirbat al-Mukhayyaṭ on Mount Nebo and those in the neighbouring Church of Kaianus in the 'Uyūn Mūsā Valley. The mosaics in the lower baptistry chapel in the west court of Madaba Cathedral complex, the lower mosaic of the Massuh Church and those on the North Church of Ḥisbān are datable to the same period. In modern Syria, an important ecclesiastic complex has been found in Ruṣāfah (ancient Sergiopolis), an episcopal seat in 434 and an important pilgrimage centre for the devotees of St Sergius (see Chapter 5). One of the three churches discovered on site, the so-called Basilica B, is dated no later than 425.[154] In the southern Ḥawrān instead, the Sergius and Bacchus Church at Umm al-Surab is precisely dated to 489, thanks to the presence of an inscription.[155]

While a good overview of the spread of Christianity in the north-west of the Arabian Peninsula is possible due to extensive research carried out in Syria and Jordan, archaeology in the Persian Gulf is still in its infancy resulting in less certainty regarding the spread of Christianity in this area. An important monastery complex built on the island of Khārg (Iran) was dated to the end of the fifth century,[156] but it is now believed to be datable to around the eighth century, similar to the monastery a at SBY-9, on the island of Sir Bani Yas (Abu Dhabi, U.A.E.).[157] The monastery in al-Qusur (Failaka Island, Kuwait) might have been founded during the late

150 H. N. Kennedy, 'Gerasa and Scythopolis: Power and Patronage in the Byzantine Cities of Bilad Al-Sham', *Bulletin d'études orientales* 52 (2000), 199–204, at p. 201.

151 Piccirillo, *Mosaics of Jordan*, 20.

152 De Vries, *Umm el-Jimal*, 230.

153 Piccirillo, *Mosaics of Jordan.*

154 Fowden, *Barbarian Plain*, 78.

155 H. C. Butler et al., *Publications of the Princeton University Archaeological Expeditions to Syria in 1904–1905 and 1909* (Leiden: Brill, 1907–1949).

156 J. Bowman, 'The Christian Monastery on the Island of Kharg', *Australian Journal of Biblical Archaeology* (1974), 49–64.

157 R. A. Carter, 'Christianity in the Gulf during the First Centuries of Islam', *Arabian Archaeology and Epigraphy* 19 (2008), 71–108.

Sasanian period. The main occupation of the site spans from the middle of the seventh and the eighth centuries. In the north-east of modern Saudi Arabia, two buildings were identified as churches in Jubayl and one in Thāj, close to the Christian cemetery of al-Hinnah, tentatively dated to the fifth century, though no proper archaeological research has offered a conclusive dating of the two buildings.[158] The churches examined in the south-western Iraqi desert have instead been defined as 'neither Sasanian nor Islamic',[159] and any attempt to date them remains unsatisfactory. This tentative dating may be a consequence of the archaeologists' scepticism to attribute Christian architecture in the region to the early Islamic period. Still, the exciting discovery of part of a large building complex in use between the mid-sixth and eighth centuries in the village cemetery at Samahij in north-east Muharraq Island (Bahrain) has the potential of changing once again our perspectives on these structures.[160] The recently discovered monastery at Sīnīya Island (Umm al-Quwain) was occupied between the middle of the sixth/seventh and the late eighth centuries. Both findings can help us to shed light on the region's co-existence of Christian and Islamic communities during the second half of the first millennium.[161] No churches have been uncovered in Qatar, though it was densely occupied in the early Islamic period.[162] As for Ḥīrah, the most important Christian centre in Mesopotamia, approximately forty churches were visible in the Abbasid period,[163] but it is unclear how many of these structures were pre-Islamic. In addition to being the seat of the Naṣrids, the city was a diocese from the fourth century onwards and Hosea, its bishop, took part in the Council

J. Bonnéric, 'Archaeological Evidence of an Early Islamic Monastery in the Centre of al-Qusur (Failaka Island, Kuwait)', *Arabian Archaeology and Epigraphy* 32 (2021), 50–61.

R. Perrogon and J. Bonnéric, "A consideration on the interest of a pottery typology adapted to the late Sasanian and early Islamic monastery at al-Qusur (Kuwait)", *Arabian Archaeology and Epigraphy* 32 (2021): 70–82.

158 J. A. Langfeldt, 'Recently Discovered Early Christian Monuments in Northeastern Arabia', *Arabian Archaeology and Epigraphy* 5 (1994), 32–60, at p. 49.

159 Y. Okada, 'Early Christian Architecture in the Iraqi South-Western Desert', *Al-Rafidan* 12 (1991), 71–83, at p. 81.

160 T. Insoll et al., 'Excavations at Samahij, Bahrain, and the implications for Christianity, Islamisation and settlement in Bahrain', *Arabian Archaeology and Epigraphy* 32 (2021), 395–421.

161 The discovery was announced in 2022 by the Sinniyah Archaeology Project, a collaboration between the Umm Al Quwain Department of Tourism and Archaeology, the Institute for the Study of the Ancient World and the Italian Archaeological Mission in Umm Al Quwain.

162 J. C. Carvajal López et al., "From Tentscape to Landscape: A Multi-Scale Analysis of Long-Term Patterns of Occupation in North-West Qatar", *Proceedings of the Seminar for Arabian Studies* 48 (2018): 31–45.

163 I. Toral-Niehoff, *Al-Ḥīra, Eine arabische Kulturmetropole im spätantiken Kontext* (Leiden: Brill, 2014), 175.

of Seleucia in 410.[164] Al-Ṭabarī, quoting Hishām ibn Muḥammad, claims that Ḥīrah's inhabitants consisted of three groups: Tanūkh; 'the inhabitants of Ḥīrah who had settled there' called 'Ibād; and al-Aḥlāf.[165] The 'Ibād were the Christians inhabiting the city.[166] They supposedly used the East Syriac *esṭrangelā* script and have thus been linked to the rise of the Arabic script.[167] However, (almost all) scholars nowadays believe that the rise of the Arabic script should instead be placed in connection with the Nabatean script.

The paucity of archaeological research in the Persian Gulf (including the dioceses of Ḥīrah before the sixth century, 'still a *desideratum*') compared to North-West Arabia is lamentable.[168] In the last decade, scholars have argued against seeing this region as a thriving Sasanian centre after the end of the Arsacid period.[169] A Late Sasanian fort at Fulayj (Oman), plausibly built around the fifth century, is the only securely dated example in Arabia.[170] The difficulty of carrying out archaeological research in some regions of the Persian Gulf undoubtedly contributes considerably to our lack of understanding of the history of this region. While many structures remain to be discovered and uncovered, others appear lost forever due to modern urbanization. Nonetheless, it is plausible that the available ratio of late antique ecclesiastical constructions in the eastern and western sides of Arabia, is accurate overall. As shown in Chapter 6, churches were more likely to be built in the allied or partner kingdoms of Rome and/or in areas politically and/or culturally linked to the Roman-Christian Commonwealth. Conversely, in the regions where Rome did not have political power, there seems to be a connection between Christian traders and church constructions. Churches discovered in the eastern side of Arabia allied to Iran were primarily located in cities with ports.[171] A similar interdependence between Christian traders and regional political authority linked to Rome is discernible in fourth- and fifth-century South Arabia (see Chapters 3–4). The Church of the East thrived in eastern Arabia as in Central Asia in the eighth and ninth centuries, and the dating to this

164 *Synodicon Orientale*, p. 275.
165 Al-Ṭabarī, *Ta'rīkh*, 1.822.
166 T. Nöldeke, *Geschichte der Perser und Araber zur Zeit der Sasaniden* (Leiden: Brill, 1879), 24 n.4.
167 J. Starcky, *Pétra et la Nabatène* (Paris: Letouzey & Ané, 1966), cols. 932–4.
168 M. Müller-Wiener et al., 'Al-Hira Survey Project: Campaigns 2015–2018', *Sumer* (2019), 84–97.
169 D. Kennet, 'The Decline of Eastern Arabia in the Sasanian Period', *Arabian Archaeology and Epigraphy* 18 (2007), 86–122.
170 N. S. Al-Jahwari et al., 'Fulayj: A Late Sasanian Fort on the Arabian Coast', *Antiquity* 92 (2018), 724–41.
171 Amm. Marc. 23.6.11.

period of the buildings securely identified as churches should not come as a surprise.[172]

The spread of Christianity gradually changed urban planning. Churches built in late antique Palestine and Arabia often marked holy places,[173] and were erected over pre-existing pagan structures or synagogues in the city's heart. However, not all temples were destroyed and had churches built in their place. The *Codex Theodosianus* mentions a penalty on anyone who performed sacrifices,[174] but temples situated outside the walls were allowed to be preserved as sites for entertainment, for example, circuses or parades.[175] In the late fourth century, the Roman Emperor Julian, himself a pagan, supposedly forced Christians to rebuild or contribute to the expenses of the planned reconstruction of the pagan temples they had demolished.[176] Although some temples were saved, church construction shaped late antique cities in Rome as in the Arabian Peninsula, especially in the fifth century when there was a conspicuous rise in the Christian population in the western side of the peninsula.

At a time when the conversion or destruction of pagan infrastructures led to the transformation of spiritual, socio-economic centres, churches became 'signs of localized economic activity' and 'centers of a wider exchange network of goods and personnel'.[177] Consequently, the imperial sponsorship of Christianity caused the rise of 'Christian architecture'. In general, the lack of Christian Arabian archaeological evidence datable to the fourth century points to a slow process of conversion of the local population, followed by a stronger foothold gained by Christianity during the fifth century. The fifth-century boom of ecclesiastical construction in north-western Arabia was spatial and temporal, as churches and monasteries quickly spread over a large territory. This phenomenon can relate to the intensification of oecumenical councils and the rise of different factions after the promulgation of the Chalcedonian creed. While a bishop named Thomas attended the Council of Chalcedon as bishop of the Syrian city of Evaria (modern Hawwarin), an anti-Chalcedonian bishop John of the Ṭayyāyē was active in the town in the same period.[178] Therefore, it

172 Christian manuscripts and inscriptions dated between the eighth to the fourteenth centuries abound in Central Asia. See L. Tang and D. W. Winkler, *Artifact, Text, Context. Studies on Syriac Christianity in China and Central Asia* (Zurich: LIT Verlag, 2020).

173 Walmsley, 'Byzantine Palestine and Arabia', 134.

174 *Cod. Theod.* 16.10.2.

175 Ibid., 16.10.3.

176 Sozom. 5.5.

177 C. A. Stewart, 'Churches', in *The Oxford Handbook of Early Christian Archaeology*, ed. W. R. Caraher, T. W. Davis and D. K. Pettegrew (Oxford: Oxford University Press, 2019), 127–46, at p. 143.

178 Trimingham, *Christianity among the Arabs*, 118–19.

is plausible that the construction of multiple ecclesiastical buildings in small centres is attributable to the competing activity of Chalcedonians, Miaphysites and the Church of the East.

Arabia became a popular destination for itinerant monks, as recounted by Sozomen[179] and Theodoret of Cyrrhus (d. 457), and well exemplified by the case of Simeon Stylites (d. 459).[180] The latter had been preceded by Hilarion (d. 371) as a healer of the 'many Saracens possessed by demons'.[181] Indeed, the desert constituted an ideal place for itinerant monks and stylites, ascetics who lived at the top of pillars (Greek *stylos*), a movement initiated by Simeon, who some believe was Arabian.[182] It also constituted the ideal setting for the racist environmental determinism of ancient and late antique writers.[183] In the wake of the Gospel narration of the temptation of Christ in the Judaean Desert,[184] Cyril of Scythopolis portrayed this space as inhabited by demons where monks have to face numerous temptations.[185] Elsewhere, Cyril described the 'Saracens' as 'formerly wolves of Arabia who then joined the rational flock of Christ',[186] recounting how a 'Christian Saracen called Thalabas' had saved a 'barbarian' possessed by a demon for having broken the door of a monastery.[187] Similarly, Cyril reported how another 'Saracen' was cured after being seized for grazing flocks in the desert.[188]

As the belief that Christianity had a 'civilizing' effect on the 'barbarian Saracens' is apparent in these ancient Christian narratives, the blatant rhetoric in such hagiographical works does not necessitate any further clarification, being self-evident. Yet, the itinerant Christian monks probably achieved resounding success with their proselytizing among the Arabians due to their apparent ability to control and tame such invisible and malign forces as the demons in the desert. The belief that the monks could cast out such demons undoubtedly fell on fertile soil, belief in such preternatural beings already being part of the Arabian culture of the time (see Chapter 6). Thus, on the one hand, Christianity became

179 Sozom. 6.38.
180 Theodoret, *Life of Symeon*, 13.
181 Sozom. 3.14; Jerome, *Life of Hilarion*, 25.
182 Trimingham, *Christianity among the Arabs*, 234.
183 For classical antiquity, see B. Isaac, *The Invention of Racism in Classical Antiquity* (Princeton: Princeton University Press, 2004), 53–253.
184 Matthew 4.1–11; Mark 1.12–23; Luke 4.1–13.
185 Cyril of Scythopolis, *Life of Sabas*, 12.
186 Cyril of Scythopolis, *Life of Euthymius*, 15.
187 Ibid., 51.
188 Ibid., 53.

an instrument to master inhospitable geographical conditions and primordial beings for the uncultured masses of the desert, and monasteries became a precious social and economic node providing resources to local societies. On the other, Christianity was viewed as a means to build special and lucrative ties with the Roman Empire, as exemplified by the case of the Tanūkh. Conversions thus came to represent a covenant of reciprocal trust. This was the case with the Arabian Zocomus, who converted to Christianity in ca. 364,[189] and possibly of the already mentioned Imru' al-Qays, who also converted to Christianity according to the Muslim historian al-Ṭabarī (d. 923).[190]

Although there are no distinguishable Christian elements in the Imru' al-Qays' epitaph and another more than possibly Christian Naṣrid by the name of Imru' al-Qays is attested (al-Ṭabarī may have confused the two),[191] it is of some significance that his epitaph was found at the Roman *limes*. An expedition by Diocletian on the edge of Syria took place in 290, and Imru' al-Qays could have been employed as a Roman ally at that time.[192] Later, in the 340s, severe persecutions against the Christians took place. It would not be surprising if Shāpūr's partner Imru' al-Qays, newly converted to Christianity, was forced to abandon the Naṣrid seat. A letter from Constantine to Shāpūr II mentions a conspicuous Christian presence in Iran,[193] who would have been deported from Roman territory during the wars of Shāpūr I.[194] Moreover, a Coptic Manichean papyrus indicates that 'Amr, supposedly Imru' al-Qays' father, allied with Iran based on the Pāikūlī inscription,[195] was a protector of Manichean Christianity,[196] further linking Imru' al-Qays to Christianity. Two centuries later, another Imru' al-Qays left Iranian employment to join the Roman forces. Attacking all the Arabians he encountered in 'that part of Arabia adjacent to Persia', he seized one Roman island and sent the bishop of his tribe, a certain Peter, as an ambassador to the Roman emperor Leo (r. 457–74), thereby gaining recognition and acceptance as a Roman ally.[197] Another chief of a tribe loyal to Iran, Aspebetos, similarly settled in Roman territory in 420,

189 Sozomen, *HE*, 6.38.
190 Al-Ṭabarī, *Ta'rīkh*, 1.834.
191 Bowersock, *Roman Arabia*, 140–1.
192 *Pan. Lat.* 11.5.4.
193 Euseb. *Vit. Const.* 1.4.9–13.
194 S. P. Brock, 'Christians in the Sasanian Empire: A Case of Divided Loyalties', *Studies in Church History* 18 (1982), 1–19, at p. 3.
195 Skjærvø and Humbach, *Sassanian Inscription.*
196 *Acts* codex, pl. 99, 28–33.
197 Malchus fr. 1.

became a Roman phylarch.[198] Before his appointment, Aspebetos converted to Christianity and attended the Council of Ephesus in 431 under the name of Peter as Bishop of Parembole.[199] A bishop in the ecclesiastical circle, Aspebetos/Peter, built a church to demonstrate his family's high status to Rome and his fellow Arabians.[200]

The public display of the Roman elites' symbol of power at the time, namely the sponsorship of ecclesiastical structures, played a multiple role in the fragmented Arabian society. Being a Christian, especially a powerful one, was a clear sign to Rome that alliances could be made with the now 'civilized' and fellow brethren in Arabia and at the same time spurred local tribes and their settlements to convert to Christianity because of the additional benefits of protection during warfare and for trading purposes. Moreover, the building of Christian churches encouraged the recognition, by both allies and subjects, of the hegemonic role of the dynasties in charge, as they were evident reminders of their influential role as patrons and protectors in both this world and, through the Church, in the next.

2.3 Concluding Remarks: Social Networks and Patterns of Conversions

At the same time as the Chinese were recruiting the Huns, fourth-century literary sources ceased to present the Arabians as a chaotic miscellanea of 'barbarians', now characterizing them either as allied functionaries or as uncivilized enemies subordinated to rival kingdoms. The empires' need for stationary troops and mercenaries to be deployed in the conflict between Rome and Iran and employed in trade, in conjunction with the fall of buffer kingdoms, created a necessity to redefine up-to-now marginalized groups as significant players in shaping new and fluid alliances. As the Noubades' raids in southern Egypt led to Rome seeking a partnership with Aksūm (in its turn eager to extend its trade monopoly, see Chapter 4), both Romans and Iranians looked to the Arabians to defend their frontiers, not only from each other but also from the reprisals of the nomads, in a similar fashion to the Han of China. Hence, while in Asia Minor and Egypt, 'peace meant prosperity',[201] in North Arabia, war lay the foundations for

198 B. H. Isaac, *The Limits of Empire: The Roman Army in the East* (Oxford: Oxford University Press, 1990), 246.

199 Cyril of Scythopolis, *Life of Euthymius*, 15. See R. Price, 'Politics and Bishops' Lists at the First Council of Ephesus', *Annuarium historiae conciliorum* (2012), 395–420.

200 Cyril of Scythopolis, *Life of Euthymius*, 14.

201 P. Sarris, *Empires of Faith: The Fall of Rome to the Rise of Islam, 500–700* (Oxford: Oxford University Press, 2011), 126.

more efficient structuring of tribal societies. And interestingly, Christianity was used both as a pretext for war and as a means of external control. Bishops, nominated by patriarchs outside Arabia from thriving centres within Arabia, became leading political figures and largely contributed to the shaping of North Arabian internal and external politics through their propagation of the concepts discussed at the first Christian councils and their regulation of the religious and social life of urban centres.

Throughout the late antique world, the edification of churches generated wealth and supported the creation of new settlements and trade nodes. Late antique churches in rural areas are usually dated later than the mid-fifth century in places like Italy.[202] Although Arabia was geographically distant from Rome's political and economic control, Christianity penetrated the peninsula despite such distance. However, in contrast to Italian churches constructed near late antique villas,[203] Arabian churches mainly were built on the sites of fortified settlements. In the harsh climatic environment of North Arabia, the choice of church locations was heavily conditioned by the availability of resources, road connections and existing social and economic networks. At the same time, the bond between ecclesiastical authorities and aristocratic families (so apparent in the Italian setting) is far less clear. While noble families in Italy understandably funded the construction of churches in/near their villas,[204] clearly adding to their social status and prestige, who was it exactly who paid for the construction of multiple churches in small rural villages in Arabia? Studies of the mosaics of late antique churches and synagogues of Arabia and the Levant have shown that the artists' names signed on the mosaics matched those of local officeholders and donors.[205] Thus, the artist and the donors were the same people.

In conclusion, the second scriptural religion spread in the Arabian Peninsula following a similar pattern to the rest of the late antique world. On the one hand, it was proffered as an economic opportunity and an instrument of salvation from the netherworld and the devilish preternatural world. On the other, it became a means for aristocracies and clergy to

[202] A. C. Arnau, 'The Archaeology of Early Italian Churches in Context, 313–569 CE', in *The Oxford Handbook of Early Christian Archaeology*, ed. W. R. Caraher, T. W. Davis and D. K. Pettegrew (Oxford: Oxford University Press, 2019), 557–80, at p. 563.

[203] Ibid., 564.

[204] E.g., Villa del Casale in Piazza Armerina.

[205] K. C. Britt, 'Early Christian Mosaics in Context', in *The Oxford Handbook of Early Christian Archaeology*, ed. W. R. Caraher, T. W. Davis and D. K. Pettegrew (Oxford: Oxford University Press, 2019), 275–95, at p. 278.

exercise control and power. Initially, scriptural and pagan traditions were merged throughout the Eurasian world, including Arabia. Although its rise was slow in fourth-century Arabia, Christianity became the main religion of the north-western side of the peninsula by the end of the fifth, under the impulses of the competing factions that emerged after the Council of Chalcedon. The patterns behind the conversions of the fourth and fifth centuries, facilitated by the late antique–born figure of the itinerant monk, helped the assimilation and integration between nomadic and sedentary populations of Arabia. The increased number of dioceses and churches in the Arabian Peninsula shows that the Arabians were attracted to this new religion of power, at least in the area long dominated by the Roman Empire. The newly built churches constituted important social centres and took on the same function as the desert oasis, becoming virtual nodes on the Arabian map, as shown by studies on sites like Umm al-Jimāl. These sites expanded extensively during the late antique period. At the same time, conversions became a form of assurance of compliance after the disappearance of buffer states at the *limes* and were a way of cementing alliances. In the 'early' late antique period, North Arabians were organized into powerful dynasties and confederations. Still, they failed in creating powerful kingdoms, as proved by the fact that narratives centred on single Arabian leaders rather than the groups they belonged to. Consequently, Christianity became a marker of *bona fides* for these entities as it did for the Goths and the Aksūmites.

Despite the probably egalitarian social structures present in late antique Arabian tribes, an increasingly hierarchical Christian framework was adopted, as suggested by the status accorded to patrons of ecclesiastical structures, and became embedded in North Arabian society from the fourth century, channelling both authority and wealth into the hands of the few. However, although the adoption of Christianity cemented the relationship between Rome and its allies, this exploitation of cults to seal alliances had, in some cases, a boomerang effect. For instance, when the Romans sent an embassy to Mavia to solicit peace, she refused to comply with the Roman requests unless a man named Moses, 'who practised philosophy in a neighbouring desert', was ordained bishop over her subjects.[206] Moses, fortunately, was willing to forgo his aesthetic lifestyle and accepted the office but refused to be ordained by the Arian see of Alexandria.[207] The Romans had no choice then but to accept Mavia's *conditio sine qua*

[206] Sozom. 6.38.
[207] Socrates Scholasticus, *Ecclesiastical History*, 4.36.

non that Moses be ordained by someone of his choosing. Sozomen claims that the converted tribe of Mavia were the direct descendants of Ishmael, son of Abraham and Hagar, and that the same group adopted the name 'Saracens' to show a direct descendant from Sarah.[208] The placement of the Arabians in the line of Abraham already in the Old Testament,[209] and works by classical authors such as Flavius Josephus (d. ca. 100),[210] plausibly legitimized the Arabians' position in the Roman Commonwealth in the eyes of late antique Christian writers and was used to promote the spread of the Gospel among Arabians, who considered themselves direct offspring of Abraham.

While Christianity became a signifier of *bona fides* among the Roman allies, Zoroastrianism did not take on any unifying role in shaping Iran's partnerships. Iranianess (*ērīh*) and Zoroastrianism were deeply connected, and the Iranians perceived themselves to be the most suited to be adherents of the 'Good Religion' (*wehdēn*). Zoroastrianism did not desire to be a universal faith. Therefore, it can be viewed as a more 'ethnic' and henotheist faith, wherein ancient pagan gods were subjected to a High One.[211] Because of this, the Sasanians rarely sought to convert their subjects. When in the first half of the fourth century, the Armenian king Trdat IV converted to Christianity, the Sasanians tried to reconvert the Armenians to Zoroastrianism, repeatedly failing and finally giving up after the battle of Avarayr (451).[212] While Christianity, with its intrinsic universal message, was well suited for being 'imported' from one region to another, the Zoroastrian particularism was a possible cause for Mazdaism's decline. Iran's sponsorship of Eastern Christianity in 410 possibly aimed to circumvent the particularistic and intrinsically Iranian character of Zoroastrianism. In contrast with the South Arabian rulers who signalled a distancing from Rome and neutrality towards Iran in the first millennium by adopting Jewish attitudes and establishing connections with the Church of the East (see Chapters 3–4), the North Arabians who were allied with Iran quietly remained pagans until the sixth century. Iran had a stronger position in Arabia, having long dominated the prosperous Persian

[208] Sozom. 6.38.
[209] Genesis 16.
[210] Joseph. *AJ.* 1.220–1.
[211] R. E. Payne, *A State of Mixture: Christians, Zoroastrians, and Iranian Political Culture in Late Antiquity* (Oakland: University of California Press, 2015), 29.
[212] A. De Jong, 'Religion and Politics in Pre-Islamic Iran', in *The Wiley Blackwell Companion to Zoroastrianism*, ed. M. Stausberg, Y. S. Vevaina and A. Tessmann (Chichester: Wiley-Blackwell, 2015), 83–101, at p. 97.

Gulf, and did not need to exploit faith to forge its long-standing alliance with the Naṣrids.

Due to the lack of a distinguishable 'Arab' identity and stable North Arabian kingdoms, Christianity (Christianities) spread in the region due to the proselytizing missions of bishops and monks serving competing factions. The economic boost caused by the construction of churches and monasteries (and roads to these centres) and by the social and economic hubs provided by these structures (especially prosperous if pilgrimages were involved) contributed to the spread of Christianity. The local establishment of a new social order commanded by clergy and powerful dynasties, who mediated between settled communities, nomad tribes and empires, further facilitated the establishment of North Arabian Christianity. However, notwithstanding the increasing prestige of Arabian bishops participating in the early oecumenical councils, there was never an 'Arabian Church' or an 'Arabian Bible', and devotees largely remained dependent on external entities usually decided on by the Arabian clergy and, to a minor extent, the political leaders of North Arabia.

CHAPTER 3

A Late Antique Kingdom's Conversion
Jews and Sympathizers in South Arabia

The cautious conversion of the kings of Ḥimyar to monotheism in the fourth century CE was influenced by the beliefs of a local Jewish community. In this chapter, I clarify the relationship between South Arabian Jews and Jewish sympathizers and offer an interpretative framework for the monotheism of fourth- and fifth-century Ḥimyar, which contextualizes the choice of South Arabia's elites to become Jewish sympathizers.[1] The process of conversion to monotheism also shares features with the first stage of Christianity in Aksūm and the Graeco-Roman world, as well as the henotheism of pre-Islamic North Arabia. I argue that the Ḥimyarite kings' cautious conversion follows a broad late antique trend which aimed to ease the transition for their subjects and/or to assume a neutral position towards the developments of the surrounding empires. In the brand new kingdom of Ḥimyar, the cult of a single, institutionalized and translocal deity provided a strong mechanism for establishing identities that were reshaped in a wider syncretistic framework through a sociopolitical exploitation of cults characteristic of the broader late antique world.

3.1 Introducing Ḥimyar and Its God(s)

Before about 275 CE, South Arabia was divided into several small kingdoms. The most powerful of these were Ḥaḍramawt and Saba', both located in the southwest corner of the Arabian Peninsula. We possess over 15,000 inscriptions coming from this area which date from the late second millennium BCE to the sixth century CE. These inscriptions employ one script, known as Sabean (so-called because it was invented in the kingdom of Saba'). The similarity of the artefacts found in the area further

[1] This chapter was submitted for publication to the *Journal of Late Antiquity* in May 2019. The article first appeared in *Journal of Late Antiquity*, Volume 13, Issue 2, Fall 2020, pages 352–82.

points to a certain degree of cultural uniformity in late antique South Arabia. However, two other cultural features point to a different picture. The South Arabian corpus is written in four different languages, named after the four most powerful kingdoms of the area (Ḥaḍramawt, Qatabān, Maʿīn and Saba'). These kingdoms also possessed distinct religious pantheons. The main god of Ḥaḍramawt was then Sayīn, of Qatabān ʿAmm, of Maʿīn ʿAthtar and of Saba' 'Almaqah.[2] Temples and sacrifices were dedicated to the main gods in each kingdom. The multiplicity of linguistic and religious features in these kingdoms mirrors the political and cultural fragmentation of the region.

Between 275 and 300, the kingdom of Ḥimyar managed to subjugate the nearby kingdoms of Saba' and Ḥaḍramawt. Ḥimyar hence unified the entire southern part of the Arabian Peninsula. The language of the ancient and renowned kingdom of Saba' was chosen as the kingdom's official language. All inscriptions dated after the fourth century are classified as Ḥimyarite. To unify their subjects culturally, the king of Ḥimyar, Malkīkarib Yuha'min (who reigned from about 375 to 400), converted to monotheism around 380. According to the fifth-century *Ecclesiastical History* by Philostorgius (d. ca. 439), a Christian religious mission of Theophilus 'the Indian' (d. 364) took place in South Arabia after the kingdom's unification:

> Constantius sent ambassadors to those formerly called Sabaeans, now known as *Homeritae* [...] They practice circumcision on the eighth day but also offer sacrifices to the sun and moon and the indigenous demons. And a significant number of Jews mingle with them [...] Having arrived among the Sabaeans, Theophilus persuaded the king (*ethnarchēs*) to become Christian, abandoning the error of the Hellenic faith. The customary malice of the Jews was decisively put to rest when Theophilus performed repeated miracles, proving the rightfulness of the Christian faith. The embassy achieved its goal as the leader of the people (*ethnos*) converted with sincere devotion and built not one but three churches.[3]

The archaeological sources prove that the rulers of Ḥimyar converted to monotheism at the time of the embassy. The king of Ḥimyar allowed at the time the construction of churches in important commercial cities such as Ẓafār and 'Aden for the use of Christian traders. The existence of Christian traders in South Arabia is confirmed by multiple sources, such as the *Chronographia*

[2] C. J. Robin, 'Before Ḥimyar: Epigraphic Evidence for the Kingdoms of South Arabia', in *Arabs and Empires before Islam*, ed. G. Fisher (Oxford: Oxford University Press, 2015), 90–127, at p. 97.

[3] Philostorgius, *Ecclesiastical History*, 3.4.

by John Malalas (d. ca. 578)[4] and the personal testimony of the Egyptian monk Cosmas Indicopleustes.[5] However, we do not possess any source other than Philostorgius claiming that 'Theophilus persuaded the king to become Christian' in the fourth century. An excerpt from the Chronicle of Bishop John of Nikiu (seventh century) briefly mentions the mission of a Christian virgin named Theognosta, who was brought as a captive from a convent for the king of Yemen.[6] She then spread Christianity in South Arabia and 'India', the equivalent of modern-day Ethiopia, as the term often refers to Aksūm and the kingdoms of South Arabia (i.e., political entities involved in trade in the Indian Ocean).[7] The mission is undated but appears to have happened after the death of Constans (350).[8] Honorius (reigned 395–423) is identified as the emperor during Theognosta's mission in India/Ethiopia-Eritrea, whose reign occurred after that of Frumentius (ca. 300–80), bishop of Aksūm.[9] Therefore, it is possible to date her mission in Ḥimyar to the end of the fourth century, but nothing more specific can be inferred (see Chapter 4 for Christianity in South Arabia).

According to Philostorgius, there were polytheists in South Arabia who practised circumcision, influenced by a Jewish community. The presence of 'circumcised pagans' and Jews in the passage by Philostorgius hints at a composite milieu in pre-Islamic South Arabia, inspired by Jews who lived in close communion with the rest of the South Arabian population. This is also suggested by the *Martyrdom of Arethas*, which describes the inhabitants of South Arabia as Jews who venerate idols,[10] and by Theodorus Lector (d. after 518), who claims that the Ḥimyarites were 'originally Jews' converted to Christianity at the end of the fifth century.[11] Furthermore, the Gəʿəz *Martyrdom of ʾAzqir* suggests that a group of Jews served the king as counsellors in the fifth century. This neglected document narrates the story of a priest named ʾAzqir who, at the time of king Shurihḇʾīl Yakkuf (roughly 468–80), 'was the first to teach Christianity in Najrān'.[12] Before the execution, ʾAzqir discusses the Bible with some Jews (*ʾayəhudə*) in front of the ruler.[13] Thereafter, one of the Jews (*rabbanāt*) convinced the king to execute ʾAzqir.[14]

[4] Malalas, *Chronicle*, 18.433.
[5] Cosmas Indicopleustes, *Topographia*, 2.56.
[6] John of Nikiu, *Chronicle*, 77.106–9.
[7] This is exemplified by Philostorgius, *Ecclesiastical History*, 2.6.
[8] Ibid., 77.105.
[9] Ibid., 77.108–12. The embassy of Frumentius in India is also found in Socrates Scholasticus, *Ecclesiastical History*, 1.19.
[10] *Martyrdom of Arethas*, 1 (hereafter *MaAr*).
[11] John Diakrinomenos, *Fragment 2*, 551–6.
[12] *Martyrdom of ʾAzqir*, 1 (hereafter *MaAz*).
[13] Ibid., 22.
[14] Ibid., 25–6.

Although the king writes about the execution to the rulers of Najrān, the Jews are the ones described as most involved during the martyrdom.[15] The presence of Jews in the king's entourage suggests that monotheism spread among the elites.

Previous scholarship has defined the monotheism of fourth- and fifth-century Ḥimyar as 'Raḥmānism'.[16] Alfred Beeston considered this creed as independent from both Christianity and Judaism, although somewhat inspired by the latter.[17] In more recent years, the monotheism of Ḥimyar has been labelled as 'Judaeo-Monotheism' by Christian Robin.[18] According to Robin, the break from polytheism by the Ḥimyarite kings was radical and abrupt,[19] and a 'massive movement of conversions made Yemen a country where Judaism was dominant for nearly 150 year'.[20] Robin argues that a significant part of the aristocracy explicitly adhered to Judaism, claiming to belong to Israel, while the remainder of the elites adhered to 'a minimalist form of Judaism'.[21] Iwona Gajda has claimed instead that three monotheistic groups inhabited South Arabia before the spread of Christianity in the area: Jews, Jewish proselytes and more neutral monotheists.[22]

I argue for the existence of two religious communities in fourth- and fifth-century South Arabia, namely local Jews and elites who were Jewish sympathizers. The first group influenced the second, which in turn chose to adopt a cautious form of monotheism. Although the conversion of the aristocracy to monotheism appears decisive in the public sphere, pagan cults likely survived among the lower classes and/or in the private sphere. No monumental inscriptions are polytheistic in their content. However, some stick inscriptions attest to the existence of pagan cults after the kings' conversion. I accordingly argue that the Ḥimyarite kings' adoption of monotheism reflects a broader trend in the late antique framework: the clever use of politically motivated conversions to cautious

[15] Ibid., 29–36.

[16] A. F. L. Beeston, 'Himyarite Monotheism', in *Studies in the History of Arabia*, Vol. 2, *Pre-Islamic Arabia, Proceedings of the Second International Symposium on Studies in the History of Arabia*, ed. A. M. Abdalla et al. (Riyadh: Jāmiʿat al-Riyāḍ, 1984), 149–54.

[17] Ibid.

[18] C. J. Robin, *Le Judaïsme de l'Arabie antique* (Turnhout: Brepols, 2015), 63.

[19] Robin, 'Before Ḥimyar', 129.

[20] C. J. Robin, 'The Peoples beyond the Arabian Frontier in Late Antiquity: Recent Epigraphic Discoveries and Latest Advances', in *Inside and Out: Interactions between Rome and the Peoples on the Arabian and Egyptian Frontiers in Late Antiquity*, ed. J. H. F. Dijkstra and G. Fisher (Leuven: Peeters, 2014), 33–82, at p. 59.

[21] C. J. Robin, 'Ḥimyar, Aksūm, and Arabia Deserta in Late Antiquity', in *Arabs and Empires before Islam*, ed. G. Fisher (Oxford: Oxford University Press, 2015), 127–71, at p. 129–30.

[22] I. Gajda, 'Remarks on Monotheism in Ancient South Arabia', in *Islam and Its Past: Jahiliyya, Late Antiquity, and the Qur'an*, ed. C. Bakhos and M. Cook (Oxford: Oxford University Press, 2017), 247–56, at p. 255.

monotheisms to gain the approval of pagan subjects and the superpowers of Late Antiquity: Rome and Iran.

I now investigate the theonyms found in the Ḥimyarite corpus and introduce some interpretative problems regarding the existence of two monotheistic communities in fourth- and fifth-century South Arabia. The Ḥimyarite inscriptions, adequately contextualized, offer valuable information about the cults of South Arabia. The terminology employed in this corpus is vague and bears a resemblance to the terminology used in other late antique contexts, where the veneration of a 'High God' and cautious sympathies towards monotheism offered a solution to the rulers' desire to reshape identities and cults in a broader, syncretistic social framework.

One feature immediately strikes the reader when analysing the Ḥimyarite monotheistic inscriptions: not only are there three different titles for the supreme deity but also these often are combined. The most common ones are: *ʾln* ('God', also spelled *ʾlhn*, *ʾlh*, or *ʾʾlhn*), *Bʿl/Mrʾ S¹myn* ('Lord of the Heaven', sometimes 'of Earth' is added), and *Rḥmnn* ('Merciful'). More than half of the inscriptions dedicated to the 'Lord of the Heaven' also possess the theonym *ʾln*. In only one case is God named just *ʾln*. However, it is specified in the same line that he is 'the one who is in heaven' (*dh-b-s¹myn*).[23] Only one inscription contains both *Rḥmnn* and *ʾln*.[24] Therefore, it looks plausible that *ʾln*, 'God', was a simple noun and not a theonym. On the other side, the theonym 'Lord of the Heaven' recurs alone more than ten times and almost the same number of times together with *Rḥmnn*. Since they often appear as a combined theonym, it is plausible that these theonyms were used by one religious community or by two or more that strongly interacted with each other. The earliest monotheistic Ḥimyarite inscriptions, dated to the last decades of the fourth century, read 'Lord of the Heaven' to indicate the monotheist god.[25] But the earliest inscription attesting to the theonym *Rḥmnn* is dated to around 432.[26] It is thus possible that *ʾln* and *Bʿl/Mrʾ S¹myn* are earlier theonyms than *Rḥmnn*.

Rḥmnn is found (as *Rḥm*) in three North Arabian Safaitic inscriptions,[27] and it also often appears in the Mishnah and the Babylonian Talmud as one of the names of God.[28] 'Lord of Heaven' is the theonym of the god venerated by the king ʿEzana of Aksūm, who supposedly converted to

[23] Ir 71.
[24] Ibrahim al-Hudayd 1.
[25] Schiettecatte-Nāʿiṭ 9; Gorge du Haut-Buraʿ 2; YM 1950.
[26] ZM 5+8+10.
[27] C 4351; AbaNS 352; C 3315.
[28] E.g., *Mishnah, Berakhot* 60b.12; *Nedarim* 51a.3; *Kiddushin* 81b.1.

Christianity around 337 to 350.[29] 'Ezana attributes his success to 'the might of the Lord of Heaven' in one monumental inscription.[30] Moreover, the theonym 'Lord of Heaven' is found seven times in a Gəʿəz inscription of the Aksūmite king.[31] 'Lord of all' appears twice in the same inscription, while 'Lord of Earth' is mentioned once. Finally, the Najrāni pagan god dhū-Samawī (*dh-S¹mwy/dh-S¹my*) bears a name that could be translated as 'Lord of Heaven'. Dhu-Samawī is attested more than fifty times in the South Arabian corpus. It is primarily mentioned in the Northern Middle Sabaic corpus,[32] and in the Central Middle Sabaic corpus,[33] and is believed to be the god of the Amir tribe, active in modern North Yemen.[34]

It seems plausible that all these lexemes evolved among one South Arabian monotheistic community or among more than one who were in contact and influenced one another. The earliest inscriptions show a combined use of the lexeme 'god' and the generic 'Lord of Heaven'. At a later point, the adjectival theonym *Rḥmnn* was employed. Some inscriptions attest to the use of 'Lord of Heaven' and *Rḥmnn* together. In the following sections, I adduce evidence for the existence of two monotheistic communities in fourth- and fifth-century Ḥimyar: a Jewish group and one composed of Jewish-sympathizing elites. These communities influenced each other and interacted closely. The Ḥimyarite kings' break with polytheism and adoption of monotheism, possibly already moving from a form of henotheism, was inspired at some point by the Jews of South Arabia. The elites adopted the same religious vocabulary as the Jewish community. However, as demonstrated in Section 3.2, some of the most explicit expressions of Judaism were mitigated.

3.2 Jewish Inscription: Israel, Jews and Hebrew

In this section, I present a group of findings that can almost certainly be attributed to Jews living in South Arabia and to some South Arabian Jews who emigrated to Palestine. As we have seen, the theonyms employed in the Ḥimyarite corpus possess blurred connotations. Any mark of identification as a community that self-identifies as Jewish is missing. For this reason, it is preferable to label their content as 'monotheistic' and not

[29] D. W. Philippson, *Foundations of an African Civilisation* (Woodbridge: James Currey, 2012), 99.
[30] RIE 189, often mentioned as DAE 11.
[31] RIE 185bis/270bis.
[32] E.g., al-Ṣilwī 1; Bāfaqīh AF 1; FB-wādī Shuḍayf 1.
[33] E.g., CIH 519; RES 4146; CIH 534.
[34] CIH 521.

'Jewish'. However, we possess around ten Ḥimyarite inscriptions, which can be attributed to Jews of Ḥimyar and point to the presence of Jews in late antique South Arabia. A part of this group is formed by inscriptions that either mention 'the People of Israel' (*s*^{2}*ʿbn Ys*^{3}*rʾl*),[35] the Jews (*Hd/Hwd/Yhd*),[36] or both.[37] An inscription also attests the formula 'Owner of the Sky God of Israel' (*Bʿ(l) S1myn ʾlh Ys*^{3}*r[ʾl]*).[38] We also possess an edict granting the construction of a Jewish cemetery (*l-qtbr b-hn ʾyhdn*),[39] and four plots 'to bury the Jews (*ʾyhdn*), with the assurance (*hymntm*, an Aramaism) that they not be buried with non-Jews (interestingly indicated as *ʾrmym*) to fulfil the obligations towards the Jews. The edict is written by the *qayl* (leader) of the Mḍḥym tribe and further grants the construction of a religious building.

In addition to these Ḥimyarite inscriptions mentioning the Jews of South Arabia, two Hebrew inscriptions have been found in South Arabia. The first is a *mishmarōt*.[40] The root of the term means 'to keep watch'. Based on a passage in the first book of Chronicles, it indicates the courses in which the priests and the Levites were organized.[41] A second small Hebrew inscription is found in the middle of a Ḥimyarite one. It mentions the 'People of Israel' and is written by a certain Yahuda', either a Ḥimyarite convert who adopted a Jewish name. The Hebrew part of the inscription reads: 'Yahūdah wrote. Remember him well. Amen, peace, amen' (*ktb Yhwdh zkwr l-ṭwb ʾmn shlwm ʾmn*).[42] Moreover, we can add two seals to the definitely Jewish corpus of South Arabia, one depicting a menorah[43] and another bearing a Jewish name.[44]

A group of epitaphs found outside South Arabia can be attributed to Jewish Ḥimyarite emigrants. Commercial relations between South Arabia and the Levant are attested from the end of the First Temple period.[45] In two manuscripts of the Arabic version and the Gəʿəz version of the

35 CIH 543; Gar Bayt al-Ashwal 1; Ibrahim al-Hudayd 1; Gar framm. 7.
36 Ry 515; Ja 1028 (dated to 523).
37 CIH 543.
38 SR-Naʿḍ 9.
39 MAFRAY-Ḥaṣī 1.
40 DJE 23.
41 1 Chr. 24–6.
42 Gar Bayt al-Ashwal 1.
43 C. J. Robin, 'Himyar et Israël', *Comptes-rendus des séances de l'académie des inscriptions et belles-lettres* 2 (2004), 831–908, at pp. 891–2.
44 P. Yule, 'Zafar: The Capital of the Ancient Himyarite Empire Rediscovered', *Jemen-Report* 36 (2005), 22–9, at p. 28.
45 A. Lemaire, 'Solomon & Sheba, Inc. New Inscription Confirms Trade Relations between Towns of Judah and South Arabia', *Biblical Archaeology Review* 36 (2010), 54–9.

Martyrdom of Arethas, the Jews are said to have inhabited South Arabia after the destruction of the Second Temple in 70 CE.[46] These contacts became more frequent after the third Jewish–Roman War and the following Jewish diaspora. In catacomb 7 of the necropolis of Beth Sheʿarīm in Lower Galilee, a Greek inscription mentions the Ḥimyarites.[47] At ṣuʿar (modern Jordan), a bilingual Palestinian inscription written in Aramaic and Ḥimyarite has been found. This inscription testifies that the South Arabian Jews who emigrated to Palestine called their god *Rḥmnn*.[48] Furthermore, the inscription shows many Aramaisms, attested in the broader monotheistic corpus of South Arabia.

There are many Hebrew and Aramaic loanwords in the Ḥimyarite inscriptions. The most recurrent one is *ʾmn* ('amen').[49] The words *s¹lwm* ('peace'),[50] *ṣlt* ('prayer'),[51] *zkt* ('grace'),[52] *gzr* ('grant')[53] and *brk* ('blessing')[54] are found fewer than five times each. These loanwords occur in the inscriptions dedicated to 'Lord of Heaven', *Rḥmnn*, or both. The existence of these loanwords might point to the presence of a Jewish community in Ḥimyar. However, it should be noted that loanwords can get easily transmitted and adopted by speakers of different languages, and Ḥimyarite inscriptions bearing Aramaisms in South Arabia need not necessarily be attributed to Jews. A Ḥimyarite-speaking community could have adopted these terms from local Jews with whom they were in close contact. In addition to the testimonies mentioned earlier clearly attesting to the presence of a Jewish South Arabian community, there are two monumental inscriptions, both dated to the sixth century during the reign of the Jewish king Yūsuf, who ruled from 522 to sometime between 525 and 530. One invokes *rb-Hwd b-Rḥmnn* ('Lord of the Jew in/with/by the aid of *Rḥmnn*'),[55] and the other *rb-Hd b-Mḥmd* ('Lord of the Jews in/with/by the aid of the Highly Praised').[56] The word *Mḥmd* ('Highly Praised') appears only in this

46 Codices 469 and 535; Arabic *MaAr.* 1.10–15; Gəʿəz *MaAr.* 1e.
47 CII 1137–8. For the catacomb 7 see M. Schwabe and B. Lifshitz, *Beth Sheʿarim*, Vol. 2 (Jerusalem: Massada Press, 1974), 89–90.
48 Naveh-Ṣuʿar 24. This Aramaic epitaph mentions a Jew who died in Ḥimyar buried in Israel (*d-gz b-Ṭfr mdynth b-ʾrʿhwn d-Ḥmyrʾy w-nfq l-ʾrʿh d-Yśrʾl*). According to Naveh, the epitaph comes from Ṣuʿar (Jordan) and is datable to 470.
49 Ry 403; Gar nuove iscrizioni 4; Ry 513; ZM 5+8+10; Ir 71.
50 Robin-Najr 1; Ry 534+MAFY/Rayda 1. Ir 71 has the monogram *S¹lwm.*
51 RES 3232–42; Gar Bayt al-Ashwal 1; Ha 11.
52 Gar antichità 9 d; Gar Bayt al-Ashwal 1; ZM 5+8+10.
53 MAFRAY-Ḥaṣī 1.
54 CIH 543; Ja 856; Ry 534+MAFY/Rayda 1.
55 Ry 515.
56 Ja 1028.

inscription in the Ḥimyarite corpus. It is hard to determine if the 'Lord of the Jews' and *Rḥmnn*/*Mḥmd* are the same god based on the syntax of the two sentences. However, since *Mḥmd* is grammatically an attributive participle and *Rḥmnn* is also an adjective, the two names could be used here as a simple apposition.

A prayer inscribed on a stone found at Ẓafār, capital of the Ḥimyarite kingdom, sheds some light on the relationship between the 'Lord of the Jews' and *Rḥmnn* while also attesting the uses of the lexemes for 'Israel' and 'Jews' together:

[b]rk w-tbrk s^{1}m Rḥmnn ḏ-s^{1}myn w-Ys^{3}rʾl w-
ʾlh-hmw rb-Yhd ḏ-hrd(ʿ) ʿbd-hmw S^{2}hrm w-
ʾm-hw Bdm w-ḥs^{2}kt-hw S^{2}ms^{1}m w-ʾl—
wd-hmy Ḍmm w-ʾbs^{2}ʿr (w)-Mʾr—
m w-kl bhṯ-h [… …]

Bless and be blessed the name of *Rḥmnn,* who is in the heaven, and Israel and
their God, the Lord of the Jews, who assisted their servant S^{2}hrm, and
his mother Bdm, his wife S^{2}ms^{1}m, and
their children ḏmm, and ʾbs^{2}ʿr and Mṣr-
m, and all his house [… …][57]

The first two lines are interesting for several reasons. First, the Hebrew formula *[b]rk w-tbrk* is attested. Second, although the invoked god is called *Rḥmnn,* it is also specified that he 'is in heaven' (*ḏ-b-s^{1}myn*). The formula recalls once again the widely attested theonym 'Lord of Heaven'. Third, the god of the Israelites is mentioned as *ʾlh-hmw Rb-Yhd* ('their God the Lord of the Jews'). It hence seems that '*Rḥmnn* who is in heaven' and 'God, Lord of the Jews' are two separate entities. This seems antithetical to the attributive use of *Rḥmnn* and *Mḥmd.* At the moment, we can only speculate that the inscriptions bearing the formulae *rb-Hwd b-Rḥmnn* and *rb-Hd b-Mḥmd* attest an early phase and that later *Mḥmd,* and especially *Rḥmnn*, ceased being adjectival forms and received the status of theonyms.

3.3 The Royal Monotheism of Ḥimyar in the Broader Late Antique Framework

As we have seen, there is considerable evidence for the existence of a Jewish community in late antique Ḥimyar. The mention of Jews and Israel, the

[57] CIH 543. Reading adapted from A. W. F. Jamme, *Miscellanées d'ancient arabe* 16 (Washington, DC, 1988), 16, 103.

presence of Hebrew inscriptions and seals, the testimonies of Jewish Ḥimyarites in Palestine and the attestation of many Aramaisms all point in this direction. Nevertheless, most of the Ḥimyarite inscriptions of the fourth and fifth centuries show a less firm adherence to monotheism. In this section, I shed some light on the monotheism of the ruling classes of the kingdom and the possible continuation of pagan cults after the fourth century. I argue that the Ḥimyarite conversion to monotheism follows a broader late antique trend, exemplified by the first stage of Christianity in Aksūm and the Graeco-Roman world, as well as by the references to a 'High God' in pre-Islamic North Arabia.

The Ḥimyarite kings' break from polytheism has been characterized as radical and abrupt.[58] Fewer than ten of the Ḥimyarite inscriptions with religious formulae are signed by kings. Other inscriptions of this kind are attributed to princes, governors[59] and 'assistants of the king.'[60] Three royal inscriptions are attributed to Malkīkarib Yuha'min (who reigned around 375 to 400) and his sons, the first kings to reject polytheism.[61] These inscriptions invoke the 'Lord of Heaven and Earth' (*ʾlhn Bʿl* S^1*myn w-ʾrḍn* or *Mrʾ (*S^1*my)[n]*). Malkīkarib Yuha'min's monotheism does not have a particular affiliation and seems generic. Almost a century later, king Shuriḥbi'īl Ya'fur, who reigned around 450 to 468, also employed the formula *ʾlhn Bʿl* S^1*myn w-ʾrḍn* in an inscription from Ma'rib commemorating a repair of the city dam.[62]

The term 'pagan monotheism' has often been used to describe a monotheism, primarily independent of Judaism and Christianity, widespread in Late Antiquity in the Near East.[63] Angelos Chaniotis has claimed that the term seems to be a paradox and reduces the matter to a question of quantity. Instead, he argues that it represents a different interpretation of the divine, and hence it is a question of quality. He has proposed to use the neologism 'megatheism'.[64] Many have adopted the term 'henotheism',

[58] Robin, 'Ḥimyar, Aksūm, and Arabia Deserta', 129.

[59] E.g., Ag 3.

[60] B 8457.

[61] RES 3383; Gar Bayt al-Ashwal 2. Ja 856, written by Malkīkarib Yuha'min, does not show any theonym but celebrates the construction of a *mkrb*. An inscription by Marthad'ilān Yun'im (YM 1200) also does not bear any theonym but commemorates the construction of a *mkrb*.

[62] CIH 540.

[63] First employed in 1999 by P. Athanassiadi and M. Frede (eds), *Pagan Monotheism in Late Antiquity* (Oxford: Oxford University Press, 1999).

[64] A. Chaniotis, 'Megatheism: The Search for the Almighty God and the Competition of Cults', in *One God: Pagan Monotheism in the Roman Empire*, ed. S. Mitchell and P. Van Nuffelen (Cambridge: Cambridge University Press, 2010), 112–40, at p. 112.

but there is not yet a universally accepted definition.[65] Comparing and contrasting monotheisms related in different degrees to the scriptural traditions during Late Antiquity can offer a valuable means to contextualize and understand the choice of the elites of Ḥimyar. What follows is an analysis of this broader late antique framework.

In some respects, the god invoked by the South Arabian kings and princes resembles the 'High God' venerated in the Graeco-Roman world and in buffer-state regions such as the already mentioned Palmyra (see Chapter 2). It has been suggested that *Theos Hypsistos* was a single, remote and abstract deity,[66] and that it was anonymous and never represented in human form.[67] Nevertheless, nothing points to the fact that the cult of *Theos Hypsistos* was unified or an empire-wide cult, and it appears that various gods were worshipped as *Hypsistos*.[68] The most interesting parallel with the 'High God' cults in the Graeco-Roman world lies in their connection to Gentile sympathizers with Judaism. We possess inscriptions to *Theos Hypsistos* redacted by both Jews and Jewish sympathizers, as in the case of the monotheism of South Arabia. Some worshippers of *Theos Hypsistos* identified themselves as *theosebeis*, 'God-fearers', also known as *metuentes* in the Latin West. God-fearers were being mentioned in the Septuagint by around 200 BCE.[69] Some of these people were Jewish sympathizers who attended services at the synagogues,[70] a feature that they shared with the kings and princes of South Arabia. Some Gentile sympathizers with Judaism also paid for the construction of religious buildings and sent money to the Temple from around 100 BCE.[71]

In 1988, a Greek inscription roughly datable to the second half of the fourth century was found at the South Arabian port city of Qanīʾ.[72] In the same town,

65 P. Van Nuffelen, 'Pagan Monotheism as a Religious Phenomenon in One God', in *One God: Pagan Monotheism in the Roman Empire*, ed. S. Mitchell and P. Van Nuffelen (Cambridge: Cambridge University Press, 2010), 16–33, at p. 18.

66 S. Mitchell, 'The Cult of Theos Hypsistos between Pagans, Jews, and Christians', in *Pagan Monotheism in Late Antiquity*, ed. P. Athanassiadi and M. Frede (Oxford: Oxford University Press, 1999), 81–148, at p. 92.

67 S. Mitchell and P. Van Nuffelen, 'Introduction: The Debate about Pagan Monotheism', in *One God: Pagan Monotheism in the Roman Empire*, ed. S. Mitchell and P. Van Nuffelen (Cambridge: Cambridge University Press, 2010), 1–15, at p. 12.

68 G. W. Bowersock, 'The Highest God with Particular Reference to North Pontus', *Hyperboreus* 8 (2002), 353–63.

69 2 Chronicle 5.6.

70 S. Mitchell, 'The Cult of Theos Hypsistos between Pagans, Jews, and Christians', in *Pagan Monotheism in Late Antiquity*, ed. P. Athanassiadi and M. Frede, 81–148 (Oxford: Oxford University Press, 1999), 81–148, at p. 115.

71 Joseph. *AJ*. 14.7.2.

72 *VDI*.

a building has been interpreted as a synagogue.[73] The inscription invokes a god (*theos*) to protect maritime trade. It mentions a 'sacred place' (*hagios topos*), often used to designate synagogues.[74] The attribute of god (*boēthos*) is also attested in Jewish or Jewish sympathizers' contexts.[75] This inscription could hence be attributed to Greek-speaking traders who were Jewish sympathizers and either lived in or traded with the inhabitants of South Arabia. This finding points to the presence of God-fearers in fourth-century Ḥimyar. Inspired by the Jews of the diaspora, it is probable that the beliefs of the late antique God-fearers were the social response to the changes of the period. The use of the theonym 'Lord of Heaven and Earth' in the kingdom of Aksūm has already been discussed. Literary sources attribute Aksūm's conversion to Christianity to the influence of the Frumentius mentioned earlier, who was consecrated bishop of Aksūm by Athanasius.[76] Frumentius' preaching is attested in a letter dated 356–7. Signed by Constantius II and addressed to ʿEzana and his brother, it is documented in the *Apology* that Athanasius addressed to Constantius II.[77] A few more words on the first stage of the Aksūmite monotheism will help understand the broader historical framework in which South Arabia's break with the region's polytheistic past must be placed.

Theonyms such as 'Lord of Heaven' are employed in Gəʿəz to refer to God.[78] It has already been noticed that a pagan deity in South Arabia shared the epithet; this was also true of the Ethiopian ʿAstar, whose name was used as 'God' in the Book of Ecclesiasticus.[79] The readaptation of the title 'Lord of Heaven' in Aksūm may have thus helped to ease the reorientations of the Aksūmite population towards monotheism. Significantly, a generic 'Lord of the World' (*ʾəgziʾabəḥer*) is used as the name of God in early literary sources such as 1 Enoch, datable between the third and the first centuries BCE.[80] A 'Lord of the World of Heaven' (*ʾəgziʾabəḥer sämayä*) is also attested.[81] ʿEzana Gəʿəz inscriptions are cautious in tone and content, resembling the sympathizing attitudes of the neighbouring

73 The interpretation of the building as a synagogue has been recently revised by Mark Letteney and Simcha Gross. The two authors argue that there are not enough information pointing to its use as a synagogue, but do not advance a different identification. See Mark Letteney and Simcha Gross, "Reconsidering the Earliest Synagogue in Yemen", *Studies in Late Antiquity* 6 (2022): 627–50.

74 G. W. Bowersock, 'The New Greek Inscription from South Yemen', in *To Hellenikon: Studies in Honor of Speros Vryonis*, ed. M. V. Anastos (New Rochelle: Artistide D. Caratzas, 1993), 3–8, at pp. 4–6.

75 Ibid., 5.

76 Rufinus, *Ecclesiastical History*, 2.5.14.

77 Athanasius, *Apology*, 29.

78 E.g., 1 Enoch 13.4.

79 Ecclesiasticus 31.8 and 37.21. See A. Dillmann (ed.), *Lexicon Linguae Aethiopicae* (New York: Frederick Ungar, 1955), 750.

80 E.g., 1 Enoch 1.2; 10.9; 18.7.

81 1 Enoch 13.4.

South Arabian kings. In contrast, in his Greek inscriptions, ʿEzana declares himself a Christian.[82] This is evident in a famous Greek inscription discovered in 1970, which reads: 'I believe in your son Jesus Christ who saved me.'[83] The Gəʿəz side of this stele commemorates ʿEzana war against the Noba, describing the expedition in detail, while the Greek narrative is vaguer. Divergences in content between inscriptions written in more than one language by the same king are not uncommon. A good example is Augustus' Greek-Latin *Res Gestae*, composed in the last year of his life (14 CE). The bilingual inscription offers two different versions of the same text, as one language does not merely translate the other.[84] The Greek version does not mention Augustus' conquests, which are emphasized in the Latin text, probably to avoid offending the communities newly conquered by Rome.[85] Interestingly, ʿEzana titulus in his Greek and Gəʿəz inscriptions also diverge, the latter being humbler in content.[86]

It is unclear why ʿEzana wrote more than his predecessors, but a likely reason lies in his ambitious plans.[87] It is plausible that the display of crosses and the Christian tones of the Greek inscriptions of Aksūm were meant to appeal to the neighbouring powers, particularly Rome. The divergences between the Greek and the Gəʿəz inscriptions of ʿEzana support this hypothesis: blatant Christian propaganda directed at the emissaries of the Roman emperors and a vague monotheism for the lower classes in the embryonic phase of the kingdom's conversion. ʿEzana and the Ḥimyarite kings aimed to please their public, and accordingly, they carefully balanced their words. This is perhaps why Philostorgius came under the impression that the South Arabian king had converted to Christianity. However, from a sociopolitical perspective, the intentions of the first kings of Aksūm and Ḥimyar diverged in the adoption of monotheism: the first did so to strengthen its relationship with an external power, Rome, while the second aimed to unify a segmented population which had recently been brought under a single rule and was not only polytheistic but also venerated different pantheons. In the case of Ḥimyar, the 'external aim' is less clear, but sympathy towards Judaism is evident. Ḥimyar likely chose to display a more timid adherence to please both Rome and Iran. In contrast with

82 Compare RIE 190 and 270.
83 Anfray 1970.
84 A. E. Cooley, *Res Gestae Divi Augusti: Text, Translation and Commentary* (Cambridge: Cambridge University Press, 2009), 26.
85 Ibid., 28.
86 See the Gəʿəz RIE 189 where he claims to be the 'King of Kings', missing in Greek inscriptions.
87 Bowersock, *Throne of Adulis*, 67.

neighbouring Aksūm, Ḥimyar was not officially allied with these powers. Both kingdoms were active in North and Central Arabia and became major participants in shaping sixth-century South Arabia. Iran even conquered South Arabia around 575.[88]

It has often been claimed that a Jewish community may have also influenced the outbreak of monotheism in Aksūm. This community supposedly migrated from South Arabia before the fourth century.[89] However, there is little proof of a significant immigration of Jews to Aksūm.[90] Arguments put forward to prove Jewish influence on Aksūmite Christianity include the coincidence of rites and lexicon, as well as a long-documented presence of Jews in the area.[91] Nevertheless, the most consistent indications of a Jewish influence on Ethiopian culture are found in literary texts translated from Greek into Gəʿəz after the conversion of ʿEzana.[92] The presence of loanwords from Jewish Palestinian Aramaic in Aksūmite Gəʿəz can likely be attributed to the contacts between Aksūm and Syro-Palestinian traders.[93] Overall, the supposed Jewish roots of Aksūmite monotheism were inspired by exegetical impulses and/or composed under the influence of later debates. Their reinterpretation of the Aksūmite past attempted to emphasize the supremacy of Ethiopian Christianity, negotiating and legitimizing the Miaphysite Ethiopian position when the quarrels among the Christian doctrinal factions were intense.

The monotheism of Ḥimyar shares features with that of the Hypsistarians and with the early phase of Aksūmite Christianity. Pre-Islamic henotheism is also attested in North Arabia (see Chapter 6). Finally, the Ḥimyarite kingdom's official conversion to monotheism shares some features with that of the first Christian emperors of the Roman Empire, mentioned in Chapter 2. Pagan cults survived in the private sphere but less openly in public. In a milieu where the distinction between religion and politics was far from insurmountable, paganism and monotheism were integrated into a mixture of sacred and profane. Pagan monotheists, megatheists and

88 Theophanes of Byzantium in Phot. 64.

89 E. Ullendorff, 'Hebraic-Jewish Elements in Abyssian (Monophysite) Christianity', in *Languages and Cultures of Eastern Christianity: Ethiopia*, ed. A. Bausi (Farnham: Routledge, 2012), 121–256, at pp. 219–28.

90 M. Rodinson, 'On the Question of "Jewish Influences" in Ethiopia', in *Languages and Cultures of Eastern Christianity: Ethiopia*, ed. A. Bausi (Farnham, 2012), 179–86, at p. 186.

91 Ibid., 180–3.

92 P. Piovanelli, 'Jewish Christianity in Late Antique Aksum and Ḥimyar? A Reassessment of the Evidence and a New Proposal', *Judaïsme ancien-Ancient Judaism* 6 (2018), 175–202, at p. 184.

93 Ibid., 187.

henotheists venerated a single 'High God' within a polytheistic framework. The religious attitude of the kings of Ḥimyar is instead monotheistic tout court: the terminology is often blurred, but there are no associators with the Lord of the Heaven/*Rḥmnn* – that is, of course, if this theonym refers to the same god. In South Arabia, a god emerged as a plenipotentiary god. Still, no other gods were reduced in importance and considered as, for example, 'angels' or 'sons/daughters' as they were in North Arabia. The god of Ḥimyar is not praised as the greatest among the gods because there *are* no other gods. This monotheism is inspired by Judaism, as possibly was the henotheism of the neighbouring Hypsistarians. However, the existence of rising henotheism in the fourth-century Near East does not exclude an evolving process towards monotheism. A blend between these two components is highly plausible and is distinctive in this period in other contexts. Moreover, the official monotheism of Ḥimyar is probably blurred only to us, as there are unfortunate *lacunae* in our knowledge. For example, it is unclear whether the new religion was imposed by force or if it was still possible to worship the pagan gods publicly. We do not possess books of religious laws, acts of councils or exegesis as in the case of the scriptural monotheisms. Although it is plausible that this monotheism was never codified, this remains nothing more than an assumption, and further archaeological investigation is needed to draw a definitive conclusion about the nature of Ḥimyarite monotheism.

Ḥimyar's becoming monotheistic was a more gradual process than previously thought, a conclusion supported by the religious vocabulary employed in the monumental epigraphic corpus. Just as paganism was not abruptly abandoned after Rome's conversion, polytheistic cults survived in Ḥimyar. This is indicated in a letter extant in Syriac and Garshuni (Arabic written in Syriac script). Two passages suggest that there were pagans (*ḥnf*) in South Arabia at the beginning of the sixth century.[94] Another indication is found in the opening section of the *Martyrdom of Arethas* mentioned earlier.[95] The monumental corpus does not shed light on the possibility that some Ḥimyarites remained polytheists after the kings' official conversion. However, some documents written on palm-leaf stalks and wooden sticks suggest that, at least in the private sphere, some inhabitants of pre-Islamic South Arabia did not convert. This corpus, comprising South Arabian minuscule inscriptions (*Korpus altsüdarabischer Minuskelinschriften*), has been partially studied by Peter Stein. Analysing some of these testimonies

[94] *Letter* 2, 2.C, line 27; 8.C, line 8.
[95] *MaAr.* 1.

housed at the Bayerische Staatsbibliothek of Munich, Stein has identified six invocations to the polytheistic gods dhū-Samawī, ʿAthtar and Almaqah.[96] He suggests that these inscriptions were written after the fourth century, though from a palaeographical perspective, it is also possible to date them to before the kingdom adhered to monotheism.[97] One of them, for example, can be dated to 469.[98] As Stein reports, even Robin, who has long argued that the end of polytheism in South Arabia was abrupt, has admitted that some polytheistic monumental inscriptions can be dated to after the end of the fourth century. A Ḥimyarite document with an invocation to dhū-Samawī,[99] mentioned in one of Robin's articles,[100] is quoted by Stein in support of this thesis.[101] Robin has revised his thesis in a publication appeared after my article in the *Journal of Late Antiquity*.[102]

This minuscule corpus of inscribed stalks and sticks can reveal whether pagan cults were still alive in the fifth century, at least in the private sphere. Additionally, since not all South Arabians were likely able to carve monumental inscriptions, we may infer from these data whether only the powerful elites converted to monotheism or the poorer social strata of society did so too. For now, at any rate, we are unable to postulate that a 'massive movement of conversion' took place.[103] Moreover, the study of more documents on sticks, at the moment still in its infancy, nevertheless promises to shed light on the creation of a Ḥimyarite monotheism in pre-Islamic South Arabia. Before drawing a general conclusion about the Ḥimyarite monotheism(s) of the fourth and fifth centuries, let us first consider the identity of the South Arabian converts and attempt to explain how and why the elites chose to become Jewish sympathizers.

96 P. Stein, 'Montheismus oder religiöse Vielfalt? Du Samawi, die Stammesgottheit derAmir, im 5. Jh. n. Chr.', in *Philologisches und Historisches zwischen Anatolien und Sokotra*, ed. A. Sima (Wiesbaden: Harrassowitz, 2009), 339–50.

97 Ibid., 344.

98 Mon.script.sab 514.

99 YM 10882.

100 C. J. Robin, 'L'institution monarchique en Arabie du Sud antique: les contributions fondatrices d'A.F.L. Beeston réexaminées à la lumière des découvertes les plus récentes', *Proceedings of the Seminar for Arabian Studies* 36 (2006), 43–52, at p. 50 n. 7.

101 Stein, 'Montheismus oder religiöse Vielfalt?', 348.

102 As previously indicated, this chapter was submitted for publication to the *Journal of Late Antiquity* in May 2019 and appeared in *JLA* 13 (2020). See Grasso, 'A Late Antique Kingdom's Conversion'. Robin has revised his position in a publication that appeared after my journal article in *JLA* and the present manuscript submission to Cambridge University Press. See C. J. Robin, 'The Judaism of an Ancient Kingdom of Ḥimyar in Arabia: A Discreet Conversion', in *Diversity and Rabbinization: Jewish Texts and Societies between 400 and 1000* CE, ed. G. McDowell, R. Naiweld and D. S. B Ezra (Cambridge: Open Book Publishers, 2021), 165–270.

103 Robin, 'The Peoples beyond the Arabian Frontier', 59.

3.4 Ḥimyarite Converts: Identities and Sympathies

The monotheistic inscriptions of Ḥimyar bear the names of rulers, princes and leaders. The elites and those close to the *rābbanat* of the kings' entourage converted,[104] at least publicly, to monotheism at the end of the fourth century. Ḥimyar's conversion to Judaism could constitute particularly fertile ground for an enquiry into 'ethnicity' during Late Antiquity, as it shows the ambiguity of the concept of 'ethnicity' at the time. The Ḥimyarite kings' monotheism was moulded to be an 'integrative monotheism'. As far as we know, there was no need to follow any ritual or behavioural rule to be a Ḥimyarite monotheist. However, could the Ḥimyarites convert fully to Judaism? The onomastics of the monotheistic Ḥimyarite corpus suggest that most of the writers of the inscriptions were Ḥimyarites, and only a few Jewish names are attested in the corpus. However, onomastics can often be misleading. For example, an inscription from late antique Hierapolis mentions seventy-six Jews, but only three have clearly Jewish names.[105] In Ḥimyar, the name Yṣḥq (Isaac) is found in an inscription[106] and in a seal from Ẓafār.[107] As Robin points out, the transliteration of the name in Ḥimyarite is different from the Aramaic version (the letter *ṣād* appears instead of *shīn*), and it is a calque from Hebrew. This may point to independence from the Jewish community of the north,[108] or it could simply be attributed to a readaptation of the word to sound more like the local Ḥimyarite. Is it possible that some people bearing biblical names were Ḥimyarites who converted to Judaism and adopted Jewish names? Enslaved men, who converted after being acquired, and women (through intermarriage) could become Jews, as in the notable case of Asenath in the pseudepigraphical *Joseph and Asenath*. In the Hebrew Bible, Gentiles convert,[109] and, according to the Talmud, such Gentiles can become 'Israelites in all respects'.[110] However, the process of complete conversion was relatively uncommon; only seven Roman laws enacted between the fourth and sixth centuries restricted conversions to Judaism.[111] Furthermore, the

[104] *MaAz.* 22–5.
[105] A. Chaniotis, 'The Jews of Aphrodisias: New Evidence and Old Problems', *Scripta Classica Israelica* 21 (2002), 209–42, at pp. 226–8.
[106] ZM 894.
[107] Yule, 'Zafar', 28, fig. 10.
[108] Robin, 'Himyar et Israël', 886–7.
[109] Judith 14.10.
[110] *Mishnah, Yevamot,* 47b.
[111] A. Linder, *The Jews in Roman Imperial Legislation* (Detroit: Wayne State University Press, 1987), 79.

converts probably were considered somehow inferior to the full-blooded Jews, or this, at any rate, is what the Jewish sources suggest.[112]

Roman imperial authorities had an influential hand in defining Jewish identity by taking steps to delineate Jews as a discrete group,[113] as testified by the tax reform (*fiscus Iudaicus*) introduced after the destruction of the Temple in 70 CE. However, during Late Antiquity, the number of Jewish sympathizers rose. Findings such as the 'donor inscriptions' of Aphrodisias (ca. 400–500 CE),[114] mentioning sixty-eight Jews, three proselytes and fifty-four *theosebeis*, attest to a composite milieu and the invention of 'categories' to redefine those belonging to Judaism.[115] The first attempts are traceable in the Talmud (completed around 400 in Jerusalem and 500 in Babylonia) and especially in the tractate *Avodah Zarah*. However, the reformation was slow, and definitions differed from place to place or even inside the same community. The exegetical phase of Judaism was likely sealed before the sixth century.[116] In a peripheral area for rabbinic Judaism, such as South Arabia, the advancements in defining identity were probably further delayed. Jews allowed conversions during Late Antiquity but, as far as we can tell, they did not set out to proselytize their neighbours to a measurable degree, or at least not on the same scale as Christians or Manicheans. They hence allowed Gentiles to form social relationships with their community and attend services in the synagogues without having to convert. The canons of the Synod of Elvira (ca. 305–6) give a glimpse into the close relationship between Gentiles and Jews in Late Antiquity.[117] Although widespread practices among Gentiles (e.g., abstaining from work on the Sabbath)[118] did not bring Gentiles and Jews closer, attending rites at the synagogue did have this effect, and in Ḥimyarite *mikrāb* ('sanctuary') were probably used by both sympathizers and Jews.[119]

Philostorgius claims that the people of South Arabia were pagans but also circumcised.[120] Already in the first century, Josephus had argued that

[112] *Mishnah, Bikkurim* 1.4.
[113] M. A. Goodman, *Mission and Conversion: Proselytizing in the Religious History of the Roman Empire* (Oxford: Oxford University Press, 1994), 125.
[114] R. S. Kraemer, 'Giving up the Godfearers', in *Crossing Boundaries in Early Judaism and Christianity*, ed. K. B. Stratton and A. Lieber (Leiden: Brill, 2016), 169–200, at p. 190.
[115] See Chaniotis, 'The Jews of Aphrodisias'. Two dedications to *Theos Hypsistos* have been also found in Aphrodisias.
[116] Fowden, *Before and after Muḥammad*, 50.
[117] E.g., Canons 16; 78.
[118] Joseph. *Ap.* 2.39.
[119] Robin, 'Ḥimyar, Aksūm, and Arabia Deserta', 129.
[120] Philostorgius, *Ecclesiastical History*, 3.4.

the Arabs, descendants of Abraham through Ishmael, practised circumcision,[121] and Christians generally conceived of the Arabs as sharing a Jewish heritage corrupted by paganism.[122] This view is also shared by later Muslim historians such as Ibn Isḥāq (d. 767),[123] and Ibn al-Kalbī (d. 821),[124] and by other literary sources such as Bardaisan's (d. 222) Syriac *Book of the Laws of Countries*.[125] In the Greek *Panarion* of Epiphanius (d. ca. 403), it is stated that the *Homēritai* observe circumcision like the Samaritans, Jews and Idumaeans.[126] In the early fifth century, Sozomen provided renewed contact with Jews as an explanation for circumcision among contemporary Arabs.[127] Outsiders' perceptions of circumcision functioned differently in time and space,[128] and in fourth- and fifth-century South Arabia, the boundaries between Gentiles and Jews were flexible. Ancient *ethnē* had permeable boundaries. Just as 'Greekness' assumed the 'function of language and culture' and ceased being 'a function of birth and geography' in the Hellenistic period,[129] a Ḥimyarite Gentile could choose to become a Jewish proselyte as long as he or she rejected polytheism and accepted the Jewish customs. This is further suggested by a fourth-century alabaster stone sculpture,[130] representing the head of a high-ranking man wearing a laurel wreath. The man also has a moustache and a single ringlet on the left cheek, indicating that he was a Jew.[131] The sculpture may represent a portrait of a Ḥimyarite king or prince who was not only a sympathizer but a Jewish proselyte. An inscription, dated to 470 and composed by writers with Ḥimyarite name, mentioning 'their tribe of Israel' (*s^{2}ʿb-hmw Ys^{3}rʾl*), corroborates this hypothesis.[132] The archaizing 'Israel' is usually preferred to 'Jew' in Ḥimyar, and this may point broadly to a representation inspired by past self-ascriptions.[133]

121 Joseph. *AJ*. 1.214.
122 Millar, *Rome, the Greek World, and the East*, Vol. 3, 372.
123 Ibn al-Kalbī, *Aṣnām*, 5–6.
124 Isḥāq, *Sīra*, 51–6.
125 Bardaisan, *Book of Law*, 56.
126 Epiphanius, *Panarion*, 1.33.3.
127 Sozom. 6.38.
128 J. Lieu, *Christian Identity in the Jewish and Graeco-Roman World* (Oxford: Oxford University Press, 2004), 125.
129 S. J. D. Cohen, 'Religion, Ethnicity and "Hellenism" in the Emergence of Jewish Identity in Maccabean Palestine', in *Religion and Religious Practice in the Seleucid Kingdom*, ed. P. Bilde, et al. (Aarhus: Aarhus University Press, 1999), 204–23, at p. 137.
130 MET 1982.317.1.
131 P. O. Harper, 'Ancient Near Eastern Art', in *MET Notable Acquisitions, 1982–1983* (1983), 5.
132 ZM 2000.
133 Lieu, *Christian Identity*, 248.

The God-fearers chose not to convert to preserve the cultural traditions inherited in their native communities.[134] Similarly, by not converting to Judaism, the rulers of South Arabia adopted a universalistic monotheism open to everyone, like Christianity, Manichaeism and later Islam. We can only speculate how the Jewish community saw the kingdom's official conversion. The relationship between the Jewish community in South Arabia and those in the Levant and Babylonia is unclear, as contemporary Jewish sources ignore this group. In late antique Ḥimyar, we see a ruling group aiming to unify an area previously defined by the territorial control of several independent kingdoms. At the beginning of the unification, their subjects did not share a language or religion. Unity was established thanks to the conversion of the kings, which proved how easy it was to overcome identity barriers, especially when permeable religious features constituted signs of identity. In the sixth century, migrations on a larger scale would further attribute to religion the crucial role in reshaping identities.

In conclusion, we can broadly identify two religious attitudes in the Ḥimyarite inscriptions of the period. The first employs generic names to indicate god and could be generally identified as sympathizers sharing features with some of the god-fearing Gentiles sympathetic to Hellenistic Judaism, as testified by the Greek inscription from Qanī',[135] and with the later Islamic *ḥunafā'*[136] who, according to the Muslim tradition, maintained the monotheism of Abraham after the introduction of polytheism in Ḥijāz.[137] The second attitude is attributable to a Jewish community, probably small but close to the king, sometimes writing in Hebrew and often mentioning Israel – and some emigrated to Palestine. A few literary sources confirm the presence of Jews in South Arabia. The *Chronicle of Seert* claims that the king of Ḥimyar was a Jew and his mother a Jewish captive in the fifth century.[138] A chapter of the sixth-century *Book of the Ḥimyarites* in Syriac is entitled 'About the Ḥimyarites and when they first received Judaism',[139] though it is now lost. The sixth-century history of Procopius (d. ca. 554) recounts that many *Homeritae* were Jews in the sixth century, and many of them professed 'the old faith nowadays called Hellenic'.[140]

134 Mitchell, 'The Cult of Theos Hypsistos', 127.
135 *VDI*.
136 The root in the first form literally means 'to revert'.
137 Isḥāq, *Sīra*, 149.
138 *Hist. nest.* 1.73.
139 *Ḥimyarites*, ch. 2.
140 Procop. *Pers.* 1.20.

The Ḥimyarite kings' choice to adopt a monotheism inspired not by Christianity but by Judaism potentially had international implications, distancing Ḥimyar from Rome, Aksūm and the Roman allies of North Arabia (i.e., the Christian Salīḥids and later the Jafnids). Ḥimyar may have aimed to strengthen its relationship with Iran (see Chapter 4). By the same token, because the kings' and princes' monotheism is often vague, Ḥimyar was able to assume a neutral posture vis-à-vis the surrounding kingdoms. The passage by Philostorgius presented at the beginning of this chapter acknowledges Rome's interest in Arabia,[141] describing the benevolent attitude of the king towards the Christian embassy. This resembles King ʿEzana stance and points again to the careful use of religion as an instrument of diplomacy and power. Little can be said regarding the result of the embassy. Using the lack of Christian inscriptions at this time as proof of the failed conversion of the ruler is an *argumentum ex silentio.* As we have seen, the monotheistic inscriptions of the kings of Ḥimyar appear to be influenced by Judaism, but they could also be partially influenced by Christianity, as the inscriptions of the neighbouring Aksūm are also vague in content. Nevertheless, the presence of a Jewish community in South Arabia serving the king, the animosity between South Arabia and Aksūm and the lack of further attested contacts with Rome seem to point to Judaism as an inspiration for the official monotheism of Ḥimyar. It is probable that the embassy mainly sought to gain the freedom to profess Christianity for the traders in commercial cities,[142] at a time when Iran was particularly hostile towards the Christian communities and Rome. The mission may have also aimed to assure South Arabia's political support against Iran, given the belligerent climate of the fourth century, and may have never had any intention to convert the inner Ḥimyar.

Like rulers of neighbouring kingdoms – for instance, Constantine, ʿEzana, Trdat III of Armenia and Mirian III of Kartli in Georgia –, Malkīkarib Yuha'min and his successors recognized the strategic importance of adopting a monotheistic religion to prevent cultural fragmentation and thereby consolidate their power. This places South Arabia within the changing world of Late Antiquity and binds it with one of the most recognizable features of the period: a careful adoption of monotheism by the ruling classes in the public sphere. The first monotheism of Ḥimyar prepared the area for the adoption of Christianity one century later, followed

[141] The renewed interest in South Arabia in the fourth century is exemplified by the Namārah epitaph.

[142] The killing of Ethiopian Christian traders is adduced as motivation for Aksūm's intervention in South Arabia. See Chapter 4, Malalas, *Chronicle*, 18.433 and *Chronicle of Zuqnīn*, 55.

later by the adoption of Islam. It is plausible that the monotheism(s) of Ḥimyar influenced the formation process of the last scriptural religion. The Ḥimyarite religious vocabulary is strikingly like that of the Qur'ān. Consider, for example, the possible adoption of the lexemes *Rḥmnn* and *mḥrb*. The first is used as one of the names of god by the Christians of South Arabia and in three Safaitic inscriptions but also by Muḥammad and his contemporary rival Musaylimah ibn Ḥabīb (see Chapter 6). The *miḥrāb*, instead, in the later Islamic tradition, came to indicate a semicircular niche in a mosque which indicates the *qiblah* (direction for praying towards the Kaʿbah). However, it is also possible that it was a Jewish or Jewish-sympathizing community active in Ḥijāz that influenced Islam and the Qur'ānic vocabulary (see Chapter 6).

The picture presented in this chapter points to the fluidity and syncretism prevalent in the Arabian cult in the broader late antique traditions. The creation of a monotheism, not openly scriptural, helped the kings create a brand new South Arabian identity and unify their infant kingdom, a procedure like that employed by Muḥammad in view of the first Muslim conquests. Ḥimyar's conversion reflects a widespread, characteristically fourth-century reorientation towards monotheism and the sociopolitical exploitation of cults among the competitive late antique empires. In South Arabia, as in the neighbouring kingdoms, the transition from polytheism to the scriptural traditions was mitigated by the syncretistic cults of sympathizers and God-fearers who the Jewish communities of the Diaspora had inspired. The fourth century thus saw the emergence of a new category of believers as a response to the social changes of the time. The kingdom of Ḥimyar, placed in a strategic position between East and West, was not exempt from the cultural transformations of Late Antiquity.

CHAPTER 4

The Shape of the Sixth Century I
The South

This chapter is the direct continuation of Chapter 3. It aims to analyse the interactions between Jews and Christians in sixth-century South Arabia, offering some reflections on the broader late antique socio-economic and political map. The first part reconstructs the spread of Christianity in South Arabia and the events leading to the massacre of the Christians of Najrān in 523, presenting a comprehensive analysis of this period through a reading of literary and epigraphic material. By looking at the Red Sea 'as an arena of human activities',[1] I argue that economic reasons were the main motivations behind the *negus*'s invasion of South Arabia and that faith was exploited as a *casus belli.* It is a recurrent *topos* for hagiographies and histories to ascribe the evangelization of a region to the arrival of a pious figure, leading to the sudden conversion of the entire population. The story of the Buddhist conversion of the Kushan ruler Kanishka in the *Fu fazang yinyuan zhuan* 付法藏因緣傳 shows that this trope was not a prerogative of Christian accounts.[2] However, conversions tended to be the cumulative result of socio-economic networks and migrations, as the exchange of ideas

[1] R. Chakravarti, 'Vibrant Thalassographies of the Indian Ocean: Beyond Nation States', *Studies in History* 31 (2015), 235–48, at p. 236.

[2] *Fu fazang yinyuan zhuan* 付法藏因緣傳, in the *Taisho Tripitaka*: T 50, no. 2058, 5. The text, also mentioned as *Fou-fa-ts'ang-in-iuen-tch'oen*, has been translated as 'Tradition of the Causes and Conditions of the Dharma-Treasury Transmission' by S. H. Young, *Conceiving the Indian Buddhist Patriarchs in China* (Honolulu: University of Hawaii Press, 2015), 69. It has traditionally been claimed that the text was translated from Sanskrit (existing as *Śri-dharma-piṭaka-nidāna-sūtra*) into Chinese in 472 CE in the Northern Wei regime by Kekaya (Ki-kia-ye) and Tanyao (T'an-aio). Building on the work of Henri Maspero, Linda Penkower has suggested that it is instead an apocryphal text, written in Chinese during the Northern Wei period. See L. Penkower, 'In the Beginning ... Guanding 灌顶 (561–632) and the Creation of Early Tiantai', *Journal of the International Association of Buddhist Studies* (2000): 245–96; H. Maspero, 'Sur la date et l'authenticite du *Foufa tsang yin yuan tchouan*', in *Melanges d'Indianisme offerts par ses eleves a M. Sylvain Levi* (Paris: Ernest Leroux, 1911), 129–49. For Bhuddist apocrypha, see also R. E. Buswell (ed.), *Chinese Buddhist Apocrypha* (Honolulu: University of Hawaii Press, 1990). For an early study of the text, see S. Lévi, *Notes sur les Indo-Scythes, Journal asiatique* 2 (1896), 475–84; for a more recent interpretation of the text as of Indian origin, see B. Kumar, *The Early Kusanas* (New Delhi: Sterling Publishers, 1973), 295. I am grateful to Scott Pearce for his bibliographical recommendation.

followed that of resources. As such, the depiction of the massacre of Najrān as a 'religious slaughter' reflects more the 'religious' character of the available literary sources than the actual unfolding of the events. The second part of the chapter focuses on the Red Sea Christianities. It examines the religious allegiances of the Aksūmite *negus* Kaleb (r. ca. 520–40) and the Ḥimyarite king Abraha (r. ca. 535–65). This section, therefore, sheds light on the several stages involved in the Christianization of these two regions and reconstructs the events that led to the collapse of Ḥimyar, arguing that the disappearance of this kingdom, in conjunction with the fall of the allied kingdoms of Jafnids and Naṣrids in North Arabia, led to a vacuum which facilitated the rise of Islam and Muḥammad's movement, thereby preparing the ground for the establishment of the Muslim Empire.

4.1 The Arrival of Christianity and the Traditional Account of the Massacre of Najrān

Christianity spread in South Arabia from the oasis of Najrān, located at the junction of the route leading to north-western and eastern Arabia. Although literary sources agree that the first Christian community of South Arabia was located in Najrān, they disagree about who exactly founded it. While the *Martyrdom of* ʾAzqir attributes the spread of Christianity in Najrān to the priest ʾAzqir ('the first to teach Christianity in Najrān'), active at the time of king Shurihbʾīl Yakkuf (ca. 468–80),[3] the *Chronicle of Seert* attributes it to a trader named Ḥannān who had converted at Ḥīrah.[4] Ḥannān's presence in South Arabia is also attested by the *Book of the Ḥimyarites*, possibly the basis for the *Chronicle of Seert* in which he appears under the name of Ḥayyān,[5] and is said to have burned synagogues.[6] Another narrative recounting the spread of Christianity in South Arabia is found in a sixth-century Syriac Christian hagiography set in fifth-century Edessa, telling the encounter between the ascetics Paul and John with a group of Ḥimyarites in Sinai, the ascetics' imprisonment in South Arabia and the conversion of the southern Arabians to Christianity.[7] During the ascetics' first night in Ḥimyar, a young girl screamed that fiery arrows were coming from the two ascetics striking her in the face. According to this recount, Paul then convinced the girl and her family to convert to Christianity to stop the arrows. However, the Ḥimyarite

[3] *MaAz.* 1.1.
[4] *Hist. nest.* 1.73.
[5] N and y look very similar in Syriac.
[6] *Ḥimyarites*, 11, p. 32b.
[7] *History of the Great Deeds*, 22–8.

king later ordered the ascetics to be sacrificed under a palm tree revered as the god of the settlement. John challenged the king to a duel, calling upon his God to defeat the ruler's idol. As soon as he finished saying a prayer, the tree was uprooted, and its branches and fruits were burned. As a result, the king himself converted, built a church and appointed priests and deacons.

The Edessan hagiography was probably the basis of the narrative by the Yemeni Wahb ibn Munabbih (d. 728/32) of the conversion of the Ḥimyarites in Najrān, as reported by Ibn Isḥāq[8] and al-Ṭabarī.[9] In both accounts, two Christians, named Faymiyūn and Ṣālih, are abducted by a group of Arabians and sold as enslaved people in Najrān, where people venerate palm trees. Faymiyūn is then challenged to prove the truthfulness of the Christian God. His ability to do this results in the wholesale conversion of the oasis's population. Ibn Isḥāq,[10] and al-Ṭabarī[11] further offer a second explanation for the spread of Christianity in South Arabia, attributing its success to the missionary activity of a disciple of Faymiyūn called ʿAbd Allāh ibn al-Thāmir.[12] Elsewhere, al-Ṭabarī claims that a fifth-century ruler of Ḥimyar 'was an adherent of the original form of Christianity but used to conceal this from his people'.[13] A fragment by the Miaphysite chronicler John Diakrinomenos (fl. early sixth century) found in the ecclesiastical history by Theodorus Lector (d. after 518) similarly dates the spread of Christianity in South Arabia to the time of Anastasius I (r. 491–518).[14]

Some recently published inscriptions also date the spread of Christianity in Najrān to the end of the fifth century.[15] One is dated to 470,[16] and the other inscriptions can be plausibly dated to the same period due to palaeographical similarities. Most of these inscriptions bear just a single name and a cross, suggesting that they are Christian epitaphs. In the single case God is mentioned, the definitive article *'l* precedes *'lh* ('the God').[17] Another inscription from the same site, possibly datable to the same

8 Ibn Isḥāq, *Sīrah*, 21.
9 Ṭabarī, *Tārikh*, 1.920–1.
10 Ibn Isḥāq, *Sīrah*, 23–5.
11 Ṭabarī, *Tārikh*, 1.923–5.
12 Ibn Isḥāq, *Sīrah*, 23–5.
13 Ṭabarī, *Tārikh*, 1.881.
14 John Diakrinomenos, Frag. 2.551–6.
15 C. J. Robin et al., 'Inscriptions antiques de la région de Najrān (Arabie Séoudite méridionale): nouveaux jalons pour l'histoire de l'écriture, de la langue et du calendrier arabe', *Comptes rendus de l'académie des inscriptions & belles-lettres* (2014), 1033–128.
16 Ḥimà-Sud PalAr 1.
17 Ḥimà-Sud PalAr 8. I find plausible that the god appearing in Ḥimà-Sud PalAr 10 constitutes part of the personal name Marthad'ilān, recurring in many Sabean inscriptions and widespread in the area.

period, mentions *ʾl-ʾlh* and a cross.[18] Although these inscriptions appear to be the only South Arabian ones bearing the name of *ʾlh* ('god') preceded by the Classical Arabic determinative article *ʾl*, other pre-Islamic transitional or Old Arabic inscriptions bear monotheistic theonym(s) in the north of the Arabian Peninsula.[19] Epigraphical evidence belonging to this corpus is a trilingual inscription (Arabic, Greek and Syriac) found on a lintel over the door to the martyrion of the church dedicated to St Sergius at Zabad (Syria) dated 512 (Chapter 1).[20] Another mention is found in an Arabic inscription dated to around 560 in the monastery of Hind the Elder at Ḥīrah preserved in two transcriptions of al-Bakrī (d. 1094)[21] and Yāqūt (d. 1229).[22] There are slight differences between the two versions,[23] but they appear authentic. More epigraphic evidence comes from north-eastern Jordan, close to Qaṣr Burquʿ, and is datable between the sixth and seventh centuries (*dkr ʾl-ʾlh yzydw ʾl-mlk*).[24] Finally, a sixth-century Old Arabic inscription from Dūmat al-Jandal, situated in a geographically prominent position linking Central Arabia and the mountains of Ḥawrān, clearly states: *dkr ʾl-ʾlh* ('May God remember').[25] The inscription contains a series of numbers, which have been interpreted to indicate the date 548–9, followed by a cross. A certain number of Christians from Ḥīrah settled in Dūmat al-Jandal.[26] At the time of Muḥammad, the leader of the city was the Christian Ḥujrid king al-Sakūnī, an ally of Rome.[27] Indeed, the Nabatean-derived script and the dating system used by the Najranite epitaphs suggest a close connection with North Arabia,[28] gesturing towards a certain degree of cultural uniformity (Chapter 1). Old Arabic is primarily attested in the north of the Arabian Peninsula, and it is possible that

[18] Ḥimà-Sud PalAr 10.

[19] For the spellings of the Christian god in the earliest Arabic versions of the Bible, see H. Kachouch, 'The Arabic Versions of the Gospels: A Case Study of John 1.1. and 1.18', in *The Bible in Arab Christianity*, ed. D. Thomas (Leiden: Brill, 2007), 9–36; and Hikmat Kashouh, *The Arabic Versions of the Gospels* (Berlin: De Gruyter, 2012).

[20] C. J. Robin, 'La réforme de l'écriture arabe à l'époque du califat médinois', *Mélanges de l'université Saint-Joseph* 59 (2006), 319–64, at p. 337.

[21] al-Bakrī, *Muʿjam* 2, p. 607.

[22] Yāqūt, *Buldān* 2.542.

[23] *Dayr* ('monastery') in Yāqūt, being *bayt* (lit. 'house') in al-Bakrī. Another small difference is constituted by the name of God, being *ʾl-Il(ā)h* in al-Bakrī, but first *ʾl-Il(ā)h* and then *All(ā)h* in Yāqūt.

[24] Al-Shdaifat 2017.

[25] L. Nehmé, 'New Dated Inscriptions (Nabataean and pre-Islamic Arabic) from a Site Near al-Jawf, Ancient Dūmah, Saudi Arabia', *Arabian Epigraphic Notes* 3 (2017), 121–64, at pp. 124–31.

[26] L. Veccia Vaglieri, 'Dūmat al-Djandal', in *The Encyclopaedia of Islam*, ed. P. Bearman, T. Bianquis, C. E. Bosworth, E. van Donzel and W. P. Heinrichs (Leiden: Brill, 2012).

[27] Al-Masʿūdī, *Tanbīh*, 248, 1.17.

[28] Following the era of the Province of Arabia.

the Christian community of Najrān adopted it as an ideological choice to distinguish themselves from the non-Christian kingdom of Ḥimyar. The currently unpublished inscriptions found by the Ṭā'if-Mecca Epigraphic Survey Project, however, may offer further insight on the matter.

Ultimately, Christianity was established in Ḥimyar at the beginning of the sixth century. In 518, the Aksūmite *negus* Kaleb,[29] described as 'a Christian and a most devoted adherent of this faith',[30] enthroned an allied king by the name of Maʿdīkarib Yaʿfur (r. ca. 518–22) in Ḥimyar. Maʿdīkarib died four years later, and the Aksūmites failed in placing another king on the South Arabian throne.[31] Hence, a Jewish Ḥimyarite leader by the name of Yūsuf (Joseph),[32] supposedly the son of a captive Jewish woman from Nisibis (Turkey) who had been sold as an enslaved man to a Ḥimyarite king,[33] proclaimed himself 'king of all the tribes', supported by the powerful Yaz'an tribal federation.[34] However, according to a small number of literary sources, he was proclaimed king directly by the Aksūmites but later rebelled.[35] Epigraphic evidence suggests that in his eagerness to free Arabia from Aksūmite control, Yūsuf began his campaigns by killing 300 Aksūmites at the Ḥimyarite capital Ẓhafār and burning its local church.[36] He then led an army to raid the South Arabian coasts of the Red Sea,[37] killing around 13,000 Christians at the church in the port city of al-Mukhā' (*Mḫwn*).[38] Yūsuf's troops blocked the entrance to the harbour of Mandab (*Mdbn*) to prevent any Aksūmite intervention. At the same time, while Yūsuf was 'guarding the coast against the Abyssinians' (*Ḥbs*^{2}*t*),[39] an army

[29] Procopius calls 'Ǝlla by a Greek adaptation of his name, Hellesthaeus (*Pers.* 1.20.), while others used a more literal adaptation (*Life of Gregentios* uses 'Elesboam', 9.1–5).In the Arabic sources, he is known as al-Isbās (*MaAr.* 1.10 et seq.), from Sabaic *'l̊ṣbḥh*(Ist 7608 bis). Kaleb and 'Ǝllä Aṣbəḥa appear together only in a Gəʿəz inscription in Sabean script (RIE 191). Moreover, Kaleb is mentioned as Andas in 18.429 et seq of the chronicle by John Malalas (d. ca. 578), and as Andug in *Chronicle of Zuqnīn*, 54 et seq.

[30] Procop. *Pers.* 1.20.

[31] 'Due to the arrival of winter' (*Chronicle of Zuqnīn*, 57–69); Pseudo-Zachariah, *Ecclesiastical History*, 8.3; Michael the Syrian, *Chronicle*, 9.12.

[32] Sabaic Yws^{1}f 's^1'r Yṯ'r (Ja 1028; Ry 507; Ry 508); Syriac *Masrūq* ('devil', not a personal name) (*Ḥimyarites*, 25 et seq.; also, in the Arabic-written *Hist. nest.* 1.73); Arabic (Zurʿah) Dhū Nuwās (Ibn Isḥāq, *Sīrah*, 26 et seq.; Ṭabarī, *Tārikh*, 1.920 et seq.) or Finḥas (*MaAr*, 1.10 et seq.), also in Gəʿəz (*MaGe.* 1c et seq.); Greek Dounaas (*MaGr.* 1.5 et seq.; also, *Life of Gregentios*, 9.1–5) or Dimnos (Malalas, *Chronicle*,18.433; *Chronicle of Zuqnīn*, 54 et seq.).

[33] *Hist. nest.* 1.73.

[34] E.g., J1028/1. See Chapter 1.

[35] *MaGr.* 258 and *MaAr.* 69.

[36] As testified by three South Arabian inscriptions dated to 523: Ry 507; Ry 508; Ja 1028.

[37] Ibid.

[38] Ibid.

[39] Ja 1028.

commanded by a Jewish *qayl* known as Sharaḥ'īl, a member of the Yaz'anite tribe (*dh-Yz'n*),[40] attacked Najrān.[41] This expedition, undertaken with the help of the tribes of Hamdān and the *ˀˁrb* of Kindah, Murād and Madḥig, was a resounding success as 12,000 Christians were killed, with spoils amounting to 11,000 prisoners and 190,000 animals.[42] Although the king probably exaggerated these numbers, many members of this community, including their leader al-Ḥārith, son of Ka'b, died in the massacre.[43]

Several literary accounts claim that the *negus* Kaleb undertook the military campaigns in Arabia to aid the Christian subjects of Ḥimyar, who the Jewish-sympathizing rulers of South Arabia were persecuting. This is, for example, suggested by the title of a chapter in the *Book of the Ḥimyarites*, reporting that a bishop named Thomas 'went to the Abyssinians and informed them that the Ḥimyarites were persecuting the Christians'.[44] The mistreatment of Christian subjects under Ḥimyarite rulers is similarly depicted by the *Martyrdom of 'Azqir*, focused on the killing of a Christian martyr by the Jews of Arabia at the end of the fifth century.[45] The most informative literary sources on the events of Najrān include the *Martyrium Sancti Arethae*[46] and two letters. The *Martyrium*, initially written in Greek around 560, describes the inhabitants of South Arabia as Jews who venerated idols and emphasizes the courage and actions of women and children during the massacre. After a siege of six months, the inhabitants of Najrān were tricked by Yūsuf into opening the city gates and were brutally killed together with the Christian leader al-Ḥārith, who had tried to warn the population of Najrān not to trust the Jewish ruler. The *Martyrium* claims that Yūsuf asked the Iranian king and the Naṣrid leader to kill the Christians living in their land in return for 3,000 dinars. Hence, at the time of the Conference of Ramla (which led to a treaty between Rome and the Naṣrids), Justin I (r. 518–27) sent a priest called Abraham to the Naṣrid leader al-Mundhir to avoid a second massacre.[47] By the end of the meeting, Abraham had managed to negotiate a peace treaty with the Naṣrids

40 A general called Dw-Yzn also appears in *Ḥimyarites*, 19, p. 26b et seq.

41 Ry 507; Ry 508; Ja 1028.

42 Ja 1028; Ry 507; Ry 508.

43 Mentioned in Greek as Arethas and in Gəʿəz as Ḥārith.

44 *Ḥimyarites*, 4.

45 *MaAz.*

46 M. Detoraki, *Le martyre de saint Aréthas et de ses compagnons* (Paris: Association des amis du Centre d'histoire et civilisation de Byzance, 2007), 98.

47 In the Arabic and Gəʿəz versions he is mistakenly called 'Constantine'. In *MaGr.* this Naṣrid leader is named *Alamoundraros* (25), while in *MaAr.* he is clearly identified as al-Nuʿmān Ibn al-Mundhir (27).

and immediately informed Justin about the seriousness of the situation in Arabia. Justin wrote to the patriarch of Alexandria and to the *negus* ordering a military intervention in Ḥimyar as his kingdom was 'too far away' for him to send troops directly.[48]

The author(s) of the *Martyrium* openly condemn the actions of the Jewish leader of Ḥimyar while also taking the opportunity to criticize the Church of the East. According to the text, when the Najrānites opened the doors of the city, Yūsuf ordered for a fire to be set to burn his Christian opponents.[49] He then invited the people of Najrān to renounce their Christian faith and become Jewish, insisting that the Romans had killed Jesus because of his blasphemous claims to be the son of God.[50] According to Yūsuf, 'the *Romaioi* ("Byzantines") known as the *Nestorianoi*' (in the Greek version), '*al-Rūm* ("the Byzantines") known as *al-Mannānīn*' (in Arabic) and '*Rome* known as *Nasätərosaqiyanə*' (in Gəʿəz) believed Jesus to be only a prophet.[51] Although this passage implies that only the Miaphysite Christian faction of Najrān was killed, the *Martyrium* aims to praise all the Christian martyrs regardless of their doctrinal preferences and celebrate Justin as 'the ruler of an undivided Christian Commonwealth'.[52] Indeed, the author(s) of the *Martyrium* display(s) a positive attitude towards Rome and the politics of the strongly Chalcedonian Justin, praisingly labelled as *tou philochristou basileusantos*.[53] Meanwhile, all the remaining Christian literary sources about the events of Najrān were written by Miaphysites, supporting the idea that the Miaphysite faction in South Arabia was the only community attacked by Yūsuf.

The *Martyrium* appears to be based on a letter dated 524.[54] The letter was written to Simeon, bishop of Gabbula, by the Miaphysite Simeon of Bēth Arsham (d. 548), found near Mesopotamian Seleucia.[55] Simeon was a Miaphysite Christian bishop and a missionary active in the Sasanian Empire and the Naṣrid kingdom,[56] as well as in Armenia,[57] where he attended the

[48] According to the Muslim tradition, it was a South Arabian called Daus Dhū Thaʿlabān who reached the Byzantine court asking for aid against Joseph. Ibn Isḥāq, *Sīrah*, 26; Ṭabarī, *Tārīkh*, 1.927.

[49] *MaGr.* 6; *MaAr.* 6; *MaGe.* 6.

[50] Ibid.

[51] Ibid.

[52] P. Wood, *'We Have No King but Christ': Christian Political Thought in Greater Syria on the Eve of the Arab Conquest (c.400–585)* (Oxford: Oxford Univerisity Press, 2010), 222.

[53] This is especially evident in one of the Greek versions of the text, belonging to the so-called γ testimony. MaGr 1.1.

[54] *Letter 1.*

[55] Bar 'Ebroyo, *Chronicle*, 3.86.

[56] John of Ephesus, *Lives*, 10.

[57] As attested in two letters by the head of the Armenian Church Babgēn I (d. 516) *Girk T'łt'oc*, 41–7. See N. Garsoïan, *L'église arménienne et le grand schisme d'Orient* (Louvain: Peeters, 1999), 441–4.

first Council of Duin in 505–6.[58] In the letter's conclusion, Simeon states that he will inform the Miaphysite bishops who had escaped to Egypt,[59] the patriarch of Alexandria (who in turn would inform the *negus* and the Aksūmite bishops), the believers of Antioch, Tarsus of Cilicia, Caesarea in Cappadocia and Edessa, about the events taking place in Najrān. According to a second letter available in Syriac and Garshuni, also dated to 524 and composed at the Jafnid camp of al-Jābiya,[60] 2,000 Christians were killed in Najrān.[61] Yūsuf had sent rabbis summoned from Tiberias[62] to promise the Najrānites that no harm would come to them, but this promise was not kept.[63] The document reveals the names of two bishops active in Najrān (both called Mār Pawlos) at the time. The first was killed in the Ẓafār persecution, while the second died before the city surrendered to Yūsuf.[64] Both bishops had been consecrated by Philoxenos (450–523), the Miaphysite bishop of Hierapolis-Mabbūg, known for his fervent attacks on Chalcedonian Christology.[65] Other important members of the Miaphysite faction are also mentioned in the text, such as John bishop of Tella (d. 538), said to have ordained the presbyter Elias subsequently 'killed in Ḥaḍramawt'.[66] These mentions give further evidence that the martyrs of Najrān were of a Miaphysite Christological position. Two more Syriac texts appear to be related to the first letter of Simeon, namely the letter by the bishop of Baṭnān Jacob of Sarug (d. 521) and the hymn by the Miaphysite John Psaltes 'Calligraphus' (d. ca. 600), abbot of the monastery of John Bar Aphtonius at Qēnneshrē (Syria). Jacob, a fervent supporter of the Miaphysite faction as suggested by a letter to the Miaphysite bishop Paul of Edessa (d. 526) dated to around 520,[67] is the author of a letter comforting the Christian Ḥimyarites.[68] Since he died in 521, his letter must refer to

58 N. Garsoïan, *Interregnum: Introduction to a Study on the Formation of Armenian Identity (ca 600–750)* (Louvain: Peeters, 2012), 73.

59 Likely referring to important Miaphysites figures such as Severus, patriarch of Antioch in 512 who fled to Alexandria in 518.

60 This letter (hereafter *Letter 2*) has also been attributed to Simeon of Beth Arshām based on structural similarity and linguistic analysis (Irfan Shahid, *Martyrs of Najrān: New Documents* (Bruxelles: Soc. des Bollandistes, 1971), 31–2). However, the letter was written anonymously in Syriac by a Miaphysite so there are no justifiable grounds for attributing its authorship with certainty to Simeon.

61 *Letter 2*, 3.A.15.

62 These are not mentioned in the first letter.

63 *Letter 2*, 2.B.15.

64 Ibid., 2.C.15–20.

65 S. Lunn-Rockliffe, 'The Invention and Demonisation of an Ascetic Heresiarch: Philoxenus of Mabbug on the "Messalian" Adelphius', *The Journal of Ecclesiastical History* 68 (2017), 455–73.

66 *Letter 2*, 2.B.15–20.

67 Jacob of Serug, *Letter to Paul of Edessa.*

68 Jacob of Serug, *Letter to the Ḥimyarites.*

persecutions before the massacre of Najrān. John Psaltes' hymn, originally written in Greek but only surviving in Syriac through a translation by Paul of Edessa, is similarly dedicated to the Christian martyrs of Najrān.[69]

Although Miaphysitism was likely the dominant Christian denomination in Najrān, other factions were active in the Arabian oasis. East Syrian Christianity had spread in Najrān by the reign of the Sasanian Yazdagird II (r. 438–57), as suggested by the *Chronicle of Seert.*[70] According to this text, a famous tradesman of the region named Ḥannān was baptized while on a journey to Constantinople when he passed through Ḥīrah, an influential bishopric of the Church of the East (Chapters 2 and 5). He later convinced his Najrānite family and acquaintances to embrace Christianity. The Chronicle further reports that Yūsuf killed only some of the Christians in Najrān (*khalqan min al-naṣārā*), thus suggesting the presence of other Christian factions. A speech by Yūsuf found in a passage of the *Book of the Ḥimyarites* encouraging the Christians of Najrān to deny Jesus Christ as he was a 'mortal man of mankind, yet spoke of himself as the son of God, the Merciful' (*Raḥmānā*),[71] ultimately ascertains that Yūsuf mostly killed the Miaphysite population of the city, and possibly suggests that the Church of the East helped Yūsuf in massacring the Miaphysites.

An echo of the massacre of Najrān is also supposedly found in the eighty-fifth *sūrah* of the Qur'ān.[72] Ibn Isḥāq claims that verses 4–8 refer to the massacre while recounting the story of 'Abdallāh ibn al-Thāmir, a Christian believer who spread Christianity to Najrān and was put to death by Yūsuf.[73] The story describes al-Thāmir as *imām.*[74] Since the Muslim sources do not mention al-Ḥārith, al-Thāmir's accounts may have been based on the narrative of the martyrdom of Ḥārith. Indeed, Muslim tradition regarding the events of Najrān appears to be based on Christian hagiography,written to comfort the persecuted Miaphysite communities but also to celebrate the Christian martyrs who were killed by a Jew, thus drawing obvious and powerful parallels with the death of Jesus Christ at the hands of the Jews.[75] Similarly, the honouring of the martyrs of Najrān in the *sūrat al-Burūj*, supposedly revealed in the Meccan period, was written

[69] John Psaltes, *Hymn.*

[70] *Hist. nest.* 1.73.

[71] *Ḥimyarites,* 13 p 13a.

[72] Q. 85.4–8.

[73] Ibn Isḥāq, *Sīrah*, 23–5.

[74] Told on the authority of Ibn Ka'b al-Quraẓī, and an unnamed 'man of Najrān'.

[75] P. La Spisa, 'Martirio e rappresaglia nell'Arabia Meridionale dei secoli V e VI: uno sguardo sinottico tra fonti islamiche e cristiane', *Adamantius* 23 (2017), 318–40.

with the intent to spur the early Muslim community to resilience. The events of Najrān became a *topos* of resistance. Nonetheless, faith played a relatively marginal role in Yūsuf's motivations for ordering the Narjān massacre and the consequent shaping of sixth-century South Arabia.

4.2 Empires on the Red Sea: Wars without Faith

If, as previously suggested, faith played a relatively marginal and even pretextual role in explaining the events that took place in sixth-century Arabia, perhaps economic reasons are a more accurate explanation for the political, social and religious upheaval in the region. South Arabia's wealth was based on trade in frankincense, perfumes and spices and was well known in ancient times. Sappho (d. 570 BCE),[76] Herodotus,[77] Horace (d. 8 BCE),[78] Virgil (d. 19 BCE),[79] Pliny the Elder (d. 79 CE)[80] and the *Periplus of the Erythraean Sea*[81] testify to its international prestige. Arabian traders are also attested in the South Arabian epigraphical records,[82] and recent publications have suggested how sixth- to eighth-century sources indicate that 'the Incense Road survived until the sixth and seventh centuries CE'.[83] On the other side of the Red Sea, Aksūm also played a significant role in ancient and late antique trade routes. According to the *Periplus*, at the Eritrean port of Adulis, ivory, tortoiseshell and rhinoceros' horn were traded for products from India and the Roman Empire.[84] A protégé of the Roman Empire since the fourth century, Aksūm experienced a period of unprecedented prosperity in the late antique period. A passage in the *Martyrium Sancti Arethae* attests to the thriving commerce of Aksūm in the sixth century, with the claim that the *negus* was able to seize six merchant ships from Rome, Iran, India and the Farasan Islands at the harbour of Gabaza in Adulis ca. 525.[85] Aksūm's dominance in the Indian Ocean trade routes is also testified by the

76 Sappho, Fragment 44.30.
77 Hdt. 3.107.
78 Hor. *Carm.* 1.29, 3.24.
79 Verg. *G.* 2. 117.
80 Plin. *HN.* 5.12.
81 *Peripl.* 8.
82 RES 3951.
83 Cosmas Indicopleustes, *Topographia*, 2.49; Jacob of Edessa, *Hexaemeron*, 115. See M. D. Bukharin, 'Mecca on the Caravan Routes in pre-Islamic Antiquity', in *The Qur'ān in Context: Historical and Literary Investigations into the Qur'ānic Milieu*, ed. A. Neuwirth, N. Sinai and M. Marx (Leiden: Brill, 2010), 115–34, at p. 131.
84 *Peripl.* 6.
85 Fifteen ships from the city of Aeila, twenty from Clysma, seven from lotabe, two from Berenike, seven from Farasan and nine from India. See *MaGr.* 29.

accounts of late antique writers who referred to India and Ethiopia-Eritrea and, to a lesser extent, South Arabia in an interchangeable way.[86] For this reason, any references to the commerce 'of green nuts, which come from India' shipping to Clysma and attested in the anonymous sixth-century diary of the 'Piacenza Pilgrim' could feasibly have referred to trade routes between Egypt and Ethiopia-Eritrea instead.[87]

Conflicts between the kingdoms of South Arabia and Aksūm, already recorded between the late second to late third centuries CE,[88] increased in frequency after Ḥimyar's victory over Saba and Ḥaḍramawt. In the fourth century, Aksūm conquered Noba, between southern modern Egypt and central Sudan, and Kasu, supposedly located in the northern Sudanese Nile Valley.[89] After the fall of the Roman buffer state of Palmyra, there was an increase in the volume of trade for Aksūm.[90] In the sixth century, Aksūm was well placed to take on a dominant role in the commercial route from India to the Roman Empire were it not for the competition it faced from neighbouring Ḥimyar.[91] The latter had annexed parts of Central Arabia by 360,[92] and, in the last years of the reign of king Abīkarib Asʿad (400–45), conquered the land of the Central Arabian tribes of Maʿadd,[93] who never managed to form a federation, similarly to the Qiang of China.[94] The financial cost of controlling a suddenly expanded territory, together with the difficulties involved in patrolling a region with such a harsh climate and having to deal with the rise of new political entities in North Arabia, swallowed up much of Ḥimyar's financial resources and made it an easy target for the expansionist policies of neighbouring Aksūm.

At the beginning of the reign of Justin I (r. 518–27), the Egyptian monk Cosmas Indicopleustes was asked by the governor of Adulis to copy two inscriptions about a past conquest of Arabia. In his work, Cosmas asserted that the *negus* was eager to conquer South Arabia and was preparing to go to war against the Ḥimyarites.[95] Other surrounding empires were similarly keen to eliminate South Arabia and gain a monopoly of the Indian Ocean

[86] *Chronicle of Zuqnīn*, 54.
[87] *Piacenza Pilgrim*, 41.
[88] Ja 574; Ja 575; Ir 69.
[89] RIE 190 and 271.
[90] E. H. Seland, 'Networks and Social Cohesion in Ancient Indian Ocean Trade: Geography, Ethnicity, Religion', *Journal of Global History* 8 (2013), 373–90, at p. 381.
[91] *MaGr.* 184; *MaAr.* 33; *MaGe.* 123.
[92] ʿAbadān 1.
[93] Ry 509.
[94] M. E. Lewis, *The Early Chinese Empires: Qin and Han* (Cambridge, MA: Harvard University Press, 2009), 147.
[95] Cosmas Indincopleustes, *Topographia*, 2.141.

trade. Interest in the Red Sea commerce between the Mediterranean and the Indian Ocean has grown recently.[96] Recent works on Roman networks,[97] the spread of Christianity,[98] and the Islamic Red Sea are changing our understanding of long-distance trade and the interaction of cultures on trading routes.[99] Evidence of contact between the people inhabiting the Indian Ocean, its inlets and the Mediterranean world is attested in the archaeological and literary sources. The proceedings of the 2022 ISAW Roundtable Seminar Series "Indian Ocean Figures that Sailed Away" will be edited by me and Divya Kumar-Dumas, and will appear in an edited volume in 2024. An excellent example of this interconnected 'globalized' world[100] is offered by a passage found in the *Chronicle of Seert* mentioning a case of piracy involving 'goods and jewels brought from the lands of India and China' investigated by the bishop of Seleucia-Ctesiphon on behalf of the Sasanian ruler Yazdgird I in the fifth century CE.[101]

Late antique economic interests in the region are attested in Procopius' *Wars*. Shortly after the massacre of Najrān, the war between Rome and Iran started again in 531, and Kavādh I defeated the Romans at Callinicum on the Euphrates. Hence, Justinian (r. 527–65) sent an ambassador named Julianus to Kaleb and the South Arabian ruler Sumūyafaʿ Ashwaʿ, an ally of Aksūm,[102] demanding that both kingdoms support the Romans in the war against the Persians 'due to their concordant religion'.[103] Rome further suggested that the Aksūmites purchase silk directly from India and sell it to the Romans. The Ḥimyarites

[96] I am currently working on an edited volume that brings together contributions from speakers and participants of the 'Indian Ocean Figures that Sailed Away' online seminar series spring 2022, which I co-organized at the Institute for the Study of the Ancient World, New York University.

[97] K. Grønlund Evers, *Worlds Apart Trading Together: The Organisation of Long-Distance Trade between Rome and India in Antiquity* (Oxford : Archaeopress, 2017); M. A. Cobb, *Rome and the Indian Ocean Trade from Augustus to the Early Third Century CE* (Leiden: Brill, 2018); E. H. Seland, *Ships of the Desert and Ships of the Sea: Palmyra in the World Trade of the First Three Centuries CE* (Wiesbaden: Harrassowitz Verlag, 2016); G. Parker, *The Making of Roman India* (Cambridge: Cambridge University Press, 2008).

[98] N. J. Andrade, *The Journey of Christianity to India in Late Antiquity: Networks and the Movement of Culture* (Cambridge: Cambridge University Press, 2018); E. H. Seland, 'Trade and Christianity in the Indian Ocean during Late Antiquity', *Journal of Late Antiquity* 5 (2012), 72–86; R. Tomber, 'Bishops and Traders: The Role of Christianity in the Indian Ocean during the Roman Period', in *Red Sea III: Natural Resources and Cultural Connections of the Red Sea*, ed. P. Starkey and J. Starkey (Oxford: BAR Publishing, 2007), 219–28.

[99] T. Power, *The Red Sea from Byzantium to the Caliphate: AD 500–1000* (Oxford: Oxford University Press, 2012).

[100] For 'globalization' in the ancient world, see Serena Autiero and M. A. Cobb, 'Introduction: Utilizing Globalization and Transculturality for the Study of the Pre-modern World', in *Globalization and Transculturality from Antiquity to the Pre-modern World*, ed. S. Autiero and M. A. Cobb (New York: Routledge 2022), 1–15.

[101] *Hist. nest.* 69.

[102] Procop. *Pers*, 1.20.9–13.

[103] Ibid., 1.20.9.

were also requested to accept a man named Caius (previously exiled for having killed a relative of Sumūyafaʿ Ashwaʿ) as leader of the people of Maʿadd and to invade Iran with a joint expedition with Aksūm. Both kings agreed to Julian's demand, but they did not carry them out. Procopius goes some way to explaining why Julian's requests were not fulfilled: he stated that it would have been impossible for the Aksūmite to buy silk from the Indians because the Sasanian merchants were always present at the harbours where the Indian ships first landed and were able to buy all the cargo due to the favourable location of their country. This picture is in line with the description of precedent Arsacid (安息)-Roman relationship found in the Chinese *Hou Hanshu*.[104] Moreover, Procopius suggests it would have been challenging for the Ḥimyarites to cross the desert land of Arabia and fight 'people much more belligerent than themselves'.[105] When Justinian and the Iranian king Khosrow I (r. 531–79) signed the first pact towards perpetual peace the following year, the expedition of Julianus in Arabia and Aksūm was concluded. Procopius elsewhere mentions another expedient pursued by Justinian in the next years to obtain silk without purchasing it from Iran: certain monks who had spent time in the country beyond the Indus explained to Justinian that certain worms are the manufacturers of silk.[106] By bringing the worm's eggs from 'Serinda' to 'Byzantium', Procopius claims that they made the Roman production of silk possible.[107] Justin II instead forged an alliance with the Turkish leader Sizabul (Istemi). Maniakh, the leader of the Sogdians, had advised Sizabul to send silk to the Romans 'because they consumed it more than anyone else'.[108]

Regardless of the Roman and Iranian attempts to subjugate the Aksūmites and the Ḥimyarites, the Red Sea trade continued to be dominated by Aksūmite and Arabian intermediaries throughout the first six centuries of the first millennium. Similarly, one of the major trade routes of the period, the inland Silk Road(s) of Central Asia (see Chapter 1), was dominated by the Sogdians, who operated not only as mediators for empires such as that of Tang-era China (618–907) but also for the nomadic groups who held political power along their routes.[109] The success of the Sogdians was undoubtedly due to their ability to connect with distant regions and adapt to the beliefs of the communities they traded with. Mazdean, Hindu,

[104] *Hou Hanshu*, 88.12.

[105] Ibid., 1.20.13.

[106] Ibid., 8.17.1–6.

[107] Ibid., 8.17.7–8.

[108] Menander, fragment 10.1.

[109] For an overview of the Sogdian traders, see E. de la Vaissière, *Sogdian Traders: A History* (Leiden: Brill, 2005). For a shorter and more recent publication, see R. McLaughlin and H. Jin Kim, 'Sogdian Ambassadors of the Göktürks and the Eastern Roman Empire', in *Rome and China: Points of Contact*, ed. H. J. Kim, S. N. C. Lieu and R. McLaughlin (Abingdon: Routledge, 2021), 43–79.

Buddhist, Christian and Manichean Sogdians travelled around Eurasia. Goods, languages and ideas travelled with them, shaping the Sogdians' syncretic culture. The Red Sea traders similarly distributed exotic goods to empires, moved between statuses while moving objects, dealt with nomads, spread beliefs and absorbed influences, transforming their kingdoms from regional actors to leading commercial entities in two centuries. Whereas the prominence of the earlier Palmyrene trade lay in the 'closed access and strong cohesion' of its 'ethnicity-based' network,[110] the success of Aksūmite and Ḥimyarite commerce is at least partially attributable to the thriving communities located along the coasts of the Red Sea. Because of the combined efforts of traders and missionaries, Christianity became the dominant faith in both regions by the end of the sixth century. While the *Chronicle of Seert* attributes the rise of Christianity in Arabia to a trader named Ḥannān,[111] a Syriac Christian hagiographical work set in Edessa,[112] Ibn Isḥāq[113] and al-Ṭabarī[114] instead attribute the spread of Christianity in the region to merchant enslaved people. Similar accounts attribute the spread of Christianity in India to the arrival of an enslaved man accompanying a merchant on a voyage to the Indo-Scythian kingdom.[115] Even the sixth-century Christian ruler of Ḥimyar, Abraha (see Section 4.3), was the enslaved man of a Greek merchant in Adulis. Undoubtedly, traders played an important role as 'faith spreaders' in the first millennium, as demonstrated by later Muslim sources attributing the spread of paganism in Arabia to traders,[116] and describing Muḥammad himself as a trader (see Chapter 6). The sea route, being cheaper, faster and, to some extent, safer than the caravan route, offered an additional benefit: it bound together individuals and fostered economic and social cohesion. For these traders, Christianity and, to a lesser extent, the use of Greek were markers of identity. As previously shown, Christian churches were erected on the Indian Ocean rim from the fourth century onwards. These buildings testify to a critical advantage of Christianity; namely that it was a 'portable religion' practised 'independently of place and primary social group'.[117]

110 Seland, 'Networks and Social Cohesion', 383.
111 *Hist. nest.* 1.73.
112 *History of the Great Deeds*, 22–8.
113 Ibn Isḥāq, *Sīrah*, 21.
114 Al-Ṭabarī, *Tārīkh*, 1.920–1.
115 *Acts of Judas Thomas*, 2.
116 Ibn al-Kalbī, *Aṣnām*, 5–6. See Chapter 6.
117 Seland, 'Networks and Social Cohesion', 384.

According to Cosmas Indicopleustes, Indian, Iranian and Aksūmite ships sailed in the Indian Ocean in the sixth century, trading Chinese silk and fragrances.[118] Iranian Christian traders settled in Sri Lanka,[119] and Egyptian merchants later ventured to the same island with the Aksūmites.[120] This explains why churches discovered on the eastern side of Arabia, allied with Iran, are primarily located in cities with ports or along important trade nodes, pointing to a strong connection between Christian traders and church construction in Arabia.[121] Philostorgius, quoted in Chapter 3, wrote about the construction of churches in South Arabia between the fourth and fifth centuries 'for the Romans who travelled there and for the locals who might convert'.[122] The main religion of the Ḥimyarites at the time was a Jewish-inspired monotheism. The by the sea location of these ecclesiastical structures suggests a connection with Christian traders active in the region. A neglected passage found in the *Martyrdom of ʾAzqir* further attests the presence of many 'foreign wayfarers' (Gəʿəz *nagd*) at the time of ʾAzqir's killing in the region.[123] The discovery of considerable quantities of Aksūmite pottery and coins dated between the fourth and fifth centuries at the port of Qanīʾ (Yemen) confirms that Aksūmite merchants were a significant presence in the region.[124] Aksūmite presence in Arabia is also mentioned in the *Chronicle of Zuqnīn*,[125] and the works by Pseudo-Zacharia (d. 536)[126] and Michael the Syrian (d. 1199).[127]

John Malalas claimed that 'it is through the country of the Ḥimyarites that the Roman traders reach Aksūm and the Indian empires',[128] citing the killing of traders coming from Aksūm and the confiscation of their goods as a cause for the Aksūm incursion in South Arabia. According to Malalas, Yūsuf had alleged that the Christian Romans were mistreating the Jews in

[118] Cosmas Indicopleustes, *Topographia*, 11.15.
[119] Ibid., 14.22.
[120] Ibid., 11.17.
[121] Undated South Arabian inscriptions have been found in Thāj (Chapter 2), located 100 km from the Persian Gulf in modern Saudi Arabia and possessing at least one church. They are probably to be attributed to traders, possibly Christian. CIH 984–5. See Gonzague Ryckmans, 'Inscriptions sud-arabes (quatrième série)', *Le muséon* 50 (1937), 239–68.
[122] Philostorgius, *Ecclesiastical History*, 3.4.
[123] *MaAz.* 12. *Nagādyān* appears in one manuscript, see Alessandro Bausi, 'Il gadla 'Azqir', *Adamantius* 23 (2017), 341–80, at p. 361.
[124] A. V. Sedov, 'New Archaeological and Epigraphical Material from Qana (South Arabia)', *Arabian Archaeology and Epigraphy* 3 (1992), 110–37, at pp. 114 and 127–8.
[125] *Chronicle of Zuqnīn*, 57–69.
[126] Pseudo-Zachariah, *Ecclesiastical History*, 8.3.
[127] Michael the Syrian, *Chronicle*, 9.12.
[128] Malalas, *Chronicle*, 18.433.

their territory.[129] A similar justification is found in the *Chronicle of Zuqnīn*, which claims that the Aksūm incursion was caused by a loss of trade for the Aksūmites after the persecution of 'Christian Roman merchants' in South Arabia:

> Since the kingdom of the Kushites [Aksūmites] was further inland than that of the Ḥimyarites, the latter opposite to Egypt and Thebes and both beyond India, the Roman merchants active in the territories of the Ḥimyarites used to cross over and enter the inner regions of the Indians [Aksūmites] called the Azuliss of India [Adulis of Aksūm], and those of the Indians and the Kushites further inland. [...] When the above-mentioned Roman merchants crossed over to the territories of the Ḥimyarites to enter the regions of the Indians and trade with them as custom, Dimnos [Yūsuf], king of the Ḥimyarites, discovered this, seized them, killed them and plundered all their merchandise, saying: 'As in the Roman territories Christians badly harass the Jews massacring them, I am killing them!' Therefore, he killed so many that they became frightened and forbidden to enter. As such, trade with the inner kingdoms of the Indians and the Kushites ceased.[130]

In response, Kaleb sent a message to Yūsuf stating: 'You did wrong by killing the Roman Christian merchants, and you stopped trade and prevented sustenance to my kingdom and other kingdoms. Especially my kingdom you have damaged.'[131] Kaleb was eager to maintain his alliance with Rome as he was aware that the massacre perpetrated by Yūsuf could put an end to his lucrative deals with Rome and thus warranted his direct intervention. The defence of the traders' faith was plausibly a minor concern. Rome and Iran were deeply engaged in promoting trade and protecting their networks. Before reporting on the partnership mentioned earlier between Justin II and the Türkic leader Sizabul, Menander notes that when a Turk-Sogdian embassy appealed to Khosrow I to allow Sogdian merchants to sell silk in Iran in 568–9, Khosrow burned their silk cargo to underline Iran's monopoly of trade.[132] The Sasanian ruler poisoned the ambassadors when a second embassy reached his court.[133] Attacks on Christian merchants were also exploited as *casus belli*. Socrates Scholasticus claimed that the ongoing war between Rome and Iran was reignited at the time of the reign of king Bahram V (420–38) because Sasanians 'would plunder Roman merchants'.[134]

[129] Ibid.
[130] *Chronicle of Zuqnīn*, 54–5.
[131] Ibid., 55.
[132] Menander, fragment 10.1.
[133] Ibid.
[134] Socrates Scholasticus, *Ecclesiastical History*, 7.18.

Just as the poor treatment of Roman merchants triggered hostilities between Rome and Iran, the mistreatment of Christian merchants in South Arabia during Yūsuf's reign caused the most significant conflict on the Red Sea in the first millennium. On the one hand, Yūsuf aimed to get rid of the (Christian) Roman-allied population of the oasis to control better the caravan trade routes which passed through the city towards Central and North Arabia. On the other hand, he wished to draw attention to his country's affiliation with the Sasanians and his hostility towards Rome and Aksūm. His alliance with the Naṣrid al-Mundhir was sealed in this context and was based on economic and political reasons as Roman-allied kingdoms surrounded both rulers. In a similar fashion to the Sasanians and the Naṣrids, Joseph tried to exploit the sympathies of the Church of the East. Arguably, Yūsuf sought external support as he lacked aristocratic blood and was surrounded by powerful external enemies. Sasanians and Naṣrids were favourably considering an alliance with the king of South Arabia, as they shared Joseph's keenness to counter the Roman-Aksūmite monopoly over the Red Sea trade route. However, they also recognized the complexities and potential repercussions of agreeing to Yūsuf's request to kill their Christian populations. And thus, they probably decided to ignore it. Meanwhile, on the other side of Eurasia, Justin I was vying with Iran for economic and political interests, both intent on controlling the trade networks between East Asia and the Mediterranean through the Arabian ports. Rome was keen to reduce Iran's presence in the Red Sea, an influence that stretched as far as modern Sri Lanka and Malaysia.[135] Iran's imperialistic policies were contingent on political, economic and cultural developments far beyond its borders.[136] Finally, the position of the Aksūmite *negus* was weakened by the loss of Ḥimyar's tribute. Because of this, he was forced to undertake the punitive mission to save his position with Rome and his subjects.

Rome, Iran, Arabia and Aksūm were also in direct competition to extend their control over Central Arabia. A Central Arabian inscription dated 521 directly testifies to an expedition carried out by Ḥimyar and Maʿadd and probably sponsored by Rome.[137] It was sent to attack Iran's allies, led by

[135] T. Daryaee, 'The Sasanian "Mare Nostrum": The Persian Gulf', *International Journal of the Society of Iranian Archaeologists* 2 (2016), 40–88, at p. 43.

[136] R. E. Payne, 'The Silk Road and the Iranian Political Economy in Late Antiquity: Iran, the Silk Road, and the Problem of Aristocratic Empire', *Bulletin of the School of Oriental and African Studies* 81 (2018), 227–250, at p. 243.

[137] Maʿdīkarib Yaʿfur was allied with Aksūm, and thus probably to Rome.

Mdhrm, the Naṣrid king al-Mundhir (ca. 503–54).[138] The campaign reached lower Iraq as suggested by the mention of the *ʿrq Kṭ* ('the plain of Kt"), with the goal of 'submitting the rebellious Arabians to him [Maʿdīkarib Yaʿfur], when Mdhrm made war with him'.[139] Similarly, the Ḥujrid leader al-Ḥārith al-Malik, allied with Ḥimyar, negotiated an alliance with Anastasius I (r. 491–518). In 531, Rome was in the powerful position to suggest that the Ḥimyarites appoint a man of their choice as the phylarch of Maʿadd.[140]

In the second half of the sixth century, faiths were exploited as a *casus belli* to remove Ḥimyar from the political and economic arena of the region. As a result of its removal, Arabia was now accessible to Rome, Iran and Aksūm. In the same way that Yūsuf and Mundhir had exploited the interests of the Jews and of the Church of the East, Kaleb, Justin I and later Justinian exploited 'the Christians'. The strongly Chalcedonian Justin and Justinian, who had previously persecuted the Miaphysites, now helped the same Miaphysites of Najrān in a convenient and pragmatic willingness to overlook the fact that the Miaphysites belonged to a rival faction because of their craving to strengthen and consolidate Roman influence in Arabia.[141] While doctrinal debates, in all likelihood, were of interest to deeply educated classes, the appeal of emperors and kings was all but relative, and one of their primary concerns was to defend their economic interests. This is not to say that trade interests undoubtedly took precedence over Christological doctrines, but rather that elites' conversion and their religious rhetorics had a profound impact on the first-millennium political map and that religious rhetoric became a valuable weapon to be used in economic warfare.

After Kaleb successful defeat of Yūsuf, and the subsequent Christianization of South Arabia, which started in 525 and lasted a little less than half a century, Rome gained an extended sphere of influence in the Arabian Peninsula. They achieved this in the north through an alliance with the Arabian Jafnids (see Chapter 5). However, Rome only managed to counter the Sasanians' expansion in the region up to 570 when Iran conquered South Arabia, thereby taking control of the area after Aksūm's interruption of Iranian commerce. Although we do not possess

[138] Ry 510.

[139] C. J. Robin, 'Les rois de Kindah', in *Arabia, Greece and Byzantium: Cultural Contacts in Ancient and Medieval Times*, ed. A. Al-Helabi, D. Letsios, M. Al-Moraekhi and A. Al-Abduljabbar (Riyadh, 2012), 59–129, at p. 95.

[140] Procop. *Pers*, 1.20.9.

[141] It is worth noticing empress Theodora's (ca. 497–548) effort to reconcile Miaphysites and Chalcedonians (Procop. *Anecd.* 10.14–23). When Simeon of Bēth Arsham visited Constantinople, he did so under her protection (John of Ephesus, *Lives*, 1.10).

conspicuous archaeological elements to evaluate Iran's commerce (the fort of Fulayj is the only securely dated Sasanian fort in Arabia, and there is a general discontinuity between Sasanian and Islamic sites), several literary sources suggest that the Sasanian played a role in maritime and inland trade.[142] Although the role of empires and kingdoms in late antique trade remains largely unclear, economic interests came into play a part in the decision to carry out the massacre of Najrān. Attestations clearly show that Christian traders were a substantial presence in the Indian Ocean, the Persian Gulf and the Red Sea throughout Late Antiquity. These traders were able to operate in South Arabia until Yūsuf's coup de force and his implementation of a protectionist policy favouring Iran and disrupting Rome and Aksūm's commerce in the region. Such policies led to the decision by the *negus* to invade Ḥimyar with the support of the Roman emperor. Kaleb and Yūsuf shared similar motivations in their bellic actions: the merchants, described as 'Romans', were persecuted (and defended) not so much because of their faith but because of their trade. Thus, the traditionally adduced 'religious motivations' for these events are primarily a concern of the literary sources available to us and were written by educated late antique men, often theologians and rabbis, whose primary focus would arguably have been religion.

As a result of Yūsuf's acts of aggression in 522, South Arabia joined the political map of Late Antiquity and became engulfed in the broader conflict between the superpowers of the time and (briefly) joined the first-millennium Christian Commonwealth. After the events of Najrān, an independent king ruled Ḥimyar for one last time, re-establishing the ancient *titulus* (see Chapter 1) and using Sabaic to commemorate victories. Nonetheless, the massacre had a significant impact on the country. It ended a millennium of political and cultural independence as evidenced, for example, by Ḥimyar's consequent adherence to the scriptural traditions of the surrounding empires: first Christianity and later Islam. Even more significantly, the massacre ended the millennial trade network of South Arabia and resulted in Aksūm gaining a short-lived monopoly on this trade.

[142] Al-Jahwari et al., 'Fulayj'. For views of Sasanian trade, see D. Whitehouse and A. Williamson, "Sasanian Maritime Trade", *Iran* 11 (1973): 29–49; J. Howard-Johnston, "The India Trade in Late Antiquity," in *Sasanian Persia: Between Rome and the Steppes of Eurasia*, ed. E. W. Sauer, 284–304 (Edinburgh: Edinburgh University Press, 2017); T. Daryaee, "The Persian Gulf in Late Antiquity: the Sasanian Era (200–700 CE)," in *The Persian Gulf in History*, ed. Lawrence G. Potter, 57–70; (New York: Palgrave Macmillan, 2009) B. Ulrich, "Oman and Bahrain in Late Antiquity: the Sasanians' Arabian Periphery", *Proceedings of the Seminar for Arabian Studies* 41 (2011): 377–385.

4.3 Christianities on the Red Sea: Kaleb of Aksūm and Abraha of Ḥimyar

4.3.1 *Kaleb and Aksūm's Christianity*

Around Pentecost of 525, Kaleb Aksūmite ships left for Ḥimyar. A Gəʿəz inscription found at Maʾrib recounts that Yūsuf was killed between 525 and 530.[143] Although some Ḥimyarites tattooed crosses on their hands after the Aksūmite invasion and begged Kaleb for mercy, thereby managing to save their lives,[144] most of the Jewish population of South Arabia was massacred. The Aksūmites, supported by the powerful Ya'zanite tribe, once Yūsuf's supporters,[145] put a Ḥimyarite prince named Sumūyafaʿ Ashwaʿ (r. ca. 530–5) on the throne.[146] Sumūyafaʿ was baptized as a Christian because Kaleb 'saw in him a good predisposition towards the faith' and Sumūyafaʿ 'had greatly desired the conversion for a long time'.[147] Kaleb added 'ruler of Ḥimyar' to his title (Chapter 1),[148] and, according to the *Book of the Ḥimyarites*, remained in Ḥimyar for seven months.[149] The *Life of Gregentios* claims instead that he stayed in Arabia for three years.[150] After his expedition, Gregentios, the sixth-century saint from Lyplianes (Ljubljana), became archbishop of Ẓafār under Justin I (r. 518–27).[151] During his stay in Ḥimyar, Kaleb 'destroyed the Jewish sanctuaries of the surrounding towns and the idol temples (*eidoleia*) of the remaining people (*ethnos*)'.[152] He then built three churches in Najrān, three in Ẓafār and three in Akana (Qānā),[153] and constructed ecclesiastical structures in 'Atarph, Legmia, Azaki and Iouze'.[154]

Kaleb is regarded as a defender of the Miaphysite faction and a saint for the universal church. The *Ethiopian Synaxarium* celebrates him on the twentieth of the month of Genbot,[155] corresponding to 28 May in the Gregorian calendar when he supposedly died. The text commemorates him for intervening during the massacre of Najrān, killing the Jews and

[143] RIÉth 195. There are multiple versions of the killing. Compare, e.g., *Ḥimyarites*, 42 and al-Ṭabarī, *Tārikh*, 1.930.
[144] *Ḥimyarites*, 44–5.
[145] CIH 621.
[146] Appearing as *Esimiphaeus* in Procop. *Pers*, 1.20.9–12.
[147] *Ḥimyarites*, 47 p 54b.
[148] RIÉth 191.
[149] *Ḥimyarites*, 48 p. 56a.
[150] *Life of Gregentios*, 9.190.
[151] Ibid., 9.1–5.
[152] Ibid., 9.140–5.
[153] Ibid., 9.145–60.
[154] These places have not been successfully identified.
[155] Also known as the *Book of the Saints*.

performing countless miracles.[156] It also claims that Kaleb became a solitary monk at the end of his life, sending his robes and crown to Jerusalem to be hung above the doors of the Church of the Holy Sepulchre.[157] Similarly, the *Martyrium* reports that Kaleb left his kingdom to live in a monastery where he did not speak to anyone and only ate bread and drank water,[158] and repeats the claim that he sent his precious crown to Jerusalem.[159] According to this account, just before he invaded Ḥimyar, Kaleb, dressed in skimpy clothing,[160] entered the church where the kings and bishops of Aksūm were buried and prayed. Since Kaleb engaged in skirmishes with Abraha, king of Ḥimyar, after his victory over Arabia and never became a monk, in reality,[161] these depictions provide more valuable insights into the writers of the sources than on Kaleb and the events described.

Kaleb importance as a protector of the Christians of Ethiopia is further attested by his mention in the Ethiopian national epic, the *Kəbrä Nägäśt.* Although the book, supposedly written in the fourteenth century but likely incorporating earlier material,[162] celebrates the glory of the kings of Ethiopia, only two rulers are mentioned: Solomon and Kaleb. The latter is mentioned towards the end, where Armenia is declared a territory of Rome and Najrān a territory of Ethiopia.[163] Accordingly, the *Kəbrä Nägäśt* claims that the 'kingdom of the Jews shall be made an end' and that the power on earth should be divided in half at Jerusalem between Ethiopia and Rome, protectors of the faith.[164] According to the text, this division was officialized by Kaleb and Justinian in a meeting in the Holy City.[165] This passage was probably based on a verse of the Psalms and aimed to emphasize the role of Ethiopia during the apocalypse.[166] Similarly, this division of the world is also found in the seventh-century Syriac apocalypse by Pseudo-Methodius (690–1),[167] who claimed that the Byzantine

156 *Ethiopian synaxarium*, 106–10.
157 Ibid.
158 *MaGre.* 39; *MaAr.* 39; *MaGe.* 39.
159 Ibid.
160 *MaGr.* 30; *MaAr.* 30; *MaGe.* 30.
161 Procop. *Pers*, 1.20.
162 D. W. Johnson, 'Dating the *Kebra Negast*: Another Look', in *Peace and War in Byzantium*, ed. T. S. Miller and J. Nesbitt (Washington, DC: Catholic University of America Press, 1995), 197–208.
163 *Kəbrä Nägäśt*, 116.
164 Ibid., 117.
165 Ibid.
166 Psalm 68.32. See George Bevan, 'Ethiopian Apocalyptic and the End of Roman Rule: The Reception of Chalcedon in Aksum and the Kebra Nagaśt', in *Inside and Out: Interactions between Rome and the Peoples on the Arabian and Egyptian Frontiers in Late Antiquity*, ed. G. Fisher and J. H. F. Dijkstra (Leuven: Peeters, 2014), 371–88, at p. 379.
167 This confirms an early date of the narrative.

emperor had Ethiopian lineage and would rescue the Christian world from the Muslims.[168] The equal division between the two rulers fits well with the sixth-century date of the passage when both empires were thriving.

However, it is disputed whether Kaleb was already Christian before the massacre of Najrān or if he converted afterwards. The lost fourth chapter of the *Book of the Ḥimyarites*, titled 'Account telling how Bishop Thomas went to the Aksūmites and informed them that the Ḥimyarites were persecuting the Christians', suggests that the king of Aksūm was already Christian at the time of Thomas' embassy, predating the massacre.[169] Nonetheless, other sources claim that Kaleb became Christian after the events of Najrān to thank God for his victory. According to the *Chronicle of Zuqnīn*, Kaleb stated at the time of the first invasion of 519: 'for if this torturer, the king of the Ḥimyarites, surrenders to me so that I conquer him, I will become a Christian'.[170] After his victory, the clergy sent by Justinian baptized him, 'urging all [the people] of the region to become Christians, and to establish churches'.[171] Similarly, John Malalas claims that Kaleb 'became a Christian',[172] making this vow just before the start of combat with the Ḥimyarites ('if I defeat Dimnos the Emperor of the Ḥimyarites, I will become Christian, for I am fighting him on behalf of the Christians').[173] After his victory, Justinian sent him a bishop named John, *paramonarios* of the Church of St John in Alexandria, who introduced him to Christianity and baptized him.[174] These accounts suggest that Kaleb converted to Christianity after the events of Najrān and thus further lend weight to the idea that economic reasons played a more prominent role than religious motivations in the invasion of South Arabia. At the same time, these narratives hint at 'a second wave of Christianisation' in Aksūm.

The introduction of Christianity in Aksūm under King ʿEzana of Aksūm was discussed in Chapter 3. It is difficult to understand fully the implications of ʿEzana conversion and to what extent the Aksūmites were Christians in the fourth century. A bishop travelling to Adulis is mentioned in the fourth/fifth-century work *On the Nations of India and the Brahmins*, which defines the negus as an 'insignificant little king of the Indians' (*basikiskos*

[168] Pseudo-Methodius, *Apocalypse*, 8.1–3 and 9.18. See F. J. Martinez, 'The Apocalyptic Genre in Syriac: The World of Pseudo-Methodius', in *Symposium Syriacum IV: Literary Genres in Syriac Literature*, ed. H. J. W. Drijvers et al. (Rome: Pont. Institutum Studiorum Orientalium, 1987), 337–52.

[169] *Ḥimyarites*, 4.

[170] *Chronicle of Zuqnīn*, 55.

[171] Ibid., 56.

[172] Malalas, *Chronicle*, 18.429.

[173] Ibid., 18.433–4.

[174] Ibid., 18.434.

mikros tōn Indōn).[175] A recent publication on the newly discovered church of Betä Sämaʿti' in Ethiopia dates the structure to the fourth century.[176] The basilica of Betä Sämaʿti' would be the oldest church in the region.[177] Various traditions point to a 'second wave of Christianisation' taking place in Aksūm at the end of the fifth century due to the efforts of 'Nine Saints',[178] supposedly 'Syrian'monks who had fled from persecution in the Eastern Roman Empire.[179] According to Shahid, Aksūm re-embraced Christianity at the beginning of the sixth century under Kaleb or his father after renouncing it in the fifth century.[180] Conversely, I argue that the depiction of a 'Christian Aksūm' in the fourth century is a direct consequence of the sources' overestimation of ʿEzana vague conversion (see Chapter 3). Hence, in a similar fashion to the depiction of the massacre of Najrān as a 'religious slaughter', these depictions are more a reflection of the 'religious' character of the available literary sources than the actual unfolding of the events. Accordingly, a sixth-century 'second wave of Christianisation' simply involved the strengthening of Aksūmite Christianity and its reshaping as Miaphysite through the intervention of exiled missionaries. Their proselytism was a collateral result of the doctrinal issues raised at the Council of Chalcedon in 451 and largely contributed to the founding of monasticism in Aksūm.[181] This 'second wave' corresponded to a 'first wave' in Ḥimyar, where Judaism had prevailed at the time of the Aksūmite 'first wave'. At the same time, the Aksūmite 'second wave' probably corresponded to the first

[175] *On the Nations of India and the Brahmins*, 4. For a fourth-century dating, see D. M. Derrett, 'The Theban Scholasticus and Malabar in ca. 355–60', *Journal of the American Oriental Society* 82 (1962), 21–31. For a fifth-century dating, see D. P. M. Weerakkody, *Taprobanê: Ancient Sri Lanka as known to Greeks and Romans* (Turnhout: Brepols, 1997), 126. For the history of the text, see also B. Berg, 'The Letter of Palladius on India', *Byzantion* 44 (1974), 5–16.

[176] M. J. Harrower et al., 'Beta Samati: Discovery and Excavation of an Aksumite Town', *Antiquity* 93 (2019), 1534–52.

[177] V. A. Grasso and M. J. Harrower, 'The Basilica of Betä Sämaʿti' in its Aksumite, Early Christian and Late Antique Context' *Journal of Near Eastern Studies* 82 (Spring 2023, forthcoming).

[178] For the sources on the 'Nine Saints' see P. Marrassini, *Storia e leggenda dell'Etiopia tardoantica* (Brescia: Paideia 2014), 83–108.

[179] This thesis was first advanced by Conti Rossini through a study of their names. See C. Conti Rossini, *Storia D'Etiopia* (Bergamo: Istituto italiano d'arte grafiche, 1928), 161. Note that 'no contemporary writing could provide reliable evidence as to either the real aims of the coming of the N.S. or their identity' (A. Brita, 'Nine Saints', in *Encyclopaedia Aethiopica*, ed. S. Uhlig, (Wiesbaden: Harrassowitz, 2003), 1188–91, at p. 1188). Brita refers to Marrassini who argued, based on linguistic elements, that 'there are no positive proofs that the Nine Saints and their colleagues were really Syrians' (P. Marrassini, 'Some Considerations on the Problem of the "Syriac Influences" on Aksumite Ethiopia', *Journal of Ethiopian Studies* 23 (1990), 35–46, at p. 42). An alternative suggestion is still a desideratum.

[180] Shahid, *Martyrs of Najrān*, 259–60.

[181] S. C. Munro-Hay, *Aksum: An African Civilization of Late Antiquity* (Edinburgh: Edinburgh University Press, 1991), 208.

real 'wave' in the Aksūmite countryside. One of the 'Nine Saints', an eremite monk called Pantalewon,[182] who Kaleb had consulted with for his Arabian expedition,[183] was active in Beta Qatin in Aksūm.[184] In a similar fashion to the majority of the 'Nine Saints', Pantalewon, nowadays saint for the Ethiopic Church,[185] was active in the countryside and operated at the crossroads of the route to Adulis, facilitating the spread of Christianity outside the circle of elites. It is impossible to tell if the first Christian missionaries of Aksūm were able to communicate in Gəʿəz with the lower class of Ethiopia. Yet, the monks who fled from the Roman Empire after Chalcedon were probably assisted by the men of faith who had arrived after ʿEzana conversion and had by then developed a Christian lexicon in Gəʿəz to proselytize all social classes of Aksūm.

The contemporary strengthening of Christianity in Ethiopia and eastern Georgia in the mid-sixth century aimed to eradicate existing cults, as recounted by the legendary Nine Saints' arrival to Aksūm and the 'Thirteen Syrian Fathers' in Iberia (Kartli).[186] Roughly at the time of the massacre of Najrān, the ruler of Georgia, Vakhtang I Gorgasali, managed to expand his kingdom for a brief period,[187] and simultaneously strengthened Christianity in his country. In a similar fashion to Kaleb 'finalization' of ʿEzana Christianity, Vakhtang Gorgasali perfected Mirian III's Christianity in Georgia, initiated in ca. 326 because of (according to legend) proselytism by a Cappadocian woman named Nino.[188] The turmoil of a 'second wave of Christianisation' in both countries provided the two rulers with some useful ideological propaganda. As we have seen, Christian propaganda was a helpful fig leaf with which to cover the more real economic reasons behind Aksūm's invasion of Arabia, such as the disappearance of the usual tribute payment after Yūsuf's coup de force and the difficult trading conditions experienced by the Roman-allied merchants. However, Kaleb and Vakhtang Gorgasali's adoption of (Miaphysite) Christianity had opposite aims. Whereas Kaleb exploited the faith to strengthen his position with Rome, Vakhtang Gorgasali used

[182] Greek Zōnaios.

[183] *MaGr.* 31; *MaAr.* 31; *MaGe.* 31.

[184] S. C. Munro-Hay, 'Saintly Shadows', in *Languages and Cultures of Eastern Christianity: Ethiopian*, ed. A. Bausi (Farnham: Routledge 2012), 221–52, at p. 138.

[185] *Ethiopian synaxarium,* 22–4.

[186] S. Matitashvili, 'The Monasteries Founded by the Thirteen Syrian Fathers in Iberia', *Studies in Late Antiquity* 2 (2018), 4–39.

[187] B. Martin-Hisard, 'Le roi géorgien Vaxt'ang Gorgasal dans l'histoire et dans la légende', *Actes des congrès de la société des historiens médiévistes de l'enseignement supérieur public* 13 (1982), 205–42.

[188] *Life of Nino* in *Moktsevai Kartlisai.*

it to signal his break with Iran, which had replaced Rome's influence in the area in the mid-fourth century.

While in the early seventh century, the Georgian Church became Chalcedonian, and the Greek language gained a prominent role in Georgian Christianity, the scattered Syriac loanwords in the Ethiopian/Eritrean scriptural traditions are a legacy of the translation of the Bible from Syriac into Gəʿəz during the fifth century.[189] Traces of Syrian influences in the Ethiopian lexicon and liturgy are more evident than in Ethiopian architecture and art.[190] Although the basilicas of Adulis and Matara evoke the Syrian churches of Kerātīn and Saint Simeon Stylites,[191] their structure is also typical in Egypt and Nubia.[192] Indeed, one of the most compelling arguments for proving the Syriac Miaphysite influence on Ethiopian Christianity is the firm position adopted by Kaleb during/after the massacre of the Miaphysites of Najrān and the importance of the Syriac sources describing these events. Kaleb was most definitely Christian at the end of his life, regardless of the dating of his conversion. All six of the Gəʿəz inscriptions attributed to him are Christian in content,[193] and present scattered quotations from biblical Scriptures such as the Gospels and the Psalms.[194] The *negus*' adoption of Miaphysite Christianity could have usefully prevented causing any animosity with Iran while at the same time not compromising his alliance with Rome. While it is impossible to exclude entirely the possibility that Kaleb identity changed in the sources later when Aksūm clearly supported the Miaphysite faction, Kaleb military intervention in Ḥimyar is prominent in the Miaphysite works on the martyrdom of Najrān written down in the sixth century.

Although Simeon Bēth Arsham believed in the existence of a 'Miaphysite commonwealth based mostly in Egypt and Syria',[195] Miaphysitism never

189 P. Marrassini, 'Once Again on the Question of Syriac Influences in the Aksumite Period', in *Languages and Cultures of Eastern Christianity: Ethiopian*, ed. A. Bausi (Farnham: Routledge, 2012), 209–17, at pp. 212–17.

190 W. Witakowski, 'Syrian Influences in Ethiopian Culture', in *Languages and Cultures of Eastern Christianity: Ethiopian*, ed. A. Bausi (Farnham: Routledge, 2012), 197–208.

191 See the rectangular apses with two side rooms, baptisteries on centralized plans and ecclesiastical buildings on the churches' sides. F. Anfray, 'Deux villes axoumites: Adoulis et Matara', in *Atti del IV congresso internazionale di studi etiopici*, ed. L. Ricci (Rome: Accademia nazionale dei Lincei, 1974), 747–65.

192 Grasso and Harrower, 'The Basilica of Betä Sämaʿti'.

193 RIE 191; 195; 263–6. Among these, RIE 191, written in the Gəʿəz language using the Sabean script, attributes the conquest of Ḥimyar to the help of God.

194 RIE 195.20–1 quoting Matthew 5.33 and RIE 195.21–5 quoting Psalms 65(66).16–17; RIE 195.26–8 quoting Psalms 19.8–9; RIE 263.29 maybe quoting Isaiah 26.19. See Marrassini, *Storia e leggenda*, 256–8.

195 Wood, '*We Have No King*', 225.

substituted the Roman state in Egypt and Syria. However, it did manage to form a 'state religion' in Ethiopia.[196] In the *Kəbrä Nägäśt*, Kaleb and Justin I are characterized as Solomon's offspring, but only the Ethiopian ruler is descended from Solomon's firstborn Menelik.[197] The passage stresses the importance of the Ethiopian Church as a defender of the faith and a protector from heresy, as well as affirming the rightfulness of the Miaphysite position. The supposed Ethiopian possession of the Ark of the Covenant provided a further justification for Kaleb role and an answer to the True Cross in Constantinople.[198] Accordingly, the Ethiopian national epic emphasized Kaleb role as a defender of Christians throughout the world, but especially as a defender of Christians inhabiting Miaphysite lands extending east of Jerusalem. Although the 'first Christian wave' washed up in Aksūm two centuries before Kaleb reign, Kaleb was the first *negus* to adopt a biblical name, taking the name of the leader of the conquest of Canaan in the Bible,[199] also alluded to in the Qur'ān.[200] The name, possibly evocative of the success of his Ḥimyarite expedition, fits well with the policy of renewal and further Christianization (rather than re-Christianization) of the country in the sixth century under the influence of the Miaphysites who had fled from the Roman Empire after the Council of Chalcedon, and in the heyday of Aksūmite political and economic power.

4.3.2 *King Abraha of Ḥimyar*

The Ḥimyarite king Sumūyafaʿ Ashwaʿ was overthrown by a group of Ḥimyarites in 535 after a five-year reign.[201] The coup d'état led to his imprisonment in a fortress, and thereafter a man called Abraha declared himself king of Ḥimyar.[202] Abraha was a Christian enslaved man of a Roman tradesman who engaged in shipping with the city of Adulis in the northern Red Sea region of modern Eritrea,[203] once again hinting at the strong ties and interactive nature between commerce, Christianity and power in the late antique Red Sea. According to Procopius, Kaleb promptly sent 3,000 men

196 Bevan, 'Ethiopian Apocalyptic', 370.
197 *Kəbrä nägäśt*, 117.
198 G. W. Bowersock, 'Helena's Bridle and the Chariot of Ethiopia', in *Antiquity in Antiquity: Jewish and Christian Pasts in the Greco-Roman World*, ed. G. Gardner and K. L. Osterloh (Tübingen: Mohr Siebeck, 2008), 383–93, at p. 392.
199 Numbers 13–4; Joshua 14–5.
200 Q. 5.23.
201 Procop. *Pers.* 1.20.
202 'Abramus' in Procopius.
203 Procop. *Pers.* 1.20.

commanded by one of his relatives against Abraha.[204] However, when the army arrived in South Arabia, they were struck by the country's beauty and started negotiations with Abraha to join his ranks and remain in Ḥimyar.[205] Kaleb sent another platoon which was also unsuccessful. When he died, Abraha agreed to pay a tribute to the new *negus*, Alla Amidas, to strengthen his position in Arabia.[206] While John Malalas claimed that Kaleb proclaimed his kin Anganes as king of Ḥimyar,[207] the *Martyrium* states that Kaleb elected Abraha as king after killing Yūsuf.[208] Muslim sources such as al-Ṭabarī's history report that when the Aksūmite general Abraha proclaimed himself ruler of South Arabia, the *negus* sent an army led by a man called Aryāṭ to reclaim South Arabia.[209] Abraha challenged Aryāṭ to engage him in single combat but tricked and killed Aryāṭ.[210] Abraha then wrote to the *negus* claiming that Aryāṭ had been disloyal to Aksūm and asked for confirmation of his office, which he received.[211] Similarly, Ibn Isḥāq claimed that Abraha disputed the authority of a viceroy called Aryāṭ, who the *negus* had chosen, and that Abraha later took his place.[212]

Fortunately, it is possible to integrate these literary accounts with the epigraphic evidence available. Two South Arabian inscriptions written by Sumūyafaʿ Ashwaʿ confirm his appointment as king of Ḥimyar and suggest that Abraha took power only later.[213] Although Abraha might have received the approval of the *negus*, it is more plausible that he seized power through a coup d'état as suggested by the accounts of Procopius and al-Ṭabarī. These accounts are based on separate traditions and claim that Kaleb tried to obstruct Abraha's coronation and later gave up. Once king, Abraha adopted the traditional titulus of Ḥimyar, as testified by four inscriptions,[214] and by one which mentions him.[215] Among Abraha's small corpus, one long monumental inscription, dated 548 and found at Ma'rib, is particularly relevant for the amount of information it provides.[216] This inscription records Abraha's *titulus* and was written after the rebellion of

[204] Ibid.
[205] Ibid.
[206] Ibid.
[207] Malalas, *Chronicle*, 18.457.
[208] MaGr. 38.
[209] Al-Ṭabarī, *Tārikh*, 1.930–4.
[210] Ibid.
[211] Ibid.
[212] Ibn Isḥāq, *Sīrah*, 26–9.
[213] CIH 621; Ist 7608 bis.
[214] Murayghān 1; CIH 541; DAI GDN 2002–20; Murayghān 3.
[215] Ja 547+Ja 546+Ja 544+Ja 545.
[216] CIH 541.

the Kindah governor appointed by Abraha. In the same year, the Ma'rib dam broke and was repaired, as similarly attested by another inscription.[217] The dam was used to capture the periodic monsoon rain which fell on the nearby mountains, irrigating the land,[218] and was precious for the inhabitants of South Arabia from the first millennium BCE onwards. The Ma'rib inscription reports that a plague spread during the repair work of the dam.[219] Another critical detail offered by this inscription is the mention of a diplomatic conference organized by Abraha after the epidemic.[220] Ambassadors from North Arabia and delegations from Rome and Iran participated, which is indicative of the international importance of Abraha and South Arabia at the time. A delegation from Aksūm also joined the embassy, suggesting that Kaleb had died by that time and that Alla Amidas had already become the *negus*.[221] Different lexemes indicate the various parties that joined the meeting, reflecting the importance of the multiple kingdoms at the time. While the *negus* and the Roman emperor (*mlk Rmn*) sent 'ministers' (*mḥs²kt*), the 'king of Persia' (*mlk Frs¹*) sent 'ambassadors' (*tnblt*). Instead, the ruler of the Naṣrids al-Mundhir, the Jafnid ḥārith and his brother Abū Karīb sent 'messengers' (*rs¹l*). No representatives from Central Arabia are mentioned, suggesting Abraha was ruling over this region at the time. Three inscriptions found at Murayghān (ca. 600 km south-west of Mecca) attest to Abraha's campaigns in this region.

In 552, four years after the punitive expedition against the rebellious governor of Kindah, Abraha raided the Maʿadd for 'a fourth time',[222] subduing them and later negotiating peace with the Naṣrid al-Mundhir who had interests in the area. Another inscription dated to the same year confirms that Abraha took possession of the Arabians of Maʿadd from al-Mundhir,[223] extending his influence over the Arabians of Hagar and Khaṭṭ in eastern Arabia, Ṭym in Central Arabia, Yathrib (Medina) in ḥijāz, and the unidentified Gzm.[224] In the 1950s, Altheim and Stiehl claimed that the expedition of Abraha recorded in the epigraphic corpus was the same as the one mentioned in the 105th *sūrah* of the Qur'ān, *al-Fīl*, 'the Elephant',[225]

[217] DAI GDN 2002–20.
[218] Yāqūt, *Buldān*, 4.383.
[219] CIH 541.
[220] Ibid.
[221] Procopius, *Pers.* 1.20.
[222] Murayghān 1.
[223] Murayghān 3.
[224] An additional inscription attests Abraha's campaigns in Tathlith. See Murayghān 2.
[225] F. Altheim and R. Stiehl, 'Araber und Sassaniden', in *Edwin Redslob zum 70 – Geburtstag: eine Festgabe*, ed. Hrsg. von Georg Rohde et al. (Berlin: E. Blaschker, 1955), 200–7; *Finanzgeschichte der Spätantike* (Frankfurt-am-Main: V. Klostermann, 1957), 145–8 and 353–5.

and later scholars have backed this hypothesis with additional documentation.[226] According to traditional Muslim sources, the pre-Islamic Meccan tribe of Quraysh used to count time, starting with the so-called year of the Elephant.[227] The Hijra took place fifty years after the year of the Elephant. This calculation fits well with the claim that Abraha undertook an expedition against Mecca in 552, the same year of the inscriptions of Murayghān.[228] As in the case of the massacre of Najrān, the Ḥimyar campaigns against Central Arabia were mainly undertaken for economic reasons, though the traditional Muslim accounts sustain religious motivations.

Ibn Isḥāq described Abraha as 'a Christian of good temperament',[229] and al-Ṭabarī also stated that he was a 'magnanimous, noble leader, attached to Christianity'.[230] Both historians recounted how he ordered the construction of the church (*qalīs*) of ṣan'ā' and wrote to the *negus* to assure him that he would not rest until he had diverted the Arabian pilgrims to it. According to this tradition, Mecca was already an important pilgrimage centre, and the Arabians were already going on pilgrimage to the Ka'bah. Hence, when an Arabian who belonged to the Banū Fuqaym read Abraha's letter, he defecated in Ṣan'ā''s Church with the explicit intention of ruining Abraha's plans through such an offensive act of provocation.[231] Another Muslim accountstates that the church was also desecrated by placing putrefying animal carcases inside.[232] Abraha thus ordered a group of Ḥijāzī Arabians to summon the people and make a pilgrimage to the church.[233] When one of the men appointed for the mission was killed, Abraha's anger increased even more, and he decided to march on Mecca to destroy the Ka'bah, aided by the Aksūmites and an elephant.[234] After defeating a group of noble Yemenites who opposed his plan, Abraha reached the territory of Khath'am, where he fought the tribes of Khath'am, Shahrān and Nāhis and continued to al-Ṭā'if. After seizing 200 camels in Mecca, he proposed to the Quraysh leader 'Abd al-Muṭṭalib, grandfather

226 Among others, M. J. Kister, 'The Campaign of Ḥulubān: A New Light on the Expedition of Abraha', *Museum* 78 (1965), 425–36; see also L. I. Conrad, 'Abraha and Muḥammad: Some Observations Apropos of Chronology and Literary "topoi" in the Early Arabic Historical Tradition', *Bulletin of the School of Oriental and African Studies* 50 (1987), 225–40.

227 Ibn Bakkār, *Nasab Quraysh*, 668.1649.

228 Ibid. Murayghān.

229 Ibn Isḥāq *Sīrah*, 29.

230 Ibid., 29–31; al-Ṭabarī, *Tārikh*, 1.934–5.

231 Part of the Ḥijāzī tribal group, which the founder of the Meccan Quraysh tribe (Quṣayy) belonged to.

232 Al-Ṭabarī, *Tārikh*, 1.942–5.

233 Ibn Isḥāq *Sīrah*, 29–31; al-Ṭabarī, *Tārikh*, 1.934–5.

234 Ibn Isḥāq *Sīrah*, 31–5; al-Ṭabarī, *Tārikh*, 1.936–41.

of Muḥammad, to let him destroy the Ka'bah to avoid any further bloodshed. However, when 'Abd al-Muṭṭalib met Abraha, he asked to have back the camels seized, claiming that his God would take care of the Ka'bah. When Abraha tried to destroy the sanctuary, his elephant refused to do so, and he was forced to retreat ignominiously to Ṣan'ā'.[235]

Both Ibn Isḥāq and al-Ṭabarī provided a very graphic and detailed description of the gruesome death of the South Arabian king and his army. They record that Abraha was struck on his body and his fingers dropped off one by one, and a 'purulent sore in its place, which exuded pus and blood' appeared at the wound of each digit.[236] Moreover, according to Ibn Isḥāq, measles and smallpox occurred in Arabia for the first time.[237] A recent study has attributed the epidemic to smallpox known as *Variola major*, whose complications include 'blindness, haemorrhages and permanent pockmark scarring'.[238]

Drawings of elephants have been found in Saudi Arabia near al-'Ulā,[239] and, more recently, near Ḥimā,[240] giving further historicity to the Muslim accounts. Fossils of an extinct elephant have been discovered in Saudi Arabia,[241] and could have played a part in the imagery of the Arabians who elaborated mythological stories on their remote past inspired by these findings. Hence, reminiscences of a Ḥimyarite expedition in Central Arabia possibly found their way into the Qur'ān. Robin has recently argued that 'the best explanation for these drawings is that an elephant passed by Ḥimà and struck the spectators with amazement'.[242] Yet, a connection between the drawings and Abraha's expedition remains speculative, as the drawings could have easily preceded the punitive mission. Abraha did lead an expedition to Central Arabia and was defeated, but it is questionable that any elephants were involved, as they had been long extinct in Arabia. For a Muslim historian living in the eighth century, Abraha's expedition, only documented by epigraphical records written in the largely incomprehensible language of South Arabia, and accounts of elephant fossils, belonged

[235] Ibn Isḥāq, *Sīrah*, 36; al-Ṭabarī, *Tārikh*, 1.945.
[236] Ibid.
[237] Isḥāq, *Sīrah*, 36.
[238] J. S. Marr et al., 'The Year of the Elephant', *WikiJournal of Medicine* 2 (2015), 1–5, at p. 5.
[239] J. Dayton, 'The Lost Elephants of Arabia', *Antiquity* 42 (1968), 42–5.
[240] Robin, 'Himyar et Israël', 1060.
[241] The Palaeoloxodon recki, known to have existed from the Middle Pliocene until the Middle Pleistocene in Africa. See C. M. Stimpson et al., 'Middle Pleistocene Vertebrate Fossils from the Nefud Desert, Saudi Arabia: Implications for Biogeography and Palaeoecology', *Quaternary Science Reviews* 143 (2016), 13–36.
[242] Robin, 'L'Arabie préislamique', in *Le Coran des historiens*, ed. M.A. Amir-Moezzi and G. Dye (Paris: Les éditions du Cerf, 2019), 51–154, at p. 113.

to the same remote and indistinct past. As a result, Abraha's *logia* were 'glossed' by eighth- and ninth-century Muslim historians who aimed to establish a comparison between the biblical narrative of the ten plagues of Egypt and the consequent freeing of the Israelites,[243] and the victory of the rising Muslim community over the surrounding empires. The battle between Abraha's army and the Quraysh hence foreshadowed and mirrored the future conflict between Muḥammad and the Romans.

The Muslim literary sources constitute a valuable enquiry tool regardless of these biases (Chapter 1). Al-Ṭabarī's account further provides a valuable description of the church of Ṣanʿāʾ and a description of the Kaʿbah as being covered by 'striped Yemeni cloth'.[244] Al-Azraqī (d. 865), the editor of a book about Mecca written by his grandfather (d. 837), claims that Ṣanʿāʾ Church was built next to the royal palace of Ghumdān, described by the Yemenite al-Hamdānī (d. ca. 945),[245] and made up of three parts called *bayt, īwān* and *qubbah*.[246] Al-Azraqī confirms al-Ṭabarī's account, reporting that red, white, yellow and black stones were used to construct the church and mentioning a frieze of marble, a copper door, painted wood columns, gold and silver nails, and decorative mosaics.[247] And lastly, the Persian polymath al-Rāzī (d. ca. 925) recounts that the Christians built a church in Ṣanʿāʾ in a place where Jesus prayed, located at the bottom of the tannery lane of Ṣanʿāʾ, opposite to a synagogue.[248] A colonnade-shaped corner of the church still survives at the end of the path to the *sūq* (market) and the Damascus district. Nevertheless, the church of Abraha was likely destroyed before the time of al-Rāzī. It is more likely that a site called *Ghurqat al-Qalīs* ('church's circular pit') located 175 metres west of the citadel wall and still visible today at Ṣanʿāʾ likely corresponds to Abraha's church.[249] Moreover, in the great mosque of ṣanʿāʾ, it is still possible today to see parts of the city's ancient church, including a door (currently in the wall of the *qiblah*), seven foliate capitals and round columns covered with vines. Four of the capitals have crosses inscribed and are identical with those found in the Church of St Mary in Zion in Aksūm, which is claimed to contain the Ark of the Covenant and was built between 372 and 424.[250] The west–east orientation of this structure, its measurements and

[243] Exodus 7–12.
[244] Al-Ṭabarī, *Tārikh*, 1.943. Based on the authority of al-Wāqidī (d. 823).
[245] Al-Hamdānī, *Iklīl 8*, p. 3–10.
[246] Al-Azraqī, *Akhbār Makkah*, 1.137.
[247] Ibid.
[248] Al-Rāzī, *Taʾrīkh*, p. 32.
[249] R. B. Serjeant and Ronald B. Lewcock, *Ṣanʿāʾ: An Arabian Islamic City* (London: World of Islam Festival Trust, 1983), 47–8.
[250] Ibid.

the construction of the walls and ceilings similar to those of the Aksūmite cathedral suggest that the contemporary Aksūmite style strongly influenced its design.[251] While the large dome is similar to that of the fourth-century Church of the Holy Sepulchre in Jerusalem, the church plan resembles that of the fourth-century Church of the Nativity in Bethlehem, hinting at significant similarities with Byzantine churches too.[252] Al-Ṭabarī reports that Abraha wrote to the Roman emperor to ask for the emperor's help in the construction of the church of Ṣanʿāʾ, and it appears possible that the emperor sent skilled artisans, mosaic cubes and marble to South Arabia.[253] A church mentioned in one of Abraha's inscriptions, written after his conquest of the *ʿrbn* in Central Arabia, further proves his involvement in ecclesiastical constructions in his kingdom.[254]

Up to this point, Abraha has been described as a zealous Christian king without any analysis being made on his doctrinal position. Three of Abraha's monumental inscriptions open with invocations to the Christian God, while only one of these opens and closes with an invocation to 'the power of *Raḥman* and his Messiah (*ms^{1}ḥ*)'.[255] Another inscription similarly states in its opening: 'with the power and the help and the support of *Raḥman*, the Lord of Heaven (*mrʾ s^{1}myn*) and the Messiah'.[256] 'Lord of Heaven' is here conceived as an attribute of *Raḥman*, similarly to the vague monotheistic inscriptions of the fourth and fifth centuries (Chapter 3). These two inscriptions are slightly in contrast with the opening of the long inscription from Maʾrib. This latter inscription invokes 'the power, the aid, and the mercy of *Raḥman*, of his Messiah', but also that of the 'Holy Spirit' (*Rḥ [q]ds^1*).[257] While in one of king Sumūyafaʿ Ashwaʿ's inscriptions, the Holy Spirit is indicated as *[mn] fs^1 qds^1*,[258] an evident borrowing from Gəʿəz,[259] Abraha's inscription indicates the 'spirit' as *rḥ*, a word of strong Syriac influence. Furthermore, the locution 'Christ the Victorious' (*Krs^{3}ts^3 ghlbn*), found in Sumūyafaʿ Ashwaʿ as well as in the inscriptions written by Kaleb and his son,[260] is completely missing

251 Ibid.; B. Finster, 'Arabia in Late Antiquity: An Outline of the Cultural Situation in the Peninsula at the Time of Muḥammad', in *The Qurʾān in Context*, ed. A. Neuwirth, N. Sinai and M. Marx (Leiden: Brill, 2010), 61–114, at p. 77.
252 Serjeant and Lewcock, *Ṣanʿāʾ*, 48.
253 Al-Ṭabarī, *Tārikh*, 1.935–6. On the authority of Hishām Ibn Muḥammad.
254 CIH 541.
255 Murayghān 1.
256 DAI GDN 2002–20.
257 CIH 541.
258 Ist 7608 bis.
259 E.g., RIE 191 and 192.
260 RIE 191.

from the epigraphic corpus of Abraha. Instead, the South Arabian king preferred to use the ancient local monotheistic name of God, *Raḥman*, and a Syriac loanword for Messiah to indicate Christ. Although in the inscription consecrating the church of Ma'rib, Syriac Aramaic loanwords are used,[261] no quotations of the Bible have been found in Abraha's inscriptions. Conversely, such biblical references abound in Kaleb inscriptions.[262] Hence, although the Muslim sources claim Abraha was Aksūmite,[263] he deliberately distanced himself from the church of Aksūm, claiming a direct Syriac lineage for his faith. At the same time, the lower recurrence of the Holy Spirit in his corpus may suggest a diplomatic attempt to soften Jewish and Christian attitudes.

An interesting passage found in the *Chronicle of Zuqnīn* sheds some light on Abraha's Christological position. According to the text, when the king learned about the introduction of the Chalcedon creed in Alexandria and the exiling of Theodosius, 'he was offended and refused to accept a bishop from Alexandria'.[264] Although the passage hints at Abraha's Miaphysite links, Carlos Segovia has claimed, in the wake of Alfred Beeston,[265] that Abraha's inscriptions display the term 'Messiah' instead of the more common *Bn* ('Son') not only to distance Ḥimyar from Aksūm but also as a sign of Abraha's inclination towards Dyophysitism.[266] It is plausible that an East Syrian community was also present in sixth-century South Arabia. Cosmas Indicopleustes claims that clergy were ordained in Iran and later sent to the 'Island of Dioscorides' (Socotra, Yemen).[267] On site, Gəʿəz inscriptions have been found alongside Palmyrene, Greek, South Arabian and Brāhmī epigraphic evidence.[268] Three of the Gəʿəz inscriptions have been dated to the period 500–75,[269] confirming the historicity of Cosmas' account. Nonetheless, Abraha's linguistic choices and his wish to politically distance himself from Aksūm are not strong enough reasons to claim he was a Dyophysite. Abraha may have preferred to use 'Messiah'

[261] See for 'consecrate the church' the use of *qds¹* (consecrate) *bʿtn* (house, sanctuary). *Qs¹s¹* (priest) is also a Syriac loanword. See CIH 541.

[262] RIE 192 and 195.

[263] Al-Ṭabarī, *Tārikh*, 1.930–4.

[264] *Chronicle of Zuqnīn*, 68.

[265] A. F. L. Beeston, 'Abraha', in *The Encyclopædia of Islam*, ed. C. E. Bosworth (Leiden: Brill, 1960), 105–6.

[266] C. A. Segovia, 'Abraha's Christological Formula Rḥmnn w-Msıḥ-hw and Its Relevance for the Study of Islam's Origins', *Oriens Christianus* 98 (2015), 52–63.

[267] Cosmas Indicopleustes, *Topographia*, 3.178–9.

[268] I. Strauch (ed.), *Foreign Sailors on Socotra: The Inscriptions and Drawings from the Cave Hoq* (Bremen: Hempen Verlag, 2012).

[269] C. J. Robin, 'South Arabia, Ethiopia and Socotra', in *Foreign Sailors on Socotra: The Inscriptions and Drawings from the Cave Hoq*, ed. I. Strauch (Bremen: Hempen Verlag, 2012), 437–46, at p. 440.

instead of 'Son' to avoid provoking anger in the Jewish community of South Arabia,[270] and this seems to be a better and more valid explanation for Abraha's lexical choice. This hypothesis could be built on in the following way: Abraha wished to create a smooth and gradual path of least resistance to conversion to Christianity for his subjects. At the same time, he was eager to avoid any further conflict with the region's Jewish *and* the various Christian communities. By using the less connotationally loaded lexeme 'Messiah' (rather than 'Son'), he avoided generating further confusion and conflict around the already much-contested nature of Christ. Keeping a low profile helped him gain the approval of the Chalcedonians (and of the Roman emperors in particular). The already mentioned Ma'rib inscription emphasizes Ḥimyar's pacific relationships with the surrounding empires and its independence from its rival on the Red Sea during the reign of Abraha.[271]

An inscription found near the Ma'rib dam attests that Abraha was still king in 558.[272] The dam collapsed for the last time in the third quarter of the sixth century, at least symbolically marking the end of the autonomy that *Arabia Felix* had enjoyed for over a thousand years. Around 575, the Sasanians of Khosrow I (r. 531–79) took advantage of Aksūm's decline in power and overthrew the Aksūmite rule of South Arabia. According to the sixth-century historian Theophanes of Byzantium, Khosrow marched against the Ḥimyarites when they 'were on friendly terms with the Romans'.[273] With the aid of the Persian general Miranes, he captured the Ḥimyarite King Sanaturces (Masruq, son of Abraha), sacked his city and enslaved the inhabitants of South Arabia. The Sasanians remained in power until ca. 630 when the Persian governor Bādhān ibn Sāsān converted to Islam. Ibn Isḥāq[274] and al-Ṭabarī,[275] as well as non-Muslim authors such as Theophanes,[276] claim that at the time, a Ḥimyarite aristocrat, Sayf ibn dhu-Yazan, petitioned for Iran to intervene to prevent the Aksūmites gaining control of South Arabia, this petition being a clear sign of the long-standing acrimony between the two Red Sea powers in the first millennium.

270 V. A. Grasso, 'Christology on the Red Sea: God and his Son in Late Antique Arabia and Ethiopia' (forthcoming).
271 CIH 541.
272 Ibid.
273 Photius, *Bibliotheca*, 64.
274 Ibn Isḥāq, *Sīrah*, 41–3.
275 Al-Ṭabarī, *Ta'rīkh*, 1.946–9.
276 Photius, *Bibiotheca*, 64.

4.4 People along Afro-Eurasian Trade Routes: A Conclusion

As trading routes and connections between the Mediterranean and West Africa plausibly influenced the early adoption of Islam in medieval western Africa,[277] trading partnerships were strengthened by conversions in the sixth-century Red Sea. Constantine's adoption of Christianity and the sociopolitical transformations convulsing the Mediterranean world at the dawn of Late Antiquity swept over the African shores of the Red Sea in the fourth century when king ʿEzanas of Aksūm converted to Christianity. His conversion marked his alliance with the powerful Roman Empire. Shortly afterwards, the South Arabian kingdom of Ḥimyar adopted a monotheism influenced by Judaism. After the massacre of Najrān, Christianity became the 'official religion' in the region.

This chapter has highlighted how economic reasons took precedence over 'religious' motivations and how the creation of economic monopolies preceded that of political and cultural regions. Through the expedition of Najrān, Romans and Aksūmites aimed to limit Iran's considerable control of the Red Sea trade networks between East Asia and the Mediterranean through the Arabian ports and take complete control of the caravan trade towards Central and North Arabia. Economic reasons played a more prominent role in these events, as hinted at by targeting the Miaphysites (like Aksūm) and not of all the various Christian factions in South Arabia. Some sources even suggest that Kaleb was not Christian at the time of the massacre, thus excluding a religious agenda behind his Arabian expedition. In this chapter, I have argued that the depiction of the massacre of Najrān as a 'religious slaughter' mostly accurately reflects the mindsets and rhetoric of the writers (theologians and men of faith) of the literary sources available than the reality of the unfolding events. Similarly, the overestimated portrayal of a 'first Christianisation' of Aksūm and the emphasis on the legendary missionary activities of the Nine Saints (recalling the Thirteen Syrian Fathers of Iberia) laid the groundwork for the divulgation of ideological propaganda which cloaked the more real but perhaps less savoury economic motivation in the mythologized narrative of religious righteousness and zeal.[278] As Judaism had prevailed at the time of the Aksūmite 'first wave', the Aksūmite

[277] S. Dueppen, 'The Archaeology of West Africa, ca. 800 BCE–1500 CE', *History Compass* 14 (2016), 247–63, at p. 255.

[278] We should place the first drafts of the Lives of the Syrian Fathers at the beginning of the ninth century. See J. Mahé, 'Les pères syriens et les origines du monachisme géorgien d'après le nouveau manuscrit sinaïtique', in *Monachismes d'Orient – Images, échanges, influences: Hommage à Antoine Guillaumont. Cinquantenaire de la chaire des' christianismes orientaux*, ed. F. Jullien and M.-J. Pierre (Turnhout: Brepols, 2011), 51–64, at p. 61.

'second wave' coincided with a 'first wave' in Ḥimyar. The sixth-century wave also co-occurred as an extensive Christianization policy in the Aksūmite countryside. Accordingly, Kaleb policy of renewal and further Christianization (rather than re-Christianization) was exaggerated by contemporary literary accounts. These accounts are often in contrast with archaeological sources and echo the difference between Roman literary accounts attributing the rapid spread of Christianity to Constantine's sudden conversion and burials attesting to a steady and silent spread of Christianity throughout the Empire well before Rome's official sponsorship of Christianity.

From its rise in the third century until its fall at the end of the sixth century, the Ḥimyarite kingdom was characterized by prosperous cities which contained cultural diversity, as testified by the conflict between Jews and Christians living in these cities. One of the most distinctive aspects of the South Arabians' success lay in the kingdom's remote location. This geographical distance ensured its independence from Rome and Iran for almost three centuries. At the same time, the support of aristocratic indigenous tribes was the 'swing vote' needed by the king of Ḥimyar to win Arabian and international battles. It is unlikely that Yūsuf's coup de force would have had the same success without the support of the powerful tribe of the Yazʾan attested from the second century onwards.[279] Moreover, the ruling elites' access to the large pool of semi-nomadic warriors of Central Arabia significantly contributed to Ḥimyar's independence. Indeed, just like the Romans and Iranians, the Ḥimyarites appointed local allies to extend their reach to Central Arabia: these allies being the so-called 'Arabians' attested in the Ḥimyarite *titulus* (Chapter 1). Ḥimyar relied on their support and incorporated them into a reliable social network. As briefly mentioned in Section 4.1, Ḥimyar and Aksūm's mobility and adaptability are similar to Sogdiana's after the Kidarite Hun invasions in the 350s and to the later Hephthalite dominance up until the Türks took over in the 550s. Like Sogdiana, Ḥimyar benefitted from fertile grounds and a privileged position in long-distance trade due to its position at the centre of several routes. And as Turanian cities grew affluent from the profits of their fertile lands and trade, so did the Ḥimyarite cities. Hence, in a similar fashion to the Sogdians, the Ḥimyarites acted as political and economic mediators, diplomats and traders between the people of the steppe and the superpowers of the day. The adaptability of Ḥimyar and Aksūm allowed them to transform their kingdoms from regional realities into leading commercial entities in only two centuries. Simultaneously,

[279] E.g., ʿAbadān 4.

Sogdia shrewdly tightened its relationship with China and Iran, and Ḥimyar found a means not to be annihilated by Aksūm, Rome and Iran.

Between the mid-sixth and the mid-ninth centuries, the Central Asian elites were 'agents of cultural communication, transmission, and appropriation' and patrons of Sogdian merchants.[280] The Türks' success lay in their ability to negotiate trade agreements with a mighty China (and maybe also with eastern Turkestan), aided by 'the specific background of the Ashinas as foreigners, as "men of the border"'.[281] This description also fits well with the profile of both Ḥimyarites and Aksūmites. Furthermore, the most significant trait shared by the elites of Central Asia and the Red Sea after the massacre of Najrān[282] is the borrowing of the first-millennium Roman elites' 'sign of power': Christianity. The cultural aura of the long-lasting civilization of South Arabia sponsored and legitimated the ruling of the Ḥimyarites, who were not extensively influenced by the surrounding empires in shaping their culture before the events of Najrān. The choice to adhere to Judaism in the region in the fourth to fifth centuries signalled the kingdom's independence from the developments in the surrounding empires. In contrast with Sogdia's absence of any political or military power and an organization structured around autonomous principalities, Ḥimyar relied on a centralized seat. From this seat, the South Arabian kingdoms thrived during the Iron Ages. Because of the 'cultural firmness' of pre-Najrān Ḥimyar, the South Arabian rulers never adopted the institutions of the neighbouring empires. They retained a 'semi-nomadic imperialism' instead based on military resources, which tied them to the semi-nomads of the steppes in a similar fashion to the Huns and the Türks.[283] The 'semi-nomadic imperialism' of Ḥimyar also has strong similarities to that of Sogdiana after the 350s. At the same time, the political hybridism of Huns and the Türks of the Iranian East has strong parallels with that of the Aksūmites, as the country's long interaction with the Roman Empire throughout the first millennium strongly influenced and shaped its cultural framework, as testified already in the mid-second–first century BCE by the imitation of Roman pottery.[284]

[280] S. Stark, 'Luxurious Necessities: Some Observations on Foreign Commodities and Nomadic Polities in Central Asia in the Sixth to Ninth Centuries', in *Complexity of Interaction along the Eurasian Steppe Zone in the First Millennium CE*, ed. J. Bemmann and M. Schmauder (Bonn: Rheinische Friedrich-Wilhems Universität, 2015), 463–502, at p. 463.

[281] Ibid., 477.

[282] And of North Arabian elites, as shown in Chapter 5.

[283] R. E. Payne, 'The Making of Turan: The Fall and Transformation of the Iranian East in Late Antiquity', *Journal of Late Antiquity* 9 (2016), 4–41.

[284] A. Manzo, 'Skeuomorphism in Aksumite Pottery? Remarks on the Origins and Meanings of Some Ceramic Types', *Aethiopica* 6 (2003), 7–46.

The Aksūmite interaction with Rome led to a sort of 'dualistic attitude' by the Aksūmite rulers. On the one hand, they appear to have adopted and internalized the culture of their powerful trading partners, while on the other, they retained their 'cultural personality'. This is exemplified by the multilingual inscriptions of ʿEzana mentioned in Chapter 3, but also by Aksūmite coin production. Although Greek is the main denomination of Aksūmite coinage, Gəʿəz legends are also noted after the fifth century.[285] While the issue of coinage bearing the Greek language may point to an attempt to appear less 'other', it might well simply indicate that it was easier to produce coinage in Greek, as pre-existing models already existed.[286] The adoption of Christianity and its firm foothold in the kingdom show a high degree of cultural permeability. Whereas Ḥimyar managed to maintain an autonomous position on the political map of Late Antiquity and retained its cultural characteristics, Aksūm was much more subject to the fluctuations and developments of the surrounding empires. However, while Ḥimyar went into decline due to physical factors and an internal crisis after Abraha's death,[287] Aksūm was never wholly subdued by external powers, as testified by Ethiopia's surviving Christianity after the Muslim conquests. Its remote location and the fact that its seat was 2,000 metres above sea level and about 300 km from the coast plausibly contributed to its longevity. A homogenized and stable religious framework mirrored the region's political stability. Nonetheless, the changes in the political map of Late Antiquity after the rise of Islam had a significant impact on Aksūm's prosperity, as a rise in piracy and a fall in trade with Rome curtailed its wealth considerably.

Analysis of pottery production in the kingdom has shown a rise in imported goods between the first and sixth centuries.[288] Similarly, glass imports rapidly fell in the sixth century.[289] The loss of a prominent position in the lucrative Red Sea trade after the rise of Islam led to the decline of Aksūm, which was probably further exacerbated by a broader climatic shift that had already started in the sixth century. Hence, the third quarter of the sixth century witnessed the eclipse of both Ḥimyar and Aksūm, albeit in different ways. Significantly enough, this also marks the time of

[285] Phillipson, *Foundations of an African Civilization*, 188–91.

[286] It is significant that the only fifth-century Aksūmite ruler to have employed Gəʿəz on his coinage copied a winged figure from the representation of Victory on Roman coins, the closest parallel being a solidus of 422 by Theodosius II. See ibid., 189.

[287] A crisis probably exacerbated by the collapse of the Marib Dam, one of the pioneering engineering wonders of antiquity.

[288] S. C. Munro-Hay, *Excavations at Aksum: An Account of Research at the Ancient Ethiopian Capital Directed in 1972–4 by the Late Dr Neville Chittick* (London: British Institute in Eastern Africa, 1989), 208.

[289] Ibid.

the collapse of the kingdom of the Jafnids in the north of the Arabian Peninsula and the Naṣrid seat shortly thereafter. As will be shown in Chapters 5 and 6, the process of the dismantlement of the old patronage system was sped up by the last Roman–Iranian war, an ecological crisis and the plague, triggering a general depopulation in the Roman East,[290] attested by the instability of the Roman imperial coinage in the period.[291]

As in the case of the Eurasian steppe empires, whose power was primarily based on the external resources they distributed,[292] Aksūm and Ḥimyar mainly relied on their trade. The label 'middlemen', often applied to indicate Sogdians and Uighurs,[293] is inadequate for both groups of traders, as it flattens their identity as traders for powerful kingdoms. They were situated 'in the middle', but their identity was either a chaotic miscellanea of other people's traits or that of passive emissaries in charge of goods' transportation. Due to their important role on the Red Sea trade routes, they never entirely constituted the 'periphery' during Late Antiquity. However, only after the events in the sixth century did these geographical areas gain sociopolitical resonance. In the Muslim collective memory and tradition, Aksūm became known as the land where the first Muslims took refuge from the Quraysh persecution in Mecca. Conversely, the glorious past of Ḥimyar and the former kingdoms of South Arabia, which partly managed to predate the unification of the Arabian Peninsula before the rise of Islam, was deliberately forgotten (with the notable exception of the works by the Muslim South Arabian scholar al-Hamdānī and, more recently, of Yemeni nationalistic propaganda).[294] In contrast with mechanisms of assimilation which characterized past conquests,[295] the Ḥimyarite Empire did not serve

[290] M. Whittow, 'Rethinking the Jafnids: New Approaches to Rome's Arab Allies', in *Les Jafnides: Des rois arabes au service de Byzance (vie siècle de l'ère chrétienne)*, ed. D. Genequand and C. J. Robin (Paris: Éditions De Boccard, 2015), 11–36, at p. 25.

[291] P. Sarris, 'The Justinianic Plague: Origins and Effects', *Continuity and Change* 17 (2002), 169–82, at p. 175. On the other side, no significant coinage decline is attested in Sasanian Iran. See J. Howard-Johnston, 'The Sasanian State: The Evidence of Coinage and Military Construction', *Journal of Ancient History* 2 (2014), 144–81.

[292] N. N. Kradin, 'Nomadic Empires in Inner Asia', in *Complexity of Interaction in Complexity of Interaction along the Eurasian Steppe Zone in the First Millennium* CE, ed. J. Bemmann and M. Schmauder (Bonn: Rheinische Friedrich-Wilhems Universität, 2015), 11–48, at p. 26.

[293] See for example P. Frankopan, *The Silk Roads: A New History of the World* (London: Bloomsbury, 2015), who defines the Sogdians as 'classic middlemen' at p. 30; Peter B. Golden, *Central Asia in World History* (Oxford: Oxford University Press, 2011), 38 and 62.

[294] V. A. Grasso, 'Perception, Representation, Memory', in *A Cultural History of the Middle East and North Africa, 450–750*, ed. N. Khalek (Bloomsbury, Cultural History series, vol. 1/6, forthcoming 2024).

[295] E.g., the Arsacids reinvention of the Seleucids. See M. P. Canepa, *The Iranian Expanse: Transforming Royal Identity through Architecture, Landscape, and the Built Environment, 550* BCE*–642* CE (Oakland: University of California Press, 2018), 93.

any scope in the Caliphate's propaganda. It was accordingly eliminated from the communal memory of the *Ummah*. This was done to give the Arabian Peninsula the same cohesion that king Malkīkarib Yuha'min reportedly had created with the introduction of monotheism two centuries before the rise of Islam. Nonetheless, the Qur'ān owes a great deal of its lexicon to the religious milieu of Aksūm, which likely reached the Ḥijāz via South Arabia.[296] In addition to some Gəʿəz loanwords found in the Qur'ān,[297] Christian canonical and non-canonical works also probably made it into the Qur'ān through Gəʿəz translations as a great extent of the Qur'ān's narratives and *topoi* bear a striking resemblance to biblical narratives belonging to Second Temple apocrypha such as the Book of Jubilees and the Book of Enoch, both canonical in Ethiopia. Ultimately, Aksūm's and South Arabia's religious frameworks and the events narrated in this chapter played a significant role in shaping the context in which the Qur'ān emerged.

[296] T. Noldeke, *Neue Beiträge zur semitischen Sprachwissenschaft* (Strassburg: Karl J. Trübner, 1910).

[297] E.g., *shayṭān, jibt* and *ṭāghūt*. For a study see M. Kropp, 'Beyond Single Words: Mā'ida-Shayṭān-Jibt and ṭāghūt – Mechanisms of Transmission into the Ethiopic Bible and the Qur'ānic Text', in *The Qur'an in Its Historical Context*, ed. G. S. Reynolds (New York: Routledge, 2008), 204–16.

CHAPTER 5

The Shape of the Sixth Century II
The North

Modern scholarship often depicts the Arabians as being at the mercy of Rome and Iran until the Muslim conquests, which provided the inhabitants of the Arabian Peninsula with a clear and unifying identity in the shape of Islam.[1] However, the pre-Islam absence of a unified pan-Arab state did not mean that the Arabians were utterly subjugated to the surrounding empires. The sixth-century skirmishes on the Arabian borders need to be contextualized and interpreted as the result of tensions both internal and external to the Arabian Peninsula. Like Rome's and Iran's leaders, Arabian dynasties made alliances to neutralize internal and alien enemies. Therefore, the antagonism between Arabian groups such as Jafnids and Naṣrids should not be solely interpreted as a reflection of the tensions between the superpowers of Late Antiquity but as an inherently Arabian phenomenon that was nonetheless part of a broader late antique political trend.

This chapter aims to present a story of North Arabia in which the Arabians play the part of the protagonist rather than the minor role in a story of empires. This is done by investigating the *Konfliktbeziehung* (conflictual relation) between empires and local dynasties and analysing the influence of foreign forces in the self-representation, cross-cultural assimilation and propaganda of the Arabian elites. In the light of the fact that Muḥammad was conspicuously not a king and that the later Umayyads were highly criticized for kingly conduct, the first part of this chapter investigates concepts of kingship among the sixth-century North Arabian dynasties allied with Rome and Iran. Hence, through a focus on degrees of participation and mediation as well as on buffer zone policies, a comparison is made between the North Arabians and those of other similar political entities in the first

[1] Shahid largely and deeply influenced this approach. See esp. the two volumes *Byzantium and the Arabs in the Sixth Century*.

millennium. As pointed out in an analysis of the interactions between Rome and the steppe empires in south-east Europe, a revision is needed of 'the model of marginal cultures striving for integration into the cultural and political structure of the dominant civilisation',[2] and the concept of centre and periphery. Accordingly, my approach is based on the belief that the mechanisms underpinning a region's development ought to be investigated by looking at the history of the area itself. Apart from a Syriac dossier,[3] no (securely dated) literary sources written by pre-Islamic North Arabians exist. However, archaeologists have assembled a small corpus of epigraphic testimonies probably composed by Jafnid rulers and their partner elites. From reading this material, I aim to avoid feeding the already conspicuous literature on 'barbarians' inhabiting the fringes of powerful empires by placing the 'peripheries' of the late antique empires at the centre.[4]

In a similar fashion to other first-millennium political entities, the Jafnids adopted the Roman *lingua franca* and its system of belief. Nonetheless, they found a way to rebrand Rome's 'identity signs' as their own, as suggested by an Old Arabic inscription's content and their adherence to Miaphysitism. Therefore, I shed light on their relationship with faith and the Church through an enquiry into their role as agents of cultural transformations in sixth-century North Arabia. In a place lacking a shared cultural identity like sixth-century North Arabia, single individuals and dynasties gained prominence and power through a shrewd exploitation of faith, which was much exploited as a *casus belli* in the same way as it was south of the Peninsula. The intelligent choice to adhere to Miaphysite rather than Chalcedonian Christianity thus provided the Jafnids with the *casus* for keeping one foot in and one foot out of the Roman sphere of control. As patrons of the Miaphysites, the Jafnids placed themselves on an equal footing (to some extent) with the Romans, patrons of the other powerful Christian faction, the Chalcedonians. Drawing a fine line between differentiating themselves from and being similar to their powerful allies, the Jafnids gained consensus among the Arabian elites, clerics and the rural classes, who acknowledged them as their political leaders and perceived them to have greater significance than the Roman emperors in their local milieu. This allowed the Jafnids to assume the role of the 'cultural lighthouse' of north-western Arabia.

[2] Schmauder, 'Huns, Avars, Hungarians', 682.

[3] BL ADD. 14.602. I am currently translating the dossier.

[4] See G. Fisher, *Between Empires: Arabs, Romans, and Sasanians in Late Antiquity* (Oxford: Oxford University Press, 2011), 12.

5.1 Intersection of Alliances: The North Arabian Frontier

During the sixth century, tensions between Rome and Iran escalated, with attacks initiated mainly by the Sasanians. Nonetheless, the Romans still welcomed Sasanian embassies, and a series of peace treaties were signed throughout the period. Accordingly, the policy towards Iran of Justinian, the most influential Roman emperor of the century, has been deemed one of 'constructive engagement'.[5] Mesopotamia, Syria and Armenia remained the preferred battleground for the two powers.[6] Hence, thanks to a seven-year truce signed in 506,[7] the Romans improved their North Arabian defence system in the first half of the sixth century, building a new fortification at Dara (north-west of Nisibis) 'for the preparation and storage of weapons and the protection of the territory of the Arabians from bands of Iranians and Ṭayyāyē'.[8] In Dara, the two parties faced each other in 530.[9] Tensions had increased due to the competition for the allegiance of the Caucasian principalities where Christianity was rapidly spreading, threatening their rulers' loyalty to Iran. The Sasanians ruinously lost this war, and a first pact of 'Eternal Peace' was signed.[10] Although the treaty signed by Khosrow I and Justinian proclaimed the two rulers 'as brothers according to the ancient custom',[11] Khosrow I invaded Roman Mesopotamia and Syria by 540, taking advantage of the fact that Justinian was busy with the Gothic wars (535–54) and reconquering Italy and Africa.[12] Rome later attacked Iran for the first time in this century in 565 under Justin II. Seven years later, the last war of the century began, only coming to an end almost twenty years later when Khosrow II (r. 590–628), son of the overthrown Hormizd IV (r. 579–90), became ruler of Iran thanks to the support of Maurice (r. 582–602), who was emulating Justinian's policy of buying off the empire's enemies.

Hugh Kennedy has argued that at the end of the sixth century, the map of this area looked similar to how it had been at the beginning of the preceding century.[13] However, the sixth-century skirmishes saw the emergence

5 G. Greatrex, 'Byzantium and the East in the Sixth Century', in *The Cambridge Companion to the Age of Justinian*, ed. M. Maas (Cambridge: Cambridge University Press, 2005), 477–509, at p. 482.
6 Procop. *Pers*, 1.7; Pseudo-Zacharia, *Ecclesiastical History*, 7.25; Malalas, *Chronicle*, 16.398; Joshua Stylite, *Chronicle*, 50.
7 Procop. *Pers*, 1.10.
8 Ibid.; Malalas, *Chronicle*, 16.399; Joshua Stylite, *Chronicle*, 90; Pseudo-Zacharia, *Ecclesiastical History*, 7.34.
9 Procop. *Pers*. 1.14; Pseudo-Zacharia, *Ecclesiastical History*, 9.92; Malalas, *Chronicle*, 18.452–3.
10 Procop. *Pers*. 1.19–22; Pseudo-Zacharia, *Ecclesiastical History*, 9.98–100; Malalas, *Chronicle*, 18.477.
11 Malalas, *Chronicle*, 18.477.
12 Pseudo-Zacharia, *Ecclesiastical History*, 10.191; Malalas, *Chronicle*, 18.479–80.
13 Kennedy, 'Syria, Palestine and Mesopotamia', 596.

of new parties which repeatedly faced each other in battle and signed alliances with Rome and Iran. For example, Justin II's war of 572 witnessed the emergence of the Türks. The latter fought side by side with the Armenians for the Romans after having conflicted with their allies, the Sasanians. Similarly, the Arabians played a vital role in the political map of the sixth century. This meant that the political map of the Arabian Peninsula at the end of the sixth century differed significantly from the political map of the fifth century. At the beginning of the sixth century, the Iran-allied Naṣrids, led by al-Mundhir III (r. 503–54), were leading a well-organized army, effectively terrorizing a wide geographical area, as recounted by Cyril of Scythopolis ('[al-Mundhir raided] in great anger against the Romans, laying everything waste, enslaving countless thousands of Romans, and committing many lawless acts').[14] In Central Arabia, the Ḥujrids of Kindah, one of the main partners of the kingdom of Ḥimyar, had subjugated the people of Maʿadd,[15] controlling a wide area including parts of the Ḥijāz and scattered locations along the Persian Gulf.[16] It was during the late fifth and early sixth centuries under the ruler al-Ḥārith ibn ʿAmr ibn Ḥujr that the Ḥujrids of Kindah power was at its height. Their territorial gains were expanded at the expense of the Naṣrids.[17] The Ḥujrids signed an alliance with Rome in 502. This alliance signalled a time when 'all Palestine, Arabia, and Phoenice enjoyed peace and calm'.[18]

In 496–7, an 'invasion of the so-called tent-dwelling Arabians into Euphratesia' is registered by Theophanes.[19] Shortly afterwards, the Romans replaced the allied Salīḥids in the northern part of the Arabian Peninsula by signing an alliance with the new rising dynasty of the Jafnids.[20] This group was thus highly likely to have taken part in the 496–7 invasion. The Abbasid geographer al-Yaʿqūbī (d. 897) claimed that the Jafnids settled in North Arabia after the Salīḥids substituted the Tanūkh as allies of the Romans in Syria.[21] A commemorative South Arabian inscription mentions

14 Cyril of Scythopolis, *Life of John the Hesychast*. 13, 211.15–19.

15 We possess a wide array of sources for this group. See Zwettler, 'Maʿadd in Late-Ancient Arabian Epigraphy'. See also P. Webb, 'Ethnicity, Power and Umayyad Society: The Rise and Fall of the People of Maʿadd 1', in *The Umayyad World*, ed. A. Marsham (Abingdon: Ashgate, 2020), 65–102.

16 L. I. Conrad, 'The Arabs', in *The Cambridge Ancient History*, Vol. 14, *Late Antiquity: Empire and Successors, A.D. 425–600*, ed. A. Cameron, M. Whitby and B. Ward-Perkins (Cambridge: Cambridge University Press, 2000), 678–700, at p. 692.

17 Ibn Ḥabīb, *Muḥabbar*, 368–9.

18 Theophanes Confessor, *Chronicle*, 144.

19 Ibid., 141.

20 Also referred to as Ghassanids, see, e.g., the already mentioned letter published by Shahid and mentioning 'the camp of Jabala king of the Ghassanids (*'sny*)'. See Chapter 1.

21 Al-Yaʿqūbī, *Taʾrīkh*, 1.233–6.

the Ghassān,[22] and another inscription dated 260 mentions 'the kings of the peoples (*mlk sh'b*) of Ghassān, al-Asd, Nizār and Madhhij'.[23] They further suggest that this group was initially located in the south of the peninsula. However, a third- or fourth-century graffito mentioning a 'Ḥārithat son of Zaydmanāt king of ʿAssān' places them 50 km south-east of al-ʿUlā (north-western Saudi Arabia).[24] After a series of failed attempts to increase the Roman military presence in the area, Anastasius I signed alliances with Ḥujrids and Jafnids to end the raids on the Arabian border. The Jafnids were then allowed to dwell in Jawlan and Balqa' (at the boundary between modern Syria and Jordan) and established their main base at al-Jābiyah, soon becoming influential in the broader area between the Euphrates and the Gulf of 'Aqaba. We are dependent on 'external' literary accounts for the emergence of the kingdom of the Jafnids, as we often are when documenting the rise of empires; for example, the Yuezhi's (大月氏) migration supposedly led to the creation of the Kushan Empire, best known by secondary late-dated sources (e.g., the fifth-century *Hou Hanshu*).[25]

Despite the Ḥujrids and Jafnids' alliances with Rome, a wide array of sources recount the Arabians' insubordination at the time.[26] More than one Roman phylarch appears to have been in control of the Arabian frontiers in the first two decades of the sixth century, as evidenced by a passage found in John Malalas' history ('the phylarch Arethas, Gnouphas, Naaman').[27] Only in 527, when the Naṣrids killed the leader of the Ḥujrids,[28] did the newly crowned Justinian decide to grant more power to the Jafnids. The constant absence of the *magister militum per Orientem* from the *limes* otherwise engaged in fighting the Iranians arguably played a role in Justinian's decision to promote the Arabian allies.[29] Hence, almost at the same time as Rome sent an ambassador to Aksūm and Ḥimyar to fight against Iran (Chapter 4),[30] the Jafnid leader al-Ḥārith was nominated phylarch (529).[31] Simultaneously, a descendant of al-Ḥārith was established as 'phylarch of the Saracens' over the people of Maʿadd in Central

[22] ʿAbadān 1.
[23] 'Inan 75.
[24] Al-Dhuyayb 65.
[25] *Hou Hanshu*, 88.13.
[26] E.g., Joshua Stylite, *Chronicle*, 88.
[27] Malalas, *Chronicle*, 18.434–5.
[28] Ibid.; Theophanes Confessor, *Chronicle*, 179.
[29] A. S. Lewin, 'L'esercito del vicino oriente nel V secolo', in *Governare e riformare l'impero al momento della sua divisione: Oriente, Occidente, Illirico*, ed. U. Roberto and L. Mecella (Rome: École française de Rome, 2016), 225–46, at p. 337.
[30] Procop. *Pers.* 1.20.9–13.
[31] Ibid., 1.17.

Arabia.[32] This appointment eventually led to the disappearance of the Ḥujrid dynasty and the Jafnids gaining undisputed control in the region.[33]

Entrusting the East to al-Ḥārith and his family was the most economical way for Rome not to lose ground to Iran and to gain a political presence in the Arabian interior. To achieve this, Justinian pitted the Jafnid ruler against the Naṣrid leader al-Mundhir, who had been raiding the sensitive territories contended over by Rome and Iran. In the first half of the sixth century, the Jafnids fought for the Romans on several occasions. For example, they were at the forefront when hostilities broke out between Samaritans, Jews and Christians in Scythopolis in 527–9,[34] right after Justinian's order to demolish Samaritan synagogues.[35] Yet, the relationship between Jafnids and Romans quickly deteriorated in the second half of the sixth century. In 562, the Naṣrid ruler Amr attacked Ḥārith's territory, and the Jafnid ruler expressed his dissatisfaction with the inefficient aid given to the Romans during his visit. In around 570, the Jafnid al-Mundhir twice defeated the Naṣrid Qābus.[36] He requested gold to hire troops but did not receive any assistance from Rome.[37] By this time, Justin II had been persuaded to have al-Mundhir assassinated.[38] The murderous plot recalled Rome's earlier dealings with Danube frontier allies. Still, it was ruined when al-Mundhir accidentally received a letter ordering his killing and managed to save himself and withdraw from defending the Roman frontier subsequently.[39] He reconciled with the *magister militum per Orientem* Justinian in Ruṣāfah only three years later in 575, 'as a Christian, grieving at the misery that had fallen upon the Roman territories, and full of anger against the Arabians of Iran'.[40] However, despite a series of successful raids, a disastrous campaign against Iran in 580 led to the end of al-Mundhir's partnership with Rome. Allegedly, when Maurice and al-Mundhir were marching together

[32] Qays (in Procopius he is known as Caisus). Photius, *Bibliotheca*, 3; Procop. *Pers.* 1.20. A Qays is also found in pre-Islamic poems, e.g., in the poetry of the famous Imru' al-Qays. See C. J. Robin, 'Abraha et la reconquête de l'Arabie déserte: Un réexamen de l'inscription Ryckmans 506 = Murayghan 1', *Jerusalem Studies in Arabic and Islam* 39 (2012), 1–93, at pp. 42–4.

[33] A late mention in a South Arabian inscription by Abraha dated to 552 suggests that the Naṣrid ʿAmr, son of al-Mundhir, had become leader of the people of Maʿadd (Ry 506). The Ḥujrids, however, appear in the later Muslim literature. See for example Ibn Ḥabīb, *Muḥabbar*, 368.

[34] Malalas, *Chronicle*, 18.446. India likely here refers to Ethiopia.

[35] *Cod. Just.* 1.5.17.

[36] The conflict is documented in detail by a Garshuni translation of the work by Michael the Syrian. See bibliography under Michael the Syrian.

[37] John of Ephesus, *Ecclesiastical History*, 3.6.3.

[38] Ibid., 3.6.4.

[39] Ibid.

[40] Ibid.

into the Sasanian dominions, they found a damaged bridge and argued with each other.[41] Two years later, al-Mundhir was arrested at Ḥuwwārīn (Syria), taken to Constantinople and exiled to Sicily.[42] Al-Mundhir's son al-Nuʿmān revolted against Maurice but was unsuccessful.[43] Hence, according to Michael the Syrian, 'the Christian Ṭayyāyē came to an end and ceased to exist because of the treachery of the Romans'.[44]

In the first half of the seventh century, some Jafnids were still allied with Rome and fighting for Heraclius (r. 610–41) against Iran, while others negotiated with the second caliph 'Umar (r. 634–44).[45] Nonetheless, they ceased to have a prominent position in the Arabian Peninsula after their fall from grace with the Romans. Despite the brief eighty-five-year alliance between the Jafnids and Rome, the Naṣrids' rule lasted for centuries. Al-Ṭabarī claims that when al-Nuʿmān met Khosrow II, the latter perceived him to be a 'hideous person'.[46] This personal repulsion notwithstanding, Khosrow still asked him to control the Arabians for him, appointing him ruler and giving him robes of honour and a crown.[47] The wealth of the Naṣrid seat, their social status and relative independence from Iran are attested by Joshua the Stylite. He hinted at the Naṣrids' deep influence on Kawad ('Kawad, king of the Persians, was considering coming against Areobindus at Edessa. The Ṭayy king al-Nuʿmān was urging him due to what had happened to his caravan').[48] Despite the Jafnids' display of power (see Section 5.2), they were never held in high esteem by their allies and did not reach the same socio-cultural advancement as their Sasanian counterpart. While the Jafnids had never established a capital for their kingdom, they did, however, found their main campsite in al-Jābiyah (Syria). This contrasts with the Naṣrids, whose centre of Ḥīrah was an important and thriving city. Being close to the Sasanian seat of Ctesiphon and strategically located by the Euphrates, Ḥīrah enjoyed the benefits of the Persian Gulf trade. Nonetheless, the Naṣrids shared a similar fate to the Jafnids and disappeared from the Arabian scene when their allies withdrew their support in 602.

41 Ibid., 3.6.16.
42 Evagrius, *Ecclesiastical History*, 6.2.
43 Ibid.
44 Michael the Syrian, *Chronicle*, 10.19.
45 Ibid. Shahid uses poetry as a primary source to argue for the ongoing Jafnid alliance with Rome.
46 Al-Ṭabarī, *Ta'rīkh*, 1.1018.
47 Ibid.
48 Not the just mentioned al-Nuʿmān but his early sixth century predecessor. See Joshua Stylite, *Chronicle*, 58.

Al-Ṭabarī suggested that the Naṣrid al-Nuʿmān had fallen into disgrace among the Sasanians for having killed ʻAdī,[49] the favourite poet of the Sasanian ruler.[50] According to the *Chronicle of Khuzistan,* however, the relationship between the Naṣrids and Sasanians deteriorated when al-Nuʿmān refused to travel with Khosrow and lend him a horse when the Sasanian ruler was fleeing from the rebel general Bahram VI Chobin.[51] As al-Nuʿmān also refused to agree to Khosrow's marriage with his daughter, Khosrow avenged himself by inviting al-Nuʿmān to dinner and serving him scraps of hay. In response to this insult, Al-Nuʿmān later sent the Maʻadd to ransack Iran. Al-Nuʿmān still agreed to meet the Sasanian ruler, convinced by one of al-Nuʿmān's ʻinterpreters from the island of Derin' (Bahrain), who had conspired with Khosrow and was then poisoned by Khosrow. Significantly, al-Nuʿmān's interpreter swore by the Gospel, assuring him that Khosrow still ʻloved him very much'. It is plausible that the Sasanians saw the disappearance of the Jafnids as an opportunity to get rid of their allies to directly extend their control over Arabia at a time when the Romans were struggling to maintain their power in the area. Al-Nuʿmān's conversion to Christianity may have also concurred with the fall from grace of the Naṣrids.[52] The disappearance of both allied groups indigenous to Arabia and the consequent weakening of (local) authority in the region in conjunction with the fall of Ḥimyar largely contributed to the rise of an Arab consciousness and a vacuum that Muḥammad's movement could fill.

Rome and Iran often exploited the skirmishes between the Arabian allies to be influential in an area that had historically proved attractive but difficult to control and to be able to position their troops elsewhere. When in 540, Khosrow I appointed the Naṣrid al-Mundhir as a ruler ʻover ʻUman, al-Baḥrayn and al-Yamāmah to al-Ṭā'if and the rest of Ḥijāz and all the Arabians of the lands in-between',[53] the Jafnid Ibn Jabala invaded al-Mundhir's territory. As al-Mundhir asked Khosrow to write to Justinian seeking justice and Justinian did not answer, war was reignited.[54] Similarly, having learned that Belisarius was gaining ground in the attempt to reconquer the Italian Peninsula for the emperor Justinian, Khosrow

49 The most well-known poet active at the court of the Naṣrid was al-Nābigha al-Dhubyānī (d. ca. 604). See his six panegyrics to al-Nuʿmān (*Dīwān* 4, 9, 14, 19, 22, 32).

50 Al-Ṭabarī, *Ta'rīkh,* 1.1018–29.

51 *Khuzistan,* 19–20.

52 *Khuzistan,* 16.

53 Al-Ṭabarī, *Ta'rīkh,* 1.958.

54 Ibid.

took advantage of a dispute between the Jafnids and the Naṣrids in 539 by raiding Roman territory.[55] Modern scholarship's portrayal of the Arabians as exploited by Rome and Iran until the Muslim conquests is largely influenced by late antique literary sources written by the educated elites of the Roman world, quite often men of faith, who cast their accounts in a rhetorical mould (Chapter 1).[56] However, despite their alliances, the North Arabian dynasties remained intrinsically independent throughout the sixth century, as demonstrated by their cultural and political choices. In fact, despite signing a treaty between Rome and Iran in 545, the Jafnids and Naṣrids remained at war for more than a decade after the treaty. Such autonomy was understandably not appreciated by the two superpowers of the time, so a subsequent peace agreement between Rome and Iran signed in 562 included a clear provision specifying 'that the Saracen allies of both empires shall also agree to this agreement and that the allies of Iran shall not attack the Romans and vice versa'.[57] This treaty, reported by a fragment by the historian Menander Protector (fl. late sixth century), further stated that Arabians and 'barbarian traders' could only travel via Nisibis and Daras and never cross foreign territory without permission.[58] In this way, Rome and Iran attempted to gain control of the Arabian trade routes. An analysis of a series of cultural choices further illustrates the North Arabians' chameleon-like alignment and their distancing from the superpowers of Late Antiquity.

5.2 North Arabian Christianity at the Dawn of Islam

The Christological controversy remained a significant issue inside and outside the Roman Empire throughout the sixth century, causing the formation of sectarian communities. Some of these communities developed a distinct cultural identity, empowered through the historical narrative of a Miaphysite Commonwealth, and enjoyed the independence of missionaries and leaders who looked for dogmatic and political assistance both to Rome and non-Roman entities.[59] With the disintegration of the Church authority, single individuals gained religious prestige and led missionary activities beyond the Roman world.[60] In particular, single individuals and dynasties

[55] Procop. *Pers*, 2.1.
[56] Again, see Shahid, *Byzantium and the Arabs.*
[57] Menander, Fragment 6, 320–5.
[58] Ibid., 330–40.
[59] Wood, *We Have No King*, 211.
[60] Ibid., 212.

gained prominence through the shrewd exploitation of cults in places lacking a common ethnicity. This analytical framework is particularly appropriate when describing the religious situation of North Arabia in the sixth century. It offers some reflection on the most prominent cultural feature of sixth-century Arabian independence: the modalities of the adoption of Christianity in the region. Some sixth-century Naṣrids bravely converted to Christianity even though they were allied with the Sasanians, who had historically shown varying degrees of tolerance/intolerance towards their Christian population. In contrast, the Jafnids, though allied with Rome, openly chose to adopt Miaphysite Christianity, exploiting the Miaphysite Arabian clergy they patronized to subordinate the 'common people' of western North Arabia. Like other emerging buffer zones such as Georgia, the Jafnid kingdom provides a significant example of the broader late antique 'social paradigm', which saw the moulding of doctrinal controversies according to each ruler's interests. The Jafnids involvement in the Christological disputes of the time had considerable repercussions in the sixth-century Arabian Peninsula, echoing in the capacious shaping of the Islamic profession of faith.

Throughout Late Antiquity, the Roman emperors pursued different and oscillating political and religious policies depending on their personal views and political strategies. Despite deposing and replacing four eastern patriarchs, the Miaphysite Anastasius I (r. 491–518) was generally a tolerant ruler. In contrast, Justin I heavily persecuted the Miaphysites. Yet his approach was not uniform: while he persecuted the monks active on the northern side of the Arabian Peninsula, he displayed a benevolent attitude towards the Miaphysite Christians based in Najrān and towards the Jafnids. This non-uniformity presumably indicated Rome's inability to gain and hold the necessary influence in the Arabian interior, which led to Rome needing to create alliances with local Arabians. The relationship between the various Christian factions considerably improved during the long reign of Justin's nephew, Justinian I (r. 482–565), who successfully exploited the benefits of missionary activities throughout his power, thereby strengthening the Roman Commonwealth under the protection of a common God. While Justinian maintained a very different approach towards his unorthodox Roman subjects, he pragmatically adopted a relatively tolerant attitude towards the doctrinological position of his allies. Moreover, while he supported the Chalcedonian faction, his wife Theodora was a strong Miaphysite supporter. The last three Roman emperors of the sixth century, Justin II (r. 565–74), Tiberius II (r. 574–82) and Maurice (r. 582–602), adopted moderate positions on religious matters. While Tiberius was disinclined to persecute the Miaphysites, Justin II even attempted to conciliate the opposing Chalcedonians and Miaphysite factions.

However, although one of his edicts opened with an invocation to 'those who believe in him' to 'gather into [the] one and only church, unanimously conceiving the true belief of Christians and withdrawing from affirming contrary views', the Church did not wholly reunite.[61] Maurice's attitude was initially relatively moderate, but he later changed his position, becoming more intransigent and repeatedly contrasting with the Jafnids.

North Arabia was not the first regional area where the Roman emperors had to placate Miaphysite tendencies to form vital alliances. For example, their differences with Aksūmite doctrine did not prevent the Romans from allying with the kingdom of Aksūm (Chapter 4). A similar conflict between Christian doctrinal perspectives at the fringe of the Roman Empire happened when Nobadia converted to Christianity at the time of Justinian. A Miaphysite missionary named Julianus was then dispatched to Nobadia by Justinian's wife, Theodora.[62] Although Justinian attempted to counter the dispatch of the unorthodox embassy,[63] Julianus successfully arrived in Nobadia around 540 and converted the kings and princes to Miaphysitism 'so that they may also walk in ways of Pope Theodosius' (d. 567), the very same pope who Justinian had previously exiled in 536.[64] Theodora also commanded to send a Miaphysite bishop by the name of Longinus to convert the neighbouring kingdom of Alodia.[65] Rome's alliances with the Miaphysite Aksūm, Nobadia and the Jafnids suggest that its need for allies was far more pressing than the need to fight 'heresies'.[66] Theodora's intervention eased the relationship between the Christian factions and was fundamental to elevating the status of the Jafnids. The Jafnids successfully exploited Christianity as a display of their powerful Roman alliance to gain the respect of the smaller tribal groups of Arabia. In fact, in contrast to Shahid's portrayal of the Jafnids, I would suggest that this group primarily aimed to control the Arabian population through a display of Roman power. Their interest in joining the Roman-Christian Commonwealth and protecting the Miaphysites was an excellent means to an end.

The date when the Jafnids became Christian is contested. It has been suggested that they converted as part of the treaty of 502 when they allied with Rome.[67] Although al-Ṭabarī points to the fact that a 'man

[61] Evagrius, *Ecclesiastical History*, 5.4.
[62] John of Ephesus, *Eccleasiastical History*, 3.4.6.
[63] Ibid.
[64] Ibid., 3.4.7.
[65] Ibid., 3.4.8; 3.4.49–53.
[66] Grasso, 'Rejoice in God!'.
[67] Wood, *We Have No King*, 246.

of Ghassan who had come from Syria who was attacked and killed by the Ḥimyarites', possibly al-Nuʿmān I (r. ca. 400–18), converted to 'the original form of Christianity' a ruler of South Arabia already in the fifth century,[68] it is implausible that Ḥimyarite kings were already Christian at that time (see Chapter 3). Nonetheless, the Jafnids were Christian for most of the sixth century, having adhered to Miaphysitism after Theodora dispatched missionaries into Arabia in 533. John of Ephesus narrates one of the first important episodes of Jafnid Christian history while recounting the mission of the eminent Miaphysite bishop of Edessa Jacob Burdʿoyo (d. 578).[69] Favoured by Empress Theodora, Jacob was ordained Bishop of Edessa by Theodosius, Patriarch of Alexandria, after the request of the Jafnid al-Ḥārith in 542:

> There was a lack of priests in the east and west lands, especially bishops. Therefore, the glorious al-Ḥārith son of Gabalā, the great king of the Arabians (*malik rab d-Ṭayyāyē*), asked with many others to the Christ-loving queen Theodora to order two or three bishops to be soon instituted in Syria by the orthodox. The believing queen wished to advance the opponents of the council of Chalcedon. Thus, she asked to ordain two capable and pious men named Jacob and Theodore, respectively, for Hirtha of the Ṭayyāyē and Edessa.[70]

This episode marks the first time the Jafnids are identified as Miaphysites. The ordination of Jacob and Theodore in the Jafnids' area sealed the establishment of a Miaphysite community and a hierarchical Church organization in North Arabia in the sixth century. Jacob's ordination of 89 bishops and 100,000 priests effectively strengthened Syrian Miaphysitism.[71] At the same time, Ḥārith's support for Miaphysite bishops in Arabia cemented his relationship with Theodora and helped foster Justinian's tolerant policy towards the Arabians. Additionally, Miaphysitism elevated the Jafnids' position equal to the Romans', thus reinvigorating their identity, even though they were not sufficiently independent from Rome to fully develop a Miaphysite policy.[72] Their sponsorship of the Miaphysites allowed the Jafnids to control better the best-educated groups of Arabia: the clerics, who acknowledged them as their political leaders and perceived them as having more local significance than the Roman emperor or the imperial tax cycle.[73]

68 Al-Ṭabarī, *Tārikh*, 1.881.
69 Jacob's name is often latinized as *Bardaeous*, and the Miaphysites are often called 'Jacobites' after him.
70 John of Ephesus, *Lives*, 50, 153–4. Hirtha is probably here the seat of the Jafnids.
71 Ball, *Rome in the East*, 105.
72 Fowden, *Empire to Commonwealth*, 130.
73 Wood, *We Have no King*, 243.

Ḥārith's Miaphysite position is recorded by the patriarch of Alexandria Cyrus of Batna (d. before 641), reported in the chronicle by Michael the Syrian. When Ephrem of Antioch visited the Jafnid leader, al-Ḥārith allegedly refused the Chalcedonian creed, saying, 'I am a barbarian and a soldier, and I cannot read the scriptures. Nonetheless, I will not eat pure meat infected by the body of a rat.'[74] He then ordered camel flesh to eat, arguing that his meal was as repugnant to the patriarch as the Chalcedonian confession was to him. A stereotypical depiction of the Arabians' 'otherness' is evident here.[75] Nonetheless, Ḥārith's support of the Miaphysite faction is corroborated by a group of forty-five Miaphysite documents, primarily letters, contained in a manuscript dated around the sixth/seventh centuries and today kept in the British Library.[76] In the corpus, we find a short letter written by al-Ḥārith to Jacob Burd'oyo after he left Constantinople in 563,[77] as well as two letters written by the bishops of Constantinople and the East (e.g., Jacob Burd'oyo and Theodore of Arabia) addressed to the Miaphysite Church[78] and that of Arabia.[79] It is followed by the reply given by the Arabian abbots of monasteries (Archimandrites), attesting Ḥārith's visit to Constantinople.[80] This letter, written around 569, the last year of Ḥārith's reign, mentions the agency of the 'Christ-loving and glorious *patrikios* al-Ḥārith' and claims that the Jafnid leader summoned the clerics of Arabia to solve the Christological controversy about 'Tritheism' in *Provincia Arabia*.[81] In the following subscriptions of the 137 Arabian archimandrites,[82] one signatory signs himself:

74 Michael the Syrian, *Chronicle*, 9.29.

75 Philip Wood and Elizabeth Fowden adopted a less sceptical view on the historicity of Michael the Syrian's work, accepting that al-Ḥārith pronounced the phrase. While Wood argued for an 'inversion of the stereotype', Fowden suggested that the passage hints at 'al-Ḥārith's knowing manipulation' of the stereotype 'from his position both "inside and Out" of Roman society'. See P. Wood, 'Christianity and the Arabs in the Sixth Century', in *Inside and Out: Interactions between Rome and the Peoples on the Arabian and Egyptian Frontiers in Late Antiquity*, ed. J. H. F. Dijkstra and G. Fisher (Leuven: Peeters, 2014), 353–68, at p. 359; and E. Fowden, 'Inside and Out: Interactions between Rome and the Peoples on the Arabian and Egyptian Frontiers in Late Antiquity by J.H.F. Dijkstra, G. Fisher (review)', *Journal of Late Antiquity* 9 (2016), 557–60, at p. 559.

76 Add. 14602.

77 *Documenta*, 143–4.

78 Ibid., 196–204.

79 Ibid., 204–9.

80 Ibid., 209–24.

81 For Monophysite Philoponian tritheism as the dominant Christology of the Najrāni bishop Abū Ḥāritha at the time of Muḥammad see C. J. Block, 'Philoponian Monophysitism in South Arabia at the Advent of Islam with Implications for the English Translation of 'Thalātha'in Qur'ān 4. 171 and 5. 73', *Journal of Islamic Studies* 23 (2012), 50–75.

82 *Documenta*, 213–24.

> Sergios priest (*qashīshā*) and head of monastery (*rīsh-dayrā*) of the monastery of ʿ*wqbtʾ*. I subscribed by the hand of the priest Eustathios, my deputy, who is the priest of the church of the glorious (*shbīḥā*) and Christ-loving patrikios (*rāḥem la-mshīḥā*) Mundhir.[83]

Another signatory contained in the same letter further mentions the head of the monastery of the land of the Ghassanids (ʿ*ysnyʾ*) together with the head of the monastery of the Arabians (ʾ*r*ʿ*bnyʾ*),[84] thus evidencing the strong Jafnid control of the Arabian clergy.

Ḥārith's successor, al-Mundhir, also had a prominent role in shaping Arabian Christianity, actively seeking possibilities for reconciliation within the Church and engaging in the dispute over the succession to the Patriarchate of Antioch. Al-Mundhir thus offered his intercessions to Tiberius II on behalf of the following Miaphysite Patriarch of Alexandria, Damianus (r. 569–605). According to John of Biclar (d. ca. 620), al-Mundhir 'went to Constantinople with his clan and hastened to Tiberius with gifts from barbarian lands'.[85] Although Tiberius received him kindly,[86] and bestowed a crown on al-Mundhir,[87] al-Mundhir's political position was compromised when Damianus violated his word and wrote anathemas against Paul, stirring up schisms everywhere.[88] Sources written in various religious contexts relate the end of al-Mundhir's alliance with Rome in different terms, either positively,[89] or by depicting al-Mundhir as a traitor.[90] According to Michael the Syrian, when al-Mundhir's son al-Nuʿmān was invited to Constantinople after his father's fall, Maurice 'Caesar of the Romans' offered him the phylarchate in exchange for conversion to Chalcedon.[91] After being asked to speak with the Chalcedonian clerics ('Synodites'), al-Nuʿmān refused Maurice's offer, claiming that 'all the tribes of the Ṭayyāyē' were then 'orthodox'.[92] Ḥārith's brother Abū Karīb similarly figures in Christian contexts. In a codex found in a monastery near Palmyra, God's mercy is invoked for the king (*mlk*) Abū

[83] Ibid., 223.15.
[84] Ibid., 224.5.
[85] John of Biclar, *Chronicle*, 37.
[86] Ibid.
[87] John of Ephesus, *Ecclesiastical History*, 4.42.
[88] Ibid., 4.43.
[89] Ibid., 6.16.
[90] Theophylact Simocatta, *History*, 3.17; Evagrius, *Ecclesiastical History*, 6.2.
[91] Michael the Syrian, *Chronicle*, 10.19.
[92] Ibid. A similar account is found in the thirteenth-century chronicle by Bar ʿEbroyo (1264–86), better known as Barhebraeus and Maphrian of the Syriac Orthodox Church. Bar ʿEbroyo, *Chronicle*, 9.2.

Karīb 'and to all their Christian brothers'.[93] Furthermore, an inscription from Sammā' mentioning Abū Karīb ('Lord God of St George protect the *endoxotatos patrikios* Abou-Chirib') is possibly derived from Psalm 120.8 ('May the Lord guard your entrance and your exit, from now on and forever').[94] And although the invocation appears similar to others found in other religious contexts,[95] it arguably hints at Abū Karīb's Christian faith.

While the Miaphysite Arabians had to deal with fickle Roman emperors, the Christians of Iran enjoyed the same tolerant climate of the preceding centuries. Only sporadic persecutions took place in the period, such as the one carried out by Khosrow II at the end of his reign.[96] In a similar fashion to that in which Theodora held sway over Justinian, the Miaphysite Christian Shirin, Iranian queen in 592, influenced Khosrow's clement disposition towards his Christian subjects. According to the seventh-century Armenian bishop Sebeos, Khosrow 'let none of the impious converts to Christianity, and none of the Christians to impiety, letting each one remain in his ancestral tradition'.[97] However, Khosrow supposedly founded a church and a monastery for Shirin, known as Mary in the *Chronicle of Seert*.[98] According to the same chronicle, as Shirin was the daughter of Maurice, Khosrow also built three churches in honour of the Roman emperor, which the patriarch of Antioch later consecrated.[99] Although the kinship between Shirin and Maurice is not attested elsewhere, the passage implies a pragmatic use of Christianity also on the part of the Iranians. Moreover, the anonymous *Life* of Mar Aḥudemmeh of Balad (d. 559), who converted the tribes of the Jazīra pastureland in northern Mesopotamia to Miaphysite Christianity, similarly suggests that the Sasanians encouraged the spread of Christianity for political ends through their support of the primary ideological opponents of Chalcedonian Christianity at the time (and possibly the establishment of a Jewish kingdom of Ḥimyar too).[100] Protecting the Church of the East was the most convenient option for the Sasanians, as the Roman emperors of the sixth

93 F. Millar, 'A Syriac Codex from Near Palmyra and the "Ghassanid" Abokarib', *Hugoye* 16 (2013), 15–35, at p. 23.

94 M. Sartre, 'Deux phylarques arabes dans l'Arabie Byzantine', *Le Muséon* 106 (1993), 145–54, at p. 151.

95 E.g., the pagan Safaitic inscriptions formulae. See, e.g., C 4068; BS 372; SIJ 912.

96 *Khuzistan*, 8, 11, 18, 26.

97 Sebeos, *Chronicle*, 85.

98 *Hist. nest.* 2.58. Shirin later became the heroine of the Iranian epic *Book of Kings*, and in the romance by the Iranian poet Niẓāmī Ganjavī (d. 1209). Ganjavī, *Dāstān-i Khusraw va Shīrīn.*

99 *Hist. nest.* 2.58. See also *Chronicle 1234*, 81; Michael the Syrian, *Chronicle*, 10.23.

100 *Aḥudemmeh.*

century were either Miaphysite or Chalcedonian.[101] Accordingly, they allowed missionaries belonging to anti-Chalcedonian factions to preach in the surroundings of their seat (e.g., Simeon of Bēth Arshām) and, after the treaty of 562, they allowed the Christians of Iran to build churches, worship freely, bury their dead in graves and stopped forcing them to take part in Magian worship.[102] Nonetheless, a reconstruction of the Naṣrids' sympathies towards Christianity is more complex than that of the Jafnids.

The Naṣrid leader al-Mundhir III (r. ca. 504–54) was the husband to the Christian Ḥujrid princess Hind the Elder. Hind was the great-granddaughter of the first of the Ḥujrid rulers from Kindah, Ḥujr ibn ʿAmr, to whom is attributed the building of a monastery in Ḥīrah. Yāqūt claims that an inscription dedicated to al-Mundhir was found inside a monastery in Ḥīrah,[103] thus suggesting that al-Mundhir at some point converted to Christianity, possibly influenced by his Christian wife. Nonetheless, 'captured one of the sons of Ḥārith in a sudden raid while he was pasturing horses, and straightaway sacrificed him to Aphrodite'.[104] Pseudo-Zachariah further claims that al-Mundhir sacrificed 400 virgins 'in one day for the worship of 'Uzzai',[105] while the anonymous Greek-written *Life of Symeon the Stylite the Younger* (d. 592) describes al-Mundhir as 'pagan and bloodthirsty'.[106] Theophanes Confessor suggests that al-Mundhir converted to East Syrian Christianity in 512–13.[107] Allegedly, when the Miaphysite Severus, bishop of Antioch (512–38), sent bishops to al-Mundhir to 'win him over to his heresy', al-Mundhir refuted them, saying: 'I received today a letter stating that the archangel Michael is dead.'[108] The bishops told al-Mundhir that this was impossible, and al-Mundhir thus asked: 'Hence how is it possible that only God was crucified, unless Christ had two natures, if even an angel cannot die?'[109] This account is in stark contrast with the narratives of the massacre of Najrān, which depict al-Mundhir as pagan and as stoking anti-Christian sentiments.[110] Although

[101] Z. Rubin, 'The Sasanid Monarchy', in *The Cambridge Ancient History*, Vol. 14, *Late Antiquity: Empire and Successors, A.D. 425–600*, ed. A. Cameron, M. Whitby and B. Ward-Perkins (Cambridge: Cambridge University Press, 2000), 638–61, at p. 651.

[102] Menander, Fragment 6, 400–10.

[103] Yāqūt, *Buldān*, 2.709.

[104] Procop. *Pers.* 2.28.13.

[105] Pseudo-Zachariah, *Ecclesiastical History*, 8.5.

[106] *Life of Symeon*, 186–7.

[107] Theophane Confessor, *Chronicle*, 159.

[108] Ibid.

[109] Ibid.

[110] *Letter 2*, 6.C.15.

al-Mundhir had a Christian wife, the passage is probably apologetic. The question regarding whether al-Mundhir adopted Christianity thus remains unsolved. The Naṣrids probably had a chameleonic ability to change their approach depending on their audiences' preferences. Nonetheless, there is a general concordance among the sources in seeing al-Nuʿmān, son of al-Mundhir, Naṣrid ruler in the last decade of the sixth century, as being openly Christian.

Evagrius Scholasticus describes al-Nuʿmān as 'a horrible and polluted pagan who even sacrificed men to his demons with his own hands'.[111] Nonetheless, he was baptized 'after the melting down in a fire a golden Aphrodite' and brought his followers to God.[112] Although the *Chronicle of Seert* states that al-Nuʿmān was attracted to paganism, adoring the star called Zuhrah (Venus) and offering sacrifices to idols,[113] it also recounts how al-Nuʿmān was healed thanks to Simeon Bishop of Ḥīrah,[114] and a monk by the name of Isho'zhka, when pagan priests failed to save him from a demon.[115] These events led to al-Nuʿmān converting in 593 and adhering to 'the healthy belief'.[116] A second version of this narrative, also found in the *Chronicle of Seert*, sees the intervention of Simeon ibn Jābir and of the Catholicus of the Church of the East Sabrisho' (d. 604) behind al-Nuʿmān's conversion to East Syrian Christianity.[117] These accounts follow the common hagiographical theme in which a ruler is healed by his Christian conversion and highlight the role of the Naṣrid seat of Ḥīrah as a thriving bishopric of the Church of the East. Choosing East Syrian Christianity over Chalcedonian or Miaphysite Christianity allowed for a smoother alliance between Naṣrids and Sasanian Iran. A passage in the Syriac *Life of Simeon Stylites*, written shortly after Simeon's death in 459, claims that an al-Nuʿmān ally of the Sasanians (but unlikely the Naṣrid leader himself) once declared: 'if I weren't a servant of the Iranian king, I would go up and become a Christian'.[118] The passage hints at the tension between the political and religious spheres in the sixth century. However, whereas this unknown al-Nuʿmān refused to convert, he allowed his people to do so.

111 Evagrius, *Ecclesiatical History*, 6.22.
112 Ibid.
113 *Hist. nest.* 2.60.
114 Later Catholicus of the Church of the East.
115 *Hist. nest.* 2.60.
116 Ibid.
117 Ibid., 265.
118 *Life of Simeon Stylites*, 597.

5.3 Kingship and Cross-cultural Assimilation: The Jafnid Epigraphic Testimonies

Only one literary source written in sixth-century North Arabia probably exists. As with the case of scholars who attempt to write 'the history of Northern Dynasties through an Inner Asian perspective' on the basis of almost exclusively Chinese-language sources,[119] Greek and Syriac literary sources heavily dominate modern scholarship on the Jafnids. Nonetheless, we possess a small corpus of epigraphic testimonies plausibly composed by the Jafnid rulers and allied elites. All but one of these inscriptions are written in Greek. While few Arabians could easily read Greek, they would have probably been able to recognize the script and perceive it as a marker of the Jafnids' close relationship with the Romans. As elaborated in Chapter 1, ethnic identity 'is not an inherent quality', and an ethnic group needs to be 'recognized from the outside', as Walter Pohl justifiably points out.[120] In the case of the Jafnids, their cultural adoption of Roman models, clearly testified by their adoption of Greek, facilitated their recognition as a Roman satellite force and their integration into the Roman Commonwealth. A recent publication by Anthony Kaldellis has briefly highlighted the Roman patriotism of provincial Arabians.[121] He mentions a letter from the Mesopotamian church of Zeugma to the church of Edessa, copied by Joshua the Stylite, concerning 'you, us, and all Romans'.[122] Indeed, Kaldellis is correct in suggesting that birth 'could be overcome by acculturation',[123] and that 'entire foreign groups' could be 'embedded within Roman institutional matrices of governance that favoured the adoption of Roman cultural norms, such as Orthodoxy, the Greek language, and identification with the Roman polity'.[124] Christianity was an incentive for 'ethnic conversion' and integration into the Roman Commonwealth through a process of assimilation. Nonetheless, the general view which sees the Jafnids' identity providentially 'constructed' one-directionally by Rome is disputable. I would instead argue that the Jafnids cleverly exploited the instruments of Roman power and control, with the primary objective of gaining the respect of and consensus from their fellow Arabians.

[119] L. Xin, 'Chinese and Inner Asian Perspectives on the History of the Northern Dynasties (386–589) in Chinese Historiography', in *Empires and Exchanges in Eurasian Late Antiquity: Rome, China, Iran, and the Steppe, ca. 250–750*, ed. N. Di Cosmo and M. Maas (Cambridge: Cambridge University Press, 2018), 166–75, at p. 172.

[120] Ibid., 192.

[121] Kaldellis, *Romanland*, 75–6.

[122] Joshua Stylite, *Chronicle*, 68.

[123] Kaldellis, *Romanland*, 68.

[124] Ibid., 126.

The Jafnid corpus mentions al-Ḥārith (twice), al-Ḥārith's brother (once), al-Mundhir (three times) and al-Mundhir's sons (twice). One of the two inscriptions mentioning al-Ḥārith was found at the Umayyad site of Qaṣr al-Ḥayr al-Gharbī (Syria) where a tower and some *spolia* were probably part of a pre-Islamic monastery,[125] which appears in a letter signed by 137 Miaphysite abbots to condemn tritheism and dated 570.[126] The inscription, dated 559, is on a lintel and is today in five separate fragments. The first and the fourth fragments attest that al-Ḥārith was titled *patricius*:

- In the name of our father Jesus Christ, saviour of the world, who erases the sin [of the world]. [At the time of an] Archimandrite and the very pious deacon Anastasios and the Phylarchate of the glorious Arethas. He should fight to be ranked among those to the right when the Lord God comes![127]
- To Fl[avius] Arethas, *patricius*, [many] years, life. [Great], beautiful, you arrived. [How much] beautiful, you came, Arethas (?)] ... the year 870 ...[128]

Ḥārith's successor al-Mundhir, on the other hand, is mentioned in (1) an undated inscription found at the entrance of an isolated tower at al-Burj (Syria);[129] (2) an inscription dated to 578 and found in a large house at al-Hayyat in the Ḥawrān;[130] and (3) among the names of the benefactors on the mosaic pavement of the sixth-century church of Saint Sergius at Tall al-ʿUmayrī (Jordan).[131]

[1] Fl[avius] Alamoundar[o]s, *paneuphēmos, patrik[ios]*, and *phylarchos* thanking Lord God and Saint Julianus for his salvation and of his children, *endoxotatoi*, built the tower.

[2] Fla[vius] Seos, administrator (*epitr[opos]*), and his son Olbanos constructed at their own cost the entire aulè from the foundations, under the illustrious (*paneuph[emos]*) Alamoundaros, *patr[ikios],* in the year 473 of the province, in the 11th indiction.

[125] D. Genequand, 'Some Thoughts on Qasr al-Hayr al-Gharbi, Its Dam, Its Monastery and the Ghassanids', *Levant* 38 (2006), 63–84.

[126] *Letter of the Archimandrites.*

[127] IGLS 5.2553b.

[128] IGLS 5.2553d.

[129] Wadd. 2562c.

[130] Wadd. 2110.

[131] My translation is based on the Greek text recently published by G. Bevan, G. Fisher and D. Genequand, 'The Late Antique Church at Tall al-ʿUmayrī East: New Evidence for the Jafnid Family and the Cult of St Sergius in Northern Jordan', *Bulletin of the American Schools of Oriental Research* 373 (2015), 49–68, at p. 54.

[3] Lord, receive the offering of the donor and the one who writes, [your servant] Mouselios with his children. The Lord Jesus Christ, God of Saint Sergius, protect the magnificent (*megaloprepestatos)* Almoundaros, the *comes.* [...]

In the first two inscriptions, al-Mundhir is titled *patrikios*, while the third names him *comes*, a Roman administrative and military rank, attested from the first century[132] and widely distributed as a generic honorific title equivalent to provincial governor.[133] Hence, the third inscription can arguably be dated earlier than those of al-Hayyat and al-Burj. Al-Mundhir did not bear the *patrikios* title yet, but that of *megaloprepestatos comes*, inferior to the *endoxotatos* title held by his father and uncle.[134] George Bevan has claimed that al-Mundhir did not inherit his father's title after al-Ḥārith's death but instead underwent 'some form of preparation by which he was made a member of the sociopolitical hierarchy of the late Roman state'.[135] However, from a reading of the available sources, no preparation seems to have taken place. John Malalas states that 'in November Arethas the *patrikios* and *phylarch* of the Saracens, came to Byzantium, since he was obliged to report to the emperor which of his sons would obtain his phylarchy after his death',[136] and a similar depiction is found in Theophanes Confessor's chronicle for the year 563–4, weakening Bevan's thesis.[137]

All Jafnid inscriptions are written in Greek, often found near ecclesiastical buildings, and show standard Roman titles to describe the Jafnid rulers. Yet, the most significant Jafnid epigraphic source is a sixth-century graffito on an isolated stone from Jabal Says (Syria) composed in Arabic language and script. Written by the leader of the al-Aws tribe, it refers to the Jafnid leader al-Ḥārith as *malik*, usually translated in English as 'king'.

1. Me (.) Rqym, son of M'rf al-'Awsī
2. sent me al-Hrith the *mlk* on
3. Usays in garrison. The year
4. 423.[138]

[132] E.g., *Not. Dign.*
[133] Sartre, *Trois études*, 108–13.
[134] Bevan, Fisher and Genequand, 'The Late Antique Church', 63.
[135] Ibid.
[136] Malalas, *Chronicle*, 18.496.
[137] Theophane Confessor, *Chronicle*, 240.
[138] M. C. A. Macdonald, 'The Old Arabic Graffito at Jabal Usays: A New Reading of Line 1', in *The Development of Arabic as a Written Language*, ed. M. C. A. Macdonald (Oxford: Archaeopress, 2010), 141–3. For a different reading, see C. J. Robin and M. Gorea, 'Un réexamen de l'inscription Arabe préislamique du Ǧabal Usays (528–529 è. chr.)', *Arabica* 49 (2002), 503–10.

This inscription, dated 528–9, constitutes one of the earliest attestations of Arabic that we possess, pointing to the cultural importance of the Jafnids, at least in their Arabian context. Indeed, two other early attestations of epigraphic Arabic are connected to the area where the Jafnids had a predominant political role. The first is the trilingual inscription in the martyrion to St Sergius at Zabad (Syria), briefly mentioned in Chapters 1 and 4. In the Zabad inscription, the Arabic part is not a direct translation from the other languages (Greek and Syriac) but is a prayer written directly in Arabic.[139] The second is a martyrion inscription (Greek and Arabic) from Lejā in north-west Ḥawrān dated to 568–9.[140] The finding of the first Arabic inscriptions in areas dominated by the Jafnids (and by Christianity) could also suggest the existence of an administrative centre where the Nabatean script evolved into cursive to compose bureaucratic documents. The inscriptions of the Jafnids are often found in churches, and this may suggest a connection between the rise of Christianity in Arabia and the development of the Arabic script. The Jafnids, having first used Greek in their monumental inscription, could have later adopted the Arabian script of the most renowned North Arabian kingdom, that of the Nabateans. However, although the use of the Nabatean script signals an attempt to declare the independence of the Jafnids from Rome, the Jabal Says text is not a monumental inscription but a simple graffito, suggesting that Greek was the most established language of power among the western North Arabians.

It is interesting to note that the two single epigraphic attestations of pre-Islamic Arabian 'kings' (i.e., the graffito from Jabal Says and the epitaph of Imru' al-Qays) have been found in Roman contexts. In the Jabal Says inscription, Ḥārith's role is defined as *mlk*, a title also found in Syriac literary sources.[141] This appellation stimulates further reflections on the role of the Jafnids in Arabia and their relationship with the surrounding empires. Does *mlk* broadly indicate a 'ruler'? Or is it possible that the Jafnids referred to themselves as kings in Arabic when speaking to their 'own people' but preferred the humbler phylarch titles when using Greek? Divergences between multilingual inscriptions are not uncommon, as demonstrated by the epigraphic corpus of king ʿEzana of Aksūm and by Augustus' bilingual *Res Gestae* (Chapter 3),[142] and this may well be another case of this phenomenon. While a late third-century bilingual inscription

[139] Sachau, *MKPAWB* (1881), 169–90. See Robin, 'La réforme de l'écriture', 331.
[140] Dussaud and Macler, *NAMSL* 10 (1902), 726. See Robin, 'La réforme de l'écriture', 332–6.
[141] E.g., John of Ephesus, *Lives*, 50, 153.
[142] Cooley, *Res Gestae*, 26.

(Greek-Nabatean) from Umm al-Jimāl mentions a certain Gadhīmat as *mlk/basileus* of Tanūkh,[143] Ammianus Marcellinus names a 'phylarch of Assanite Saracens' as 'Malechus Podosacis',[144] a name probably deriving from the Arabic *mlk*. Accordingly, while the Roman allies did not rule over a well-defined region (with a well-defined seat), they held honorific titles that were probably perceived purely as *de iure* on the Roman side. These attributes were perceived as both *de iure* and *de facto* for the Arabians.

Procopius' historical accounts offer two further passages that clarify the title conferred to the Arabians by their allies. After stating that the Naṣrid al-Mundhir held the position of the king (*basileus*) over the Iranian 'Saracens', he mentions Ḥārith's role as follows:

> Neither any commander of Roman troops, whom they call *dukes* nor any leader (*hegumen*) of the Saracens allied with the Romans, called *phylarchoi,* was strong enough to fight Alamoundaras with his men, as the troops in the districts were not able to resist the enemy. Hence the king (*basileus*) Justinian put Arethas, the son of Gabalas, who ruled over the Saracens of Arabia, in command of many clans and bestowed upon him the dignity of king (*basileus*), a thing which among the Romans had never been done.[145]

A second passage states that Ḥārith's brother Abū Karīb was appointed as '*basileus phylarchos* over the Saracens in Palestine' by the Roman emperor, enabling him to rule over the coast beyond the boundaries of Palestine in Ḥijāz (Roman *Palestina Tertia*).[146] Abū Karīb further appears as a leader in one of the Petra papyri,[147] and in the already mentioned 548 diplomatic mission to Abraha next to Ḥārith.[148] Both al-Ḥārith and his brother are viewed as *basileus* by Procopius, who uses the lexeme to broadly indicate a man of high rank ruling over a land. It is reasonable to look for apologetic intentions in Procopius' passages, as the benevolent attitude of the Roman emperor towards the Arabian allies in naming al-Ḥārith as 'king' would have emphasized the supposed treason of Ḥārith. Nonetheless, a comparison with the Germanic titles allows for a categorical exclusion of such a hypothesis as Procopius also uses the title for the Vandals Ilderic.[149] Instead, the titulus *patrikios* was more specific, and a ceremony usually celebrated its

[143] F.038.02.
[144] Amm. Marc. 22.2.4.
[145] Procop. *Pers.*, 1.17.
[146] Ibid., 1.19.
[147] M. P. Kaimio, 'Petra inv. 83: A Settlement of a Dispute', *Atti del XXII congresso internazionale di papirologia. Firenze, 23–29 Agosto 1998* (2001), 719–24.
[148] CIH 541.
[149] Procop. *Pers.* 3.9.

conferment. Accordingly, John of Ephesus claims that when 'the illustrious Moundir' was honoured with the title of *patrikios* at the time of his visit to the capital,[150] he was received 'with great pomp and endless honours' and that the Roman emperor gave him royal gifts, letting him wear the royal crown and bestowing military titles on his sons.[151] John specifies that this was the first time an Arabian had received such an honour ('the right of wearing it had never been conceded before to any of the chiefs of the Arabs. They were only allowed to wear on their heads a simple circlet').[152]

Like material objects gifted in steppe empires in Inner Asia,[153] al-Mundhir's crown symbolized dependence and prestige and raised his public status in Arabia. While literary sources refer to him as *basileus*,[154] *phylarchos*[155] and *basiliskos*,[156] his sons are titled *endoxotatoi* in the inscription from al-Burj. A bronze plaque mentioning al-Mundhir's son al-Nuʿmān states: 'Nuʿmān *endoxotatos stratēlatēs* and *phylarchos*',[157] a title equivalent to the Latin *vir gloriosus*, which was the highest, yet very common, rank available for the Roman aristocracy at the time. Indeed, the ranks of *magnificentissimus* (Gr. *megaloprepestatos*), *gloriosissimus* (Gr. *endoxotatos*) and *famosissimus* (Gr. *paneuphemos*) introduced after Valentinian I's reforms (r. 364–75) made the titles of *clarissimus*, *illustris* and *spectabilis* the only available ones for employees of the emperor. The rank of *endoxotatos* was thus superior to that of *lamprotatos*, usually conferred on provincial phylarchs,[158] and attested in a mosaic floor from Nitl in Jordan ('[*lamprotatos*] Thaalaba the *phylarchos*').[159] Abū Kārib, although referred to as *basileus* by Procopius,[160] and as *malik* in the codex from Palmyra,[161] is also labelled *endoxotatos* in the already mentioned inscription from Sammāʾ,[162] possibly suggesting that the title was adopted to indicate those Jafnid members who were not the main leader of the dynasty (Table A.5).

150 John of Ephesus, *Ecclesiastical History*, 3.4.39–42.
151 Ibid.
152 Ibid., 3.4.42.
153 Kradin, 'Nomadic Empires in Inner Asia', 26.
154 Procop. *Pers.* 1.17 and 1.18.
155 IGLS 4.1550.
156 MaAr.
157 IGLS 4.1550.
158 A. S. Lewin, 'Did the Roman Empire Have a Military Strategy and Were the Jafnids Part of It?', in *Les Jafnides. Des rois arabes au service de byzance (vie siècle de l'ère chrétienne)*, ed. D. Genequand and C. J. Robin (Paris: Éditions De Boccard, 2015), 155–92, at p. 172.
159 Piccirillo 2001.
160 Procop. *Pers.* 1.19.
161 Millar, 'A Syriac Codex', 16.
162 IGLS 13/2.9843.

A transitional inscription from Eilat (Israel), datable to the late fifth century and written by a *mlk* by the name of Thaʿlaba, has been recently linked to the tribe of the Ghassān.[163] Moreover, the same publication mentions more than ten *Arabia Deserta mlk* reigning between the second and fifth centuries,[164] and ruling over tribes such as Qaḥṭān, Madhḥig and Kiddat.[165] The lack of mention of a tribe/territory for four Arabian *mlk* (in addition to Thaʿlaba) was attributed to the disappearance of 'kings ruling over a particular tribe' from the fourth century onwards due to the creation of Roman, Iranian and Ḥimyarite phylarchates.[166] Indeed, through the promotion of the Jafnids, the Roman emperors encouraged the creation of a unified North Arabian frontier. However, they still maintained a suspicious attitude towards their Arabian allies. For example, when the Romans were soundly defeated at Callinicum by the Sasanians, the Romans immediately attributed the failure to the betrayal of their Arab allies.[167] While Procopius claims that al-Ḥārith was the first to flee from battle, John Malalas states that he fought till the end, and the one who abandoned his army to escape by boat was the Roman Belisarius.[168] Shahid has made a case for preferring Malalas' over Procopius' account.[169] Geoffrey Greatrex later contested his position.[170] Still, Shahid's case appears more convincing when considering the broader political climate of the period, a time marked by political tension and double agents. This climate is also hinted at by Procopius in 550 when the capture of the Naṣrid al-Mundhir and the killing of one of the sons of the Jafnid leader ('from this, it was known that Arethas was not betraying the Romans to the Persians').[171]

The Romans' caution towards the Jafnids is further confirmed by the existence of other North Arabian sixth-century Roman allies. This scenario is in stark contrast with the narrative, which sees the Jafnids as the uncontested rulers of the region at the time. While the Arabic side of a bilingual inscription found on a lintel in the village of Lajā' (Ḥawrān) was written by a certain Sḥyl br ẓlmw, the Greek part of the inscription, dated 567 and commemorating a martyrion, is signed by a Saraelos Talemou *phylarch(os)*.[172] As Saraelos

163 Avner 2013.
164 Ibid.
165 Ja 635/26–27; Ja 576/2.
166 Avner, Nehmé and Robin, 'A Rock Inscription', 253.
167 Procop. *Pers.* 1.17; Malalas, *Chronicle*, 18.463–5.
168 Malalas, *Chronicle*, 18.465.
169 Shahid, *Byzantium and the Arabs in the Sixth Century*, 1.134–42.
170 G. Greatrex, *Rome and Persia at War, 502–532* (Leeds: Francis Cairns, 1998), 200–7.
171 Procop. *Pers.* 2.28.
172 For a recent study see Robin, 'La réforme de l'écriture', 332–6.

does not seem to have been a member of the Jafnid dynasty, there may have been more than one *phylarchos* in 567 North Arabia. Although in the early years of Justinian's reign, the Roman administration of the Arabian groups in charge of North Arabia became more complex, and the Roman authorities officially recognized several men as phylarchs,[173] Justinian did not feel comfortable enough to promote al-Ḥārith to the point where no other leader could compete with him.[174] His *Novellae*, issued after the promulgation of Justinian's Code in 534 and thus after Ḥārith's elevation as 'supreme phylarch' in 529, shed further light on the interactions between Romans and Arabians in the sixth century. One of these documents concerns Roman Arabia and states that the governor should not permit 'the prestigious duke or the *phylarchos*' to inflict any damage.[175] The explicit subordination of the *phylarchos* to the Roman governor points to the fact that Ḥārith's titles were indeed only honorary. The Roman emperor granted him the 'dignity of a king', as the Sasanians had done with the Naṣrid counterpart, but nothing substantial changed in the relationship between Arabians and allies. Significantly, Jafnid leaders could never fill the position of *magister militum per Orientem*, the actual figure in command of the Eastern Roman arm. Al-Ḥārith's social climbing stopped after holding the positions of *stratelatos*, *comes*, *endoxotatos* and *patrikios*. His son, al-Mundhir, managed to rise one step further, becoming *paneuphemos*, while his grandson was *endoxotatos*, *phylarchos* and *stratelatos*. However, although Justinian bestowed Roman titles on the Arabian leaders, he did not grant them the title of *magister militum*, a role in part similar to that of the 'Inspecting Commandant who Protects the Wuhuan', the Han supervisor of the Wuhuan at the dawn of the first millennium.[176]

On the one hand, Ḥārith's ruling title was conceived by the Romans as being merely symbolic. Still, on the other, far away from Constantinople, it probably served to gain respect and prestige in the Arabian Peninsula. Hence, the literary representations of groups such as the Jafnids and Naṣrids found in 'external sources' need to be contextualized with their author's personal bias and sympathies. Accordingly, the description of al-Ḥārith as 'king' may have overestimated his influence, while conversely, most of the Greek-written sources downgraded him and his role. His name, mentioned together with Khosrow, Justinian and Abraha among the 'kings who are

[173] Lewin, 'Did the Roman Empire Have a Military Strategy?', 174.

[174] G. Greatrex, 'Les Jafnides et la défense de l'empire au vie siècle', in *Les Jafnides: Des rois arabes au service de Byzance (vie siècle de l'ère chrétienne)*, ed. D. Genequand and C. J. Robin (Paris: École française de Rome, 2015), 121–54, at p. 140.

[175] *Nov. Just.* 102.1.

[176] Lewis, *The Early Chinese Empires*, 150.

famous', can be explained by a possible Miaphysite origin of the passage by Pseudo-Dionysius.[177] Indeed, the Jafnids' inscriptions were subordinated to kings' propaganda and tended to overstate their power. And although they probably sponsored the construction of the religious buildings beautifully ornamented with mosaics found in their areas of jurisdiction, they were not the only Arabian family involved in construction in areas of significant Roman settlement,[178] and there is no distinguishable 'Jafnid architecture'.[179] Al-Iṣfahānī's list of Jafnid rulers and their construction is partially unreliable due to its mention of 32 rulers over 616 years and most of the buildings' wrong dating.[180] However, even though scholarship on Jafnid material culture is nowadays conceived as an 'eminently speculative exercise',[181] a list of sites was associated with the Jafnids thanks to the finding of inscriptions mentioning them in situ (i.e., the already mentioned inscriptions from Jordan at Nitl and Tall al-ʿUmayrī, and from Syria at Ruṣāfah, al-Burj, Hayyāt, Jabal Says, Qaṣr al-Ḥayr al-Gharbī, al-Gharbi and Sammāʾ). At least four of these sites possess churches or monasteries (Nitl and Tall al-ʿUmayrī in Jordan, and Ruṣāfah, Burj and Qaṣr al-Ḥayr al-Gharbī in Syria). Ruṣāfah,[182] found in Euphratesia along the line of the 200 mm isohyet, is the most important of these sites.

Mentioned in the second-century map of Ptolemy,[183] and later in the fourth-century *Notitia Dignitatum*,[184] Ruṣāfah became an important religious site for the inhabitants of the Near East affiliated with Rome during Late Antiquity as the place of the supposed burial of Sergius, a military officer who suffered martyrdom after refusing to renounce Christianity. The cult of Sergius, shared by both Miaphysites and Dyophysites, became widely renowned in the sixth century, and Ruṣāfah became a prominent shrine for pilgrims, as witnessed by the description of an anonymous Latin traveller from Piacenza.[185] The Jafnids were closely associated with the cult, centred in the Syrian steppe,[186] where seasonal migration, trade, warfare and pilgrimage

177 *Chronicle of Zuqnīn*, 110.
178 Fisher, *Between Empires*, 105.
179 Genequand, 'Some Thoughts', 80–1.
180 Al-Iṣfahānī, *Taʾrīkh*, 117–21. See H. Munt, 'Arabic and Persian Sources for pre-Islamic Arabia', in *Arabs and Empires*, ed. G. Fisher (Oxford: Oxford University Press, 2015), 434–500, at p. 471.
181 D. Genequand, 'The Archaeological Evidence for the Jafnids and the Naṣrids', in *Arabs and Empires*, ed. G. Fisher (Oxford: Oxford University Press, 2015), 172–213, at p. 175.
182 Also known as Sergiopolis.
183 Ptol. *Geog.* 5.15.
184 *Not. Dign.* 33.27.
185 *Piacenza Pilgrim.*
186 Procop. *Pers*, 2.5.2.

had given prominence to points of convergence around water sources.[187] While soldiers, pastoralists, farmers and traders found a socio-economic 'focal point' in the centre,[188] Ruṣāfah was also an important display of the Jafnids' power, as exemplified by al-Mundhir's on-site meeting with the patrician Justinian.[189] An isolated basilica north of the city, known as the 'Mundhir building' due to an inscription in situ,[190] was probably also used as an audience hall,[191] as secular and religious symbolism was often merged in late antique religious structures.[192] In the building, the depiction of an eagle visually emphasized the phylarch's temporal and heavenly authority.[193] As suggested by Pliny the Elder, the eagle was a known Roman symbol of power.[194] In sixth-century North Arabia, Jafnids appropriated the symbol to strengthen their connection to Rome through their iconography of power. There was no 'intrinsic attractiveness of the Roman way of life seen through the eyes of the indigenous population'.[195] 'Romaness' (i.e., 'Roman culture'), in all its forms and expressions, was a simple means to an end.

Comparing and contrasting the Arabians with their counterparts in the West and the East can further elucidate these people's identity and their role in the broader late antique political map. Points of contact between the allies of West and East are evident. For example, the title *Flavius* was shared by the Lombard ruler Authari (584–90),[196] as well as by the Jafnid al-Ḥārith and al-Mundhir. Throughout the first millennium, widespread instruments of diplomacy and control commonly involved Rome's and Iran's granting of titles to the 'barbarians' with grandiose ceremonies.[197] Hence, similar to the Germanic leaders of Late Antiquity, the Naṣrids and Jafnids advanced their

[187] Fowden, *Barbarian Plain*, 3.

[188] E. Fowden, 'Shrines and Banners: Paleo-Muslims and Their Material Inheritance', in *Beiträge zur Islamischen Kunst und Archäologie: Band 6*, ed. L. Korn and Ç. İvren (Wiesbaden: Dr. Ludwig Reichert, 2020), 5–24, at p. 11.

[189] John of Ephesus, *Ecclesiastical History*, 3.

[190] The lower band of the moulding over the apse window bears a Greek inscription: 'The fortune of Alamoundaros triumphs' (Wadd. 2110.79; SEG 7.188). A similar formula, common in the eastern provinces and widely attested from the fifth to the seventh centuries, has been found on a column in the north gate of the same site of Ruṣāfah ('The faith of the Christians triumphs', SEG 41 (1991) 1531d.).

[191] J. Sauvaget, 'Les Ghassanides et Sergiopolis', *Byzantion* 14 (1939), 115–30.

[192] E. Fowden, 'An Arab Building at Rusafa-Sergiopolis', *Damaszener Mitteilungen* 12 (2000), 303–24.

[193] Fowden, *Barbarian Plain*, 155. See most recently Thilo Ulbert, *Forschungen in Resafa-Sergiupolis* (Berlin: De Gruyter, 2016).

[194] Plin. *HN.* 10.5.

[195] R. MacMullen, *Romanization in the Time of Augustus* (New Haven: Yale University Press, 2000), 134.

[196] Paulus Diaconus, *Historia longobardorum*, 3.16.

[197] E. Nechaeva, 'Patterns of Roman Diplomacy with Iran and the Steppe Peoples', in *Empires and Exchanges in Eurasian Late Antiquity: Rome, China, Iran, and the Steppe, ca. 250–750*, ed. N. Di Cosmo and M. Maas (Cambridge: Cambridge University Press, 2018), 357–68, at p. 358.

position and gained wealth by taking advantage of the wars between Rome and Iran while owing their power (and symbols of rulership) to the patronage of their allied superpowers. And, as the Romans eliminated the Germanic leaders hoping to absorb their ranks into an army under their direct control, they did likewise with their Eastern allies. At the same time, the Germanic and Jafnid experiences diverged in various aspects. The Germanic rulers became allies after settling in areas that Rome had historically dominated. In contrast to the Germans, who successfully broke the Roman yoke and built their own governmental and legislative social structure, the Jafnids never set up a political organization due to Rome's more powerful position in the Middle East throughout the late antique period. In the East, client kingdoms were sometimes incorporated into the empire, becoming provinces of the Roman Empire, as in the case of Armenia. This did not happen in North Arabia, which unified instead under a third party, a phylarch. This was due to Rome's desire to emulate the success of the Naṣrids' political system, whereby a military governor called *marzpān* (lit. *marz* 'frontier' and *-pān* 'guardian'), attested from the Achaemenid period, ruled for the *Shahanshah*, the Iranian King of Kings. The Jafnids also differed from the Germanic leaders through the existence of an increasingly independent Miaphysite Church that provided 'literate clergy' and 'radical political thought'.[198] Although it is unclear how many of the clergy were literate,[199] the development of a Miaphysite identity shaped and gave cultural prominence and independence to the Jafnids during the sixth century. Finally, while most of those groups labelled by the Romans as 'barbarians' had little or no individual identity at all',[200] this is not the case of the Jafnid leaders, who were well identified and better known than the groups they belonged to.

Another significant parallel case to that of the Jafnid kingdom is provided by the Türks, as both dynasties appropriated the symbols of legitimacy belonging to their surrounding empires for representational purposes. The Türkic Bugut stela, dated to 584 and found in the Ikh-Tamir district of Arkhangai Province (Mongolia), also attests to the 'appropriation' and 'adaptation' by the ruling Turkish elite of Chinese symbols of legitimacy found in high officials' steles since the Eastern Han period.[201] The stela

198 Wood, *We Have No King*, 245.

199 Tannous, *Making of the Medieval Middle East*, 11–46.

200 R. W. Mathisen, 'Catalogues of Barbarians in Late Antiquity', in *Romans, Barbarians, and the Transformation of the Roman World*, ed. R. W. Mathisen and D. Shanzerpp (Farnham: Ashgate, 2011), 17–32, at p. 18.

201 D. C. Wong, *Chinese Steles: Pre-Buddhist and Buddhist Use of a Symbolic Form* (Honolulu: University of Hawai'i Press, 2004), 27.

displays the typical Chinese iconographies while bearing two inscriptions in the Sogdian and Brahmi scripts. Their use emphasizes the 'Turk's claim to imperial status',[202] while assimilating to and distancing themselves from the Chinese. Even in the site of Khöshöö Tsaidam (Mongolia), inhabited by the late Ashinas-Türk rebels against China, there is a vast display of Chinese craftsmanship exploited as a symbol of power.[203] Moreover, while Iranian influences are found in the Xiao Hongnahai memorial (Xinjiang, China), Sogdian, Iranian and Roman iconographies are attested in western Turkic copper coins from Chăch in modern Uzbekistan.[204]

Sandwiched between China and Iran, the Türks merged different worlds, giving rise to a largely emulative and, at the same time, creative propaganda designed for their multiethnic subjects. While external forces granted them titles, they also claimed titles as symbols of power for themselves. Similarly, the Jafnids adopted and adapted Rome's language of power to make it their own and adhered to a Miaphysitism instead of the Chalcedonian creed. Furthermore, the Jafnids' inscriptions and buildings gave the same 'appearance of legitimacy', which has been attributed to the Huns by the supply of Sasanian coins with their heraldry, enabling them to retain the nomads' military services and collect taxes from their subordinated settled peoples.[205] More similarities with other first-millennium political entities can be made. At the end of the sixth century, the Chinese established a buffer zone coinciding with the Eastern Türkic Empire.[206] The inhabitants of this zone later took advantage of the internal crisis in China, achieving unprecedented power under Shibi Khan (r. 609–19) and proving unsuccessful China's use of the northern Ordos zone 'to settle nomadic allies'.[207] Similarly, Rome and Iran held off the belligerent northern Arabians by employing (some of) them to patrol their frontiers. Nonetheless, both empires removed their Arabian allies from their position at the end of the sixth century, thus creating a power vacuum in the region, which Muḥammad's followers later filled. In fact, by erasing the

202 S. Stark, 'Aspects of Elite Representation among the Sixth- and Seventh-Century Türks', in *Empires and Exchanges in Eurasian Late Antiquity: Rome, China, Iran, and the Steppe, ca. 250–750*, ed. N. Di Cosmo and M. Maas (Cambridge: Cambridge University Press, 2018), 333–56, at p. 344.

203 Stark, 'Luxurious Necessities', 492.

204 Stark, 'Aspects of Elite Representation', 344–50.

205 Bonner, *Last Empire of Iran*, 100.

206 E. De la Vaissière, 'Away from the Ötüken: A Geopolitical Approach to the Seventh Century Eastern Türks', in *Complexity of Interaction along the Eurasian Steppe Zone in the First Millennium CE*, ed. J. Bemmann and M. Schmauder (Bonn: Rheinische Friedrich-Wilhems Universität, 2015), 453–62, at p. 457.

207 Ibid.

Arabians from the political map of Late Antiquity, the superpowers of the period (including Aksūm) unintentionally created a more powerful rival in the region.

Dynasties such as the Jafnids and the Naṣrids needed the empires' support to gain prominence in Arabia among other local tribes and among the Ḥimyarites who were similarly interested in controlling Central Arabia and the caravan routes. Parallels can be drawn with the relationship between steppe nomad groups and sedentary empires in the region 'between the Chinese Wall and the Great Hungarian Plain'.[208] Both sides, the steppe tribes on the one hand and the empires on the other, dealt with the other with suspicious apprehension, and the relationship soon turned into a *Konfliktbeziehung* (conflictual relation).[209] A similar pattern can be seen in the interactions between the North Arabians and surrounding empires, explaining the general climate of apprehension and mistrust. The Romans were more sceptical than the Iranians, having made multiple alliances with the Arabians and dealt with numerous riots in the past (Chapter 2). However, the 'surge of imperialist ambition',[210] which took place in the sixth century, underlined both empires' need to collaborate with allied Arabians.

On the one hand, Iran felt vulnerable vis-à-vis Rome and desired to protect Mesopotamia, its economic powerhouse, from Rome, while Rome felt an equally pressing need to protect Syria from Iran. Nonetheless, although the involvement of Rome and Iran indeed had significant repercussions, the two main groups in the landscape of sixth-century Arabia remained largely independent throughout this period, in combat with each other without having to seek the approval of their respective allied empires. They also made the most of their positions as Roman/Iranian allies to maintain and extend their local consensus. Thus, not so differently from fortified settlements, inscriptions became symbols of power throughout the first millennium, and the interaction with foreign forces affected the self-representation and the 'royal' propaganda of the Arabians. In a similar fashion to the policies of the elites of the steppe in the sixth to ninth centuries, the policy of the Arabians was the adaptation and spread of narratives and iconographies.

208 T. Stickler, 'The Gupta Empire in the Face of the Hunnic Threat: Parallels to the Late Roman Empire?', in *Complexity of Interaction along the Eurasian Steppe Zone in the First Millennium* CE, ed. J. Bemmann and M. Schmauder (Bonn: Rheinische Friedrich-Wilhems Universität, 2015), 659–70, at p. 659.

209 Ibid.

210 G. W. Bowersock, *Empires in Collision in Late Antiquity* (Waltham: Brandeis University Press, 2012), 6.

According to a model based on dynamics in East Asia, nomadic groups developed an imperial organization due to contact with organized agricultural-urban societies. These contacts resulted in the nomadic groups deciding to emulate such organizational systems to achieve the same socio-economic position.[211] This model indicates a solid statistical regularity between a location near a steppe frontier and 'frequency of imperiogenesis',[212] and emphasizes the reciprocity of social interactions. In contrast with biased Western narratives, which depict nomads and 'exotic' dynasties as 'barbarians', the interaction between Arabians and empires was bidirectional, more or less equally affecting both entities, similar to the 'feed-back loops' between East Asian steppe confederations and empires.[213] These considerations thus call for an urgent reassessment of the terminology when speaking about the Arabian allies as a whole. Was al-Ḥārith the ruler of a well-structured kingdom, or was he ruling over Arabian 'tribes'? According to Chris Wickham, a 'state' is defined by five main criteria: (1) authority centralization (justice and the army); (2) governmental hierarchy; (3) a concept of public power; (4) independent and stable resources for rulers; and (5) a class-based system of surplus-extraction and stratification.[214] As far as we know, none of these criteria applies to the sixth-century Jafnid and Naṣrid kingdoms, and thus they cannot be conceived as 'states'. Therefore, perhaps a more neutral word is preferable to indicate these realities in sixth-century North Arabia. I would suggest that 'federations', a lexeme less connoted than 'kingdom', not as modern as 'state' and less biased than 'tribal structure', could serve well for this purpose.

At least as far back as the Ruwāfa inscription (Chapter 1), 'confederations' were present in the Arabian Peninsula. Among these groups, the Jafnids were neither outside nor inside the Roman Empire, always remaining 'in-between'.[215] It is difficult to ascertain the degree to which the establishment of the allied rulers of Arabia was a consequence of the political map of Late Antiquity and to assess what the influence of Rome and Iran was in shaping the sixth-century Arabian Peninsula. It is equally complicated to determine how influential Jafnids and Naṣrids were in developing Arab identity and language. Nonetheless, it is plausible that the politics and culture of these groups had profound repercussions on the fragile

211 P. Turchin, 'A Theory for Formation of Large Empires', *Journal of Global History* 4 (2009), 191–217.
212 Ibid.
213 Ibid., 199.
214 C. Wickham, *Framing the Early Middle Ages: Europe and the Mediterranean, 400–800* (Oxford: Oxford University Press, 2005), 303.
215 Fisher, *Between Empires*, 12.

political equilibrium of Late Antiquity, contributing to the ideological ferment that led to the rise of a unified Arabian kingdom. Significantly, Jafnid cultural choices were more dependent on Rome than on neighbouring Ḥimyar and Aksūm. Still, we are not in front of a form of indirect formal rule.[216] Arabia is one peninsula today, but Central Arabia was perceived as a political and cultural barrier in the first millennium, a barrier that could only be overcome from inner Ḥijāz. However, as pointed out for the Türkic regions, the lack of 'large structures, impressive cities, and major literary accomplishments' should not mislead scholars into thinking of these areas as '"insubstantial" or "empty"'.[217] North Arabia was neither desert nor at the mercy of its neighbouring powers. Although unity was not achieved in Arabia before Islam, fragmentation mainly resulted from internal antagonism and not external pressures.

5.4 Final Remarks

Rome and Iran long aimed to control Arabia directly. However, in the sixth century, both empires were occupied with defending other sensitive areas (e.g., the Sasanians against the Hephthalites and the Romans against the Germans) and chose to rely on the Arabians' help to control their frontiers. The consequent exploitation of warfare led to various advantages for the two superpowers. Still, the reorganization of both sides' borders also had beneficial repercussions for the Arabians, leading to career advancement for some Arabian allies. According to Mark Whittow, the critical factor of the latter's success was their position in a zone of 'aristocratic land purchase and investment'.[218] They did not possess an 'irreducible ethnic resistance to Rome', but their presence in an area with an economic upturn with different characteristics from the Armenian frontier or the lands of Huns and Goths made them dangerous competitors for the Romans to have in Late Antiquity.[219] Whittow is right in underlining the importance of the strategic location of the Jafnids' seat. However, his claim that the Jafnids were distinct from their peers and rivals because they could 'play up their Arab identity and draw on Bedouin support' cannot

[216] Governance 'entrusted to members of the native elite under the supervision of imperial governors'. M. W. Doyle, *Empires* (Ithaca, NY: Cornell University Press, 1986), 38.

[217] M. R. Drompp, 'Infrastructures of Legitimacy in Inner Asia: The Early Türk Empires', in *Empires and Exchanges in Eurasian Late Antiquity: Rome, China, Iran, and the Steppe, ca. 250–750*, ed. N. Di Cosmo and M. Maas (Cambridge: Cambridge University Press, 2018), 302–16, at p. 316.

[218] Whittow, 'Rethinking the Jafnids', 29.

[219] Ibid.

be fully supported as there was no communal Arab consciousness in pre-Islamic times.[220] Conversely, the skirmishes on the Arabian borders of the sixth century must be contextualized and interpreted as the internal and external tensions in the Arabian Peninsula. In a similar fashion to Rome and Iran, the Arabians exploited their alliances with the colossi of Late Antiquity to do away with their enemies, as well testified by the disappearance of Central Arabian dynasties after the signing of the Roman–Jafnid alliance. Accordingly, we should not conceive of the tensions between Jafnids and Naṣrids as a microcosm of the war between Rome and Iran but as a characteristic Arabian phenomenon.

The sixth-century outbreak of hostilities concurred with high 'levels of investment' in Rome's desert frontier and significant levels of urban development, not experienced again until the twentieth century.[221] A peak of economic growth and an increase in settled population was registered in the northern parts of the Arabian Peninsula at the beginning of the sixth century, as evidenced by the sixth-century Greek papyri from Petra, which describe farms owned by wealthy landlords.[222] In this period, families in southern Syrian rural villages became more prominently associated with monasteries, the main cultural and economic centres of the Arabian Peninsula. Churches (especially martyria) and monasteries extended their importance as social nodes in the sixth century. The explosion of church building was a symptom of new ways devised by families and clans to invest surplus money derived from the export of agricultural goods. In the steppe, an intensification of agricultural settlement policy contributed to the political security offered by the Jafnids on the caravan trade routes. At the same time, it provided the economic growth necessary for the emergence of developed political governance. The centre of Ruṣāfah is an excellent example of such social dynamics behind the making of a 'religious node' in the Arabian Peninsula and a witness to the economic prosperity linked to an increase in the construction of ecclesiastical buildings.

According to Procopius, Justinian surrounded a church in Ruṣāfah with a wall, stored up water, provided the city with supplies and established a garrison of soldiers there,[223] later erecting a church for Sergius in Constantinople.[224] The frontier zone cult of Sergius in Ruṣāfah allowed

220 Ibid., 26.
221 Ibid., 25.
222 S. T. Parker, 'An Empire's New Holy Land: The Byzantine Period', *Near Eastern Archaeology* 62 (1999), 134–180, at p. 142.
223 Procop. *Aed.* 2.9.
224 CIG 4.8639.

Justinian to have control of the loyalty of Arabian allies while at the same time allowing him to monitor the pilgrimage of the anti-Chalcedonians. This solved two of his most pressing preoccupations: the reconciliation between Chalcedonians and their opponents and the security of the eastern frontier.[225] The cult of Sergius was also widespread in Iran, though the Sasanian rulers' treatment of the cult was eclectic. When, in 540, Khosrow I took Sura on the Euphrates, Candidus, bishop of Ruṣāfah, was offered the opportunity by the Iranian ruler to ransom 12,000 captives in exchange for 200 pounds of gold.[226] Candidus failed to obtain the sum and proposed to Khosrow to empty the treasury of Ruṣāfah's shrine instead,[227] including the gold cross dedicated to Sergius by Justinian and Theodora.[228] Khosrow nonetheless besieged the city, which was only saved later by an Arabian Christian named Ambrus.[229] According to the *Life of Aḥudemmeh*, Khosrow imprisoned the Syrian Orthodox (Miaphysite) Metropolitan of the East Aḥudemmeh (d. 575),[230] who had tried to divert attention away from the shrine of Ruṣāfah by building a church in his seat at Bēth ʿArbāyē (sixty miles north-west to Mosul).[231] The city assumed instead an essential role under Khosrow II, who chose the Christian Roman military commander at Ruṣāfah Abū Jafna ibn al-Mundhir as his mediator with Maurice,[232] and prayed to Sergius for having a child with his wife Shirin, sending to his shrine a golden cross with a Greek inscription.[233] The Sasanians had by then understood the attraction of controlling Christianity and its value as a political tool. Hence, in a similar fashion to Theodora, Shirin became involved in sponsoring the non-Chalcedonians. And just as Justinian did, Khosrow II maintained an ambiguous relationship with the Miaphysites, letting his wife offer them glimmers of toleration.

Broader late antique patterns, such as the integration of tribal identities through the establishment of churches and monasteries, are also attested among Jafnids and Naṣrids.[234] Even though Christianity had become a Roman imperial phenomenon by the time of Justin, three out of the four

225 Fowden, *Barbarian Plain*, 133.
226 Procop. *Pers.* 2.5.
227 Ibid., 2.20.
228 Evagrius, *Ecclesiastical History*, 5.28.
229 Procop. *Pers.* 2.20.
230 *Aḥudemmeh*, 5–8.
231 Ibid., 4.
232 Michael the Syrian, *Chronicle*, 10.23; *Chronicle of 1234*, 90.
233 Evagrius, *Ecclesiastical History*, 6.21; Theophylact Simocatta, *History*, 5.14.
234 G. Fisher, P. Wood, et al., 'Arabs and Christianity', in *Arabs and Empires*, ed. G. Fisher (Oxford: Oxford University Press, 2015), 276–372, at p. 372.

main Christian movements of Late Antiquity, Arianism, Miaphysitism and East Syrian Christianity were more tolerated in Iran than in Rome. This interplay between politics and religion is visible in the Arabian Peninsula, as in the wider late antique map. On the one hand, the Jafnids relied on the support of the Roman emperors, who aimed to monitor the empire's border by creating an alliance strong enough to counterbalance Iranian power in the region and the increasing Aksūmite presence. On the other hand, the Jafnids had the support of the Miaphysite Commonwealth, which was becoming particularly strong in the Red Sea thanks to the preaching of exiled missionaries (Chapter 4). It may well be no coincidence that Miaphysite Aksūm expanded its influence in Arabia during the Jafnids' Golden Age. It is perhaps of equal significance that the Jafnids disappeared from the political map of Arabia roughly at the same time as the collapse in the south of the peninsula, where the Iranians gained power in around the 570s. The elimination of the Naṣrid seat possibly took place in the same political framework as the Naṣrids were no longer of political use to the Iranian rulers, who now had direct control of the Arabian routes and were no longer in competition with Rome for hegemony in the area. The Jafnids and the Naṣrids disappear at the time of one of the most impactful wars between Rome and Iran. The war plausibly played a role in their ultimate collapse. As the unification of China had led to the creation of the nomadic empires and China's dissolution had caused their descent,[235] the Jafnids and the Naṣrids' faiths were ultimately bounded to Rome and Iran.

Past scholarship conceived Arabia at the end of Late Antiquity as a 'centre of religious competition'.[236] Despite the Iranian-sponsored East Syrian component in eastern Arabia and its islands and sporadic Jewish communities, the extreme north and south of the Arabian Peninsula were dominated by Miaphysite Christianity at the dawn of Islam. The Jafnid federation and the Christian kingdom of Ḥimyar concurrently advanced the spread of Miaphysitism in sixth-century Arabia on the wave of a 'second Christianisation' likely involving a vast portion of the late antique world (Chapter 4). In this regard, I would contest Shahid's view that Miaphysitism came to Najrān through the Jafnids.[237] A plausible explanation could be that Miaphysitism migrated from South Arabia with the Jafnids after reaching the southern part of the Arabian Peninsula through the same Syrian

[235] A. Bell-Fialkoff, *The Role of Migration in the History of the Eurasian Steppe: Sedentary Civilization vs. 'Barbarian' and Nomad* (New York: Palgrave Macmillan 2000), 4.

[236] J. P. Berkey, *The Formation of Islam: Religion and Society in the Near East, 600–1800* (Cambridge: Cambridge University Press, 2002), 45.

[237] Shahid, *Byzantium and the Arabs in the Fifth Century*, 373.

missionary expeditions that started a Christian revival in Aksūm. Thereafter, Christian impulses made their way into Ḥijāz from both the northern Jafnid seat and the southern kingdom of Ḥimyar. Justin's persecution of Christian monks and their consequent flight from the empire expanded the Christians' preaching into the unexplored and inaccessible areas of the Arabian Peninsula, as reported in Pseudo-Zachariah's claim that the desert was 'supplied with a population of believers' in this period.[238] At the same time, the Ḥijāzī commercial routes were another possible vehicle for the spread of Christianity. It is a recurrent topos for hagiographies and histories to ascribe the evangelization of a region to the arrival of a lone itinerant figure who abruptly converted its entire population. However, this trend was the cumulative result of socio-economic networks and migrations, as the exchange of ideas followed that of resources. Accordingly, slavery probably played a more prominent role in the spreading of Christianity than the activity of a visionary monk in the Arabian desert (even the adopted son of Muḥammad was a Christian enslaved man).[239]

Overall, it is inconceivable to depict 'the Arab world during the first six centuries AD' as 'dormant', as argued by Trimingham.[240] It is equally unconvincing to see the Arabians as untouched or unaffected by the surrounding religious and political conflicts.[241] Trimingham claimed that Christianity did not reach the nomad Arabians as 'the nomad quite simply does not need religion'.[242] Although it is outside the scope of this monograph to illustrate the reasons behind the adoption of a particular faith, it is essential to stress the pragmatic gap that religion filled in pre-Islamic Arabia, namely, that caused by the lack of a unitarian political structure and an apparent Arab ethnicity, as well exemplified by the attestation of a wide array of languages in the region throughout Late Antiquity. As elsewhere, the clever use of 'religion' surmounted division in clans and dynasties. Christianization thus strengthened political partnerships during the sixth century both in the Germanic West and in the Arabian East. There is continuity from this perspective; Miaphysitism spread among the Arabians allied with Rome, while East Syrian Christianity spread in Iran. However, a series of significant changes took place in the sixth century.

238 Pseudo-Zacharia, *Ecclesiastical History*, 8.81.

239 Ibn Isḥāq, *Sīrah*, 160; al-Ṭabarī, *Tārikh*, 1.1168. On slavery in pre-Islamic Arabia, see V. A. Grasso, "Slavery in pre-Islamic Arabia as Reconstructed from the Epigraphic Corpora" (forthcoming, presented in 2022 at the QaSLA Project Conference – Epigraphy, the Qur'ān, and the Religious Landscape of Arabia).

240 Trimingham, *Christianity among the Arabs*, 308.

241 Ibid.

242 Ibid., 309.

First, the rural provinces assumed a role of prominence and synods were now held in village monasteries. From a certain point of view, sites such as Ruṣāfah had a more prominent role than Antioch. The hall and the churches that al-Mundhir built in Ruṣāfah attest the prominence of the site and its strategic position in a sensitive zone. Second, a general increase in missionary expeditions was registered in the sixth century. This is well testified by the expansion of Christianity in Aksūm, Arabia and Georgia, which was primarily due to the efforts of persecuted Miaphysites.

After Constantine, Roman emperors and neighbouring kings became prominent 'religious mediators', though they were never ordained. The religious milieu of pre-Islamic Arabia was similarly heavily politicized. The powerful dynasties emerging in the north in the sixth century had strong ties with the spiritual life of their subjects. This significantly contributed to the spread of Miaphysitism in rural areas where the grip of the Chalcedonians was less firm. Although Christianity quickly spread in Arabia, it was only through the indigenous experiment of Islam that an Arab consciousness was achieved. In the same way that Jafnids and Naṣrids remained 'outsiders' in the eyes of their allied kingdom, so too did the Romans and the Iranians with their long-established hierarchies and cults in the eyes of the Arabians. Accordingly, Islam partly emerged in response to the rise of aristocracies sponsored by foreign powers.

Fergus Millar has claimed that the Jafnids' control of a whole region was a fantasy.[243] Others, like Irfan Shahid, have argued that they were a 'principal pillar in the Byzantine defence system in Oriens'.[244] I believe that both the Jafnids and Naṣrids played a significant role, being especially essential for maintaining order in areas that were otherwise inaccessible. However, their role was primarily relevant in their indigenous Arabian federations, which became the first breeding ground to exert power and control as well as successful political propaganda in North Arabia. Michael Drompp has recently pointed out a series of 'strategies of cohesion and control' employed by rulers of the Türk and Uyghur empires revolving around the enhancement of military structure, diplomacy, trade, the close connections between ruling elites and subject peoples, exploitation of language and the use of other symbols of power.[245] All these expedients can also be traced in the propaganda of southern (Ḥimyar) and northern (Jafnids) Arabians.

243 Millar, 'Christian Monasticism', 107.

244 Shahid, *Byzantium and the Arabs in the Sixth Century*, 1.646.

245 M. R. Drompp, 'Strategies of Cohesion and Control in the Türk and Uyghur Empires', in *Complexity of Interaction along the Eurasian Steppe Zone in the First Millennium* CE, ed. J. Bemmann and M. Schmauder (Bonn: Rheinische Friedrich-Wilhems Universität, 2015), 437–52, at p. 447.

Studies comparing pre-Islamic Arabian groups with surrounding empireless people are still in their infancy. Works comparing pre-Islamic Arabian dynasties with each other have focused on Jafnids and Naṣrids. Still, a comparison between northerners and southerners can offer some valuable insights into Arabian kinship mechanisms at the rise of Islam. In a similar fashion to literary sources concerning the Türk and Uyghur empires, the Ḥimyarite inscriptions attest: (1) the existence of a strong army able to carry out raids in Central Arabia; (2) diplomatic embassies with Rome, Iran and North Arabians; (3) a prominent role in trading operations in the Red Sea and the Persian Gulf; and (4) a clever adherence to monotheism to unify its population (Chapter 4). Similarly, the Jafnids: (1) led a powerful army that repeatedly engaged in war with Iran; (2) had an alliance with Rome and held a series of strategic locations where their power was emphasized by inscriptions in Greek and Roman-inspired buildings; (3) had a role in the caravan trade routes and as protectors of the pilgrimage connected to St Sergius; and (4) exploited Miaphysite patronage to tighten the relationship with their subjects who were instructed in Christianity by a clergy independent from Rome.[246] The Old Arabic graffito defining the Jafnid ruler as king testifies to the Jafnids' use of propaganda, echoed centuries later in al-Iṣfahānī's (d. 967) work referring to the Jafnids as 'kings of the Arabians' (*mulūk ʿarab al-shām*) allied with Rome over Syria.[247]

As pointed out by Bryan Miller when discussing the southern Xiongnu in northern China, it is more helpful to 'speak of degrees of participation, rather than integration',[248] and of 'mediations between cultures by interceding individuals' rather than of 'transformations of whole groups or cultures'.[249] The Western non-Roman and the Eastern non-Chinese 'barbarians' needed centuries to establish their reigns and managed to do so only after the fall of Rome and the Xiongnu and Han empires.[250] Similarly, the Arabian tribes internally unified from the centre to fight their external enemies only after the fall of the Ḥimyarites in the second half of the sixth century, the subsequent Iranian invasion of South Arabia and the collapse

[246] We do not possess Naṣrid direct testimonies.

[247] Al-Iṣfahānī, *Aghānī*, I.114–115.

[248] B. K. Miller, 'The Southern Xiongnu in Northern China: Navigating and Negotiating the Middle Ground', in *Complexity of Interaction along the Eurasian Steppe Zone in the First Millennium* CE, ed. J. Bemmann and M. Schmauder (Bonn: Rheinische Friedrich-Wilhems Universität, 2015), 127–98, at p. 162.

[249] Ibid., 186.

[250] Ibid., 186.

of Jafnids and Naṣrids. The pre-Islamic Arabians interacted with various political entities. While moving objects, they also moved between social statuses. Their disappearance was necessary to create a more robust political polity in the first millennium, as in the case of the Ordos Mongols.[251] In a similar fashion to the eclipse of centralized power in China, which led to the formation of political systems in Manchuria,[252] the Arabians responded to the tiresome war between Rome and Iran and the disappearance of local Arabian dynasties with the transformation of their tribal systems into an imperial confederation. Furthermore, like the Avars, who initially allied with Rome, later becoming one of the greatest enemies of the Roman emperors,[253] the Arabians of the fourth, fifth and sixth centuries switched from being valuable allies for Rome and Iran to be a thorn in the side of both empires.

At the dawn of Late Antiquity, the number of Chinese Buddhist believers increased. In the first century CE, the Chinese believed Buddha to be a 'miracle-performing deity', similar to their Daoist gods.[254] Despite Emperor Huan's (147–66) sacrifices to Buddha, it was only in the third century that we witnessed a rise in Buddhist Chinese believers thanks to missionary activities.[255] According to Valerie Hansen, Buddhism spread throughout China because of gifts and tax exemptions from rulers like General Shi Le (r. 330–3).[256] Northern kingdom rulers explicitly showcased their support of Buddhism through their art,[257] as exemplified by the most giant early gilt-bronze Chinese sculpture known today, a Buddha Maitreya commissioned in honour of the Empress Wenming in 486 (442–90).[258] Despite missionaries' adaptations of some of Buddha's teachings, Buddhist foundations 'remained unquestionably foreign'.[259] Buddhism's 'vertical

251 Ibid.

252 Kradin, 'Nomadic Empires in Inner Asia', 24.

253 M. Maas, 'How the Steppes Became Byzantine: Rome and the Eurasian Nomads in Historical Perspective', in *Empires and Exchanges in Eurasian Late Antiquity: Rome, China, Iran, and the Steppe, ca. 250–750*, ed. N. Di Cosmo and M. Maas (Cambridge: Cambridge University Press, 2018), 19–34, at p. 23.

254 V. Hansen, *The Silk Road* (Oxford: Oxford University Press, 2012), 25–55.

255 V. Hansen, 'The Synthesis of the Tang Dynasty: The Culmination of China's Contacts and Communication with Eurasia, 310–755', in *Empires and Exchanges in Eurasian Late Antiquity: Rome, China, Iran, and the Steppe, ca. 250–750*, ed. N. Di Cosmo and M. Maas (Cambridge: Cambridge University Press, 2018), 108–22, at p. 114.

256 Ibid.

257 M. Deeg, 'The Spread of Buddhist Culture to China between the Third and Seventh Centuries', in *Empires and Exchanges in Eurasian Late Antiquity: Rome, China, Iran, and the Steppe, ca. 250–750*, ed. N. Di Cosmo and M. Maas (Cambridge: Cambridge University Press, 2018), 220–34, at p. 233.

258 A. F. Howard et al., *Chinese Sculpture* (New Haven: Yale University, 2006), 229, fig. 3.30.

259 Hansen, 'The Synthesis of the Tang Dynasty', 114.

spread', thanks to missionary preaching and royal support, shares some features with the spread of Roman Christianity. Nonetheless, although the Romans shrewdly 'assimilated Christianity' (more than 'appropriated') to the point scholarship now interchangeably uses locutions such as 'Christian Commonwealth' and 'Roman Commonwealth', Christianity, to quote Hansen again, 'remained unquestionably foreign' for some of the Roman allies who converted to Christianity. Despite the Arabian network of ecclesiastical structures and contacts with the Christian Syriac and Roman Worlds, the Jafnid epigraphic corpus, all written in Greek except for one inscription, highlights the intrinsic 'otherness' of Christian and royal representations in sixth-century North Arabia.

In contrast with the Jafnids, who primarily drew inspiration from the Romans' symbols of power (e.g., adopting Greek in their inscriptions) as well as with the Türks, who 'consciously and explicitly reproduced dynamics of internal organization, expansion, and diplomacy that harkened back to the early Xiongnu Empire',[260] Muḥammad never presented himself as a *malik*, promoting the religious element of his message over the secular one. A century later, the Umayyads were criticized for their kingly conduct. It is thus possible that while the Jafnid emphasis on mundane political power led to their disappearance, Muḥammad's propaganda, based more on his prophetic career than on his role as a military leader, lawgiver and ruler, laid the seed for the creation of the long-lived Muslim Empire. As argued by Nikolai Kradin in an article on nomadic empires in Inner Asia, empires emerged 'if economical advisability, personal pretensions, and concourse of accidental circumstances' coincided.[261] Chapter 6 shows that these circumstances were precisely at the core of Muḥammad's Ḥijāzī movement and consequently explain the success of Arabian Islam in its autochthonous Arabia.

[260] N. Di Cosmo, 'The Relations between China and the Steppe: From the Xiongnu to the Türk Empire', in *Empires and Exchanges in Eurasian Late Antiquity: Rome, China, Iran, and the Steppe, ca. 250–750*, ed. N. Di Cosmo and M. Maas (Cambridge: Cambridge University Press, 2018), 35–53, at p. 36.

[261] Kradin, 'Nomadic Empires in Inner Asia', 25.

CHAPTER 6

The Ḥijāzī Islam

Narratives and Frameworks Re-Examined

According to traditional Muslim sources, the latest scriptural tradition originated in the Ḥijāz, a region in modern Saudi Arabia bordered on the north by Jordan, on the west by the Red Sea, on the east by the plateau of the Najd and on the south by the 'Asir region.[1] The name Ḥijāz – 'The Barrier' – refers to the mountain range between the dry narrow coastline and the fertile hinterland. The presence of oases connected to wadis (dry valleys except in the rainy season) allowed for settled agriculture from early times. For this reason, the Ḥijāz is a relatively thriving region compared with its Central Arabian surroundings. At the same time, its position on the inland caravan trade routes from the south of the peninsula into Jordan and parallel to the sea routes guaranteed a monopoly on goods exchanged between the region and the Mediterranean and South Arabia, as well as the Indian Ocean. Because of its flourishing geoeconomical characteristics, the Ḥijāz had been of interest to various people throughout the ages. The importance of locations such as the oasis of Tayma, recorded in the Neo-Assyrian annals from the eighth century BCE,[2] is suggested by the presence of the last king of the Neo-Babylonian Empire, Nabonidus (ca 556–39 BCE) in the city.[3] Echoes of the city's importance are also found in the Hebrew *Tanakh*.[4]

Between the third century BCE and the beginning of the second century CE, the Ḥijāz was controlled by the Nabateans. The largest Nabatean settlement after the capital Petra, in modern Jordan, was

[1] A wide portion of this chapter was part of my first-year examination (23 July 2018). It was later presented at the Nangeroni meeting June 2019 and submitted for publication in December 2019. It later appeared as V. A. Grasso, 'The Gods of the Qur'ān: The Rise of Ḥijāzī Henotheism during Late Antiquity', in *The Study of Islamic Origins: New Perspectives and Contexts*, ed. M. B. Mortensen, G. Dye, T. Tesei and I. Oliver (Berlin: De Gruyter, 2021), 297–324.

[2] Tiglath-pileser III, 42, 44, 47.

[3] Nabonidus Chronicle.

[4] Isaiah 21.13–14; Jeremiah 25.23; Job 6.19,20.

Madā'in Ṣāliḥ,[5] known in Antiquity as Ḥegra and located in the Ḥijāzī region. An indication of its importance can be found in the Qur'ān, where it is referred to as the land of the Thamud during the days of the Arabian prophet Ṣāliḥ.[6] Nabatean cultic monuments, strongly resembling those found in Taymā',[7] were found in the city and its surroundings.[8] When the Nabatean Kingdom became part of the Roman province of Arabia in 106 CE, the north of the Ḥijāz was annexed, and Madā'in Ṣāliḥ became a Roman city, inhabited at least until the fifth century. However, the Romans lost control of the city after the third century.[9]

Both Mecca and Medina, the holiest cities of Islam, are found in the Ḥijāz. Medina, ancient Yathrib, is better attested than Mecca as it fell under the control of the Ḥimyarites around 552 (Chapter 4).[10] Later on, it also fell under the power of the Iranians through the Naṣrids, according to the Iranian geographer Ibn Khurradādhbih (d. 912).[11] There is virtually no independent historical information for the Ḥijāz during Late Antiquity. Though it is possible to reconstruct the history of the south and the north of the Arabian Peninsula through an analysis of non-Muslim literary accounts and thanks to an abundance of archaeological material, it is not possible to do the same for the history of late antique Ḥijāz as few or no archaeological sources exist from this area dated to this period. The existing non-Muslim sources show explicit apologetic intents and a clear objective to reduce the extent of Muḥammad's impact. We are thus forced to rely on the detailed though late Muslim literary accounts available and the scattered references found in the Qur'ān. For this reason, the history of late antique Ḥijāz and the rise of Islam cannot be understood in isolation. It is only through a comparative analysis of this region with the historical material on the better-documented milieux of south and north Arabia that a satisfactory historical reconstruction can be made of the cultural environment at the beginnings of Muḥammad's career.

5 L. Nehmé, 'Towards an Understanding of the Urban Space of Madā'in Ṣāliḥ, Ancient Ḥegrā, through Epigraphic Evidence', *Proceedings of the Seminar for Arabian Studies* 35 (2005), 155–75, at pp. 171–2.

6 Q. 7.73–9; 11.61–9; 15.80–4; 141–58; 54.23–31; 91.11–15.

7 R. Eichmann, H. Schaudig, and A. Hausleiter, 'Archaeology and Epigraphy at Tayma (Saudi Arabia)', *Arabian Archaeology and Epigraphy* 17 (2006), 163–76, at pp. 167–8.

8 L. Nehmé et al., 'Mission archéologique de Madain Saleh (Arabie Saoudite): Recherches menées de 2001 à 2003 dans l'ancienne Hijrah des Nabatéens (1)', *Arabian Archaeology and Epigraphy* 17 (2006), 41–124, at pp. 91–101.

9 K. Alhaiti et al., 'Madâ'in Sâlih, Ancient Hegra: Archaeological Work 2014/5', *Bulletin of the British Foundation for the Study of Arabia* 20 (2015), 36–8, at p. 38.

10 Murayghān 3.

11 Ibn Khurradādhbih, *al-Masālik wa-al-mamālik*, 128.

Having previously investigated the political and religious milieux of the north and the south of the Arabian Peninsula, I now shed some light on the history of the Ḥijāz at the time of the rise of Islam. In this chapter, I aim to answer the following questions: what factors made the Ḥijāz a favourable environment for the emergence of a third scriptural monotheism? What was the religious context of sixth- and seventh-century Ḥijāz? What picture emerges from a comparative reading of the epigraphical and literary sources? I discuss the polytheistic milieu of pre-Islamic Arabia immediately after the introduction. This discussion includes an analysis of the Qur'ānic passages which mention pagan idols, and I argue the case for the existence of a henotheist Ḥijāz at the end of the sixth century. In Section 6.3, an overview of the scriptural communities documented in the Ḥijāz is given. These scriptural groups heavily influenced and shaped the rise of Islam, as evident from even a superficial reading of the Qur'ān. Finally, in Section 6.4, I analyse Muḥammad's prophetic career.

6.1 Introduction: The Ḥijāz, Mecca and the Kaʿbah

According to traditional Muslim sources, the prophet Muḥammad was born in the Ḥijāzī city of Mecca in ca. 570. The town is described as a prominent political, economic and spiritual centre thanks to the astute leadership of the powerful tribe of Quraysh. The income of the inhabitants of Mecca has been the subject of debate since the publication of Patricia Crone's *Meccan Trade and the Rise of Islam* in 1987.[12] This publication reassessed the city's role in luxury trade, arguing that the Meccans mainly traded in leather goods and had no role in the trade of spices to the Mediterranean at the time of Muḥammad.[13] A heated debate followed the dissemination of Crone's work.[14] Recent publications have cast doubt on Crone's position since they show that southern Ḥijāz was, in reality, affected by the caravan trade from the second century BCE onwards, revealing that the incense road had an impact on Mecca's wealth at least until the seventh century CE,[15] and that the incense trade did not end with Christianization. Indeed the importation and exportation of incense to Arabia continued well into

[12] See also F. E. Peters, 'The Commerce of Mecca before Islam', in *A Way Prepared: Essays on Islamic Culture in Honor of Richard Bayley Winder*, ed. F. Kazemi and R. D. McChesney (New York and London: New York University Press, 1988), 3–26.

[13] Crone, *Meccan Trade.*

[14] Serjeant, *Meccan Trade.* Followed by Crone, *Serjeant and Meccan Trade.*

[15] Bukharin, 'Mecca on the Caravan Routes'.

the fifteenth century.[16] Although it is unlikely that Mecca was the primary Arabian trade node,[17] it did not have enough natural resources to sustain its entire population based solely on agriculture. Thus, despite its remote location making it less than ideal for a caravan trade led by camels, Mecca had no choice but to rely heavily on trade for its survival. Contemporarily, it also relied for economic survival on the fact that it was a cultic centre,[18] revolving around a significant shrine in pre-Islamic times and later the core of Islam: the Kaʿbah.

The location of a shrine is usually much pondered, and one shrine location is preferred to another for its commercial and natural features. For example, a Christian site such as that of Sergius in Ruṣāfah owed much of its influence to its location at a watered intersection in central Syria-Mesopotamia.[19] Shrines also often have a holy significance due to an event taking place close by, such as in the case of the Holy Sepulchre of Jerusalem. Finally, these sites were chosen to make a connection between the pilgrimage, and the holiness and supramundane, instilling in the pilgrim a sense of awe and the sublime. For this reason, impressive geographical conformations were often chosen as a site, as in the case of the Tigray churches, which were built in the mountains of Ethiopia. In the case of the Kaʿbah, it is possible that Mecca was designated a worthy site because of its meteorite impact craters. The Black Stone of the Kaʿbah is not the only meteorite in the area, as scientists have found and studied meteorite craters in the surrounding region.[20] Early Muslim literary accounts further corroborate modern scientific research in the region. A passage in the ninth-century history by the Meccan historian al-Fākihī claims, on the authority of Ibn ʿAbbās, that the Quraysh discovered two stones on the summit of Abū Qubays mountain, next to Mecca.[21] These are described as 'brighter and more beautiful than any other stones', one stone being yellow and the other white.[22] Al-Fākihī reports that the Quraysh claimed: 'By God, these stones do not belong to the stones of our country, nor of any other country we know. They

[16] S. Le Maguer, 'The Incense Trade during the Islamic Period', *Proceedings of the Seminar for Arabian Studies* (2015), 175–83.

[17] Mecca is not mentioned in any Roman source.

[18] On the two 'pillars' of Mecca. See also M. Robinson, *Marriage in the Tribe of Muhammad: A Statistical Study of Early Arabic Genealogical Literature* (Berlin: De Gruyter, 2019), 166–78.

[19] Fowden, *Barbarian Plain*, 69.

[20] E. Thomsen, 'New Light on the Origin of the Holy Black Stone of the Ka'ba', *Meteoritics* 15 (1980), 87–91.

[21] Al-Fākihī, *Ta'rīkh*, 276.

[22] Ibid.

must have descended from the sky.'[23] After the loss of the yellow stone, the Quraysh kept the white stone, and when they built the Ka'bah, it was placed inside.[24] According to Muslim tradition, another stone, known as *maqām Ibrāhīm* ('station of Abraham'), was found in the same mountains, containing the imprint of Abraham's feet.[25]

As shown in Chapter 5, pilgrimage to a shrine led to economic growth and was an opportunity for thriving commerce in the surrounding area. In the 1970s, Avraham Negev suggested that the Nabatean temple of Hegra played a banking role linked to the royal treasury.[26] In more recent years, Leonardo Gregoratti has highlighted the connection between trade and the temple in ancient Palmyra, hypothesizing the existence of a 'banking network' connecting long-distance trade and the shrines of the Syrian city.[27] Moreover, the presence of a pilgrimage site is arguably as fundamental as the redaction of a text to the ignition of a new faith. As mentioned in Chapter 4, it was very likely that the site of Mecca was already a vital pilgrimage centre at the time of Abraha of Ḥimyar (d. 570). Redefining the religious nature of the Ka'bah from a pagan to an Islamic shrine was perhaps easier and preferable to creating a new pilgrimage site (and trade) route in the region. Hence, there was a merging of the polytheist past of the Ḥijāz and the rising strict monotheism of Islam to smooth the path to and ease the conversion process. The readaptation of the Ka'bah from a pagan shrine to the core of the Islamic world should in no way seem surprising. Narratives on the creation of shrines become part of the scriptural edification of the belief itself and often eased the potentially tricky transition from paganism. Therefore, the Qur'ān attributes the edification of the Ka'bah to Abraham and Ishmael,[28] and various accounts of its rebuilding are scattered throughout Muslim sources.[29] According to Muslim tradition, the Ka'bah housed an idol by the name of Hubal and other lesser pagan deities.[30] For the Muslim historian Ibn al-Kalbī, Hubal was the main god of the Meccan tribe of Quraysh,[31] but this is only certain

23 Ibid.
24 Ibid.
25 Ibid., 277.
26 A. Negev, 'The Nabateans and the Provincia Arabia', *Aufstieg und Niedergang der römischen Welt* 2 (1977), 520–686.
27 L. Gregoratti, 'Temples and Traders in Palmyra', in *Capital, Investment, and Innovation in the Roman World*, ed. Paul Erdkamp (Oxford: Oxford University, 2020), 461–480.
28 Q. 2.127.
29 E.g., Ibn Isḥāq, *Sīrah*, 122–7.
30 Al-Azraqī, *Ka'ba*, 54.23.
31 Ibn al-Kalbī, *Aṣnām*.

in one Nabatean inscription invoking curses from 'Dushara, Hubal and Manat' (*Dwshrʾ w-Hblw w-l-Mnwtw*).[32] Since this is the only inscription mentioning the god Hubal and is devoid of the repetition of the preposition *l* ('from') in front of the theonym Hubal, it is possible that Hubal was an epithet of the main Nabatean god Dushara, widely attested in the Nabatean corpus and also found in the Ḥijāz. The name is elsewhere found in the Safaitic,[33] Dadanitic[34] and Taymanitic corpora.[35]

At the beginning of the twentieth century, Julius Wellhausen suggested that Hubal could be identified as Allāh based on his presence in the Kaʿbah.[36] However, this is not corroborated in the Qur'ān or in the early Muslim sources, which merely depict the god Hubal as being venerated inside the Kaʿbah along with other betyls at the time of Muḥammad. While these accounts postulate the existence of a stable polytheistic environment in pre-Islamic times, the pre-Islamic *talbiyāt* point to a more complex and evolving situation in late antique Mecca. According to François De Blois, the pilgrimage to Mecca, as well as the circumambulation around the Kaʿbah and the kissing of the Black stone, are all manifestations of a 'remnant of the pagan past'.[37] But how remote was the pagan past of *Jāhilīyah*? In Section 6.2, I (re)consider the intertextuality between two products of Late Antiquity: the pre-Islamic inscriptions and the Qur'ān, where strands of genres and traditions are pulled together. Stories of pre-Islamic idols recount a cultural past that was subsequently revised to accentuate the prophetic nature of Muḥammad's career in a polytheistic environment. I argue that Muḥammad built his career on the existing basis of flexible henotheism, professing a strict monotheism similar to those of the surrounding scriptural communities and very much inspired by their preaching, but which developed autonomously in the distinctive Arabian milieu.

6.2 Idolatry in Late Antique *Jāhilīyah*: Evolving Cults and Literary Forgeries

Muslim accounts such as those written by al-Ṭabarī, Ibn al-Kalbī and Ibn Isḥāq have been favourite sources for the polytheistic cults of Arabia

[32] JSNab 16.8.
[33] E.g., LP 559; CSNS 718; KRS 2245.
[34] E.g., Al-Saʿīd 1419/1999, 27–8, no. 4.
[35] JSTham 556.
[36] Wellhausen, *Reste arabischen Heidentums*, 75–6.
[37] F. De Blois, 'Islam in Its Arabian Context', in *The Qurʾān in Context: Historical and Literary Investigations into the Qurʾānic Milieu*, ed. A. Neuwirth, N. Sinai and M. Marx (Leiden: Brill, 2010), 615–24, at p. 621.

during the last century,[38] and still are for some.[39] As previously mentioned, this material broadly describes most Arabians contemporary to Muḥammad as idolatrous. The inhabitants of Arabia are said to have once been *ḥunafāʾ* (lit. 'those inclined'), '[a] loan-word from Aramaic through Nabatean'.[40] This term denotes those Arabians who professed the *dīn* or *millat Ibrahīm*, 'creed of Abraham',[41] who 'was no idolater' (*mushrik*),[42] but a follower of the 'straight path' (*al-ṣirāṭ al-mustaqīm*) and 'right religion' (*dīn qiyām*).[43] Little is known of this peculiar Arabian monotheistic creed, and what little information we can deduce is often controversial. The *ḥunafāʾ*'s belief was at a certain point corrupted by a man called ʿAmr Ibn Luḥayy, who went to Syria, gathered some idols there and erected them around the Kaʿbah in Mecca. Afterwards, people started worshipping stones and irremediably forgot the true religion of Abraham.[44] This story is reported by the biographer of the prophet Ibn Isḥāq[45] and by Ibn al-Kalbī.[46] Another version by Ibn al-Kalbī claims that the corruption of monotheism in Arabia was established once the inhabitants of Mecca left the city due to its overpopulation; no one then left Mecca without a stone from the *ḥarām* ('holy shrine'), and after a while, these were mistaken for idols.[47] A similar story is found in a non-Muslim source, namely the fifth-century ecclesiastical history by Sozomen, which claims that the Ishmaelites, descendants of Abraham and Hagar and possibly found further to the north, assumed the name of Saracens pretending to descend from Sara, the wife of Abraham.[48] Like the Jews, this group practised circumcision and refrained from the use of pork. Accordingly, all their 'deviations' from the Jews are 'ascribed to the lapse of time and their intercourse with neighbouring people'.[49] In fact, due to the lapse of time, 'their ancient customs fell into oblivion', and only due to their contacts with the Jews some of them returned to 'their true origin'.[50]

38 Wellhausen, *Reste arabischen Heidentums*.
39 M. Lecker, 'Idol Worship in pre-Islamic Medina (Yathrib)', *Le muséon* 106 (1993), 331–46.
40 P. Hitti, *History of the Arabs: From the Earliest Times to the Present* (London: Macmillan, 1970), 108.
41 Q. 6.161.
42 Ibid.
43 Ibid.
44 Ibn al-Kalbī, *Aṣnām*, 5–6.
45 Ibn Isḥāq, *Sīrah*, 51–6.
46 Ibn al-Kalbī, *Aṣnām*, 5–6.
47 Ibid., 4.
48 Sozom. 6.38.
49 Ibid.
50 Ibid.

The Qur'ān often engages in polemic with a group called *al-mushrikūn* ('those who associate [with Allāh]',[51] and 'make [equal] with Allāh another deity'),[52] often translated as 'polytheists'. The presence of this group altogether, with the mentions of idol names and betyls in the Muslim Holy Book, contributed to early Muslim historians' understanding of the Ḥijāzī milieu at the rise of Islam as extensively polytheist. This view is further reflected in later Muslim and Western scholarship and is still in vogue today.[53] With this section, I shed light on the idols mentioned in the Qur'ān, assessing the presence of paganism in the Ḥijāzī milieu at the rise of Islam. In his groundbreaking book *The Idea of Idolatry and the Emergence of Islam*, Gerald Hawting claimed that the identification of the *mushrikūn* as polytheists is dependent upon Muslim tradition and absent in the Qur'ān.[54] Moving from the teaching of his mentor John Wansbrough, who had claimed that the Qur'ān must have gone through a period of oral transmission within Judeo-Christian communities,[55] Hawting pointed out that hyperbolic charges of 'idolatry' were standard in monotheistic polemics and that monotheists generally tend to describe monotheist competitors as idolatrous. Quoting John of Damascus,[56] Hawting highlighted that the Arabians used to call the Christians 'associators' (*hetairiastas*) because of the belief in the trinitarian dogma,[57] arguing that the Qur'ānic *mushrikūn* were Jews or Christians and that the Qur'ānic polemic against this group reflects a debate among monotheists not necessarily taking place in Arabia.[58]

If the redaction of the Qur'ān in Arabic would not be enough to make it an Arabian product, the presence of deities widely attested in the Arabian Peninsula unequivocally links the Qur'ān to its Arabian background. Archaeological sources discovered in the Arabian Peninsula in the last decades have attested the eight pagan deities mentioned in the Qur'ān. While the three goddesses al-Lāt, al-'Uzzā and Manāt mentioned in *sūrah* fifty-three are primarily attested in the northern and central part of the peninsula, the southern epigraphic corpora mention the five

[51] Q. 3.64; 12.108.
[52] Q. 15.96.
[53] E.g., Howard-Johnston who describes Muḥammad's milieu as 'predominantly polytheistic Beduin world'. See J. Howard-Johnston, *Witnesses to a World Crisis: Historians and Histories of the Middle East in the Seventh Century* (Oxford: Oxford University Press, 2010), 448.
[54] Hawting, *Idea of Idolatry*, 5.
[55] Wansbrough, *Qur'ānic Studies*.
[56] John of Damascus, *On Heresies*.
[57] Hawting, *Idea of Idolatry*, 84. An example of this polemic is found in the famous inscriptions inside the Dome of the Rock, dated to the time of Abd al-Malik (692) ('Believe in God and his messenger and do not say "three" [...]').
[58] Ibid., 16 and 137.

deities found in *sūrah* seventy-one, hinting at the existence of localized polytheistic cults throughout Arabia. Therefore, it is unreasonable to locate the Qurʾānic context outside of Arabia. But what about Hawting's claim that the Qurʾānic polemic against the *mushrikūn* reflects a debate among monotheists? Although I agree with Hawting's suggestion that the Qurʾānic *mushrikūn* are not polytheists, I argue that these were not Jews or Christians and that the Qurʾānic idols were not angels. A Qurʾānic verse found in *sūrat al-Hajj* mentions Jews, Sabeans, Christians, Magians and *mushrikūn*,[59] implying the presence of different communities in the religious milieu at the rise of Islam. As the *sūrat al-Hajj* considers the *mushrikūn* as a separate category, I argue that the *mushrikūn* were sympathizing monotheists who venerated Allāh. This was a pagan god who assumed biblical character due to the intense proselytizing activity of monotheistic communities active in Arabia (see Chapters 2–5). The presence of the idols in *sūrat al-Najm*, a few verses before the polemic against angels, is a direct consequence of the assembly of orally transmitted *logia* at the time of the written composition of the Qurʾān.

6.2.1 *The Goddesses of Sūrat Al-Najm*

The *sūrat al-Najm* ('The Star') mentions three Arabian goddesses, al-Lāt, al-'Uzzā and Manāt, as follows: 'Have you considered al-Lāt and al-'Uzzā? and Manāt, the third, the other? What, have you males, and He females?'[60] The Muslim tradition reports in this regard a story known as *Qiṣṣat al-Gharānīq* ('Story of the Cranes'), found in the exegetical literature on the authority of Ibn ʿAbbās as well as in the *Maghāzī* ('Stories of Military Expeditions'). This *qiṣṣah* narrates that after *sūrat al-Najm* was revealed to Muḥammad, he recited it in front of the pagan tribe of the Quraysh. However, when he got to the names of the 'Daughters of Allāh' venerated by this powerful tribe, he supposedly added the phrase: 'Indeed they are the high cranes, and indeed their intercession is to be desired',[61] having been misled during a moment of inattention. That this was a possibility is acknowledged in the Qur'ān,[62] and other versions of this story are also found in the works by al-Ṭabarī[63] and Ibn al-Kalbī.[64]

59 Q. 22.17.
60 Q. 53.19–21.
61 E.g., *Tafsīr al-Jalālayn*.
62 Q. 22.52.
63 Al-Ṭabarī, *Taʾrīkh*, 1.1192–6.
64 Ibn al-Kalbī, *Aṣnām*, 12.

Al-Lāt, al-ʿUzzā and Manāt are mentioned as the 'Daughters of Allāh' (*banāt Allāh*) in the Muslim sources based on a Qurʾānic passage,[65] and other Semitic deities were also considered as the daughters of a High God in other contexts.[66] The Qurʾānic triad is attested in the pre-Islamic poetic corpus (e.g., in the encyclopaedic collection by al-Iṣfahānī explicitly mentioning the custodian of al-ʿUzzā),[67] and in non-Muslim accounts produced between the fifth century BCE and the late Middle Ages. For instance, while the Arabian cult of Aphrodite is connected with al-Lāt by Herodotus ('the "heavenly" Aphrodite [...] is called by the Assyrians Mylitta, by the Arabians Alilat'),[68] the Syrian bishop of Cyrrhus Theodoret (d. ca. 466) argued one millennium later that the 'Ishmaelites' converted to Christianity renouncing the 'ceremonies for Aphrodite'.[69] Procopius recorded the Arabians' veneration of Aphrodite when narrating the conflict between the Naṣrid leader al-Mundhir and the Jafnid leader al-Ḥārith during the sixth century, stating that the first captured the son of the second and then 'sacrificed him to Aphrodite'.[70] There are also attestations of Aphrodite's cult among the Arabians in the later work of the Syrian priest John of Damascus (d. in the 740s) ('they used to be idolaters and worshipped the morning star and Aphrodite, whom in their language they called *Khabar*, which means great'),[71] and in the anonymous Arabic *Chronicle of Seert* mentioning the Naṣrid leader al-Nuʿmān's conversion to Christianity and his former veneration of 'the star named Venus (*al-Zohra*)'.[72] Like many Semitic idols, the 'Daughters of Allāh' possessed astral characteristics.[73] Hence, al-ʿUzzā was probably seen as a personification of Venus, no differently from the Greek Aphrodite. Therefore, since Herodotus also associated Alilat (i.e., al-Lāt) with the Greek goddess, scholars have postulated that al-Lāt and al-ʿUzzā were in an initial phase attributes of the same female goddess.[74]

65 Ibid. See Q. 16.57.

66 C. J. Robin, 'Les 'filles de Dieu' de Saba' à la Mecque: réflexions sur l'agencement des panthéons dans l'Arabie ancienne', *Semitica* 50 (2000), 113–92. See also C. J. Robin, 'L'Arabie préislamique', in *Le Coran des historiens*, ed. M. A. Amir-Moezzi and G. Dye (Paris: Les éditions du Cerf, 2019), 51–154, at pp. 109–14.

67 Al-Iṣfahānī, *Aghānī*, 21.57–8.

68 Hdt. 1.131.3.

69 Theodoret, *Ecclesiastical History*, 26.13.

70 Procop. *Pers.* 2.28.20.

71 John of Damascus, *On Heresies*, 218.

72 *Hist. nest.* 60.

73 D. Nielsen, *Die altarabische Mondreligion und die mosaische Ueberlieferung* (Strasbourg: K. J. Trübner, 1904).

74 J. Starcky, 'Allath, Athèna et la déesse syrienne', in *Mythologie gréco-romaine, mythologies périphériques: Études d'iconographie*, ed. L. Kahil and C. Augé, 119–39 (Paris: Editions du Centre national de la recherche scientifique, 1981), 120.

Three works attest the worship of al-'Uzzā instead during the fifth and sixth centuries. This is the case of the fifth-century Syriac work of Isaac of Antioch and the sixth-century chronicle attributed to Pseudo-Zachariah Rhetor, bishop of Mytilene. While the first states that 'the Arabians sacrifice to 'Uzzāi when they worship',[75] Pseudo-Zachariah Rhetor mentions the veneration of al-'Uzzā in connection with the violent raids of the Naṣrid leader al-Mundhir claiming that al-Mundhir 'brought down with him four hundred virgins who were suddenly made captive from the assembly of the apostle Thomas at Emesa (?), whom he sacrificed in one day for the worship of 'Uzzāi'.[76] Another mention of the veneration of al-'Uzzā/Aphrodite appears in the West Syrian recension of the legend of the Christian monk Sergius/Baḥīrā, said to have recognized Muḥammad in Syria as the prophet-to-be. The Christian version of this story is found in two Syriac (one eastern 'Nestorian' and one western Syrian 'Jacobite') and two Arabic versions, dated between the eighth and the twelfth century CE. These versions consist of various parts that must have circulated independently.[77] Muslim versions of this material are scattered all over Islamic literature. The story is, for example, contained in Ibn Isḥāq's *sīrah* mentioned earlier. Whereas two of the three 'Daughters of Allāh' are mentioned in the Muslim account ('Baḥīrā got up and said to him: 'Boy, I ask you by al-Lāt and al-'Uzzā to answer my question'),[78] only one of them (al-'Uzzā) is found in the (Christian) West Syrian recension. Correspondence between the two deities is established ('the star al-'Uzzā, who is Aphrodite Venus').[79]

According to the archaeological sources, the cult of at least two of the three goddesses mentioned in *sūrat al-Najm* was widespread in the northern and central parts of the Arabian Peninsula. The three deities are invoked to protect the sanctity of tombs and grant asylum in the same fashion to other pagan gods attested in the area. Already in the first millennium BCE, inscriptions attesting to the veneration of al-Lāt are widely distributed. This is because the name means 'the goddess', as al-Lāh means 'the god'.[80] Although the main archaeological sites where the cults of this deity and 'her sisters' are attested belonged to the Nabateans, their corpus is dated too early to offer helpful information on the religious milieu of Arabia

[75] Isaac of Antioch, *Homilies*, 11.101.
[76] Ps.-Zachariah, *Ecclesiastical History*, 8.5.78.
[77] K. Szylágyi, 'Muḥammad and the Monk: The Making of the Christian Baḥīrā Legend', *Jerusalem Studies in Arabic and Islam* 34 (2008), 169–214, at p. 201.
[78] Ibn Isḥāq, *Sīrah*, 116.
[79] *West-Syrian Recension*, 49a.31.
[80] In Semitic languages *t* is usually the feminine suffix.

just before the rise of Islam. Moreover, barring the onomastic of the later 'Nabateo-Arabic' or 'transitional' inscriptions (e.g., JSNab 17, dated to 267 and mentioning a certain 'Abd-Manātw), there is no epigraphic attestation of the 'Daughters of Allāh' in this later corpus and using names as indicators is risky.[81] On the other hand, in the Safaitic corpus, a deity named *'Lt* or *Lt* is mentioned more than a thousand times. Furthermore, there are ca. 100 mentions of *Lt* in the Hismaic corpus,[82] dated to the same time as the Safaitic. *Mny*, literally meaning 'fate' and possibly treated as its personification,[83] recalls the name Manāt.[84] The theonym al-'Uzzā is also found in pre-Islamic South Arabian inscriptions.[85] These inscriptions are all dated before the end of the fourth century CE. Moreover, among the thirty-two 'transitional' texts dated to the period 200–500 CE and analysed by Laïla Nehmé,[86] only one mentions a deity, a very generic 'Lord of Eternity' (*mry 'lm*).[87] Neither have polytheistic *formulae* been found in the nine inscriptions, which Michael Macdonald defines as 'Epigraphic Old Arabic'.[88]

We do not possess many inscriptions dated between the fourth and sixth centuries CE. The inhabitants of the northern part of the Arabian Peninsula decreased their habit of writing on rocks, asking for the protection of pagan deities. Yet there are consistent epigraphic mentions for this period of Allāh in association with those Christian communities which inhabited the Arabian Peninsula during Late Antiquity (see Chapters 4–5). As for material culture, portraits of al-Lāt, sometimes represented with the same iconography as the Greek Athena,[89] are scattered all over Arabia, but they are not dated after the third century. We also lack testimonies of pagan temples dated after the fourth century. Nabatean temples and later temples with architectural Nabatean influences with cult niches and steles have been found in the north.[90]

81 A similar comment in M. C. A. Macdonald, 'Personal Names in the Nabatean Realm: A Review Article', *Journal of Semitic Studies* 44 (1999), 251–89.

82 Formerly Thamudic E.

83 Al-Jallad, *Outline*, 328.

84 A mention is even found in a Latin inscription written by a Roman Palmyrene soldier in Hungary. See J. F. Healey, *The Nabatean Tomb Inscriptions of Mada'in Salih* (Oxford: Oxford University Press, 1993), 119.

85 E.g., A-50–506; A-50–858; CIAS 35.21/o 6. Qatabanic: e.g., CIAS F 24/s 4/95.11; CIAS 95.11/o 2; H 2c.

86 Nehmé, 'Glimpse of the Development of the Nabatean Script'.

87 JSNab 17.

88 OCIANA.

89 Hoyland, *Arabia and the Arabs*, 187; al-Azmeh, *The Emergence of Islam*, 170.

90 J. Patrich, *The Formation of Nabatean Art: Prohibition of Graven Images among the Nabateans* (Jerusalem: Magnes Press, 1990), 50–113.

However, only one of these, located at Umm al-Jimāl, can be dated to the fourth century.[91] Therefore, there is no archaeological evidence for the veneration of polytheistic deities after the fourth century. The Muslim literary sources claim that Manāt was the first deity of the three to be venerated in the Ḥijāz, followed by Allāt and later al-ʿUzzā.[92] Cults, as al-Azmeh suggests, would probably have assigned a pre-eminent position to the first in the sequence.[93] However, this is mere speculation as the information may have entirely been fabricated *a posteriori*. The lack of archaeological sources for late antique Ḥijāz cannot help us verify the statement. Nonetheless, the contemporary presence of all these deities in the inscriptions from surroundings dated to the early late antique period and the scattered attestation in the non-Muslim sources do not seem to point in this direction. Furthermore, these deities seem to have had an equal position in the Muslim tradition and the Qurʾān. The three gods of *sūrat al-Najm* constitute a triad, and even more eloquently, they are sisters. Conversely, progressive adoption of these deities' cults would have meant the prominence of an older deity over another.

6.2.2 *The Gods of* Sūrat Nūḥ

In addition to the 'Daughters of Allāh', the Qurʾān mentions five pagan deities in the *sūrat Nūḥ*, where Noah complains to God that his people venerate Wadd, Suwāʿ, Yaghūth, Yaʿūq and Nasr ('[a]nd [the people of Noah] said, "Never leave your gods and never leave Wadd or Suwāʿ or Yaghūth and Yaʿūq and Nasr"').[94] Three of these deities are connected to South Arabia by Ibn Isḥāq[95] and Ibn al-Kalbī.[96] The latter claims that the Quraysh, the Thaqīf, the Aws, the Khazraj and all the northern and Central Arabian tribes preferred al-Lāt, al-ʿUzzā and Manāt to other deities. Moreover, according to al-Kalbī, these tribes did not hold the five idols of *sūrat Nūḥ* in the same regard.[97] As such, these idols were conceived as less important than the 'Daughters of Allāh' because they were revered far away from the Ḥijāzī milieu ('for their distance from them').[98] Wadd,

[91] J. F. Healey, *The Religion of the Nabateans: A Conspectus* (Leiden: Brill, 2001), 65; Peter Alpass, *The Religious Life of Nabataea* (Leiden: Brill, 2013).
[92] Ibn al-Kalbī, *Aṣnām*.
[93] Al-Azmeh, *Emergence of Islam*, 179.
[94] Q. 71.23.
[95] Ibn Isḥāq, *Sīrah*, 52. Suwāʿ was also venerated by the Banū Hudhayl in al-Ḥijāz.
[96] Ibn al-Kalbī, *Aṣnām*, 6–7.
[97] Ibid., 16.
[98] Ibid., 17.

for example, was the national god of the Mineans,[99] and was possibly also venerated in Dūmat al-Jundal, the capital of Kindah.[100] In addition to representing the moon, he was also a fertility deity.[101] This god also appears in the *Dīwān* (collection of poems by one author) of the pre-Islamic poet al-Nābigha (ca. 535–604),[102] and is mentioned in an inscription found in al-ʿUlā recording the offering of a young enslaved boy by a priest of *Wd* and his two sons to the chief god of the kingdom of Liḥyān.[103] The veneration of *Wd* is further attested in the south of the Arabian Peninsula by more than a hundred inscriptions composed in Ḥaḍramitic, Sabaic, Qatabanic and Minaic and dated up to the late third century CE. Ibn al-Kalbī heard Suwāʿ's name in a 'poem by a man from Yemen'.[104] On the other hand, while al-Kalbī states that he never heard the names of Yaʿūq and Nasr,[105] other Muslim accounts attest that Nasr was venerated in Ḥimyar.[106]

As shown in Chapter 3, King Malkīkarib Yuha'min (r. 375–400) and the ruling class of Ḥimyar adopted monotheism around 380. Thereafter, no monumental inscription attests the survival of polytheism. Hence, differently from the segmentary and chaotic picture we possess of North Arabian society, we can safely say that there were no public polytheistic cults in South Arabia at the time of Muḥammad's prophetic career. As in the case of the three 'Daughters of Allāh', no archaeological source attests the cult of the gods of *sūrat Nūḥ* after the fourth century. However, Muslim historians claim that pre-Islamic Arabia's inhabitants were mainly idolatrous on the eve of Islam and the Qurʾān itself mentions the belief in eight pagan deities. For their part, the non-Muslim authors argue that some leaders of the Arabians began converting to Christianity from the fifth century onwards and the names of the pagan deities which these authors mention correspond to those named by Muslim scholars and the Qurʾān itself. Overall, if the literary extracts convey the idea of the existence of widespread polytheistic beliefs in pre-Islamic North Arabia, the archaeological material points to a lack of polytheism during Late Antiquity. Of course, this lack of material is not to be used as an *argumentum ex silentio*; polytheistic inscriptions simply

[99] J. Ryckmans, 'Le panthéon de l'Arabie du Sud préislamique: état des problèmes et brève synthèse', *Revue de l'histoire des religions* (1989), 151–69, at p. 163.
[100] Ibn al-Kalbī, *Aṣnām*, 9.
[101] Ryckmans, 'Le panthéon de l'Arabie', 164.
[102] C. A. Nallino, 'Il verso d'Annabigah sul dio Wadd', *Rendiconti accademia nazionale dei Lincei* 29 (1921), 283–90.
[103] JSLih 049a.
[104] Ibn al-Kalbī, *Aṣnām*, 6.
[105] Ibid., 7.
[106] Ḥabīb, *Muhabbar*, 317.

could not have been found yet. However, at the moment, we register an abrupt epigraphic disappearance of polytheistic deities and the dismissal of pagan temples from the fourth century onwards. A closer engagement with the literary sources could shed light on these developments.

6.3 A Henotheist Ḥijāz?

I have previously mentioned that the Qurʾān directly testifies that most of the people living at the time of its revelation were *mushrikūn*,[107] 'those who set up with Allāh [the God] another god',[108] and often translated in English as 'idolaters'. The Muslim Holy Book thus implies that these were not *tout court* 'polytheists' because they believed in Allāh, using different terms to refer to idols worshipped concurrently with Allāh. In addition to *andād* ('equals') and *shurakāʾ* ('partners'), these idols were named *ṭāghūt*, *jibt*, *anṣāb*, *awthān* or *aṣnām*. Ibn al-Kalbī explains that if statues were made of wood, gold or silver and resembled human forms, they were called *aṣnām*.[109] Instead, if they were made of stones, they were called *awthān*.[110] While all the Qurʾānic passages mentioning the *aṣnām* ('idols') relate to an old past and are part of accounts of Abraham,[111] or the Children of Israel, the two occurrences of idols as *awthān* are more ambiguous. Although the first, found in Q. 29.17 and 25, may also be placed in the context of Abraham's narrative,[112] the situation is particularly complicated for the mention in the *sūrat al-Ḥajj*. We read: 'Whoever honours the sacred rites of Allāh – it is best for him in the sight of his Lord. And permitted to you are the grazing livestock, except what is recited to you. So, avoid the abominations of idols and avoid false statements.'[113] Since the *sūrah* also mentions Sabians, Christians, Magians and 'those who associate' (*alladhīna ashrakū*),[114] its historical context is unclear, and the encouragement to 'avoid false statements' can be interpreted in various ways.[115]

Ibn al-Kalbī claims that the inhabitants of Arabia were 'fond of worshipping idols' (*al-aṣnām*).[116] However, if we closely analyse the relevant sources

[107] E.g., Q. 15.94.
[108] Q. 15.96.
[109] Ibn al-Kalbī, *Aṣnām*, 33. See also 21.
[110] Ibid.
[111] Q. 6.74; 14.35; 21.57; 26.71.
[112] Q. 29. 17 and 25.
[113] Q. 22.30.
[114] Q. 22.17.
[115] E.g., Al-Ṭabarī, *Tafsīr*, 17.113.
[116] Ibn al-Kalbī, *Aṣnām*, 21.

on the creeds of the *Jāhilīyah* and attentively search for mention of Allāh as a High God, we obtain unexpected results. From (polemic) Qur'ānic passages, we can infer that the 'pagans of *Jāhilīyah*' were accustomed to associating lesser beings with a High God only when not in need of protection, thus offering substantial evidence of the existence of a pagan belief in Allāh:

> When they embark on the ships, they call on
> God; making their religion sincerely His.
> but when He has delivered them to the land,
> they associate others (*yushrikūn*)
> with Him.[117]

> When some affliction visits humankind, they
> call unto their Lord, turning to Him; then,
> when He lets them taste mercy from Him,
> lo, a party of them assign associates (*yushrikūn*)
> to their Lord.[118]

> They [the evildoers, *al-ẓālimūn*] appoint to God of the tillage and cattle
> that He multiplied, a portion, saying,
> 'This is for God' - so they assert - 'and
> this is for our associates (*shurakā'*)'. So, what is
> for their associates reaches not God; and
> what is for God reaches their associates.
> Evil is their judgement![119]

Similar Qur'ānic passages postulate the concurrent belief in a High God named Allāh and in other preternatural beings associated with him. Pre-Islamic formulae of ritual invocation further attest that pre-Islamic Arabians repeatedly invoke and pray to Allāh. It has been almost one century since S. M. Husain's article collected twenty-five pre-Islamic *talbiyāt*, utterances during the Meccan pilgrimage.[120] A later paper by M. J. Kister, moving from Husain's pioneering work, claimed that the pre-Islamic *talbiyāt* of the tribe association of the Ḥums (including the Quraysh) expounded 'clearly their belief in the authority of Allāh over the principal Arab deities'.[121] While Kister claimed that the *talbiyāt* reflect the ideas of

[117] Q. 29.65. Prayers to grant protection in maritime trade are common in the ancient world. See the Greek Arabian inscription of Qanī' mentioned in Chapter 3. On the Qur'ānic references to the sea, see P. Crone, 'How Did Quranic Pagans Make a Living?', *Bulletin of the School of Oriental and African Studies* 68 (2005): 387–99.

[118] Q. 30.33.

[119] Q. 6.136.

[120] S. M. Ḥusayn, 'Talbiyat al-jahiliyya', *Proceedings of the Ninth All-India Oriental Conference* (1937), 361–9.

[121] M. J. Kister, 'Labbayka, Allāhumma, Labbayka: On a Monotheistic Aspect of a Jāhiliyya Practice', *Jerusalem Studies in Arabic and Islam* 2 (1980), 33–57, at p. 36.

the existence of Allāh as a supreme god in pre-Islamic times, al-Azmeh has suggested in more recent years that these acclamations are 'generic, intensified and superlative affirmation of devotion, used for a variety of deities and for any deity'.[122] Al-Azmeh has thus claimed that Allāh was an undefined god, invoked in particular ritual moments, far from being conceived as a cosmocratic deity.

An enlightening passage by Ibn al-Kalbī points to belief in an Arabian *Urmonotheismus*, reporting that the North Arabian tribe Nizār commonly said:

> 'Here I am, Allāh! Here I am! (*Labbayka Allāhumma! Labbayka!*)
> Here I am! You have no partner (*sharīk*) save one who is yours!
> You have dominion over him and over what he possesses.'
> They were used to declare his unity through the *talbiyāt* while associating their gods with him, placing their affairs in his hand.[123]

This and the passages mentioned earlier clearly attest the simultaneous belief in Allāh and in the intermission of lesser beings used as auxiliaries during the pilgrimage to Mecca. These intercessors may have assumed different forms. For example, they may have been perceived as 'angels with the names of females',[124] much like the three goddesses of *sūrat al-Najm.* But the same preternatural beings may have also been conceived as demons. Ibn al-Kalbī regards the aforementioned al-'Uzzā as such: 'al-'Uzzā was a demon (*shayṭān*) which used to frequent three trees in the valley of Nakhla'.[125] The passage continues with the description of the mission of the companion of Muḥammad, Khālid ibn al-Walīd, who was ordered to cut down the trees of al-'Uzzā at al-Ṭā'if (in modern Saudi Arabia). Around one of these trees, al-Walīd saw an 'Abyssinian' woman gnashing her teeth.[126] Once Khālid had severed her head in two, she crumbled into ashes.[127]

It is improbable that Allāh's associates were perceived as independent gods, as depicted by the later Muslim authors ('When a traveller stops to sleep, he would take four stones, pick the finest one and adopt it as his lord').[128] The supposed polytheism of the pre-Islamic Arabians was thus limited to the request of vague forms of intercession to a High God to whom all creatures were subordinated ('Those on whom you call apart

[122] Al-Azmeh, *Emergence of Islam*, 231.
[123] Ibn al-Kalbī, *Aṣnām*, 4.
[124] Q. 53.27; 17.40; 37.149–50.
[125] Ibn al-Kalbī, *Aṣnām*, 15.
[126] Ibid., 16.
[127] Ibid.
[128] Ibn al-Kalbī, *Aṣnām*, 21.

from God, are servants the likes of you; call them and let them answer you, if you speak truly').[129] The lack of a well-organized Ḥijāzī pantheon and the inconsistent, scattered mentions of guardians and temples found in literature corroborate this thesis. Arabian animism and the veneration of a supreme god in pre-Islamic Arabia, also suggested by the reiterated supremacy of al-Ka'bah,[130] are further documented in the Qur'ān and other Muslim sources (e.g., 'By Allāt and al-'Uzzā and those who believe in them, and by Allāh, indeed he is greater than both').[131] I have previously argued that polytheistic cults are only conspicuously attested until the fourth century, *terminus ad quem* of the North Arabian Inscriptions, and the moment in which the kings of Ḥimyar adhered to monotheism. The inscriptions of the Arabian Peninsula dated after the fourth century attest the mention of more than one recurrent name to indicate god. This imperfect terminology is reflected in the Qur'ān. I now briefly move to analyse the nature of this Ḥijāzī High God.

In the Qur'ān, both the words *Raḥmān* and *Allāh* appear in Medinan and Meccan *suwar* with no particular proportions to indicate the god of Islam. While *Rabb* also often seems to indicate the god of Muḥammad, false gods are instead mentioned as *ilah*. *Raḥmān* instead usually appears as an epithet. We encountered this theonym in Chapter 3–4 while looking at the epigraphic corpus of South Arabia. The theonym is also attested in the *Book of the Ḥimyarites*,[132] and in the first letter of Simeon (Chapter 4).[133] According to al-Azmeh, a god named *Raḥmān* was assimilated to Allāh from the second Meccan period.[134] Al-Azmeh has further claimed that 'Allāh had the distinct advantage of not having been anyone's cultic deity'.[135] Although epigraphy has shown that Allāh was the god of the Christians, al-Azmeh is correct in suggesting that the genesis of Allāh can be seen as a historical process whereby a specific deity came to emerge as singular.[136] Indeed, some passages of the Qur'ān give the impression that *Raḥmān* was not only an epithet of Allāh. In *sūrah* twenty-five, for example, *Raḥmān* is perceived with aversion by Muḥammad's contemporaries ('And when it is said to them, "Prostrate to al-Raḥmān", they

129 Q. 7.194.
130 Ibn al-Kalbī, *Aṣnām*, 21. Also in Ibn Isḥāq, *Sīrah*, 55.
131 Ibn al-Kalbī, *Aṣnām*, 11.
132 *Ḥimyarites*, 13 p 13a.
133 *Letter 1*, 503.
134 Al-Azmeh, *Emergence of Islam*, 313.
135 Ibid., 314.
136 Ibid., 47.

say, "And what is the al-Raḥmān? Should we prostrate to that which you order us?" And it increases them in aversion').[137] As previously shown, *al-Raḥmān* appears in inscriptions from the north and the south of the Arabian Peninsula and more than fifty South Arabian inscriptions and three Safaitic inscriptions bear this attestation (Chapters 4–5).[138] The name is used in both Christian and Jewish inscriptions from South Arabia and recurs in pre-Islamic *talbiyāt*,[139] and in the traditional Muslim literature on the attack of Abraha of Ḥimyar (Chapter 4). Conversely, a deity named *Lh*, 'god', is mentioned in the Ancient North Arabian corpora. Most of the time, he is mentioned singularly,[140] but sometimes he is not.[141] It is, however, uncertain whether this deity corresponded to Allāh since his name was not attached to the North Arabian determinative article *h-*.[142] Nabatean inscriptions attesting the veneration of Allāh have been found at Umm al-Jimāl,[143] and Old Arabic inscriptions dated to the sixth century mention Allāh with the Classical Arabic determinative article (*'l-'lh*) (Chapter 4).[144] Overall, though the attestation of Lah appears widespread, the veneration of Raḥmān is more confined to the south. Thus, it seems plausible that this god was imported to the Ḥijāz from the south after the kingdom's collapse at the end of the sixth century.

A close inspection of the Qur'ān confirms the identification of *Raḥmān* as a proper theonym and not as a mere epithet of Allāh. The Qur'ān tries to merge these two gods ('Say: Invoke Allāh or invoke *al-Raḥmān*. Whichever you invoke, to Him belong the best names. And do not be too loud in your prayer or quiet but seek between that a [intermediate] way'),[145] but it is still possible to find some echoes of the tension between the two.[146] In fact, *Raḥmān* is present mainly in Meccan *suwar*,[147] and Allāh is not mentioned at all in the *sūrat al-Raḥmān*. Allāh is also missing in Meccan *sūrat al-Naba'*, where *al-Raḥmān* is found twice.[148] Any explanation for *Raḥmān*'s prominence in early and middle Meccan suwar would

137 Q. 25.60.
138 C 4351; AbaNS 352; C 3315.
139 Kister, 'Labbayka Allāhumma Labbayka'.
140 For example, KRS 2301; RSIS 30; SIJ 284; HSIM 49218.1.
141 For example, KRS 2298; KRS 1974; C 2816; C 3712.
142 Al-Jallad translates 'Lh' with 'Allāh' while analysing some theophoric names. Al-Jallad, *Outline*, 58.
143 Bert De Vries, 'Between the Cults of Syria and Arabia: Traces of Pagan Religion at Umm el-Jimal', *Studies in the History and Archaeology of Jordan* 10 (2009), 177–91, at p. 188.
144 Nehmè, 'New Dated Inscriptions'.
145 Q. 17.110.
146 See already mentioned Q. 25.60.
147 Six Medinan, ten Meccan.
148 Q. 78.37–8.

be tentative. Still, the mention of *Raḥmān* probably reflects the nomenclature employed at an embryonic phase of the formation of Islam. In Medina, a change in Muḥammad's perception of god is signalized by the adoption of the more generic Allāh over *Raḥmān*. This procedure does not reflect the abandonment of Allāh as a 'dreadful and inflexible Justiciary' or Muḥammad's renunciation of being an apocalyptic prophet for being a legislator.[149] Instead, it indicates Muḥammad's recognition that a generic name would better fit Islam's universalistic message. Possibly accustomed to the nomenclature struggle dividing the Christian churches at the time, Muḥammad may have opted to employ a firm but straightforward name and interpretation of God over a more subjective and complex one.

Already in the nineteenth century, Julius Wellhausen had proposed seeing Allāh as 'der eigentliche Inhaber der Göttlichkeit' ('the true bearer of divinity') and as the Supreme God of pre-Islamic Arabia.[150] He accordingly claimed that the inhabitants of Arabia believed Allāh had created the world and postulated that Allāh was a syncretistic abstraction of other local deities and that his cult was intertribal. Carl Brockelmann later proposed to read the genesis of Allāh as a primitive *Urmonotheismus*; this was thus not an abstraction of other deities but a primitive Arabian god resembling a *Deus Otiosus*.[151] The discussion was reinstigated in the 1970s by the works of Javier Teixidor and William Montgomery Watt. The former postulated the existence in the Hellenistic and Roman Near East of a main god who controlled lesser divine beings,[152] while Watt proposed seeing Allāh as a *Deus Otiosus*.[153] This deity is similar to the active Supreme God of the Near East offered by Teixidor,[154] and a similar genesis and interpretation were proposed for *al-Raḥmān* in Chapter 3 when discussing the beliefs of fourth- and fifth-century South Arabia. The merging of the two high gods bearing similar attributes arguably took place in Ḥijāz, at the centre of the Arabian Peninsula, a location familiar with merging cultures and exchanging goods and ideas due to the caravan trade. A Ḥijāzī High God,

[149] C. J. Robin, 'L'Arabie préislamique', in *Le Coran des historiens*, ed. M. A. Amir-Moezzi and G. Dye (Paris: Les éditions du Cerf, 2019), 51–154, at pp. 104–5.

[150] Wellhausen, *Reste arabischen Heidentums*, 217.

[151] C. Brockelmann, 'Allah und die Götzen, der Ursprung des islamischen Monotheismus', *Archiv für Religionswissenschaft* 21 (1922), 99–121.

[152] Teixidor, *Pagan God.*

[153] W. M. Watt, 'The Qur'ān and Belief in a "High God"', in *Proceedings of the Ninth Congress of the Union Européenne ses Arabisants et Islamisants: Amsterdam, 1st to 7th September 1978*, ed. R. Peters (Leiden: Brill, 1981), 228–34. For an earlier exposition, see W. M. Watt, 'Belief in a "High God" in pre-Islamic Mecca', *Journal of Semitic Studies* 16 (1971), 35–40.

[154] Teixidor, *Pagan God.*

simply called *al-Lāh* ('the God'), had always been primitively venerated in Arabia, but became prominent from the fifth century onwards, when it was merged with the southern, better defined, High God by the name of *Raḥmān*. It then started assuming the attributes of a biblical God under the evident influence of Jewish-Christian communities. A recently published late South Arabian graffito in a North Arabian dialect found at al-Ḍāliʿ (Yemen) records the first pre-Islamic attestation of the Islamic *basmala* ('In the name of God, the Most Gracious, the Most Merciful') as '[i]n the name of Allāh, the Raḥmān, have mercy upon us, Lord of Heaven (*rb* *sɪmwt*) [...]'.[155] The formula bears strong reminiscence of the Psalms and mentions Raḥmān and the Lord of Heaven in addition to Allāh, pointing to the slow emergence of the Islamic Supreme God and the fusion of South and North Arabian instances.

Before assessing the influences of the scriptural communities over the Ḥijāzī milieu of Muḥammad, I now offer some reflections on the Qurʾānic *jinn* as re-elaborations of pagan creatures which grew to represent interfaces between the sacred and secular spheres and were adapted to serve the strictly hierarchical Qurʾānic cosmology. For an extended study, see V. A. Grasso, "Historicizing Ontologies: Qurʾānic Preternatural Creatures between Ancient *Topoi* and Emerging Traditions", *Journal of Late Antiquity* (Spring 2023). Three main groups of preternatural beings indeed appear in the Muslim Holy Book: *jinn* occurring thirty-one times,[156] and *shayāṭīn* ('satans') and *malāʾikah* ('angels'), each appearing eighty-eight times. The identity of preternatural beings had long fermented in the Arabian milieu but gradually lost ground to external scriptural influences, either expunged from Muḥammad's prophecy or shrewdly reshuffled as in the case of the liminal *jinn*. The *jinn* are thus found exclusively in Meccan *suwar* with one exception, namely *sūrah* fifty-five, *al-Raḥmān*. In contrast, *malāʾikah* and *shayāṭīn* appear in both Medinan and Meccan *suwar*, though more prominently in the latter. Because Meccan *suwar* are dated earlier and *malāʾikah* and *shayāṭīn* mostly appear in *logia* belonging to Jewish-Christian traditions, it seems with the confluence of scriptural trends into the Arabian milieu, devils and *jinn* were increasingly merged. Although a few Qurʾānic passages distinguish the two or at least discern the 'devils from mankind' from the *jinn*,[157] others assimilated these two preternatural beings, as exemplified by *sūrah* eighteen, which mentions

[155] Al-Hajj 2018.
[156] The word *janna/jannāt* comes from the same root but means 'paradise'.
[157] Q. 6.112.

the Devil (Iblīs/Satan) as 'one of the jinn' in a verse of strong biblical reminiscences.[158]

According to the Islamic tradition, the *jinn* were created from smokeless fire,[159] a *topos* which recalls a statement found in a New Testamentarian Apocryphon titled *Cave of Treasures*, describing Satan as a being 'of fire and spirit'.[160] Because of their creation from light, they are more tangible than the angels but less so than humankind, as men were created from clay. As such, the *jinn* can be anthropomorphic or zoomorphic manifestations or appear in the form of shadows. As men, they eat, drink, sleep and have sexual intercourse (among *jinn* but also with humans). And like humans, but contrary to angels and demons, they have free will. As suggested in the *sūrat al-Jinn* (number seventy-two), good *jinn* listened to the teachings of Muḥammad and accepted Islam, becoming part of the *Ummah* (Muslim community).[161] Because of the intransigent monotheism promulgated by Muḥammad and synthesized in the *tawḥīd* (profession of faith), these preternatural beings are thus identified as closer to men than God and are thus often named together.[162] Al-Azmeh has argued that preternatural beings such as the *jinn*, with whom polytheistic Arabs had lived 'in a continuum of familiarity',[163] did not have a cultic infrastructure in pre-Islamic times and were later 'Islamised and made to be subservient to and created by the Supreme Being'.[164] I prefer to see the *jinn* and the other preternatural beings found in the Qur'ān and the later Muslim literature as already subjected to a henotheistic High God in pre-Islamic times. As such, among the partners of Allāh, that is, the intercessors, we may also include the *jinn*.[165] After being denigrated, they were integrated into the brand new monotheistic system of Islam and reduced from powerful preternatural beings, similar to the Latin *genii loci*, to creatures at the service of God and even of humans. Nonetheless, opponents of Muḥammad, himself a self-proclaimed *rasūl* (lit. 'messenger', no ontological explanation provided or needed), still worshipped them and claimed their companionship to Allāh, al-Raḥmān and al-Rabb 'on a par in indicating a polyonymous personal deity'.[166]

158 Q 18.48–50. Compare Q. 7.14–18 and Job 1.8–12.
159 Q. 15.27; 55.15.
160 *Cave of Treasures*, 53.
161 Q. 46.29.
162 Q. 46.18; 51.56; 55.39; 114.6.
163 Al-Azmeh, *Emergence of Islam*, 206.
164 Ibid., 327.
165 Q. 6.100. Ibn al-Kalbī also claims that an Arab tribe worshipped the 'demons' known as *jinn*. See *Aṣnām*, 22.
166 Al-Azmeh, *Emergence of Islam*, 312.

Whereas the Qurʾānic *mushrikūn* were 'imperfect monotheists', the members of Muḥammad's monotheist movement originated as 'perfected' monotheists who associated Allāh only with his epithets. As the genesis of Allāh from polyonymous being to one and only God was long and complex, the emergence of the Qurʾānic *jinn* was characterized by a long process of systematization, including the dissolving of their most salient divine features and their imposed Islamization. The inconstancy of nomenclature of the first Meccan *suwar* was thus gradually eradicated, and the *jinn*'s taxonomy was supplemented when the divine Jewish-Christian beings were adopted and adapted. This is not to say that the *mushrikūn* were 'monotheists' or that 'monotheism' is the 'natural' evolution from 'polytheism'.[167] Instead, I suggest that Muḥammad's movement, especially the Caliphate and the Muslim Commonwealth raised in the name of 'Arab' identity and of a 'universal faith', saw the need for a higher degree of uniformity. Therefore, the preternatural creatures not incorporated into the emerging Islamic theological system were rigidly condemned. Nonetheless, the celestial beings the Qur'ān dooms are not the ones belonging to the alien Jewish-Christian world, such as Michael or Gabriel, but those indigenous to Arabia, such as al-Lāt and al-ʿUzzā. Others, like the *jinn*, were instead transfigured and reclassified. This process was continuous, and the transition was likely less abrupt than that illustrated by the later Muslim literary sources. Overall, the opponents of Muḥammad mainly were accused of 'association' with beings which are most of the time whitewashed under one vague umbrella term: 'partners' (*shurakāʾ*). These included preternatural beings henotheistically subordinated to Allāh already in pre-Islamic times and the Christian Messiah, as suggested by the famous inscription in the Dome of the Rock. In fact, while Christian communities were actively discussing the nature of Christ, an Arabian man prophesied the existence of One God, who had no sons or daughters, sweeping away local beliefs and surrounding controversies.

The Qur'ān is a multistrand text(s) composed of a series of *logia* collected during different periods and across various places,[168] but likely all originating in Arabia. The blended arrangement of the Qurʾānic macrotext merged strands of traditions whose boundaries were already vague. Muḥammad thus gave birth to a dynamic adaptation process and reshaping of pre-existing pagan and scriptural narratives. However, these systems were often merged in an imprecise way, either consciously to blur doctrinal differences or because the rapid *mise en place* of the Qur'ān did not allow much space for

[167] Strict categorizations are mostly useful for pedagogical purposes.
[168] Wansbrough, *Qur'ānic Studies.*

polishing and editing single narratives within the macrotext. The Meccan *sūrah* twenty-seven is an excellent example of the active merging of strands of traditions anchored to their Arabian milieu with other material featured in the Bible. In the *sūrah*, stories about Moses and Ibrahim as well as the prophets Noah and Lot intertwine with those having as main protagonists three Arabian prophets, named Hūd, Ṣāliḥ and Shuʿayb. A similar merging is evident in the narratives revolving around Solomon. In the same *sūrah* twenty-seven, Solomon is given the ability to speak to *jinn*, humans and birds by God in a passage strongly recalling 1 Kings.[169] These beings thus constitute Solomon's 'soldiers', or army.[170] Whereas in *sūrah* twenty-seven Solomon interacts with the *jinn*,[171] in other Qurʾānic passages he mingles with the *shayāṭīn*.[172] The merging of pagan deities with scriptural mediators is characteristic of the Mediterranean basin and Arabia (see Chapter 2 on *Sol Invictus*). Supplementing local beliefs, these beings carried on pre-existing conversations between men and God. More than a millennium before Muḥammad's prophetic career, Plato reported the philosopher Diotima of Mantinea as saying: 'God does not mingle with man; only through means of demons (*daimones*) all intercourse and conversation between man and gods is carried on.'[173] Associated with angels and demons but less binary than the Qurʾānic *shayāṭīn* and *malāʾikah*, the *jinn* became the smokeless and more powerful counterparts of men.[174] Nonetheless, the *jinn*'s faith was subjected to Allāh, the one and only God (*lā ilāha illā Allāh*).

6.4 'O People of the Book! Come to Common Terms as between Us and You': An Overview of the Ḥijāzī Scriptural Traditions

Before starting his prophetic career, Muḥammad worked for his wife Khadīja, mostly trading with Syria ('Muḥammad went on business to the lands of Palestine, Arabia and Phoenicia of the Tyrians'),[175] allegedly the exact location from which paganism was imported according to the Muslim tradition.[176] Around 610, he started preaching One God. The

169 1 Kings 5:13.
170 Q. 27.17.
171 Ibid. and 27.39. The *jinn* work for Solomon by the permission of his Lord also at 34.12–13.
172 Q. 2.102; 27.82.
173 Pl. Symp. 203a.
174 Q. 72.5.
175 Jacob of Edessa, *Chart Fragments*, 326.
176 'O People of the Book! Come to Common Terms as between Us and You' in the section title is from Q. 3.64.

hostile response of the polytheist ruling tribe of Quraysh in Mecca led to a first *hijrah* ('departure') of Muḥammad and his followers to Aksūm in 615, followed by the second more famous *hijrah* to Medina in 622. After the victorious battle against the Quraysh held at Badr in 624 and his victorious return to Mecca in 630, Muḥammad was able to become the unchallenged leader of an Arabian *Ummah*, overcoming tribal division. Muslim and non-Muslim sources narrating the origins of Islam are not always in antithesis.[177] In fact, according to both traditions, Muḥammad's prophethood was first recognized by a Christian monk by the name of Sergius, also called Baḥīrā, whom he met outside of the Ḥijāz. Muslim traditional sources composed by authoritative writers such as Ibn Isḥāq,[178] al-Ṭabarī[179] and al-Wāqidī claim that Baḥīrā was the first to have recognized Muḥammad as a prophet and to have instructed him in monotheism.[180] Ibn Isḥāq narrates the encounter between the two, attributing its circumstances to a business trip in a merchant caravan directed to the Syrian town of Buṣrā, shortly before Muḥammad's marriage to Khadījah. Therein, Muḥammad allegedly showed that he was responsive and open to the monk's preaching, staunchly refusing polytheistic cults for the 'Daughters of Allāh' ('Baḥīrā said: 'Boy, I ask you by al-Lāt and al-'Uzzā to answer me'. He mentioned them only because he had heard his people swearing by these gods. The prophet answered, '[d]o not ask me by al-Lāt and al-'Uzzā, for by Allāh, nothing is more hateful to me than these words').[181] Thereafter, Baḥīrā asked Abū Ṭālib to protect Muḥammad from the Jews in the Ḥijāz ('If they see him and know about him what I know, they will harm him!').[182] As previously mentioned, this story is reported in four Christian accounts,[183] dated between the eighth and the twelfth centuries. An echo of this narrative is found in non-Muslim sources, such as in the work of John of Damascus ('A false prophet named Muḥammad has appeared in their midst. This man, after having chanced upon the Old and New Testaments and likewise, it seems, having conversed with an Arian monk, devised his heresy').[184] It has been

177 See Hoyland, *Seeing Islam as Others*; and S. W. Anthony, *Muhammad and the Empires of Faith: The Making of the Prophet of Islam* (Oakland: University of California Press, 2020).
178 Ibn Isḥāq, *Sīrah*, 114–19.
179 Al-Ṭabarī, *Ta'rīkh*, 1.1125–6.
180 Al-Wāqidī, *Futūḥ*, 2.20–1.
181 Ibn Isḥāq, *Sīrah*, 116.
182 Ibid.
183 B. Roggema, *The Legend of Sergius Baḥīrā: Eastern Christian Apologetics and Apocalyptic in Response to Islam* (Leiden: Brill, 2009).
184 John of Damascus, *On Heresies*, 218.

recently demonstrated that the Christian version of the legend of Sergius the monk comprises various unconnected parts that must have circulated independently,[185] and it is at the moment impossible to tell whether the legend originated in a Muslim or a non-Muslim milieu. Although a possible interpretation that the legend was dismissing the Arabians as *mushrikūn*, unable to recognize the signs of the divine due to their 'pagan error', all interpretations remain tentative.

Even a superficial reading of the Qurʾān points to the presence and broad knowledge of Judeo-Christian Scriptures. Jews, Christians and, more generally, what the Qurʾān labels as *Ahl al-Kitāb* ('People of the Book') are at the centre of the Qurʾānic discourse, and the multiple allusions to parts of the Bible undoubtedly presume an audience familiar with Judeo-Christian preaching. Numerous scholars have investigated how Muḥammad had such knowledge of the Bible. Although it is generally accepted that Muḥammad elaborated essential material which came to him from Jewish sources,[186] it is still disputed if these reached him directly[187] or through Christian channels.[188] Theodor Nöldeke suggested that Muḥammad's primary source of information must have been uncanonical liturgical and dogmatic literature, such as the apocryphal gospels, and not the Bible itself.[189] Recent studies have shown that the Qurʾānic Meccan chapters appear to have been formulated in line with Jewish liturgical material,[190] and Nöldeke's view is still widely accepted. Research on the existence of an Arabic Bible in pre-Islamic times has produced only partial results.[191] Both Jews and Christians are directly addressed in the Qurʾān, and it is thus plausible to imagine that both groups were present in the Ḥijāz at the time of Muḥammad.[192] Muslim sources such as the history by Ibn Isḥāq indicate their presence in the surroundings of Mecca and Medina.[193] Although this presence is not conspicuously attested, absence

[185] Szylágyi, 'Muḥammad and the Monk', 192–202.

[186] On this matter, see the recent H. M. Zellentin (ed.) *The Qur'an's Reformation of Judaism and Christianity: Return to the Origins* (Abingdon: Ashgate, 2019).

[187] Torrey, *Jewish Foundation of Islam.*

[188] Bell, *The Origin of Islam.*

[189] Nöldeke, *Geschichte des Qorans.*

[190] A. Neuwirth, 'Qurʾānic Readings of the Psalms', in *The Qurʾān in Context: Historical and Literary Investigations into the Qurʾānic Milieu*, ed. A. Neuwirth, N. Sinai and M. Marx (Leiden: Brill, 2010), 733–78.

[191] S. H. Griffith, *The Bible in Arabic: The Scriptures of the 'People of the Book' in the Language of Islam* (Princeton: Princeton University Press, 2013).

[192] The Qurʾānic codex post-dates Muḥammad but Jews and Christians were present in Ḥijāz already at his time.

[193] E.g., Ibn Isḥāq, *Sīrah*, 130–6.

of evidence is not evidence of absence. However, as shown in Chapters 2–5, the Ḥijāz was surrounded by active scriptural communities in the north and the south. It is, therefore, plausible to presume scriptural infiltration in the Ḥijāz, especially after the ecological and political crisis in the second half of the sixth century.

A Christian presence in the north and the south of the Arabian Peninsula in the sixth century has been extensively discussed in the preceding chapters. The Qurʾān often engages in polemics against Christians, reflecting the tensions between the monotheistic communities of the time and their internal struggles in Arabia (e.g., '[t]hey disbelieve (*kafara*) who say: Allāh is one of three in the Trinity: for there is no god except one God').[194] Virulent criticism of the Christian doctrines of Incarnation and Trinity are predominantly found in various sources such as in Muslim literary accounts ('they claim that God is Christ the son of Mary and Christ addressed the disciples "my brothers". Nevertheless, if the disciples have sons, God would be their uncle'),[195] and early Islamic coins,[196] and the famous early Islamic inscription found in the Dome of the Rock,[197] drawing from the Qurʾān.[198] Close interaction with the Christians of Mecca can be traced by the reported presence of portraits of Mary and Jesus inside the Kaʿbah, though such reports might well belong to a later tradition.[199] Christians are referred to as *al-naṣārā* in the Qurʾān, a word that has been connected to the village of Nazareth where Jesus lived, as well as to the Arabic root *n-ṣ-r*, 'to help'.[200] Several attempts have been undertaken to identify this group better,[201] but it is still unclear.

The Qurʾān acknowledges the conflict between various Christian positions at the time of its composition ('And from those who say, "We are Christians", we took their covenant; but they forgot a portion of that of which they were reminded. So, we caused among them animosity and

194 Q. 5.73.
195 Al-Jāḥiẓ, *Naṣārā*, 233.
196 R. Hillenbrand, *Islamic Art and Architecture* (London: Thames and Hudson, 1999), 24.
197 M. Milwright, *Dome of the Rock and Its Umayyad Mosaic Inscriptions* (Edinburgh: Edinburgh University Press, 2016).
198 Q. 4.171.
199 G. D. R. King, 'The Paintings of the pre-Islamic Kaʿba', *Muqarnas* 21 (2004), 219–29.
200 S. H. Griffith, 'The Qurʾān's "Nazarenes" and Other Late Antique Christians: Arabic-Speaking "Gospel People" in Qurʾānic Perspective', in *Christsein in der islamischen West*, ed. S. H. Griffith and S. Grebenstein (Wiesbaden: Harrassowitz, 2015), 81–106, at p. 89.
201 E.g., S. H. Griffith, 'Christian Lore and the Arabic Qur'an: The "Companions of the Cave" in Surat al-Kahf and in Syriac Christian Tradition', in *The Qur'an in Its Historical Context*, ed. G. S. Reynolds (London: Routledge, 2008), 109–38.

hatred until the Day of Resurrection').[202] Criticism in the Qur'ān may have focused on one particular Christological position and interpretations of the Trinity through a denial of God's absolute oneness.[203] In fact, the main points of the polemic against the Christians involve the definition of Jesus as only a man ('To Allāh Jesus is like that of Adam. He created Him from dust; then He said to him: "Be". And he was'),[204] and a simple messenger,[205] as Jesus is only the son of Mary and not of God for Islam.[206] Once again, the diatribe creating division in Christianity at the Council of Chalcedon and at the centre of discussion in the Second (553) and Third Councils of Constantinople (680–1) undoubtedly reached and reverberated around the Arabian milieu, stimulating the debate around the nature of Christ traceable in the Qur'ān. Indeed, an excellent example of the Qur'ānic engagement with the Christological quarrel is found in *sūrat al-Ikhlāṣ*, which reformulates the Nicaeno-Constantinopolitan declaration of faith to stress the absolutism of the Islamic God ('Say, "He is Allāh the one (*aḥad*), Allāh the absolute (*ṣamad*), He neither begets nor is begotten, Nor is there to Him any equivalent"').[207] The Qur'ān is equally critical of the Jewish conception of the nature of God, as exemplified by a verse of *sūrat al-Tawba*:

> The Jews (*al-yahūd*) say: 'Ezra is the son of Allāh', and the Christians (*al-naṣārā*) say: 'The Messiah is the son of Allāh'. That is their statement from their mouths, imitating the saying of those who disbelieved (*kafarū*) in the past. May Allāh destroy them; how are they deluded?
>
> They have taken their scholars (*aḥbār)* and monks (*ruhbān)* as lords (*arbāb*) besides Allāh, and the Messiah, the son of Mary. And they were not commanded except to worship one God; there is no god except Him. Exalted is He above whatever they associate with Him (*yushrikūn*).[208]

The word *aḥbār* appears four times in the Qur'ān, and it is used in connection with *rabbāniyūn* to refer to the Jewish leaders,[209] or with *ruhbān*,[210] indicating Christian monks.[211] Accordingly, it probably refers to the top

[202] Q. 5.14.
[203] Q. 5:72–5.
[204] Q. 3.59.
[205] See again, Q. 5.75.
[206] Ibid.; 3.45.
[207] Q. 112.1–4. See A. Neuwirth, 'The Qur'ān as a Late Antique Text', in *In the Shadow of Arabic: The Centrality of Language to Arabic Culture*, ed. B. Orfali (Leiden: Brill, 2011), 495–509.
[208] Q. 9:30–1.
[209] Q. 5.44 and 5.63.
[210] Q. 9.31 and 9.34.
[211] On these 'official titles' see H. M. Zellentin, *The Qur'ān's Legal Culture: The Didascalia Apostolorum as a Point of Departure* (Tübingen: Mohr Siebeck, 2013), 207–28.

leaders of the *Ahl al-Kitāb* communities. Recurrent polemics against the Jews challenges their perception of themselves as the 'chosen people'.[212] They are also accused of killing prophets,[213] and failing to observe the Torah.[214] Just as Christians accused the Jews of corrupting the Bible,[215] they were also accused in the Qur'ān of altering Jewish Scripture.[216] In addition to engaging in polemics with Judeo-Christian groups, the Qur'ān shows some familiarity with the religious buildings of these groups as synagogues (*ṣalawāt*), monasteries (*ṣawāmiʿ*) and churches (*biyaʿ*) are all mentioned in the Qur'ān.[217] In the preceding chapters, Christian presence outside of the Ḥijāz has been extensively discussed. Unfortunately, we do not have Christian archaeological material directly connected with the Ḥijāz. The closest Christian archaeological finding is the already mentioned inscription from the region of Dūmat al-Jandal.[218] In contrast, Jewish presence in the Ḥijāz is attested by both literary and archaeological sources.

A small corpus of inscriptions, primarily written in Nabatean Aramaic and found at Madā'in Ṣāliḥ and al-ʿUlā (the latter at ca. 350 km from Medina), is dated between the third century BCE and the fifth century CE. Although only one inscription of this corpus, an epitaph from Madā'in Ṣāliḥ, is clearly Jewish ('This is the tomb which Shubaytu son of 'Ali'u, the Jew (*Yhwdy*), for himself and his children and for 'Amirat, his wife'),[219] the onomastics of other inscriptions hint at a Jewish redaction. A group of Safaitic inscriptions also mention Jewish communities living between Ḥawrān and North Arabia.[220] Furthermore, the South Arabian corpus also mentions Medina, under the control of the Christian Ḥimyarites around 552.[221] The city is also found in two Hellenistic South Arabian inscriptions, and it is thus plausible that interactions between Medina and Ḥimyar took place during the Jewish period.[222] Traditional material further indicates that a flourishing Jewish community inhabited Medina at the time of Muḥammad. Perhaps the most significant proof pointing to the presence of a Jewish community in the Ḥijāz at the time of Muḥammad is offered by

212 Q. 62.6.
213 Q. 3.181.
214 Q. 62.5.
215 *Nov. Just.* 146.
216 Q. 2.75.
217 Q. 22.40.
218 Nehmé, 'New Dated Inscriptions'.
219 JS nab4.
220 E.g., ASWS 217; C 3360; KRS 37.
221 Muraygħān 3.
222 Ma'in 93–A/4 and 95/12.

the so-called 'Constitution of Medina' (*Dustūr al-Madīnah*). Found in various Muslim histories,[223] the *Dustūr* regulates tribal matters such as warfare between the leading tribes of Medina, the Aws and Khazraj, and those who emigrated with Muḥammad from Mecca to Medina in 622. A treaty with the Jews of Medina, the Banū Qurayẓah, Banū Naḍir and Banū Qaynuqaʿ is also included in the document. The faith of the Jews is recognized in the constitution of the *Ummah*, which institutionalized religious pluralism in Islam.[224] The absence of Medina in Ibn al-Kalbī's work assigning a polytheist deity to prominent cities of North, Central and South Arabia is possibly indicative of a dominant monotheism in the town.[225]

The Jewish community of the Ḥijāz may also have played an essential role in inspiring the belief of the *ḥunafāʾ*, the already mentioned 'followers of Abraham's faith', attested both in Medinan and Meccan *suwar*.[226] The *ḥunafāʾ* are sometimes mentioned in diatribes against the 'People of the Book',[227] and at other times they are mentioned in invectives against the *mushrikūn*.[228] Ibn Isḥāq recounts how four Ḥijāzī men converted to monotheism, seeking the 'religion of Abraham'.[229] Three of these men converted to Christianity during their search for the religion of Abraham. A man named Zayd ibn ʿAmr ibn Nufayl 'accepted neither Judaism nor Christianity' while also abstaining from the pagan sacrifice of infant daughters, hence becoming a *ḥanīf*.[230] Zayd ibn ʿAmr is believed to have been the first to suggest Muḥammad to adopt the Kaʿbah as *qiblah* (the direction faced when a Muslim prays) instead of Jerusalem ('This is the *qiblah* of Abraham and Ishmael. I do not worship stones and do not pray towards them and do not make sacrifices to them, and do not eat what is sacrificed to them and do not draw lots with arrows. I will only pray towards this House till I die').[231] Although the Quraysh, the most fervid opponents of the Islamic prophet, are described as infidels in some *ḥadīth*,[232] they

223 Ibn Isḥāq, *Sīrah*, 341–6.
224 S. A. Arjomand, 'The Constitution of Medina: A Sociolegal Interpretation of Muhammad's Acts of Foundation of the Umma', *International Journal of Middle East Studies* 41 (2009), 555–75, at p. 560. On this text, see also M. Lecker, '*The Constitution of Medina': Muhammad's First Legal Document* (Princeton: Princeton University Press, 2004); and F. Donner, 'From Believers to Muslims: Confessional Self-identity in the Early Islamic Community', *Al-abāth* 50–1 (2002–3), 9–53.
225 Robin, 'L'Arabie préislamique', 135.
226 Medinan: 2; 3; 4; 22; 98. Mecca: 6; 10; 16; 30.
227 Q. 3.67; 4.125; 98.5.
228 Q. 6.79; 10.105; 16.120–3; 22.31.
229 Ibn Isḥāq, *Sīrah*, 143–50.
230 Ibid., 144.
231 Ibn Saʿd, *Al-ṭabaqāt al-kubrā*, 3.380.
232 *Sunan ʾAbī Dāwūd*, 20, 73, 77; *Ṣaḥiḥ al-Bukhārī*, 78, 231.

are also described as *ḥunafāʾ* elsewhere. According to this portrayal, they rejected Muḥammad's mission purely for economic reasons, fearing losing their hegemony in the *ḥajj* and in the associated trade and administration of the Kaʿbah ('Quraysh carried out for us the obligation of the religion which ʾIsmāʿīl bequeathed us'),[233] hinting once again at the intersection between economy and religion in pre-Islamic late antique Arabia.

Overall, eclectic monotheistic presences are registered in the Ḥijāz and its surroundings at the dawn of Islam. Hawting is right to emphasize that Islam 'should be understood as the result of an intra-monotheist polemic'.[234] Nonetheless, he is too eager to place the formative stage of Islam in Syria/Palestine and Iraq, 'where the tradition of monotheism was firmly established'.[235] Even without accepting as historically accurate the early Muslim sources (and the Qurʾān), it is impossible not to notice a high degree of probability for the presence of monotheist communities in the Ḥijāz. Jewish and Christian inscriptions found in the surroundings strengthened this hypothesis. Although the possibility of carrying out archaeological research in Mecca and Medina is very slight, future work on surrounding Ḥijāzī sites may clarify the extent of scriptural infiltration in the area. The fall of the political entities of North and South Arabia in the sixth century arguably played a role in the migration of people in the region and the consequent spreading of beliefs in the Ḥijāz. As we will soon see, additional factors intensified the movement of people and the spreading of a prophetic and eschatological climate.

6.5 Crisis and Prophets: Muḥammad's Prophetic Career, Musaylimah and Others

Two centuries before the preaching of Muḥammad, idolatry was in decline, and the sociological milieu of Arabia was changing under external influences. In the fifth and sixth centuries, while neighbouring empires increased their impact on the tribal communities of Arabia, extensive monotheistic movements flourished and echoed into the Peninsula along the trade routes. At that time, Arabia was also experiencing a political crisis. After the disappearance of the South Arabian kingdom and the allied kingdoms of the north, a prophetic monotheistic movement attempted to respond to an age of rampant fragmentation. Unlike Jesus, a biographically

[233] Ḥabīb, *Muḥabbar*, 264.
[234] Hawting, *Idea of Idolatry*, 7.
[235] Ibid., 13.

elusive figure located in a well-known historical milieu, Muḥammad is a biographically tangible figure who operated in a historical gap.[236] It is virtually impossible to assess the historicity of the prophets operating in Arabia at the time. Nonetheless, the familiarity with Judeo-Christian preaching implied in the Qur'ān makes it plausible to imagine the activity of more than one prophet in the region.

Muḥammad is not the only prophet to appear in the Qur'ān, as well-known Judeo-Christian prophets such as *Ilyās* (Elijah) and *Zakarīya* (Zachariah) are also found in the Muslim Holy Book. Three indigenous Arabian prophets are also mentioned. An entire *sūrah*, number eleven, is named after Hud, the prophet for the people of ʿAd, described as people who forsook God and adopted idols and were therefore killed by God with a thunderous storm.[237] A second Arabian prophet, Shuʿayb, operated in Midian and was cut down by an earthquake for not having listened to Shuʿayb's preaching.[238] The same destiny is assigned by God to the people of Thamud, to whom he sent the third Arabian prophet Ṣāliḥ in their city of Madā'in Ṣāliḥ (later named after the prophet).[239] The presence of cities in ruin, such as Madā'in Ṣāliḥ, together with the spread of Judeo-Christian eschatological and apocalyptic literature arguably available in the north and the south of the Arabian Peninsula, influenced and stimulated the creative content of the Qur'ān. A third element may have played a role in the rise of a prophetic movement in sixth-century Arabia. The Arabian political crisis in the second half of the sixth century is mirrored and possibly also accentuated by a broader ecological crisis in the same period.

Historians such as Procopius claimed that around 536, the sun 'looked very similar to the sun in eclipse', and 'men were free neither from war nor pestilence nor any other thing leading to death'.[240] Indeed, according to recent scientific enquiries, two significant volcanic eruptions took place in this period.[241] The first eruption took place in 535 or early 536, releasing large quantities of sulphate and ash into the atmosphere in the northern hemisphere.[242] The second eruption took place in 539–40 and was right before the Justinian plague of 541–3, which quickly spread along the trade routes,

[236] De Blois, 'Islam in Its Arabian Context', 620.
[237] Q. 46.24–5.
[238] Q. 7.85–91.
[239] Q. 15.80–4.
[240] Procop. *Pers.* 4.14.
[241] M. Sigl et al., 'Timing and Climate Forcing of Volcanic Eruptions for the past 2,500 years', *Nature* 523 (2015), 543–9.
[242] Ibid., 547.

causing a reduction in population in the Mediterranean basin.[243] At the time of the eruptions, a series of earthquakes were also registered in the Near East.[244] Hence, the destruction of the people of ʿAd, Midian and Thamud by a thunderstorm and two earthquakes, as narrated in the Qurʾān, may reflect these climatic and atmospheric phenomena. Recent work on the so-called late antique Little Ice Age shows that the total annual precipitation in Arabia and East Africa declined abruptly at the beginning of the sixth century, with the most severe droughts occurring during the 520s.[245] Droughts undoubtedly led to competition over limited resources, as well as to social conflict and migrations.[246] The ecological crisis of the sixth century could thus be linked to the collapse of Ḥimyar in the south of the Arabian Peninsula.[247] The most significant evidence of a pestilence[248] affecting pre-Islamic Arabians is found in poems by the Medinan Ḥassān ibn Thābit (d. 659). Although the verses of this *Dīwān* differ in style, content and quality, and it is thus plausible that some of them might not be attributable to Ibn Thābit, the corpus presents valuable historical information. Two of his poems[249] have been shown to reference the spread of a plague in the Ḥawrān during the sixth century.[250] Archaeological material has confirmed a decrease in rural and urban settlements in the region during this period.[251] Accordingly, literary and archaeological sources are not contradictory,[252] and modern scientific research on the sixth-century crisis further corroborates these findings.

It is also plausible that the war of 603–30 stimulated the eschatological message at the core of Muḥammad's preaching[253] and the prophetic movement that supposedly spread in this region during these centuries as the

[243] Ibid., 548.
[244] Y. Hirschfeld, 'The Crisis of the Sixth Century: Climatic Change, Natural Disasters and the Plague', *Mediterranean Archaeology and Archaeometry* 6 (2006), 19–32, at p. 24.
[245] J. Haldon and D. Fleitmann, 'Drought and the End of Himyar? Complexity, Determinism and the Limits of Explanation' (forthcoming).
[246] Ibid.
[247] Ibid.
[248] Haldon and Fleitmann question the plague's impact. For an opposite opinion, see P. Sarris, *Plague in the Time of COVID-19* (forthcoming). Both plague and drought arguably contributed to the fall of Ḥimyar.
[249] Ibn Thābit, *Dīwān*, 1.228.105; 1.225.123.
[250] L. I. Conrad, 'Epidemic Disease in Central Syria in the Late Sixth Century: Some New Insights from the Verse of Assān Ibn Thābit', *Byzantine and Modern Greek Studies* 18 (1994), 12–59.
[251] H. N. Kennedy, 'Justinianic Plague in Syria and the Archaeological Evidence', in *Plague and the End of Antiquity: The Pandemic of 541–750*, ed. L. K. Little (Cambridge: Cambridge University Press, 2006), 87–96, at p. 95.
[252] Ibid.; see also P. Sarris, 'Bubonic Plague in Byzantium', in *Plague and the End of Antiquity: The Pandemic of 541–750*, ed. L. K. Little (Cambridge: Cambridge University Press, 2006), 119–32; and Sarris' forthcoming article.
[253] The war is mentioned in Q. 30.2–5.

natural outcome of a widespread and oppressive malaise.[254] The Muslim sources claim that six prophets preached in Arabia ca. 575–634, operating in different geographical areas of the peninsula. Accordingly, Ibn Sayyād, conceived by the Muslim tradition as a *Masīḥ Dajjāl* ('false Messiah'), was active as the 'apostle of God' among the Jews of Medina. Khālid ibn Sinān instead, acknowledged as a *nabī* ('prophet') by the Islamic tradition, supposedly lived one generation before Muḥammad and fought paganism in the Ḥijāz. Kaʿb al-ʿAnsī preached in modern Yemen in the first decade of the Muslim era, 'speaking' in the time of Muḥammad (*kāna takallama fī ʿahd rasūl Allāh*),[255] though many perceived him to be a traditional Arabian soothsayer (*kāhin*) rather than a prophet (*nabī*). An Arabian prophetess by the name of Sajaḥ bint al-Ḥārith ibn Suwayd is also recorded. Sajaḥ married Musaylimah ibn Ḥabīb, the most well-known prophet preaching at the time of Muḥammad, who belonged, perhaps not entirely by chance, to a clan called Banū Ḥanīfah.[256]

Known in the Muslim sources as 'the liar' (*al-Kadhdhāb*), Musaylimah began his religious career in Haddār. Like Muḥammad, he received a revelation from God transmitted by *Jibrīl* (Gabriel) and wrote his own Qur'ān. 'Qur'ān' is a technical lexeme meaning 'liturgical recitation' and relates to the Syriac *qeryānā*. Hence, the possible existence of a Qur'ān other than Muḥammad's, as well as the loan of the Syriac lexeme itself, further attests Arabian familiarity with the scriptural communities. Musaylimah never denied Muḥammad's prophethood, claiming he was granted a 'share' in prophethood.[257] Al-Ṭabarī reports on the authority of Abū Bakr a message written by Musaylimah (*rasūl Allāh*) to Muḥammad (*rasūl Allāh*) claiming that 'half of the land belongs to us and the other half belongs to Quraysh'.[258] Although the possibility that the *mushrikūn* were supporters of Musaylimah's claim to prophethood has not been explored, future enquiries could shed further light on their identity.[259] Furthermore, it is

254 Howard-Johnston, *Witnesses to a World Crisis*, 436–54.
255 Ibn Isḥāq, *Sīrah*, 964.
256 Ibid., 946.
257 Ibid.
258 Al-Ṭabarī, *Taʾrīkh*, 1.1749.
259 Another interesting interpretation of the term could come out from its comparison with the Middle Persian term *agdēn*, often translated as 'infidel' and associated 'with the changing of an individual's identity to or from Zoroastrianism, especially in cases of conversion and intermarriage' (J. Mokhtarian, 'The Boundaries of an Infidel in Zoroastrianism: A Middle Persian Term of Otherness for Jews, Christians, and Muslims', *Iranian Studies* 48 (2015), 99–115, at p. 115). Further studies need to clarify if the term *mushrikūn* could have been used to define dissident members of the same community or attitudes of 'others'.

also significant that the Muslim tradition states that Musaylimah adopted the name of *Raḥmān* before the birth of Muḥammad's father. The pre-existing belief in *Raḥmān* in pre-Islamic Arabia lends authenticity to this claim, and the already mentioned passages in the Qur'ān, such as Q. 25:60, confirm the composite belief in an Arabian High God. He was simultaneously called Allāh and Raḥmān both by Muḥammad and by Musaylimah, as exemplified by the two letters mentioned earlier. Musaylimah's belief in *Raḥmān* was possibly influenced by his predecessor as leader of the Banū Ḥanīfah, Hawdha ibn 'Alī (d. 630), who was a Christian.

Musaylimah operated in Yamāmah, to the east of the Najd plateau in modern-day Saudi Arabia. Robert Serjeant has argued that Arabian cities, having acquired ascendancy over neighbouring tribes and regions, would form a *ḥaram*, a nucleus gathering an indefinite number of tribes.[260] A given town or region would be thus recognized as a sanctuary, in which no blood could be shed and where intertribal matters could be discussed and trade conducted. According to Serjeant, several *ḥarams* are known to have existed in seventh-century Arabia. These include al-Ṭā'if, al-Yamāmah and Mecca. There is no objective evidence stating that Musaylimah established a *ḥaram* in Yamāmah – or that Musaylimah existed. Nonetheless, assuming he did, it is possible that his preaching attempted to provide a religious and political framework for a principality based in Yamāmah and independent of the surrounding empires of Iran, Rome and Aksūm and its Arabian competitors.

Christian Robin has recently identified a series of characteristics common to the late antique Arabian prophets: (1) a revelation in a rhymed language; (2) the preference for naturalistic images or 'signs' of divine power; (3) the need for an intermediary to face the divine omnipotence; and (4) the need for a community.[261] In this need for a community, the message of Musaylimah and Muḥammad essentially diverge. In fact, differently from Muḥammad's universalistic vision, Musaylimah's message is confined to the settled population of Yamāmah. This could indicate a society closer to the pattern of intertribal relations or more strictly kin-based. Muḥammad's prophecy was more closely inspired by Christianity's universalistic and messianic spirit and did not seem to be addressed purely

[260] R. B. Serjeant, 'Ḥaram and Ḥawṭah, the Sacred Enclave in Arabia', in *The Arabs and Arabia on the Eve of Islam*, ed. F. E. Peters (London: Routledge, 1999), 167–84.

[261] C. J. Robin, 'Les signes de la prophétie en Arabie à l'époque de Muhammad (fin vie siècle et début VIIe siècle de l'ère chrétienne)', in *La raison des signes: présages, rites, destin dans les sociétés de la méditerranée ancienne*, ed. S. Georgoudi, R. K. Piettre and F. Schmidt (Leiden: Brill, 2012), 433–76.

to the Meccan community. The word Mecca is only used once in the Qur'ān ('And it is He who withheld their hands from you and your hands from them within Makkah after He gave you victory over them. And ever is Allāh of what you do, seeing').[262] The Arabian prophets share the same ambition. This was to contrast their prophetic visions with the disorders that Arabia experienced in the sixth century, that is, the dissolution of the kingdom of South Arabia and the allied kingdoms of the North. Far from being the culmination of the distantly biblical prophetism of Ṣāliḥ, Shuʿayb or Hūd, their prophetic messages were well anchored to their sociological milieu. Therefore, Muḥammad and his rivals' preaching was the comforting, though pragmatic, response to a geological and political change in the Arabian milieu. Muḥammad and the pan-tribal nature of his message were more successful than the others, who were aiming to convince only specific tribal groups.

[262] Q. 48:24. With the possible addition of 'Bakka' in Q. 3.96.

CHAPTER 7

Conclusion

This book traced the late antique cultural, economic and political developments which would eventually lead to the formation of Arab communal identity, the emergence of Arabic and the rise of Islam, offering an interpretative framework that contextualizes the religious choices of pre-Islamic late antique Arabians. In doing so, my analysis illustrated the region's impact on the first-millennium world. It highlighted the region's actualization of broader late antique trends, which cemented the identity of emerging political entities vying to maintain political control and gain economic advantages. A focus was placed on the Arabian exploitation of cults, a marker of the region's attitudes towards neighbouring superpowers that eased the transition for their subjects. The sociopolitical exploitation of cults, aimed at controlling and shaping a common identity, mirrors a broad late antique trend. The sociopolitical and economic structures of late antique pre-Islamic Arabia were not immune to adopting this *instrumentum regni.*

The two-centuries-long incubation period between the last dated Arabian pagan inscriptions and the establishment of the Islamic *Ummah* witnessed the rise of incipient henotheism and the spread of scriptural traditions in Arabia, as well as a series of internal and external attempts to create a unified empire. However, none of these endeavours was done to unify the 'Arabs'. In fact, the inhabitants of South Arabia perceived themselves to be Ḥimyarites (after the name of their kingdom during Late Antiquity), and only some disputed traces of 'Arabness' can be found among (some) northern and Central Arabian dynasties. I have thus argued that it is inaccurate to use the term 'Arabs' before the rise of Islam, thus framing pre-Islamic Arabia as an Arab-less land. Nonetheless, it was neither a 'desert' nor an area at the mercy of neighbouring powers but a region featuring some relatively common traits. Despite its political fragmentation, it was an active participant in the broader developments of Late Antiquity. As such, it had much influence on the political map of the period.

Pre-Islamic Arabia was characterized by a perpetual state of fragmentation caused by internal antagonisms and external pressures. Except for its south-western corner, the social fabric of the Arabian Peninsula was structured around a series of tribes and dynasties throughout Late Antiquity. Some scholars have argued that what made pre-Islamic 'Arabs' distinct from other people was language,[1] describing them as 'personnes ou groupes de langue arabe'.[2] However, it would be more semantically appropriate to refer to the region's inhabitants in pre-Islamic times as 'Arabians' since the use of 'Arab' as an ethnicon, and a distinguishable 'Arabness', are only traceable after the birth of the Islamic community in the seventh century. Before Arabia's process of ethnicization, a process of unification was in its infancy in the southern region under the kingdom of Ḥimyar. Like contemporary Sogdians, the Ḥimyarites were surrounded by multiple political entities and powerful empires. This meant they needed to defend themselves militarily. They did so based on a 'semi-nomadic imperialism', negotiating their presence by forming solid relationships and alliances to avoid complete annihilation. Roughly at the same time as the unification of Ḥimyar in the fourth century, Rome and Iran started recruiting North Arabian groups to defend their empires' borders from each other, as well as from independent Arabians. Thanks to these newly formed alliances and the draining wars between Rome and Iran, North Arabians managed to regain (part of) the autonomy that they had lost with the disappearance of the Nabatean Kingdom at the beginning of the second century. They remained largely independent also because of Arabia's geographical configuration. Nonetheless, they failed to unify into a single entity and form solid regional kingdoms, as hinted at by the presence of narratives on single Arabian leaders and not on the broad groups to which these figures belonged.

While in Asia Minor and Egypt, 'peace meant prosperity',[3] war laid the foundations for more efficient structuring of the tribal societies of North Arabia. And Christianity channelled both authority and wealth by providing the pretext for starting wars and controlling the Arabians. Churches were most likely built in Rome's allied or partner kingdoms and/or areas politically and/or culturally linked to the Roman-Christian Commonwealth. On the one hand, the public display of elite Roman symbols of power, such as the sponsorship of ecclesiastical structures, signalled the possibility of signing alliances with the newly 'civilized' Arabians. On

[1] Hoyland, *Arabia and the Arabs*, 230.
[2] Robin, 'La pénétration des Arabes nomads', 71.
[3] Sarris, *Empires of Faith*, 126.

the other hand, it stimulated the conversion of local tribe members and their settling around nodes that were strategic for warfare or trade and led to them being controlled by Roman-allied dynasties. Hence, ecclesiastical buildings facilitated recognition of the hegemonic role played by local dynasties in charge of negotiations both with the external superpowers and with the internal substrata who looked towards the church's patrons to gain protection both in this world and perhaps in the next. Accordingly, the spread of the second scriptural religion in the Arabian Peninsula followed a similar pattern to that of the rest of the late antique world. On the one hand, Christianity was viewed as an economic opportunity and an instrument of salvation from the netherworld and the devilish preternatural world. On the other, it became a means for aristocracies and clergy to exercise control. Despite the initial syncretism between scriptural and pagan traditions, the rise of Christianity was overall relatively slow in fourth-century Arabia. Nonetheless, by the end of the fifth century, Christianity became the main religion in the Near East under the impulses of the competing factions emerging after the Council of Chalcedon. The high number of churches in places like Syria, attributable to the proselytizing missions of bishops and monks, arguably served competing factions. The consequent economic boom caused by the construction of churches and monasteries (and roads to these centres) and the social and economic hubs provided by these structures (especially prosperous if pilgrimages were involved) hugely contributed to the Arabians' acceptance of Christianity. Such approval was facilitated by the lack of 'Arab' identity and stable kingdoms. Notwithstanding the local establishment of a new social order underpinned by clergy and powerful dynasties mediating between settled communities, nomad tribes and empires, and the increasing international prestige of Arabian bishops participating in early oecumenical councils, there was never an 'Arabian Church', and devotees largely remained dependent on external entities.

While Christianity spread in North Arabia, the South Arabian elites cautiously became Jewish sympathizers. The fourth- and fifth-century Ḥimyaritic adoption of monotheism also follows a broad late antique trend which allowed for a gradual transition towards monotheism and the adoption of a neutral position towards the developments of the surrounding empires. In the brand new kingdom of Ḥimyar, the cult of a single, institutionalized and translocal deity thus provided a robust mechanism for establishing identities. Identities were then reshaped in a broader syncretistic framework through a sociopolitical exploitation of cults, which shared features with the first stage of Christianity in Aksūm and the

Graeco-Roman world, as well as with the henotheism of pre-Islamic North Arabia. Nonetheless, in the wake of the turmoil caused by a 'second wave of Christianisation' in Aksūm, proselytized by Miaphysite monks in flight from persecution in the Roman Empire after the Council of Chalcedon and particularly during the darkest hour of the anti-Chalcedonian persecution between 518 and 520,[4] South Arabia eventually converted to Christianity. In a similar fashion to Vakhtang Gorgasali and the Thirteen Syrian Fathers, who built on Mirian III's introduction of Christianity to Georgia in the sixth century, Kaleb and the Aksūmite Nine Saints finalized 'Ezana adoption of Christianity in Aksūm. While Vakhtang Gorgasali aimed to signal his break with Iran, Kaleb exploited Christianity to strengthen his position with Rome. A programme of renewal and further Christianization of the country (rather than re-Christianization) took place at the height of Aksūmite political and economic power, affecting Arabia and the wider late antique political map. Aksūm and Ḥimyar never entirely constituted a 'periphery' during Late Antiquity because of their fundamental role in the Red Sea trade routes. However, only after the events in the sixth century did these geographical areas gain a broad sociopolitical resonance when Christianity provided Aksūm with an ideal weapon of ideological propaganda to justify Aksūmite intervention in South Arabia. 'Faith reasons' were a rhetorical cloak to disguise the deeper economic reasons behind this military intervention. Economic reasons possibly played a role in the shift from paganism to monotheism in Arabia as elsewhere; temples' treasuries were often remitted to the kings after their closure, and controlling pilgrimage meant being in control of offers and profits along 'holy routes'. Therefore, 'seizing' and closing pagan temples also meant seizing their wealth and better controlling the kingdom's finances.

The events that took place in Najrān and the subsequent embassies from Rome, Iran and their Arabian allied kingdoms attest the impact of the Red Sea political entities in the wider late antique world. Despite Rome and Iran's interests in the region, Arabian leaders remained largely independent from surrounding empires and each other. The adoption of Judaism in the south and Miaphysitism and East Syrian Christianity in the north testify to the exploitation of faith as a mark of 'otherness' in the first millennium and the Arabians' relative autonomy from Rome and Iran. While Arabian elites emulated the surrounding empires' adoption of

[4] For the persecutions, see L. Van Rompay, 'Society and Community in the Christian East', in *The Cambridge Companion to the Age of Justinian*, ed. M. Maas (Cambridge: Cambridge University Press, 2005), 239–66, p. 242.

one language and one faith to foster social cohesion, they also understood the usefulness of imported beliefs to signal their position in the broader African and Euro-Asian World. In some cases, imported faiths could also become a *casus belli* to defeat competing elites, advance positions and gain better trading options. The borrowing of Rome's chief 'symbol of power', Christianity, became one of the most significant trait shared by the elites of Central Asia and the Red Sea after the massacre of Najrān. However, while Ḥimyar managed to maintain an autonomous position in the first half of the first millennium and retained its cultural characteristics, Aksūm was more heavily subjected to the fluctuations and developments of the surrounding empires, as shown by the high degree of cultural permeability attested by Christianity's deep penetration into the region – the presence of Christianity in the area surviving even the spread of Islam.

Monasticism was a crucial factor in the growth of Arabian and Aksūmite Christianity. In the sixth century, the lack of a codified monastic rule resulted in Christian monasticism being flexible and transplantable. Because of this, Arabian monasticism quickly incorporated the region's structures of kinship and clientele, providing a secure haven much like Irish monasticism. Arabian churchmen pledged their allegiances to Antioch similarly to Irish churchmen professing allegiance to Rome due to the lack of a 'Celtic Church'. It is virtually impossible to say 'what made a Christian' in late antique Arabia. Was smashing a pagan temple enough? Was building a church sufficient for a ruler to join the Christian Commonwealth? Was launching a military campaign to impose the faith enough? The expansion of Christianity is attributable primarily to its predominantly urban social setting. As such, church construction boomed in the urban communities of sixth-century North Arabia and much less so in the barren lands of inner Arabia. For example, in an urban setting such as Umm al-Jimāl, fifteen churches were built on site, whereas the 'gods of the more distant imperial powers, Greece and Rome', did not manage to harvest local pagan deities.[5] Eight of these fifteen constructions have been attributed to private contexts,[6] supporting the hypothesis that the establishment of Christianity was mainly an urban and elite phenomenon in Arabia. The Christian patronage of holy sites and the protection of pilgrimage routes lay at the intersection of religion, politics and economics. While churches were built by small elites in the village communities of the north, widespread construction of ecclesiastical buildings in the south

[5] De Vries, 'Between the Cults of Syria and Arabia', 189.
[6] De Vries, 'Continuity and Change', 41. Only the cathedral looks like a public church.

took place only after the adoption of Christianity in the sixth century. Meanwhile, the rise of Christianity is less documented in the Persian Gulf, where the Romans had little or no influence. There is an urgent need to excavate the surroundings of the churches to examine the milieu in which religious buildings were constructed.

Late Antiquity also saw an acceleration of trade, as demonstrated by the enormous output of Sasanian silver coinage.[7] According to Procopius, the Romans could never equal Iran's trading monopoly, despite their alliance with Aksūm.[8] Iran undoubtedly benefitted from the addition of Characene to the Sasanian Empire and the destruction of Palmyra in the third century, which put an end to the Roman merchants' access to the Persian Gulf. Traders played an essential role in spreading faiths in the first millennium (Muḥammad himself was a trader). Christianity created a social network of commerce facilitated both by trading diasporas (permanent settlements of merchants on foreign soil)[9] and by the establishment of a Christian Commonwealth, formed by communities partnered with Rome. Christian merchants were found in Sri Lanka, southern India, Socotra, Iran, Aksūm and South Arabia.[10] However, while the world of Late Antiquity became increasingly globalized through its intertwining trade routes, people not only exchanged goods and ideas but also illnesses such as the bacterium *Yersinia pestis*, causing the sixth-century pandemic, which had allegedly originated in Egypt in 541. This plague contributed to the sixth-century crisis, exacerbated by ecological factors and constant warfare.

At the time, while the kingdom of Aksūm extended its influence in Arabia, Rome promoted the Jafnids in response to Iran's promotion of the Naṣrids. Rome and Iran both had the goal of creating and controlling buffer political entities to defend themselves from each other and counterbalance the increasing presence of the Aksūmites and the Ḥimyarites in Arabia. After experiencing the height of their power(s) simultaneously, the Jafnids and Aksūmites were eclipsed when the Iranians assumed control of Arabia in the 570s. Only vague memoirs by antiquarians of the millennial kingdoms of South Arabia still exist today. In a similar fashion to other Arabian regions, these antiquarians described the identities of the Ḥimyarites in a way that initially framed the Arabians as Ishmaelites

[7] T. Daryaee, 'The Persian Gulf Trade in Late Antiquity', *Journal of World Hist*ory 14 (2003), 1–16, at p. 1.

[8] Procop. *Pers.* 1.20.12.

[9] P. D. Curtin, *Cross Cultural Trade in World History* (Cambridge: Cambridge University Press, 1984).

[10] Cosmas Indicopleustes, *Topographia*, 3.65, 11.14.

and thereafter depicted the Arabians as Muslims. The Iranian (and later Roman-adopted) model of controlling peripheries by tightening alliances with one supratribal authority proved ineffective in Arabia. At the end of the sixth century, such a policy was no longer necessary and was no longer used. This led to the wiping out of the Naṣrids, as they were unable to extend their control from their lower Mesopotamian seat of Ḥīrah over a vast area characterized by harsh geographical conditions and by the presence of warring multitribal entities. Interpersonal conflicts triggered by misunderstandings and deep cultural incompatibilities such as those sparked by faith controversies inevitably caused relationships between clients and superpowers to deteriorate. The conquest of Ḥimyar and the dismantlement of the regional federations of the Jafnids and Naṣrids led, to some extent, to the dismantlement of the wider late antique world and, consequently, to a power vacuum and the resulting formation of the Caliphate. In fact, the collapse of these political entities (and on a smaller scale, the fall of the Aksūmites and the earlier fall of the people of Maʿadd in Central Arabia and buffer states such as Palmyra) after their adoption and re-elaboration of surrounding ideas, networks and structures, had the unexpected sociopolitical result of creating one intraregional superpower under the leadership of Muḥammad. Iran underestimated the effectiveness of faith as a deterrent against political division and as an instrument of power (see also Iran's loss of Armenia to Christianity). Its lack of desire to impose a monopoly on culture within its empire created fertile ground for the rise of Islam. Such conditions were exploited by those Arabians who saw Muḥammad's movement as a valuable means to free themselves from the Sasanians (who plausibly a more prominent political role on the Arabian Peninsula at the time than Rome). Most significantly, Islam arose in the Arabian region, which was less involved in the broader late antique developments: the Ḥijāz.

According to Michael Doyle's models of imperial expansion, three concurrent factors are necessary for the rise of an empire among the following features: (1) the existence of a highly differentiated metropole; (2) the 'transnational extension of the economy, society, or culture' of the latter; (3) the existence of a periphery (either tribal, patrimonial, feudal, fractionated or settler); and (4) the presence of an international system.[11] Yet, the tribal Ḥijāzī society – with its limited social differentiation – managed to become an imperial metropole. The *conditio sine qua non* for the rise of

[11] M. W. Doyle, *Empires* (Ithaca, NY: Cornell University Press, 1986), 128–35.

the Ḥijāzī movement was the pericentric explosion of the north and the south of the peninsula, resulting in the formation of the Ḥimyarite Empire and of the establishment of entities such as the Jafnid kingdom. Indeed, Rome's and Iran's reaction to their Arabian peripheries led to the latter's expansion, and eventually, the peripheries overrode the centre's policies. The client kingdoms that both superpowers had supported throughout Late Antiquity made a considerable military contribution to the empires' survival. Governing territory by proxy undoubtedly had the advantage of avoiding routine deployment of troops but also entailed high costs in terms of the necessary large-scale crisis management. The Arabian clients' status was often demoted considering mutations in the political map of Late Antiquity, and the arbitrary comings and goings of externally nominated kings and officials exacerbated already existing fault lines in Arabian society, eventually contributing to a widespread malaise and clearing the path for the making of the Muslim Empire. Although Islam partially emerged in response to the rise of neighbouring aristocracies sponsored by foreign powers, it originated in the deep inland of the peninsula as an indigenous Arabian phenomenon kindled by competing tribes, regions and prophets. Contrary to Aksūm's literal adoption and internalization of the culture of its powerful trading partners (thus inevitably and involuntarily linking its destiny to Rome's decline), Arabia, though fragmented, remained largely autonomous throughout Late Antiquity. The success of Islam lay precisely in the fragmentation of pre-Islamic political and religious entities. These factors allowed for the emergence of Islam in a region located in a declining 'continent', albeit probably less affected than its surrounding empires by the crisis of the second half of the sixth century. Hence, the 'insularity' of the Ḥijāz was precisely the critical factor in the rise of the Muslim community: a close-knit community that was less subjected to external influences and located in a region isolated not only outside Arabia but also inside Arabia from the north and south of the peninsula.

The Roman and Iranian administrations and faiths remained intrinsically 'other' in the Arabian Peninsula. In some respects, late antique pre-Islamic Arabia could be compared with Korea. Korea appeared in Chinese histories before the region developed their historiography, similarly to the Arabians. While Chinese neighbours adopted Hans' bureaucratic system, script and culture, the Koreans expelled the North Korean Chinese administration introduced in the late second century BCE and started forming their kingdoms in 106 CE.[12] In the third century CE, the Chinese

[12] Lewis, *The Early Chinese Empires*, 151.

Wei later formed strategic alliances with Korean groups such as the Puyŏ against their common enemy Goguryeo.[13] Groups such as the Goguryeo are described as 'barbarian' in the Chinese records in the first century BCE but appear to have assimilated a certain degree of Chinese culture and called their rulers using the Chinese lexeme for 'king' in the first century CE. The interaction between the Han and the Korean Lolang gave rise to the trading centre of Sorabol, which became the capital of Silla (Kyongju), one of the Three Kingdoms of Korea that managed to unify the peninsula in the seventh century, shortly after the trading centre of Mecca unified Arabia. As 'Roman culture' and Christianity seeped into Arabia during Late Antiquity, Chinese culture and Buddhism seeped into Korea during the Three Kingdoms period to centralize royal authority,[14] but the experiment was not met without resistance. Buddhism had 'only shallow roots in Goguryeo',[15] and so did Christianity in Arabia.

As the Chinese writing system was adopted in Korea, Greek was adopted by the Christian north-western Arabian kingdom of the Jafnids for their monumental inscriptions. Yet, by the end of the sixth century, the 'Nabatean-transitional' script had become popular among Christian communities in the north and south of the Arabian Peninsula. It is likely that, with the advance of Christianity in the region, a 'pan-Arabian' identity of some sort was forged around the Ḥijāz. Indeed, Arabic increasingly became a marker of identity. The lack of a pre-Islamic Arabic Bible and the consequent plausible adoption of 'external' liturgical languages (Syriac or Gəʿəz) in the region hint at: (1) the marginal penetration of Christianity; and (2) the prominent position of Syriac in the Arabian Peninsula similar to its prominence along the 'Silk Road(s)',[16] where it became the 'vehicle for the communication of Christian literature'.[17] A biblical translation appeared among the Goths in the mid-fourth century,[18] and in the

[13] For the Puyŏ, see M. E. Byington, *The Ancient State of Puyŏ in Northeast Asia: Archaeology and Historical Memory* (Leiden: Brill, 2020).

[14] J. W. Best, 'Buddhism and Polity in Early Sixth-Century Paekche', *Korean Studies* 26 (2002), 165–215.

[15] J. Jorgensen, 'Goguryeo Buddhism: An Imported Religion in a Multi-ethnic Warrior Kingdom', *The Review of Korean Studies* 15 (2012), 59–107.

[16] See Chapter 1.

[17] S. F. Johnson, 'The Languages of Christianity on the Silk Roads and the Transmission of Mediterranean Culture into Central Asia', in *Empires and Exchanges in Eurasian Late Antiquity: Rome, China, Iran, and the Steppe, ca. 250–750*, ed. N. Di Cosmo and M. Maas (Cambridge: Cambridge University Press, 2018), 206–19, at p. 206.

[18] C. Falluomini, *The Gothic Version of the Gospels and Pauline Epistles: Cultural Background, Transmission and Character* (Berlin: De Gruyter, 2015).

fifth, an Armenian Bible emerged,[19] followed by a Gəʿəz version.[20] But 'la democratizzazione della cultura' through the agency of the Christian Church, a hallmark of Late Antiquity as advocated by Santo Mazzarino,[21] only marginally reached Arabia. The fall of the Nabateans (to some extent 'inventors' of the Arabic script) and increased intervention from outside coincided, in fact, with a decrease in epigraphic activity from the fourth century onwards. The 'civilizing' role promised by Rome and Iran resulted in a very marginal 'democratizazzione della cultura' in the region, as suggested by the late *mise par écrit* of the two most important pre-Islamic macrotexts of *logia* (each *suwar* could be further considered a macrotext in itself) only after the seventh century: the Qur'ān, a retelling of pre-Islamic circulating Scriptures, and pre-Islamic poetry, which also originated orally. Similarly, traditional customs, such as marriage and the disposal of the dead, arguably remained unaffected by attempts of 'Romanization' (and to a lesser degree 'Iranization') in the region. As the social conformity required for joining the Roman Commonwealth occurred at the upper echelons of society, cultural change in Arabia was not unilateral or unilinear, and 'Romanization' was not unidirectional but a dynamic process, which proceeded vertically and horizontally, engaging various social strata of the same community as well as multiple regions. Although Roman culture became an artefact of the provinces as much as of the metropolitan centre,[22] the negotiation of identities of every province was different, and concepts such as acculturation and emulation are too simplistic and narrow to explain the complex and multiphased making of commonwealths and empires. This is illustrated by the composite epigraphic milieu of the Jordanian city of Umm al-Jimāl, where Safaitic, Nabatean and Greek/Latin inscriptions have been attributed to Arabian nomads, sedentary people and external superpowers.

Like languages and scripts, faith filled a void in pre-Islamic Arabia, a region marked by the lack of a unitarian political structure and an apparent Arab ethnicity. Accordingly, Islam was not an alien product of Late Antiquity and did not mark the beginning of a new periodization.

[19] S. P. Cowe, 'The Armenian Version of the New Testament', in *The Text of the New Testament in Contemporary Research*, ed. B. D. Ehrman and M. W. Holmes (Leiden: Brill, 2013), 253–292.

[20] A. Bausi, 'Intorno ai vangeli etiopici di 'Enda- 'Abba- Garima- presso Adua', *La parola del passato* 65 (2010), 460–71.

[21] S. Mazzarino, 'La democratizzazione della cultura nel basso impero', *XIe congrès international des sciences historiques, Stockholm 21–28 août* (1960), 35–54.

[22] S. Keay and N. Terrenato (ed.), *Italy and the West: Comparative Issues in Romanization* (Oxford: Oxford University Press, 2001), 113.

However, it did mark the end of an era extensively marked by the diatribes concerning the nature of Christ. Islam, largely perceived not as a 'new religion' but as a 'new heresy' in the Christian world, took a strong position on the nature of Christ, rejecting both the incarnation and the divinity of Jesus. Hence, it could be seen as the most tangible result of centuries of debates and polemics lacerating the Christian world, and their final resolution far from the control of both episcopates and political leaders. Both Arabian henotheistic god(s) and scriptural beliefs contributed to the making of the Qurʾānic God, who slowly became more structured and defined. As early Ḥijāzī monotheism incorporated pagan elements (e.g., the *ḥajj*), the Qurʾānic opponents of Muḥammad, the *mushrikūn*, were 'imperfect monotheists' and the members of Muḥammad's monotheist movement originated as 'perfect monotheists', who associated Allāh only with his epithets (e.g., al-Raḥmān and al-Rabb). *Raḥmān* was arguably the monotheistic God of South Arabia (possibly also appearing twice in the North Arabian Corpus) who emerged as a deity after Ḥimyar's unification in the 380s. Just as the Nabatean Dushara was hellenized when the Nabatean merchants of Arabia reached southern Italy,[23] and 'safaiticized' when the Arabian Nabateans mingled with the also-Arabian Safaitic writers, so too was the South Arabian *Raḥmān* Islamized as Allāh when the Ḥimyarites came into contact with the people of the Ḥijāz. Allāh's attributes moved from the universal to the particular, encompassing early pagan substrata and gradually taking on the resemblance of the biblical God. To a certain degree, this process is similar to the making of the Christian God in Rome, rising from a blend of *Sol Invictus*, Neoplatonic influxes and vague henotheistic stances merged with the rigidly monotheistic features of the Old and New Testament God.

With the proclamation of one single God and his 'messenger', Muḥammad became the supreme leader of the tribe of the Quraysh in the Ḥijāz and thereby controlled Meccan pilgrimage and trade, as well as the fragmented political world of Arabia; a world finally unified by the identification of one common 'other': the unbelievers. The 'others' ceased to be rival tribes but were now those who did not believe in Allāh. This new othering allowed for faith to be seen as the main prerequisite for cultural uniqueness, belonging and the construction of an Arabian identity. Processes of legitimization are often binary; when the Christian community of Rome was legitimized by Constantine, for example, the polytheist

[23] G. Lacerenza, 'Il dio Dusares a Puteoli', *Puteoli – Studi di storia antica* 12–13 (1988–9), 119–49.

believers were delegitimized. Indeed, faith can be exploited to legitimize authority and give credibility to rulers and ministers, a means to challenge the status quo and deconstruct outdated paradigms and frameworks. An entire community can be rehabilitated and find a new accommodating place in the elites' propaganda and social framework through legitimization. Syncretistic instances can smooth this process of identity formation and allow for the taking of neutral positions. Because of the transience of the legitimization process at the time, it was only when the Arabians managed to 'legitimize' their identity, relying exclusively on their tools, that they succeeded in establishing a sociopolitical apparatus, paving the way for the shaping of the medieval Muslim world.

In a similar fashion to Arabian Christianities and Jewish attitudes, Islam was, to some extent, also a 'political response' to a broader crisis, accentuated *in loco* by disputes between nomad and settled populations. Moreover, like the Roman Empire, the Muslim Empire had claims of cultural monopoly early on. In the south, politics based on religious coercion had failed. In fact, sponsored by neighbouring superpowers, the Christian minority of Najrān triumphed over the Jewish sympathizers of the south. A hundred years later, another religious minority, that of Muḥammad's followers at the time of the Medinan *hijrah*, defeated the Ḥijāzī elites. A prophet, who could simultaneously wear the cloak of a general and assume the traits of a ruler, was successful because of his emphasis on the universal aspirations of his people. It was a universal appeal that triumphed over the particularities separating these people from their neighbours.

Rome never ceased viewing Arabians as 'barbarians'. Not even Christianity's universal message succeeded in the Arabians' full integration into the Commonwealth. In some ways, Muḥammad's career *e contrario* mirrors that of Constantine, the first advocate of Christendom. Whereas Constantine outrightly rejected the cloak of a pagan ruler to sit at the first Ecumenical Council and preside over the shaping of the Christian creed, Muḥammad's trajectory followed the opposite direction, his career starting as a prophet. The sixth-century world was vastly different from that of the fourth century. The last Roman–Iranian war (602–28) wore out Eurasia and inspired apocalyptic writings. Lasting most of Muḥammad's lifetime (571–632), this war profoundly impacted his prophetic inspiration and found echoes in the Qur'ān.[24] The Arabians took advantage of the wars, which had left the two empires economically bankrupt. The success

[24] See Howard-Johnston, *Witness to a World Crisis*; and T. Tesei, 'Heraclius' War Propaganda and the Qur'ān's Promise of Reward for Dying in Battle', *Studia Islamica* 114 (2019), 219–47.

of Muḥammad's movement thus lay in his channelling of political knowledge (the Arabians were accustomed to Rome, Iran and Aksūm's instruments of control and internal logistics) and of the scriptural traditions into his message, adapting them to Arabia. At the same time, Muḥammad moulded Arabian elements for the broader public of Late Antiquity. In fact, much like Christianity had been exploited as a *signifiant* of *bona fides* in the Roman Commonwealth, Islam became both a key instrument for the negotiation of identities in the Muslim Commonwealth and the most significant religious legacy originating in Late Antiquity. Nevertheless, if becoming Christian meant, to a certain extent (and not under the Sasanids), 'becoming Roman', becoming Muslim never meant becoming Arabian. Like the Iranians, Romans, Chinese and Türks, the Arabians understood the importance of developing their tradition of a divinely inspired hegemony. By favouring eschatological premises over geographical claims, the 'political prophet' Muḥammad gained leverage through the promise of a new spiritual world.

Appendix

Table A.1 *Mention of the ʿrb/ʿrbn*

Inscription name	Date	Text
Ja 560	first c. BCE–early second c. CE	the country of the ʿ**rbn**
FB-al-ʿAdān 1	first c. BCE–early second c. CE	the wars and the razzias of the ʿ**rbn** of the region of the East
Ja 629	late second c. CE–late third c. CE	they attacked and pursued the Ḥaḍramis and the ʿ**rbn** that had marched to the vicinity of Tmnʿ
CIH 343	late second c. CE–late third c. CE	He saved them from the land of Ḥimyar and the ʿ**rbn**
CIH 350	late second c. CE–late third c. CE	he led and auxiliary column of ʿ**rbn**
CIH 79	late second c. CE–late third c. CE	he moved against the ʿ**rbn** in the region of Mnhtm;
Ir 32	late second c. CE–late third c. CE	his contingent of ʿ**rbn**: three hundred ʿ**rbn** soldiers
Ja 788+Ja 671	late second c. CE–late third c. CE	expedition at the head of the army of ʿ**rbn**
Gr 124	late second c. CE–late third c. CE	Ḥm]yrm, Ḥḍrmwt and ʿ**rbn**
Ir 12	late second c. CE–late third c. CE	mounted an offensive against them and with him there were one hundred and seventy men among the ʿ**rbn**
ʿAbadān 1	late second c. CE–late third c. CE	ʿ**rbn**
CIH 541	fourth c.–sixth c. CE	so that the ʿ**rbn** who had not returned with Yzd would submit themselves + after he had sent out the summons and the ʿ**rbn** submitted themselves
Ry 507	fourth c.–sixth c. CE	ʿ**rbn**

Table A.2 *Mention of the ʾʿrb*

Inscription name	Date	Text
CIH 353	late second c. CE–late third c. CE	ʾʿ**rb** Mrb w-D̲bn
Gl 1177	late second c. CE–late third c. CE	ʾʿ**rb**
Ir 32	late second c. CE–late third c. CE	S¹ʿdtʾlb Ytlf bn Gdnm kbr ʾʿ**rb** + ʾʿ**rb** king S¹bʾ w-Kd—t w-Ngrn w-S¹fln((s¹fln))
Ja 561bis	late second c. CE–late third c. CE	ʾʿ**rb**
Ja 629	late second c. CE–late third c. CE	Whbʾl bn Mʿhr and d̲-H̬wln and Ḥaḍramawt and Qataban and Rdmn and Mḏḥym and all the soldiers and the ʾʿ**rb** who supported them against their lords the kings of Sabaʾ
Ja 665	late second c. CE–late third c. CE	S¹ʿdtʾlb Ytlf bn Gdnm kbr ʾʿ**rb** king S¹bʾ w-Kdt w-Md̲ḥgm w-Ḥr— mm w-Bhlm w-Żydʾl and all the ʾʿ**rb** S¹bʾ w-Ḥmy— rm w-Ḥḍrmt w-Ymnt + his contingent of the ʾʿ**rb** of Sabaʾ and Kindah and the inhabitants of Ns²qm and Ns²n
ʿAbadān 1	late second c. CE–late third c. CE	ʾʿ**rb** + ʾʿ**rb** Ḥḍrmt
MAFRAY-al-Miʿsāl 4	late second c. CE–late third c. CE	ʾʿ**rb** who were in the town of Shabwa
Ry 509	fourth c.–sixth c. CE	going down to the lowland with their lieutenants and their ʾtly, their hunters, their leaders, their ʾʿ**rb** of Kindah, S¹wd, Wlh
Murayghan 3	fourth c.–sixth c. CE	he took possession of the ʾʿ**rb** of Mʿdm, from Md̲rn, he drove out ʿmrm, son of Md̲rn, and he took possession of all the ʾʿ**rb** of Mʿdm, Hgrm, H̬ṭ, Ṭym, Yt̲rb and Gzm

Table A.3 *The South Arabian rulers' titles (375–565)*

Ruler	*Titulus*	Inscription reference number
Malkīkarib Yuha'min (375–400) and his sons	king of Saba', ḏu-Raydān, Ḥaḍramawt, Yamanat	RES 3383
Abīkarib As'ad (ca. 400–45) et alia	king(s) of Saba', ḏu-Raydān, Ḥaḍramawt and Yamanat	Ry 534+MAFY/Rayda 1; Gar BSE
Abīkarib As'ad (ca. 400–45)	king of Saba', ḏu-Raydān, Ḥaḍramawt, Yamanat and Ṭwdm and Thmt king of Saba', ḏu-Raydān, Ḥaḍramawt, Yamanat **and their ''*rb* of Ṭwdm and Thmt**	BynM 17 Ja 516
Abīkarib As'ad (ca. 400–45) and his son Ḥaśśān Yuha'min (ca 445–50)	kings of Saba', ḏu-Raydān, Ḥaḍramawt, Yamanat **and the ''*rb* of Ṭwdm and Thmt**	Ry 509
Shurihbị'īl Ya'fur (ca. 450–68)	king of Saba', ḏu-Raydān, Ḥaḍramawt, Yamanat and their ''*rb* of Ṭwdm and Thmt	CIH 45+CIH44; CIH 540; Dostal 1; Gar framm. 3; Gar Sharahbil A; Ẓafār Iz10-016
Shurihḅ 'īl Yakkuf and his sons (ca. 468–80)	king of Saba', ḏu-Raydān, Ḥaḍramawt, Yamanat and their ''*rb* of Ṭwdm and Thmt	CIH 537+RES 4919; CIH 644; Gl 1194; RES 4969; Ẓafār Iz10-003
Marthad'ilān Yun'im (ca. 480–5)	king of Saba', ḏu-Raydān, Ḥaḍramawt, Yamanat and their ''*rb* of Ṭwdm and Thmt	CIH 620; YM 1200
Marthad'ilān Yanūf (ca. 500–15)	king of Saba', ḏu-Raydān, Ḥaḍramawt, Yamanat and their ''*rb* of Ṭwdm and Thmt	CIH 596; DhM 287; Fa 74
Ma'dīkarib Ya'fur (ca. 519–22)	king of Saba', ḏu-Raydān, Ḥaḍramawt, Yamanat and their ''*rb* of Ṭwdm and Thmt	Ja 2484; Ry 510
Yūsuf/Joseph/Dhū Nuwās (ca. 522–30)		
Aksūmite ruler Sumūyafa' Ashwa' (ca. 531–5)		
Abraha (ca. 535–65)	king of Saba', ḏu-Raydān, Ḥaḍramawt, Yamanat and their ''*rb* of Ṭwdm and Thmt	CIH 541; DAI GDN 2002–20; Murayghān 3; Ry 506

Table A.4 *Joint Epigraphic attestation of ʿrb and ʾʿrb*

Inscription name	Date	Text
Ry 508	fourth c.–sixth c. CE	the armies of the ʾzʾn, with the tribes of ḏ-Hmdn: their citizens and their ʿ**rb,** and the ʾʿ**rb** of Kindah, Murād, Madhḥig
Ja 1028	fourth c.–sixth c. CE	he was in guard against Nagrān with the tribe of Hamdān, citizens and ʿ**rbn**, and the assault troops of ʾzʾnn and the ʾʿ**rb** of Kindah, Murād, Madhḥig, while the qayls, his brothers, with the king, were mounting guard
Ja 561bis	late second c. CE–late third c. CE	they intervened in war against groups of ʿ**rbn** on the frontier of the tribe Ḥs²dm, and in certain territories of the ʿ**rbn,** the ʾʿ**rb** who had committed offences against their lords
Ry 510	fourth c.–sixth c. CE	in order that he submitted the rebellious ʿ**rbn** to him + he undertook this expedition with his tribes Sabaʾ, Ḥimyar, Rḥbtn, Ḥaḍramawt and Yḥn, with their ʾʿ**rb** of Kindah and Mḏḥgm and with the banū Ṯʿlbt, Mḍr et S¹bʿ

Table A.5 *The Jafnids' epigraphic corpus*

Ruler name	Place	Text
Al-Ḥārith (r. 528/9–568/9)		
528–9	Jabal Says	al-Hrith the *mlk*
559	Qasṛ al-Ḥayr al-Gharbī	Fl[avius] Arethas *patrikios, endoxotatos, stratelatos*
Al-Mundhir (r. 568/9–581/2)		
528/9	Tall al-ʿUmayrī	*megaloprepestatos* Almoundaros, the *komes*
Undated	Al-Burj	Fl[avius] Alamoundar[o]s, *paneuphēmos, patrik[ios],* and *phylarchos*
578	al-Hayyat	*paneuph[emos]* Alamoundaros, *patr[ikios]*
Abū Kārib (Ḥārith's brother)		
Undated	Sammāʾ	*endoxotatos phylarchos* Aboou Chirib
al-Mundhir's sons		
Undated	al-Burj	his children, *endoxotatoi*
al-Nuʿmān ibn al-Mundhir		
Undated	Unknown	Nuʿmān *endoxotatos stratēlatēs* and *phylarchos*

Note: Two more inscriptions coming from the nave mosaic of the central church Nitl (Jordan) are probably part of the Jafnids' epigraphic corpus. One simply invokes 'Arethas son of Arethas', while the second invokes the salvation of the Thaalaba, the phylarch son of Audelas. Piccirillo, *Church of Saint Sergius.*

Bibliography

Epigraphic Sources

South Arabian Inscriptions

(Accessible on the Digital Archive for the Study of pre-Islamic Arabian Inscriptions, http://dasi.cnr.it/index.php?id=14&prjId=1&corId=0&colId=0&navId=0.)

- ʿAbadān 1.
- ʿAbadān 4.
- ʿInan 75.
- A-50-506.
- A-50-858.
- Ag 3.
- Al-Ṣi lwī 1.
- B 8457.
- Bāfaqīh AF 1.
- CIAS 35.21/o 6.
- CIAS 39.11/o 2 n° 8.
- CIAS 95.11/o 2.
- CIAS F 24/s 4/95.11.
- CIH 45+CIH 44.
- CIH 151+CIH 152.CIH 519.
- CIH 521.
- CIH 534.
- CIH 540.
- CIH 541.
- CIH 543.
- CIH 621.
- CIH 984–5.
- DAI GDN 2002–20.
- Dostal 1.
- FB-wādī Shuda yf 1.
- Gar Antichità 9 d.
- Gar Bayt al-Ashwal 1.

- Gar Bayt al-Ashwal 2.
- Gar framm. 3.
- Gar framm. 7.
- Gar Nuove Iscrizioni 4.
- Gar Sharahbil A.
- Gl 1194.
- H 2c.
- Ha11.
- Ir 69.
- Ir71.
- Ist 7608 bis.
- J1028/1.
- Ja 516.
- Ja 547+Ja 546+Ja 544+Ja 545.
- Ja 574.
- Ja 575.
- Ja 629.
- Ja 635.
- Ja 856.
- Ja 1028.
- JSLih 049a.
- Ma'in 93-A/4 and 95/12.
- MAFRAY-Ḥasī 1.
- Murayghān 1.
- Murayghān 2.
- Murayghān 3.
- RES 3232–42.
- RES 3383.
- RES 3951.
- RES 4146.
- Robin-Najr 1.
- Ry 403.
- Ry 506.
- Ry 507.
- Ry 508.
- Ry 509.
- Ry 510.
- Ry 513.
- Ry 515.
- Ry 520.
- Ry 534+MAFY/Rayda 1 – SR-Naʿḍ9.
- Sh 31.
- Wellcome A 103664.
- YM 1200.
- YM 10882.

- ZM 2000.
- ZM 5+8+10.

See also:

Ḥimà-Sud. See Robin, C. J. et al. 'Inscriptions antiques de la région de Najrān (Arabie Séoudite méridionale): nouveaux jalons pour l'histoire de l'écriture, de la langue et du calendrier arabe', *Comptes rendus de l'academie des inscriptions & belles-lettres* (2014), 1033–128.

Mon.script.sab 514. See Stein, P. 'Montheismus oder religiöse Vielfalt? Du Samawi, die Stammesgottheit der Amir, im 5. Jh. n. Chr.', *Philologisches und Historisches zwischen Anatolien und Sokotra*, ed. W. Arnold et al., 339–50. Wiesbaden: Harrassowitz, 2009.

Naveh-Ṣuʿar 24. See Naveh, J. 'A Bilingual Burial Inscription from Saba', *Lĕsonénu* 5763 (2003), 117–20.

North Arabian Inscriptions

(Accessible on the Online Corpus of the Inscriptions of Ancient North Arabia, http://krc.orient.ox.ac.uk/ociana/index.php/database.)

- AbaNS 352.
- Al-Mafraq Museum 14.
- Al-Saʿīd 1419/1999: 27–8, no. 4.
- ASWS 217.
- BS 372.
- C 2816.
- C 3315.
- C 3360.
- C 3712.
- C 4068.
- C 4351.
- C 4448.
- C 4866.
- CSNS 424.
- CSNS 718.
- HSIM 49218.1.
- JSTham 556.
- KhNSJ 6.
- KRS 37.
- KRS 995.
- KRS 1974.
- KRS 2245.
- KRS 2298.
- KRS 2301.
- KRS37.

- LP 94.
- LP 157.
- LP 559.
- RMSK 1.
- RSIS 30.
- SIJ 78.
- SIJ 88.
- SIJ 284.
- SIJ 293.
- SIJ 912.
- ZeGA 1.
- ZNam 6.

Aksūmite Inscriptions

See Bernand, E. et al. *Recueil des inscriptions de l'Éthiopie des périodes pré-Axoumite et Axoumite*. Paris: Académie des inscriptions et belles-lettres, 1991.

- RIE 190.
- RIE 191.
- RIE 192.
- RIE 195.
- RIE 263.
- RIE 264.
- RIE 265.
- RIE 266.
- RIE 271.

Greek Inscriptions

See Waddington, W. H. *Inscriptions grecques et latines de la Syrie*. Paris: F. Didot, 1870.

- Wadd. 2076.
- Wadd. 2110.
- Wadd. 2124.
- Wadd. 2203.
- Wadd. 2497.
- Wadd. 2558.
- Wadd. 2562c.

See in Jalabert, L., Mouterde, R. and Mondésert, C. *Inscriptions grecques et latines de Syrie*. Paris: P. Geuthner, 1929–59.

- IGLS 4.1550.
- IGLS 5.2553b.
- IGLS 5.2553d.

- IGLS 13/2.9843.
- IGLS 16.1385–1414.

See in Pleket, H. W. et al. *Supplementum epigraphicum graecum*. Leiden: Brill, 1923.

- SEG 7.188.
- SEG 36 (1986), 1386.
- SEG 41 (1991) 153Id.

See also:

Anfray 1970. See Anfray, F., Caquot, A. and Nautin, P. 'Une nouvelle inscription grecque d'Ezana, roi d'Axoum', *Journal des Savants* 4 (1970), 260–74.

CIG 4.8639. See Mango, C. A. 'The Church of St. Sergius and Bacchus at Constantinople and the Alleged Tradition of Octagonal Palatine Churches', *Jahrbuch der Österreichischen Akademie der Wissenschaften* 21 (1972).

Littman 752. See Littman, E., Magie, D. and Stuart, D. R. *Greek and Latin Inscriptions*, no. 752. Leiden: Brill, 1921.

OGIS 129. See Dittenberger, W. *Orientis graeci inscriptiones selectae*. Leipzig: S. Hirzel, 1903–59.

Piccirillo 2001. See Piccirillo, M. 'The Church of Saint Sergius at Nitl: A Centre of the Christian Arabs in the Steppe at the Gates of Madaba', *Liber annuus* 51 (2001), 267–84, at p. 282.

VDI. See Vinogradov, A. P. and Sedov, A. V. 'Grecheskaja nadpis iz Yuzhnoy Aravii.', *Vestnik Drevnei Istorii* 2 (1989), 162–9.

Hatran and Edessean Inscriptions

Aggoula 353. See Aggoula, B. 'Remarques sur les inscriptions hatréennes, XVI', *Syria: Archéologie, art et histoire* 67 (1990), 397–421.

As36, As47 and As49. See Segal, J. B. 'Some Syriac Inscriptions of the 2nd–3rd Century A.D.', *Bulletin of the School of Oriental and African Studies, University of London* 16 (1954), 13–36.

Drijvers 25. See Drijvers, H. J. W. *Old-Syriac (Edessean) Inscriptions*. Leiden: Brill, 1972.

H336b and H343. See Healey, J. F. *Aramaic Inscriptions and Documents of the Roman Period*. Oxford: Oxford University Press, 2009.

Nabatean, Nabateo-Arabic and Old Arabic Inscriptions

Al-Dhuyayb 65. See Al-Dhuyayb, S. *Nuqūsh nabaṭiyya fī al-Jawf, al-ʿUlā, Taymāʾ, al-mamlaka al-ʿArabiyya al-Saʿūdiyya*. Al-Riyāḍ, 2005.

Al-Hajj 2018. See Al-Hajj, M. A. and Faqʿas, A. A. 'Naqsh Jabal Dhabūb: naqsh jadīd bi-Ḫaṭṭal-Zabūr al-Yamānī fī al-istiʿāna bi-al-Llāh wa-taqwī-hi li-al-ʾīmān', *Al-ʿibar li-al-dirāsāt al-tārīkhiyyah wa-al-ʾāthāriyya* 2 (2018), 12–43.

Al-Shdaifat 2017. See Al-Shdaifat, Y. et al. 'An Early Christian Arabic Graffito Mentioning "Yazīd the King"', *Arabian Archaeology and Epigraphy* 28 (2017), 315–24.

Avner 2013. See Avner, U., Nehmé, L. and Robin, C. J. 'A Rock Inscription Mentioning Thaʿlaba, an Arab King from Ghassān', *Arabian Archaeology and Epigraphy* 24 (2013), 237–56.

F.038.02. See 197–8 in Hackl, U., Jenni, H. and Schneider, C., *Quellen zur Geschichte der Nabatäer: Textsammlung mit Übersetzung und Kommentar*. Freiburg: Universitätsverlag Freiburg, 2003.

JS Nab 4, 16 and 17. See Savignac, R. and Jaussen, A. *Mission archéologique en Arabie*. Paris: P. Geuthner, 1909–22.

Lejā. See Dussaud, R. and Macler F. 'Rapport sur une mission scientifique dans les régions désertiques de la Syrie soyenne', *Nouvelles archives des missions scientifiques et littéraires* 10 (1902), 411–744.

Zabad. Sachau, E. 'Eine dreisprachige Inskription von Zébed', *Monatsberichte der Königlich Preussischen Akademie der Wissenschaften zu Berlin* (1881), 169–90.

Iranian Inscriptions

Ardashīr's relief. See Herrmann, G. (ed.) *The Sasanian Rock Reliefs at Naqsh-i Rustam*. Berlin: Reimer, 1989.

Paikuli inscription. See Skjærvø, P. O. and Humbach, H. *The Sassanian Inscription of Paikuli*, 3: 77–139. Munich: Wiesbaden, 1983.

Shapur I' inscription at Ka'ba-ye Zartosht, 2–3. See Huyse, P. *Die dreisprachige Inschrift Šabuhrs I. an der Kaba-i Zardust (ŠKZ)*, 1: 19–24. London: School of Oriental and African Studies, 1999.

Manichean, Parthian and Sogdian Fragments

M2 I R I 1–33 and MM II, 301–2. See Asmussen, J. P. *Manichaean Literature: Representative Texts Chiefly from Middle Persian and Parthian Writings*. Delmar: Scholars' Facsimiles & Reprints, 1975.

MMTKGI, 2.5 (170–87), 26 and MMTKGI, 3.3 (441–515), 41–5. See Sundermann, W. *Mitteliranische manichäische Texte kirchengeschichtlichen Inhalts*. Berlin: Akademie-Verlag, 1981.

Assyrian Annals

Eph'al, I. *The Ancient Arabs: Nomads on the Borders of the Fertile Crescent, 9th–5th Centuries BC*. Leiden: Brill, 1982.

Luckenbill, D. D. *Ancient Records of Assyria and Babylonia*. Chicago: University of Chicago Press, 1926.

Tadmor, H. and Yamada, S. *The Royal Inscriptions of Tiglath-pileser III (744–27 BC) and Shalmaneser V (726–2 BC), Kings of Assyria*. Winona Lake: Eisenbrauns, 2011.

Literary Primary Sources

Acta Conciliorum Oecumenicorum, ed. E. Schwartz and J. Straub. Berlin: De Gruyter, 1960–2012.

Acts codex, see Pedersen, N. A. (ed.), 'A Manichaean Historical Text', *Zeitschrift für Papyrologie und Epigraphik* 119 (1997), 193–201.

Acts of Judas Thomas, see *The Acts of Thomas*, ed. A. F. J. Klijn. Leiden: Brill, 1962.

Aḥudemmeh (Life of), see *Histoires d'Ahoudemmeh et de Maroutha*, ed. F. Nau. Paris: Firmin-Didot et cie, 1905.

Al-Azraqī, *Akhbār Makkah wa-mā jā'a fīhā min al-āthār*, ed. R. Malḥas. Mecca, 1983.

Al-Azraqī, Kaʿba, see *La Kaʿbah tempio al centro del mondo (Akhbār Makkah)*, ed. R. Tottoli. Trieste: Societa Italiana Testi Islamici, 1992.

Al-Bakrī al-Andalusī, *Muʿjam mā istaʿjama min asmā al-bilād wa-al-mawāḍiʿ*, ed. M. al-Shaqqā. Cairo: Maṭbaʿat lajnat al-ta'līf wa-al-tarjamah wa-al-nashr, 1945–9.

Al-Fākihī, *Ta'rīkh Makkah*. MS Leiden, Or. 463.

Al-Hamdānī, *Iklīl*, ed. N. A. Faris. Princeton: Princeton University Press, 1940.

Al-Iṣfahānī, *Kitāb al-aghānī*, ed. R. E. Brünnow. Leiden: Brill, 1888.

Al-Iṣfahānī, *Ta'rīkh sinī mulūk al-arḍ wa-al-anbiyā '*, ed. I. M. E. Gottwaldt. Leipzig, 1844.

Al-Jāḥiẓ, *Naṣārā*, in *Majmūʿ rasā'il al-Jāḥiẓ*, ed. P. Kraus, M. Ṭ. Ḥajiri. Cairo, 1943.

Al-Masʿūdī, *Kitāb al-tanbīh wa-al-ishrāf*, ed. M. J. de Goeje. Leiden: Brill, 1893.

Al-Masʿūdī, *Murūj al-dhahab*, ed. C. Barbier de Meynard and P. de Courteille. Paris: Société asiatique, 1868–74.

Al-Nābigha al-Dhubyānī, *Dīwān*, see *Diwans of the Six Ancient Arabic Poets*, ed. W. Ahlwardt. London: Trübner, 1870.

Al-Qalqashandī, *Ṣubḥ al-aʿshā fī ṣināʿat al-inshā'*, ed. M. A. al-Rasūl Ibrāhīm. Cairo, 1913–20.

Al-Rāzī, *Ta'rīkh madīnat Ṣanʿā'*, ed. Ḥ. A. al-Amrī. Ṣanʿā ', 1974.

Al-Ṭabarī, *Tafsīr al-jalālayn*, ed. M. M. Tāmir. Cairo, 2004.

Al-Ṭabarī, *Ta'rīkh al-rusul wa-al-mulūk*, ed. M. J. de Goeje. Leiden: Brill, 1879–1901.

Al-Wāqidī, *Futūḥ al-Shām*. Beirut, 197?.

Al-Yaʿqūbī, *Ta'rīkh*, ed. M. T. Houtsma. Leiden: Brill, 1883.

Ammianus Marcellinus, *Res Gestae*, see *Histoire*, ed. G. Sabbah et al. Paris: Les Belles Lettres, 1978–99.

Arnobius of Sicca, *Adversus nationes*, see *Studio introduttivo ai sette libri di Arnobio [Afro] contro i Pagani*, ed. B. Amata. Rome: LAS/Libreria Ateneo salesiano, 2012.

Athanasius, *Apology*, see *Athanasius Werke, CPG, 2090–309*. Berlin: De Gruyter, 1934–2010.

Athanasius, *History of the Arians*, see *Ton hagion Athanasion kata Areianōn logoi: The Orations of St. Athanasius against the Arians*, ed. W. Bright. Oxford: Oxford University Press, 1884.

Aurelius Victor, *Liber de Caesaribus*, ed. F. Pichlmayr and R. Gruendel. Leipzig: B. G. Teubner, 1970.

Ban Gu, Han shu, ed. *Zhonghua shuju bianjibu*. Beijing: Zhonghua shuju, 2002.

Bar 'Ebroyo, *Chonicle*, see *The Chronography of Gregory Abu'l Faraj, the Son of Aaron, the Hebrew Physician, Commonly Known as Bar Hebraeus: Being the First Part of His Political History of the World*, ed. E. A. W. Budge. Oxford: Oxford University Press, 1932.

Bardaiṣān, *Book of the Laws of Countries*, see *W. Cureton in Spicilegium Syriacum*. London: Rivingtons, 1855.

BL ADD. 14.602, see *Documenta ad origenes monophysitarum illustrandas*, ed. J.-B. Chabot. Paris: e Typographeo Reipublicae, 1907.

Canons 16; 78, see *Die Canones der Synode von Elvira*, ed. E. Reichert. Hamburg: E. Reichert, 1990.

Cassius Dio, *Roman History*, ed. E. Cary. Cambridge, MA: Harvard University Press, 1914–27.

Cave of Treasures, see *The Book of the Cave of Treasures: A History of the Patriarchs and the Kings Their Successors from the Creation to the Crucifixion of Christ Translated from the Syriac Text of the British Museum Ms. Add. 25875*, ed. E. A. W. Budge. London: The Religious Tract Society, 1927.

Chronicle of 1234, see *Chronicon anonymum ad annum Christi 1234 pertinens*, ed. J. B. Chabot, et al. Paris: Corpus Scriptorum Christianorum Orientalium, 1916–74.

Chronicle of Zuqnīn = Incerti auctoris chronicon anonymum Ps-Dionysianum vulgo dictum, ed. J.-B. Chabot. Paris: E Typographeo Reipublicae, 1927–89.

Codex Justinianus, ed. P. Krueger. Berlin: Weidmann, 1877.

Codex Theodosianus, see *Theodosiani libri XVI*, ed. T. Mommsen and P. M. Meyer. Berlin: Deutsche Akademie der Wissenschaften zu Berlin, 1905.

Commonitorium of Vincentius of Lerins, see 'Commonitorium', in *Corpus christianorum: Series latina*, ed. R. Demeulenaere. Turnhout: Brepols, 1985.

Cosmas Indicopleustes, see *La topographie chrétienne de Cosmas Indicopleustés*, ed. W. Wolska. Paris: Presses universitaires de France, 1968–73.

Cyril of Scythopolis, *Life of Euthymius*; *Life of John the Hesychast*; *Life of Sabas*, see *Kyrillos von Skythopolis*, ed. E. Schwartz. Leipzig: Hinrichs, 1939.

Diodorus Siculus, *Bibliotheca historica*, ed. F. Vogel and C. T. Fischer. Leipzig: In aedibus B. G. Teubneri, 1888–1906.

Ecclesiasticus, ed. N. Schmidt. London: Dent, 1903.

Enoch, see *The Book of Enoch*, ed. R. H. Charles. Oxford: Oxford University Press, 1893.

Ephrem the Syrian, *Hymns*, see *Des Heiligen Ephraem des Syrers*, ed. E. Beck. Louvain: Secrétariat du Corpus SCO, 1955–79.

Epiphanius, *Panarion*, ed. K. Holl. Leipzig: Hinrich, 1915–80.

Epitome de Caesaribus, see *Aurelii victoris liber de Caesaribus: Incerti auctoris Epitome de Caesaribus*, ed. L. Cardinali. Hildesheim: Olms-Weidmann, 2012.

Ethiopian Synaxarium, see *The Book of the Saints of the Ethiopian Church: A Translation of the Ethiopic Synaxarium Made from the Manuscripts Oriental 660 and 661 in the British Museum*, ed. E. A. W. Budge. Cambridge: Cambridge University Press, 1928.

Eusebius, *Ecclesiastical History*, see *Kirchengeschichte*, ed. E. Schwartz. Leipzig: J. C. Hinrich, 1902–3.

Eusebius, *Vita Constantini*, see *Das Leben Konstantins*, ed. B. Bleckman. Turnhout: Brepols, 2007.

Eusebius of Caesarea, *Commentary on Isaiah*, see *Der Jesajakommentar*, ed. J. Ziegler. Berlin: De Gruyter, 1975.

Eusebius of Caesarea, *The Onomasticon: Palestine in the Fourth Century a.d.*, ed. J. E. Taylor. Jerusalem: Carta, 2003.

Eutropius, *Breviarium*, see *Eutropii Breviarium ab Urbe Condita: Eutropius, Kurze Geschichte Roms seit Gründung*, ed. F. L. Müller. Stuttgart: F. Steiner, 1995.

Evagrius Scholasticus, *Historia Ecclesiastica*, see *Kirchengeschichte*, ed. A. Hübner. Turnhout: Brepols, 2007.

Ganjavī, *Dāstān-i Khusraw va Shīrīn*, ed. A. Ayatī. Teheran, 1974.

Girk T'lt'oc (Book of Letters), ed. Y. Ismireanc'. Tblisi, 1901.

Herodian, *History of the Empire from the Death of Marcus = Geschichte des Kaisertums nach Marc Aurel*. Stuttgart: Steiner, 1996.

Herodotus, *Herodoti historiae*, ed. C. Hude. Oxford: Oxford University Press, 1926–7.

Ḥimyarites, see *The Book of the Himyarites: Fragments of a Hitherto Unknown Syriac Work*, ed. A. Moberg. Lund: C. W. K. Gleerup, 1924.

Hist. nest., see *Histoire nestorienne inédite*, ed. A. Scher and R. Griveau. Paris: Firmin-Didot et cie, 1908–19.

Historia Augusta, see *Scriptores Historiae Augustae*, ed. E. Hohl. Leipzig: Teubner: 1965.

History of the Great Deeds of Bishop Paul of Qenṭos and Priest John of Edessa, ed. H. Arneson et al. Piscataway: Gorgias Press, 2010.

Horace, *The Odes*, ed. K. Quinn. Basingstoke: Macmillan, 1980.

Hou Hanshu, see *Through the Jade Gate – China to Rome*, Vol. 1, ed. J. E. Hill, 2015. Ibn Al-Kalbī, *Kitāb al-Aṣnām*, ed. R. Klinke-Rosenberger. Leipzig: O. Harrassowitz, 1941.

Ibn Bakkār, *Jamharat Nasab Quraysh wa-Akhbārihā*, ed. M. M. Shākir. Al-Riyāḍ, 1999.

Ibn Ḥabīb, *Muḥabbar*, ed. I. Lichtenstädter. Hyderabad, 1942.

Ibn Isḥāq [Ibn Hishām], *Sīrat Rasūl Allāh*, ed. M. al-Saqqā, I. al-ʾAbyārī and ʾA. Shalba. Cairo, 1937; English translation: A.Guillaume, *The Life of Muhammad: A Translation of ʾIshāq's Sīrat Rasūl Allāh*, 1st edition, Oxford, 1967. Oxford: Oxford University Press, 2004.

Ibn Khurradādhbih, *al-Masālik wa-al- mamālik*, ed. M. J. de Goeje. Leiden: Brill, 1889.

Ibn Sa'd, *Kitāb al- ṭabaqāt al-kubrā*, ed. I. Abbās. Beirut, 1960.

Ibn Thābit, *Dīwān*, ed. W. Arafat. London: Luzac, 1971.

Isaac of Antioch, *Homily*, see *Homiliae S. Isaaci Syri Antiocheni,* ed. P. Bedjan. Paris: Otto Harrassowitz, 1903.

Jacob of Edessa, *Chart Fragments*, see *Chronica minora 3*, ed. E. W. Brooks, I. Guidi and J.-B. Chabot. Paris: E Typographeo Reipublicae, 1903–7.

Jacob of Edessa, *Hexaemeron: Commentary on Creation*, ed. J. Y. Çiçek. Piscataway: Gorgias Press, 2010.

Jacob of Serug, *Homiliae selectae Mar-Jacobi Sarugensis*, ed. P. Bedjan and S. Brock. Piscataway: Gorgias Press, 2006.

Jacob of Serug, *Letter to Paul of Edessa* in J. P. P. Martin, 'Lettres de Jacques de Saroug aux moines du couvent de Mar Bassus, et à Paul d'Edesse, relevées et traduites', *Zeitschrift der Deutschen Morgenländischen Gesellschaft* 30 (1876), 217–75.

Jacob of Serug, *Letter to the Ḥimyarites* in R. Schröter, 'Trostschreiben Jacob's von Sarug an die Himjaritischen Christen', *Zeitschrift der Deutschen Morgenländischen Gesellschaft* 31 (1877), 369–85.

Jerome, *Life of Hilarion*, see *Trois vies de moines: Paul, Malchus, Hilarion*, ed. E. M. Morales. Paris: Cerf, 2007.

John Diakrinomenos, *Fragment in Theodoros Anagnostes, Kirchengeschichte*, ed. G. C. Hansen. Berlin: De Gruyter, 1995.

John of Biclar, *Chronicle*, see *Victoris Tunensis chronicon. Consularibus Caseraugustanis. Iohannis Biclarensis chronicon*, ed. C. de Hartmann and R. Collins. Turnhout: Brepols, 2001.

John of Damascus, *On Heresies in John of Damascus and Islam: Christian Heresiology and the Intellectual Background to Earliest Christian-Muslim Relations*, ed. P. Schadler. Leiden: Brill, 2017.

John of Ephesus, *Lives of the Eastern Saints*, ed. E. W. Brooks. Paris: Firmin-Didot et cie, 1923–6.

John of Ephesus, *The Third Part of the Ecclesiastical History of John, Bishop of Ephesus*, ed. W. Cureton. Oxford: Oxford University Press, 1853; see also, *Extracts from the Ecclesiastical history of John, Bishop of Ephesus*, ed. J. P. Margoliouth. Leiden: Brill, 1909.

John of Nikiu, *Chronicle*, see *La chronique de Jean, eveque de Nikou*, ed. H. Zotenberg. Paris: Imprimerie Nationale, 1879.

John Psaltes, *Hymn* in R. Schröter, 'Trostschreiben Jacob's von Sarug an die himjaritischen Christen', *Zeitschrift der Deutschen Morgenländischen Gesellschaft* 31 (1877), 402–3.

Joseph et Aséneth, ed. M. Philonenko. Leiden: Brill, 1968.

Josephus, *Against Apion*, see *The Life against Apion*, ed. H. St J. Thackeray. Cambridge, MA: Harvard University Press, 2014.

Josephus, *Jewish Antiquities*, ed. H. St J. Thackeray. London: W. Heinemann, 1930.

Joshua the Stylite, *Chronicle*, see *The Chronicle of Joshua the Stylite*, ed. W. Wright. Cambridge: Cambridge University Press, 1882.

Kebra Nagast: die Herrlichkeit der Könige; aus dem äthiopischen Urtext zum ersten mal in's Deutsche übersetzt, ed. C. Bezold. Munichn: Akademie der Wissenschaften, 1905.

Khuzistan, see *Chronicon anonymum*, ed. I. Guidi. Leuven: Secrétariat du CorpusSCO, 1960–1.

Lactantius, *De mortibus persecutorum*, ed. J. L. Creed. Oxford: Oxford University Press, 1984.

Letter 1, see I. Guidi, 'La lettera di Simeone Vescovo di Bêth-Arśâm sopra i martiri omeriti', *Atti della reale accademia dei Lincei: Memorie della classe di scienze morali, storiche e filologiche* 3 (1880–1), 471–515.

Letter 2 in I. Shahid, *The Martyrs of Najran: New Documents*, 33–111. Bruxelles: Soc. des Bollandistes, 1971.

Letter of the Archimandrites in Documenta ad origenes monophysitarum illustrandas, ed. J.-B. Chabot. Paris: e Typographeo Reipublicae, 1907.

Life and Works of Saint Gregentios, Archbishop of Taphar, ed. A. Berger. Berlin: De Gruyter, 2005.

Life of Nino in Moktsevai Kartlisai, see *Le nouveau manuscrit géorgien sinaïtique N Sin 50: édition en fac-similé*, ed. Z. Aleksidze and J.-P. Mahé. Louvain: Peeters, 2001.

Life of Symeon the Stylite the Younger, see *La vie ancienne de S. Syméon le Jeune*, ed. P. Van Den Ven. Bruxelles: Soc. des Bollandistes, 1962–70.

Malalas, *Chronicle*, see *Chronographia*, ed. J. Thurn. Berlin: De Gruyter, 2000.

Malchus in *The Fragmentary Classicising Historians of the Later Roman Empire*, ed. R. C. Blockley. Liverpool: Liverpool University Press, 1981–3.

Martyrdom of 'Azqir, see A. Bausi, 'Il gadla 'Azqir', *Adamantius* 23 (2017), 341–80.

Martyrdom of Arethas (first Arabic and Geʿez versions), see *Tradizioni orientali del 'Martirio di Areta': La prima recensione araba e la versione etiopica*, ed. A. Bausi and A. Gori. Florence: Dipartimento di linguistica, Università di Firenze, 2006.

Martyrdom of Arethas (Greek version), see *Le martyre de Saint Aréthas et de ses compagnons*, ed. M. Detoraki. Paris: Association des amis du Centre d'histoire et civilisation de Byzance, 2007.

Menander, *Fragment*, see *The History of Menander the Guardsman*, ed. R. C. Blockley. Liverpool: Liverpool University Press, 1985.

Michael the Syrian, *Chronicle*, see *Text and Translations of the Chronicle of Michael the Great*, ed. G. A. Kiraz. Piscataway: Gorgias Press, 2009–11.

Mishnah (Berakhot; Bikkurim; Nedarim; Kiddushin; Terumot, Yevamot) see The William Davidson Talmud, www.sefaria.org/william-davidson-talmud.

Nabonidus Chronicle in A. K. Grayson, *Assyrian and Babylonian Chronicles*. Locust Valley: J. J. Augustin, 1975.

Notitia dignitatum accedunt notitia Urbis Constantinopolitanae et Laterculi prouinciarum, ed. O. Seeck. Berlin: Weidmann, 1876.

Novellae Just, see *Corpus iuris civilis III*, ed. R. Schöll and W. Kroll. Berlin: Berolini, Apud Weidmannos, 1954. See also *The Novels of Justinian: A Complete Annotated English Translation*, ed. D. J. D. Miller and P. Sarris. Cambridge: Cambridge University Press, 2018.

On the Nations of India and the Brahmins, see *Palladius de Gentibus Indiae et Bragmanibus*, ed. W. Berghoff. Meisenheim am Glan: Anton Hain, 1967.

Panegyrici latini, ed. R. A. B. Mynors. Oxford: Oxford University Press, 1964.
Paulus Diaconus, *Historia Longobardorum*, ed. L. Capo. Milan: Mondadori, 1992.
Periplus Maris Erythraei, ed. L. Casson. Princeton: Princeton University Press, 1989.
Philostorgius, *Ecclesiastical History*, see *Kirchengeschichte: Mit dem Leben des Lucian von Antiochien und den Fragmenten eines Arianischen Historiographen*, ed. J. Bidez. Leipzig: J. C. Hinrichs, 1913.
Photius, *Bibliotheca*, see *Bibliothèque*, ed. R. Henry. Paris: Bibliothèque nationale, 1959–91.
Piacenza Pilgrim, see P. Geyer (ed.), *Itineraria et alia geographica*, 129–53. Turnhout: Brepols, 1965.
Plato, *Symposium*, see *Platonis opera*, ed. J. Burnet. Oxford: Oxford University Press, 1903.
Pliny, *Natural History*, ed. H. Rackham. London: Heinemann, 1938–63.
Procopius. *Aed., Anecd., and Wars (inc. Pers.)*, see *Procopii Caesariensis opera omnia*, ed. J. Haury, rev. G. Wirth. Leipzig: Teubner, 1963.
Pseudo-Methodius, *Apocalypse*, see *Die Syrische Apokalypse des Pseudo-Methodius*, ed. G. J. Reinink. Leuven: E. Peeters, 1993.
Pseudo-Zachariah, *Ecclesiastical History*, see *Historia ecclesiastica Zachariae Rhetori vulgo adscripta*, ed. E. W. Brooks. Paris: E Typographeo Reipublicae, 1919–24.
Ptolemy, *Geographia*, ed. C. F. A. Nobbe. Leipzig, 1898–1913.
Rufinus, *Ecclesiastical History*, see *Eusebius Werke II/1, 2, 3,* ed. Th. Mommsen, in E. Schwartz, T. Mommsen, and F. Winkelmann, *Die Kirchengeschichte*. Berlin: De Gruyter, 1999.
Sappho, *Fragments*, see *Saffo: Frammenti*, ed. A. Aloni. Florence: Giunti, 1997.
Sebeos, *Chronicle, see Patmut'iwn Sebēosi*, ed. G. V. Abgaryan. Erevan, 1979.
Socrates Scholasticus, *Ecclesiastical History*, see *Histoire Ecclésiastique*, ed. G. C. Hansen, P. Périchon and P. Maraval. Paris: Cerf, 2004.
Sozomen, *Ecclesiastical History*, see *Kirchengeschichte*, ed. J. Bidez, rev. G. C. Hansen. Berlin: De Gruyter, 1995.
Strabo, *Geography*, see *Strabons Geographika*, ed. S. L Radt. Göttingen: Vandenhoeck & Ruprecht, 2002–11.
Synodicon Orientale, ou recueil de synodes nestoriens, ed. J. Chabot. Paris: Imprimerie nationale, 1902.
Taisho Tripitaka, http://tripitaka.cbeta.org/en/T50n2058_006.
Theodoret, *Life of Syméon*, see *Histoire des moines de Syrie*, ed. P. Canivet and A. Leroy-Molinghen. Paris: CERF, 1979.
Theophanes Confessor, *Chronicle*, see *Chronographia*, ed. C. de Boor. Hildesheim: Georg Olms, 1963–5.
Theophanes of Byzantium in Photius, *Bibliotheca*, ed. N. G. Wilson. London: Duckworth, 1994.
Theophylact Simocatta, *History*, see *Theophylacti Simocattae Historiae*, ed. C. De Boor, rev. P. Wirth. Leipzig: Teubner, 1972.Virgil, *Georgics*, ed. R. F. Thomas. Cambridge: Cambridge University Press, 1988.
West-Syrian Recension in *The Legend of Sergius Baḥīrā*, ed. B. Roggema, 311–73. Leiden: Brill, 2009.

Xenophon, *Anabasis*, ed. A Tzartzanos and K. Arapopoulos. Athens: Epistēmonikē Hetaireia tōn Hellēnikōn Grammatōn Papyros, 1938–54.
Yāqūt, *Kitāb muʿjam al-buldān*. Beirut, 1955–7.

Secondary Sources

Ahlwardt, W. *Bemerkungen über die Echtheit der Alten Arabischen Gedichte*. Greifswald: L. Bamberg, 1872.
Al-Azmeh, A. *The Emergence of Islam in Late Antiquity: Allāh and His People*. Cambridge: Cambridge University Press, 2017.
Al-Ghabban, A. I. et al. (ed.), *Roads of Arabia*. Paris: Musée du Louvre, 2010.
Alhaiti, K. et al. 'Madâ'in Sâlih, Ancient Hegra: Archaeological Work 2014/5', *Bulletin of the British Foundation for the Study of Arabia* 20 (2015), 36–8.
Alizadeh, K. 'Overlapping Social and Political Boundaries: Borders of the Sasanian Empire and the Muslim Caliphate in the Caucasus', in *Archaeology of Medieval Islamic Frontiers*, ed. A. Eger, 139–67. Louisville: University Press of Colorado: 2019.
Alizadeh, K. 'Borderland Projects of Sasanian Empire', *Journal of Ancient History* 2 (2014), 93–115.
Al-Jahwari, N. S. et al. 'Fulayj: A Late Sasanian Fort on the Arabian Coast', *Antiquity* 92 (2018), 724–41.
Al-Jallad, A. *An Outline of the Grammar of the Safaitic Inscriptions*. Leiden: Brill, 2015.
Al-Jallad, A. 'New Epigraphica from Jordan II: Three Safaitic-Greek Partial Bilingual Inscriptions', *Arabian Epigraphic Notes* 2 (2016), 55–66.
Al-Jallad, A. "ʿArab, ʾAʿrāb, and Arabic in Ancient North Arabia: The First Attestation of (ʾ) ʿrb as a Group Name in Safaitic', *Arabian Archaeology and Epigraphy* 31 (2020), 422–35.
Alpass, P. *The Religious Life of Nabataea*. Leiden: Brill, 2013.
Altheim, F. and Stiehl, R. 'Araber und Sassaniden', in *Edwin Redslob zum 70 – Geburtstag: eine Festgabe*, ed. H. von Georg Rohde et al., 200–7. Berlin: E. Blaschker, 1955.
Altheim, F. and Stiehl, R. *Finanzgeschichte der Spätantike*. Frankfurt-am-Main: V. Klostermann, 1957.
Andrade, N. J. *The Journey of Christianity to India in Late Antiquity: Networks and the Movement of Culture*. Cambridge: Cambridge University Press, 2018.
Andræ, T. *Der Ursprung des Islams und das Christentum*. Uppsala: Almqvist & Wiksells, 1926.
Anfray, F. 'Deux villes axoumites: Adoulis et Matara', in *Atti del IV congresso internazionale di studi etiopici*, ed. L. Ricci, 747–65. Rome: Accademia nazionale dei Lincei, 1974.
Anthony, S. W. *Muhammad and the Empires of Faith: The Making of the Prophet of Islam*. Oakland: University of California Press, 2020.
Arberry, A. J. *The Seven Odes: The First Chapter in Arabic Literature*. London: G. Allen & Unwin, 1957.

Arjomand, S. A. 'The Constitution of Medina: A Sociolegal Interpretation of Muhammad's Acts of Foundation of the Umma', *International Journal of Middle East Studies* 41 (2009), 555–75.

Arnau, A. C. 'The Archaeology of Early Italian Churches in Context, 313–569 CE', in *The Oxford Handbook of Early Christian Archaeology*, ed. W. R. Caraher, T. W. Davis and D. K. Pettegrew, 557–80. Oxford: Oxford University Press, 2019.

Asmussen, J. P. *Manichaean Literature: Representative Texts Chiefly from Middle Persian and Parthian Writings. Delmar: Scholars' Facsimiles & Reprints*. Delmar, NY: Scholars' Facsimiles & Reprints, 1975.

Athanassiadi, P. and Frede, M. (ed.) *Pagan Monotheism in Late Antiquity*. Oxford: Oxford University Press, 1999.

Autiero, S. and Cobb, M. A. 'Introduction: Utilizing Globalization and Transculturality for the Study of the Pre-modern World', in *Globalization and Transculturality from Antiquity to the Pre-modern World*, ed. S. Autiero and M. A. Cobb, 1–15. New York: Routledge 2022.

Avner, U., Nehmé, L. and Robin, C. J. 'A Rock Inscription Mentioning Thaʿlaba, an Arab King from Ghassān, *Arabian Archaeology and Epigraphy*, 24 (2013), 237–56.

Ball, W. *Rome in the East: The Transformation of an Empire*. London: Routledge, 2000.

Bardill, J. *Constantine, Divine Emperor of the Christian Golden Age*. Cambridge: Cambridge University Press, 2012.

Bausi, A. 'Intorno ai vangeli etiopici di 'Enda- 'Abba- Garima- presso Adua', *La parola del passato* 65 (2010), 460–71.

Bausi, A. 'Il gadla ʾAzqir', *Adamantius* 23 (2017), 341–80.

Beeston, A. F. L. 'Abraha', in *The Encyclopædia of Islam*, ed. C. E. Bosworth, 105–6. Leiden: Brill, 1960.

Beeston, A. F. L. 'Himyarite Monotheism', in *Studies in the History of Arabia*, Vol. 2, *Pre-Islamic Arabia, Proceedings of the Second International Symposium on Studies in the History of Arabia*, ed. A. M. Abdalla et al., 149–54. Riyadh: Jāmiʿat al-Riyāḍ, 1984.

Beeston, A. F. L. 'Languages of pre-Islamic Arabia', *Arabica* 28 (1981), 178–86.

Bell, R. *The Origin of Islam in Its Christian Environment*. Edinburgh: Edinburgh University Press, 1925.

Bellamy, J. A. 'Arabic Verses from the First/Second Century: The Inscription of 'En ʿAvdat', *Journal of Semitic Studies* 35 (1990), 73–9.

Bellamy, J. A., 'A New Reading of the Namārah Inscription', *Journal of the American Oriental Society* 105 (1985), 31–51.

Bell-Fialkoff, A. *The Role of Migration in the History of the Eurasian Steppe: Sedentary Civilization vs. 'Barbarian' and Nomad*. New York: Palgrave Macmillan 2000).

Berg, B. 'The Letter of Palladius on India', *Byzantion* 44 (1974), 5–16.

Berkey, J. P. *The Formation of Islam: Religion and Society in the Near East, 600–1800*. Cambridge: Cambridge University Press, 2002.

Best, J. W. 'Buddhism and Polity in Early Sixth-Century Paekche', *Korean Studies* 26 (2002), 165–215.

Bevan, G. 'Ethiopian Apocalyptic and the End of Roman Rule: The Reception of Chalcedon in Aksum and the Kebra Nagaśt', in *Inside and Out: Interactions between Rome and the Peoples on the Arabian and Egyptian Frontiers in Late Antiquity*, ed. G. Fisher and J. H. F. Dijkstra, 371–88. Leuven: Peeters, 2014.

Bevan, G., Fisher, G. and Genequand, D. 'The Late Antique Church at Tall al-ʿUmayrī East: New Evidence for the Jafnid Family and the Cult of St. Sergius in Northern Jordan', *Bulletin of the American Schools of Oriental Research* 373 (2015), 49–68.

Biella, J. C. *Dictionary of Old South Arabic Sabaean Dialect*. Chico: Scholars Press, 1982.

Block, C. J. 'Philoponian Monophysitism in South Arabia at the Advent of Islam with Implications for the English Translation of 'Thalātha'in Qurʾān 4. 171 and 5. 73', *Journal of Islamic Studies* 23 (2012), 50–75.

Bonner, M. *The Last Empire of Iran*. Piscataway: Gorgias Press, 2020.

Bonnéric, J. 'Archaeological Evidence of an Early Islamic Monastery in the Centre of al-Qusur (Failaka Island, Kuwait)', *Arabian Archaeology and Epigraphy* 32 (2021), 50–61.

Bowden, W. 'The Early Christian Archaeology of the Balkans', in *The Oxford Handbook of Early Christian Archaeology*, ed. W. R. Caraher, T. W. Davis and D. K. Pettegrew, 538–56. Oxford: Oxford University Press, 2019.

Bowersock, G. W. *The Crucible of Islam*. Cambridge, MA: Harvard University Press, 2017.

Bowersock, G. W. 'From Emperor to Bishop: The Self-conscious Transformation of Political Power in the Fourth Century A.D.', *Classical Philology* 81 (1986), 298–307.

Bowersock, G. W. *Empires in Collision in Late Antiquity*. Waltham: Brandeis University Press, 2012.

Bowersock, G. W. 'Helena's Bridle and the Chariot of Ethiopia', in *Antiquity in Antiquity: Jewish and Christian Pasts in the Greco-Roman World*, ed. G. Gardner and K. L. Osterloh, 383–93. Tübingen: Mohr Siebeck, 2008.

Bowersock, G. W. 'The Highest God with Particular Reference to North Pontus', *Hyperboreus* 8 (2002), 353–63.

Bowersock, G. W. 'The New Greek Inscription from South Yemen', in *To Hellenikon: Studies in Honor of Speros Vryonis*, ed. M. V. Anastos, 3–8. New Rochelle: Artistide D. Caratzas, 1993.

Bowersock, G. W. 'A Report on Arabia Provincia', *Journal of Roman Studies* 61 (1971), 219–42.

Bowersock, G. W. *Roman Arabia*. Cambridge. MA: Harvard University Press, 1983.

Bowersock, G. W. *The Throne of Adulis: Red Sea Wars on the Eve of Islam*. New York: Oxford University Press, 2013.

Bowersock, G. W., Brown, P. and Grabar, O. (eds) *Interpreting Late Antiquity*. Cambridge, MA: Harvard University Press, 2001.

Bowman, J. 'The Christian Monastery on the Island of Kharg', *Australian Journal of Biblical Archaeology* 2 (1974), 49–64.

Briant, P. *État et pasteurs au moyen-orient ancien*. Cambridge: Cambridge University Press, 1982.

Brita, A. 'Nine Saints', in *Encyclopaedia Aethiopica*, ed. S. Uhlig, 1188–91. Wiesbaden: Harrassowitz, 2003.

Britt, K. C. 'Early Christian Mosaics in Context', in *The Oxford Handbook of Early Christian Archaeology*, ed. W. R. Caraher, T. W. Davis and D. K. Pettegrew, 275–95. Oxford: Oxford University Press, 2019.

Brock, S. P. 'Christians in the Sasanian Empire: A Case of Divided Loyalties', *Studies in Church History* 18 (1982), 1–19.

Brockelmann, C. 'Allah und die Götzen, der Ursprung des islamischen Monotheismus', *Archiv für Religionswissenschaft* 21 (1922), 99–121.

Brown, P. *The World of Late Antiquity*. London: Thames and Hudson, 1971. See also Brown, P. *The World of Late Antiquity*. New York: Norton, 1989.

Bukharin, M. D. 'Mecca on the Caravan Routes in pre-Islamic Antiquity', in *The Qur'ān in Context: Historical and Literary Investigations into the Qur'ānic Milieu*, ed. A. Neuwirth, N. Sinai and M. Marx, 115–34. Leiden: Brill, 2010.

Burbank, J. and Cooper, F. *Empires in World History: Power and the Politics of Difference*. Princeton: Princeton University Press, 2010.

Buswell, R. E. (ed.) *Chinese Buddhist Apocrypha*. Honolulu: University of Hawaii Press, 1990.

Butler, H. C. et al. *Publications of the Princeton University Archaeological Expeditions to Syria in 1904–1905 and 1909*. Leiden: Brill, 1907–49.

Byington, M. E. *The Ancient State of Puyŏ in Northeast Asia: Archaeology and Historical Memory*. Leiden: Brill, 2020.

Cameron, A. (ed.) *Late Antiquity on the Eve of Islam*. Abingdon: Routledge, 2013.

Cameron, A. and Hall, S. G. *Eusebius: Life of Constantine*. Oxford: Oxford University Press, 1999.

Cameron, A. 'Bitter Furies of Complexity', *Times Literary Supplement* (20 September 2019), 28–9.

Canepa, M. P. 'Iran under the Parthian and Sasanian Dynasties', in *The Oxford World History of Empire*, Vol. 2, *The History of Empires*, ed. C. A. Bayly, P. Bang and W. Scheidel, 290–324. Oxford: Oxford University Press, 2020.

Canepa, M. P. *The Iranian Expanse: Transforming Royal Identity through Architecture, Landscape, and the Built Environment, 550 BCE–642 CE*. Oakland: University of California Press, 2018.

Carvajal López, J. C. et al., 'From Tentscape to Landscape: A Multi-Scale Analysis of Long-Term Patterns of Occupation in North-West Qatar', *Proceedings of the Seminar for Arabian Studies* 48 (2018), 31–45.

Carter, R. A. 'Christianity in the Gulf during the First Centuries of Islam', *Arabian Archaeology and Epigraphy* 19 (2008), 71–108.

Cereti, C. G. and Terribili, G. 'The Middle Persian and Parthian Inscriptions on the Paikuli Tower: New Blocks and Preliminary Studies', *Iranica antiqua* 49 (2014), 347–412.

Chabbi, J, *Le seigneur des tribus : l'islam de Mahomet*. Paris: CNRS Éditions, 2013.

Chaichian, M. A. *Empires and Walls: Globalization, Migration, and Colonial Domination*. Leiden: Brill, 2014.

Chakravarti, R. 'Vibrant Thalassographies of the Indian Ocean: Beyond Nation States', *Studies in History* 31 (2015), 235–48.

Chaniotis, A. 'The Jews of Aphrodisias: New Evidence and Old Problems', *Scripta Classica Israelica* 21 (2002), 209–42.

Chaniotis, A. 'Megatheism: The Search for the Almighty God and the Competition of Cults', in *One God: Pagan Monotheism in the Roman Empire*, ed. S. Mitchell and P. Van Nuffelen, 112–40. Cambridge: Cambridge University Press, 2010.

Chelhod, J. *Le sacrifice chez les Arabes: recherches sur l'évolution*. Paris: Presses universitaires de France, 1955.

Clark, V. A. 'The Roman Castellum of Qasr Bshir', in *The Roman Frontier in Central Jordan*, ed. S. T. Parker, 457–95. Oxford: Oxford University Press, 1987.

Clines, D. J. A. (ed.) *Dictionary of Classical Hebrew*. Sheffield: Phoenix Press, 1993.

Cobb, M. A. *Rome and the Indian Ocean Trade from Augustus to the Early Third Century CE*. Leiden: Brill, 2018.

Cohen, S. J. D. 'Religion, Ethnicity and "Hellenism" in the Emergence of Jewish Identity in Maccabean Palestine', in *Religion and Religious Practice in the Seleucid Kingdom*, ed. P. Bilde, et al., 204–23. Aarhus: Aarhus University Press, 1999.

Collins, S. 'Where Is Sodom? The Case for Tall el-Hammam', *Biblical Archaeology Review* 39 (2013), 32–41.

Conrad, L. I. 'Abraha and Muḥammad: Some Observations apropos of Chronology and Literary "Topoi" in the Early Arabic Historical Tradition', *Bulletin of the School of Oriental and African Studies* 50 (1987), 225–40.

Conrad, L. I. 'The Arabs', in *The Cambridge Ancient History*, Vol. 14, *Late Antiquity: Empire and Successors, A.D. 425–600*, ed. A. Cameron, M. Whitby and B. Ward-Perkins, 678–700. Cambridge: Cambridge University Press, 2000.

Conrad, L. I. 'Epidemic Disease in Central Syria in the Late Sixth Century: Some New Insights from the Verse of Assān ibn Thābit', *Byzantine and Modern Greek Studies* 18 (1994), 12–59.

Conrad, L. I. and Cameron, A. (eds) *The Byzantine and Early Islamic Near East I: Problems in the Literary Source Material*. Princeton: Princeton University Press, 1992.

Conti Rossini, C. *Storia D'Etiopia*. Bergamo: Istituto italiano d'arte grafiche, 1928.

Cooley, A. E. *Res Gestae Divi Augusti: Text, Translation and Commentary*. Cambridge: Cambridge University Press, 2009.

Cowe, S. P. 'The Armenian Version of the New Testament', in *The Text of the New Testament in Contemporary Research*, ed. B. D. Ehrman and M. W. Holmes, 253–92. Leiden: Brill, 2013.

Cracco Ruggini, L. 'Il Tardoantico: per una tipologia dei punti critici', *Storia di Roma, 3/1*. Torino: Einaudi, 1993.

Crone, P. 'How Did Quranic Pagans Make a Living?', *Bulletin of the School of Oriental and African Studies* 68 (2005), 387–99.

Crone, P. *Meccan Trade and the Rise of Islam*. Princeton: Princeton University Press, 1987.

Crone, P. 'Serjeant and Meccan Trade', *Arabica* 39 (1992), 216–40.

Crone, P. and Cook, M. *Hagarism: The Making of the Islamic World*. Cambridge: Cambridge University Press, 1977.

Curtin, P. D. *Cross Cultural Trade in World History*. Cambridge: Cambridge University Press, 1984.

Daryaee, T. 'The Persian Gulf Trade in Late Antiquity', *Journal of World History* 14 (2003), 1–16.

Daryaee, T. 'The Persian Gulf in Late Antiquity: The Sasanian Era (200–700 CE)', in *The Persian Gulf in History*, ed. Lawrence G. Potter, 57–70. New York: Palgrave Macmillan, 2009.

Daryaee, T. 'The Sasanian "Mare Nostrum": The Persian Gulf', *International Journal of the Society of Iranian Archaeologists* 2 (2016), 40–88.

Dauge, Y. *Le Barbare: Recherches sur la conception romaine de la barbarie et de la civilization*. Bruxelles: Latomus, 1981.

Dayton, J. 'The Lost Elephants of Arabia', *Antiquity* 42 (1968), 42–5.

De Blois, F. 'Islam in Its Arabian Context', in *The Qur'ān in Context: Historical and Literary Investigations into the Qur'ānic Milieu*, ed. A. Neuwirth, N. Sinai and M. Marx, 615–24 Leiden: Brill, 2010.

De Jong, A. 'Religion and Politics in Pre-Islamic Iran', in *The Wiley Blackwell Companion to Zoroastrianism*, ed. M. Stausberg, Y. S. Vevaina and A. Tessmann, 83–101. Chichester: Wiley-Blackwell, 2015.

De la Vaissière, E. 'Away from the Ötüken: A Geopolitical Approach to the Seventh Century Eastern Türks', in *Complexity of Interaction along the Eurasian Steppe Zone in the First Millennium CE*, ed. J. Bemmann and M. Schmauder, 453–62. Bonn: Rheinische Friedrich-Wilhems Universität, 2015.

De la Vaissière, E. *Sogdian Traders: A History*. Leiden: Brill, 2005.

De la Vaissière, E. 'Trans-Asian Trade, or the Silk Road Deconstructed (Antiquity, Middle Ages)', in *The Cambridge History of Capitalism*, Vol. 1, *The Rise of Capitalism: From Ancient Origins to 1848*, ed. J. G. Williamson and L. Neal, 101–24. Cambridge: Cambridge University Press, 2014.

De Vries, B. 'Between the Cults of Syria and Arabia: Traces of Pagan Religion at Umm el-Jimal', *Studies in the History and Archaeology of Jordan* 10 (2009), 177–91.

De Vries, B. 'Continuity and Change in the Urban Character of the Southern Hauran from the 5th to the 9th Century: The Archaeological Evidence at Umm al-Jimal', *Journal of Mediterranean Archaeology* 13 (2000), 39–45.

De Vries, B. *Umm el-Jimal: A Frontier Town and Its Landscape in Northern Jordan*, Vol. 1, *Fieldwork 1972–1981*. Portsmouth: Journal of Roman Archaeology, 1998.

Deeg, M. 'The Spread of Buddhist Culture to China between the Third and Seventh Centuries', in *Empires and Exchanges in Eurasian Late Antiquity: Rome, China, Iran, and the Steppe, ca. 250–750*, ed. N. Di Cosmo and M. Maas, 220–34. Cambridge: Cambridge University Press, 2018.

Derrett, D. M. 'The Theban Scholasticus and Malabar in c. 355–60', *Journal of the American Oriental Society* 82 (1962), 21–31.

Detoraki, M. *Le Martyre de Saint Aréthas et de ses Compagnons*. Paris: Association des amis du Centre d'histoire et civilisation de Byzance, 2007.

Di Cosmo, N. 'China–Steppe Relations in Historical Perspective', in *Complexity of Interaction in Complexity of Interaction along the Eurasian Steppe Zone* in *the First Millennium* CE, ed. J. Bemmann and M. Schmauder, 49–72. Bonn: Rheinische Friedrich-Wilhems Universität, 2015.

Di Cosmo, N. 'The Relations between China and the Steppe: From the Xiongnu to the Türk Empire', in *Empires and Exchanges in Eurasian Late Antiquity: Rome, China, Iran, and the Steppe, ca. 250–750*, ed. N. Di Cosmo and M. Maas, 35–53. Cambridge: Cambridge University Press, 2018.

Dignas, B. and Winter, E. *Rome and Persia in Late Antiquity*. Cambridge: Cambridge University Press, 2007.

Dillmann, A. (ed.) *Lexicon linguae aethiopicae*. New York: Frederick Ungar, 1955.

Donner, F. 'From Believers to Muslims: Confessional Self-identity in the Early Islamic Community', *Al-abāth* 50–1 (2002–3), 9–53.

Doyle, M. W. *Empires*. Ithaca, NY: Cornell University Press, 1986.

Drompp, M. R. 'Infrastructures of Legitimacy in Inner Asia: The Early Türk Empires', in *Empires and Exchanges in Eurasian Late Antiquity: Rome, China, Iran, and the Steppe, ca. 250–750*, ed. N. Di Cosmo and M. Maas, 302–16. Cambridge: Cambridge University Press, 2018.

Drompp, M. R. 'Strategies of Cohesion and Control in the Türk and Uyghur Empires', in *Complexity of Interaction* in *Complexity of Interaction along the Eurasian Steppe Zone in the First Millennium* CE, ed. J. Bemmann and M. Schmauder, 437–52. Bonn: Rheinische Friedrich-Wilhems Universität, 2015.

Dueppen, S. 'The Archaeology of West Africa, ca. 800 BCE–1500 CE', *History Compass* 14 (2016), 247–63.

Edwards, M. *Religions of the Constantinian Empire*. Oxford: Oxford University Press, 2015.

Eichmann, R., Schaudig, H. and Hausleiter, A. 'Archaeology and Epigraphy at Tayma (Saudi Arabia)', *Arabian Archaeology and Epigraphy* 17 (2006), 163–76.

Elsner, J. 'The Birth of late Antiquity: Riegl and Strzygowski in 1901', *Art History* 25 (2002), 361–70.

Esders, S. '"Faithful Believers": Oaths of Allegiance in post-Roman Societies as Evidence for Eastern and Western "Visions of Community"', in *Visions of Community in the post-Roman World: The West, Byzantium and the Islamic World, 357–74*, ed. W. Pohl, C. Gantner and R. E. Payne, 357–74. London: Routledge, 2012.

Evers, K. G. *Worlds Apart Trading Together: The Organisation of Long-Distance Trade between Rome and India in Antiquity*. Oxford: Archaeopress Publishing Ltd, 2017.

Fahd, T. *Arabie préislamique et son environnement historique et culturel*. Leiden: Brill, 1989.

Falluomini, C. *The Gothic Version of the Gospels and Pauline Epistles: Cultural Background, Transmission and Character*. Berlin: De Gruyter, 2015.
Fiema, Z. T. and Nehmé, L. 'Ecclesiastical Architecture in Petra', in *Arabs and Empires before Islam*, ed. G. Fisher, 390–2. Oxford: Oxford University Press, 2015.
Finster, B. 'Arabia in Late Antiquity: An Outline of the Cultural Situation in the Peninsula at the Time of Muḥammad', in *The Qurʾān in Context*, ed. A. Neuwirth, N. Sinai and M. Marx, 61–114. Leiden: Brill, 2010.
Fisher, G. *Between Empires: Arabs, Romans, and Sasanians in Late Antiquity*. Oxford: Oxford University Press, 2011.
Fisher, G., Wood, P. et al. 'Arabs and Christianity', in *Arabs and Empires*, ed. G. Fisher, 276–372. Oxford: Oxford University Press, 2015.
Fisher, G. (ed.) *Arabs and Empires before Islam*. Oxford: Oxford University Press, 2015.
Ford, R. B. *Rome, China, and the Barbarians: Ethnographic Traditions and the Transformation of Empires*. Cambridge: Cambridge University Press, 2020.
Fowden, E. 'An Arab Building at Rusafa-Sergiopolis', *Damaszener Mitteilungen* 12 (2000), 303–24.
Fowden, E. *The Barbarian Plain: Saint Sergius between Rome and Iran*. Berkeley: University of California Press, 1999.
Fowden, E. 'Constantine and the Peoples of the Eastern Frontier', in *Cambridge Companion to the Age of Constantine*, ed. N. Lenski, 377–98. Cambridge: Cambridge University Press, 2005.
Fowden, E. 'Inside and Out: Interactions between Rome and the Peoples on the Arabian and Egyptian Frontiers in Late Antiquity by J.H.F. Dijkstra, G. Fisher (review)', *Journal of Late Antiquity* 9 (2016), 557–60.
Fowden, E. 'Shrines and Banners: Paleo-Muslims and Their Material Inheritance', in *Beiträge zur Islamischen Kunst und Archäologie: Band 6*, ed. L. Korn und Ç. İvren, 5–24. Wiesbaden: Dr. Ludwig Reichert, 2020.
Fowden, G. *Before and after Muḥammad: The First Millennium Refocused*. Princeton: Princeton University Press, 2014.
Fowden, G. *Empire to Commonwealth: Consequences of Monotheism in Late Antiquity*. Princeton: Princeton University Press, 1993.
Frankopan, P. *The Silk Roads: A New History of the World*. London: Bloomsbury, 2015.
Frankopan, P. 'Why We Need to Think about the Global Middle Ages', *Journal of Medieval Worlds* 1 (2019), 5–10.
Fück, J. 'Die Originalität des Arabischen Propheten', *Zeitschrift der Deutschen Morgenländischen Gesellschaft* 90 (1936), 509–25.
Gajda, I. 'Remarks on Monotheism in Ancient South Arabia', in *Islam and Its Past: Jahiliyya, Late Antiquity, and the Qur'an*, ed. C. Bakhos and M. Cook, 247–56. Oxford: Oxford University Press, 2017.
Gallagher, W. R. *Sennacherib's Campaign to Judah: New Studies*. Leiden: Brill, 1999.
Garbini, G. *Introduzione all'epigrafia semitica*. Brescia: Paideia, 2006.
Garsoïan, N. *Interregnum: Introduction to a Study on the Formation of Armenian Identity (ca 600–750)*. Louvain: Peeters, 2012.

Garsoïan, N. *L'église arménienne et le grand schisme d'Orient*. Louvain: Peeters, 1999.

Gawlikowski, M. 'Arabes et Arabies dans l'antiquité', *Topoi: Orient-Occident* 14 (2006), 41–6.

Geiger, A. *Was hat Mohammed aus dem Judenthume Aufgenommen?* Bonn: F. Baaden, 1883.

Genequand, D. 'The Archaeological Evidence for the Jafnids and the Naṣrids', in *Arabs and Empires*, ed. G. Fisher, 172–213. Oxford: Oxford University Press, 2015.

Genequand, D. 'Some Thoughts on Qasr al-Hayr al-Gharbi, Its Dam, Its Monastery and the Ghassanids', *Levant* 38 (2006), 63–84.

Ghilardi, M. 'Alle origini del dibattito sulla nascita dell'arte tardoantico', *Mediterraneo antico* 5 (2002), 117–46.

Gibbon, E. *The History of the Decline and Fall of the Roman Empire*. London, 1776.

Gignoux, P. *Les quatre inscriptions du mage Kirdīr*. Paris: Association pour l'avancement des études iraniennes, 1991.

Goldziher, I. *Die Richtungen der Islamischen Koranauslegung*. Leiden: Brill, 1920.

Goldziher, I. *Muhammedanische Studien*. Halle: Max Niemeyer, 1889–90.

Goodman, M. A. *Mission and Conversion: Proselytizing in the Religious History of the Roman Empire*. Oxford: Oxford University Press, 1994.

Görke, A. 'Prospects and Limits in the Study of the Historical Muḥammad', in *Transmission and Dynamics of the Textual Sources of Islam*, ed. N. Boekho-van der Voort, K. Versteegh and J. Wagemakers, 137–51. Leiden: Brill, 2011.

Graf, D. F. *Rome and the Arabian Frontier: From the Nabataeans to the Saracens*. Aldershot: Ashgate, 1997.

Graf, D. F. 'The Saracens and the Defence of the Arabian Frontier', *Bulletin of the American Schools of Oriental Research* 229 (1978), 1–26.

Grasso, V. A. 'Christology on the Red Sea: God and His Son in Late Antique Arabia and Ethiopia' (Spring 2023, forthcoming).

Grasso, V. A. 'The Gods of the Qur'ān: The Rise of Ḥijāzī Henotheism during Late Antiquity', in *The Study of Islamic Origins: New Perspectives and Contexts*, ed. M. B. Mortensen, G. Dye, T. Tesei and I. Oliver, 297–324. Berlin: De Gruyter, 2021.

Grasso, V. A. 'Historicizing Ontologies: Qur'ānic Preternatural Creatures between Ancient Topoi and Emerging Traditions', *Journal of Late Antiquity* (Spring 2023, forthcoming).

Grasso, V. A. 'A Late Antique Kingdom's Conversion: Jews and Sympathisers in South Arabia', *Journal of Late Antiquity* 13 (2020), 352–82.

Grasso, V. A. 'On the Jafnid al-Ḥārith, from the Jafnid al-Ḥārith: A Translation and Commentary of Syriac Miaphysite Letters from the Sixth Century' (forthcoming).

Grasso, V. A. 'Rejoice in God! Five Miaphysite Letters from Sixth Century Alexandria', in *Bishops and Bishoprics in Egypt, Nubia and Ethiopia*, ed. A. Tsakos and R. Seignobos (forthcoming).

Grasso, V. A. and Fowden, G. 'Review of G. Fisher (ed.), *Arabs and Empires before Islam*, and G. Bowersock, *The Crucible of Islam*', *Journal of Roman Studies* 108 (2018), 317–20.

Grasso, V. A. and Harrower, M. J. 'The Basilica of Betä Säma'ti' in Its Aksumite, Early Christian and Late Antique Context', *Journal of Near Eastern Studies* 82 (Spring 2023, forthcoming).

Grasso, V. A. 'Perception, Representation, Memory', in *A Cultural History of the Middle East and North Africa, 450–750,* ed. N. Khalek. London: Bloomsbury (Cultural History series, vol. 1/6, forthcoming 2024).

Grasso, V. A. 'Slavery in pre-Islamic Arabia as Reconstructed from the Epigraphic Corpora' (forthcoming, presented in 2022 at the QaSLA Project Conference – Epigraphy, the Qur'ān, and the Religious Landscape of Arabia).

Grasso, V. A. 'Christology on the Red Sea: God and His Son in Late Antique Arabia and Ethiopia' (forthcoming).

Greatrex, G. 'Byzantium and the East in the Sixth Century', in *The Cambridge Companion to the Age of Justinian*, ed. M. Maas, 477–509. Cambridge: Cambridge University Press, 2005.

Greatrex, G. 'Les Jafnides et la défense de l'empire au vie siècle', in *Les Jafnides: Des rois arabes au service de Byzance (vie siècle de l'ère chrétienne)*, ed. D. Genequand and C. J. Robin, 121–54. Paris: École française de Rome, 2015.

Greatrex, G. *Rome and Persia at War, 502–532*. Leeds: Francis Cairns, 1998.

Gregoratti, L. 'Temples and Traders in Palmyra', in *Capital, Investment, and Innovation in the Roman World*, ed. Paul Erdkamp, 461–80. Oxford: Oxford University, 2020.

Grenet, F. *La geste d'Ardashir fils de Pâbag*. Paris: Éditions A Die, 2003.

Griffith, S. H. *The Bible in Arabic: The Scriptures of the 'People of the Book' in the Language of Islam*. Princeton: Princeton University Press, 2013.

Griffith, S. H. 'Christian Lore and the Arabic Qur'an: The "Companions of the Cave", in Surat al-Kahf and in Syriac Christian Tradition', in *The Qur'an in Its Historical Context*, ed. G. S. Reynolds, 109–38. London: Routledge, 2008.

Griffith, S. H. 'The Qur'ān's "Nazarenes" and Other Late Antique Christians: Arabic-Speaking "Gospel People" in Qur'ānic Perspective', in *Christsein in der islamischen West*, ed. S. H. Griffith and S. Grebenstein, 81–106. Wiesbaden: Harrassowitz, 2015.

Grouchevoy, A. G. 'Trois niveaux de phylarques: Étude terminologique sur les relations de Rome et de Byzance avec les Arabes avant l'Islam', *Syria* 72 (1995), 105–31.

Gysens, J. C. 'Safaitic Graffiti from Pompeii', *Proceedings of the Seminar for Arabian Studies* 20 (1990), 1–7.

Haldon, J. and Fleitmann, D. 'Drought and the End of Himyar? Complexity, Determinism and the Limits of Explanation' (forthcoming).

Halsberghe, G. H. *The Cult of Sol Invictus*. Leiden: Brill, 1972.

Hansen, V. *The Silk Road*. Oxford: Oxford University Press, 2012.

Hansen, V. 'The Synthesis of the Tang Dynasty: The Culmination of China's Contacts and Communication with Eurasia, 310–755', in *Empires and Exchanges in Eurasian Late Antiquity: Rome, China, Iran, and the Steppe, ca. 250–750*, ed. N. Di Cosmo and M. Maas, 108–22. Cambridge: Cambridge University Press, 2018.
Harper, P. O. 'Ancient Near Eastern Art', in *MET Notable Acquisitions, 1982–1983*, ed. The Metropolitan Museum of Art, with a foreword by Philippe de Montebello, 5. New York: The Metropolitan Museum of Art, 1983.
Harrower, M. J. et al. 'Beta Samati: Discovery and Excavation of an Aksumite Town', *Antiquity* 93 (2019), 1534–52.
Hatke, G. *Aksum and Nubia. Warfare, Commerce, and Political Fictions in Ancient Northeast Africa*. New York: New York University Press, 2013.
Hawting, G. R. *The Idea of Idolatry and the Emergence of Islam*. Cambridge: Cambridge University Press, 1999.
Healey, J. F. *The Nabatean Tomb Inscriptions of Mada'in Salih*. Oxford: Oxford University Press, 1993.
Healey, J. F. *The Religion of the Nabateans: A Conspectus*. Leiden: Brill, 2001.
Hillenbrand, R. *Islamic Art and Architecture*. London: Thames and Hudson, 1999.
Hirschfeld, H. *Beitrage Zur Erklärung des Koran*. Leipzig: O. Schulze, 1886.
Hirschfeld, Y. 'The Crisis of the Sixth Century: Climatic Change, Natural Disasters and the Plague', *Mediterranean Archaeology and Archaeometry* 6 (2006), 19–32.
Hitti, P. *History of the Arabs: From the Earliest Times to the Present*. London: Macmillan, 1970.
Honigmann, E. 'La liste originale des pères de Nicée: a propos de l'évêché de "Sodoma" en Arabie', *Byzantion* 14 (1939), 17–76.
Hornkohl, A. D. *Ancient Hebrew Periodization and the Language of the Book of Jeremiah*. Leiden: Brill, 2014.
Horovitz, J. *Koranische Untersuchungen*. Berlin: De Gruyter, 1926.
Howard, A. F. et al. *Chinese Sculpture*. New Haven: Yale University, 2006.
Howard-Johnston, J. 'The Sasanian State: The Evidence of Coinage and Military Construction', *Journal of Ancient History* 2 (2014), 144–81.
Howard-Johnston, J. *Witnesses to a World Crisis: Historians and Histories of the Middle East in the Seventh Century*. Oxford: Oxford University Press, 2010.
Howard-Johnston, J. 'The India Trade in Late Antiquity', in *Sasanian Persia: Between Rome and the Steppes of Eurasia*, ed. E. W. Sauer, 284–304. Edinburgh: Edinburgh University Press, 2017.
Hoyland, R. G. *Arabia and the Arabs from the Bronze Age to the Coming of Islam*. London: Routledge, 2001.
Hoyland, R. G. *The Late Antique World of Early Islam: Muslims among Christians and Jews in the East Mediterranean*. Princeton: Princeton University Press, 2015.
Hoyland, R. G. *Seeing Islam as Others Saw It: A Survey and Evaluation of Christian, Jewish and Zoroastrian Writings on Early Islam*. Princeton: Princeton University Press, 1997.
Hoyland, R. G. 'Writing the Biography of the Prophet Muḥammad: Problems and Solutions', *History Compass* 5 (2007), 581–602.

Ḥusayn, S. M. 'Talbiyat al-jahiliyya', *Proceedings of the Ninth All-India Oriental Conference* (1937), 361–9.

Ḥusayn, Ṭ. *Fi al-shiʿr al-jāhilī*. Cairo, 1926.

Imrie, A. *The Antonine Constitution: An Edict for the Caracallan Empire*. Leiden: Brill, 2018.

Insoll, T. et al. 'Excavations at Samahij, Bahrain, and the Implications for Christianity, Islamisation and Settlement in Bahrain', *Arabian Archaeology and Epigraphy* 32 (2021), 395–421.

Intagliata, E. E. *Palmyra after Zenobia AD 273–750: An Archaeological and Historical Reappraisal*. Oxford: Oxford University Press, 2018.

Isaac, B. *The Invention of Racism in Classical Antiquity*. Princeton: Princeton University Press, 2004.

Isaac, B. *The Limits of Empire: The Roman Army in the East*. Oxford: Oxford University Press, 1990.

Jamil, N. *Ethics and Poetry in Sixth-Century Arabia*. Cambridge: Cambridge University Press, 2017.

Jamme, A. W. F. *Miscellanées d'ancient arabe 16*. Washington, DC: 1988.

Johnson, D. W. 'Dating the Kebra Negast: Another Look', in *Peace and War in Byzantium*, ed. T. S. Miller and J. Nesbitt, 197–208. Washington: Catholic University of America Press, 1995.

Johnson, S. F. 'The Languages of Christianity on the Silk Roads and the Transmission of Mediterranean Culture into Central Asia', in *Empires and Exchanges in Eurasian Late Antiquity: Rome, China, Iran, and the Steppe, ca. 250–750*, ed. N. Di Cosmo and M. Maas, 206–19. Cambridge: Cambridge University Press, 2018.

Johnson, S. F. (ed.) *The Oxford Handbook of Late Antiquity*. Oxford: Oxford University Press, 2012.

Jones, C. P. 'ἔθνος and γένος in Herodotus', *The Classical Quarterly* 46 (1996), 315–20.

Jorgensen, J. 'Goguryeo Buddhism: An Imported Religion in a Multi-ethnic Warrior Kingdom', *The Review of Korean Studies* 15 (2012), 59–107.

Kachouch, H. 'The Arabic Versions of the Gospels: A Case Study of John 1.1. and 1.18', in *The Bible in Arab Christianity*, ed. D. Thomas, 9–36. Leiden: Brill, 2007.

Kaimio, M. P. 'Petra inv. 83: A Settlement of a Dispute', *Atti del XXII congresso internazionale di papirologia, Firenze, 23–9 Agosto 1998* (2001), 719–24.

Kaldellis, A. *Romanland: Ethnicity and Empire in Byzantium*. Cambridge, MA: Harvard University Press, 2019.

Kashouh, H. *The Arabic Versions of the Gospels*. Berlin: De Gruyter, 2012. Keay, S. and Terrenato, N. (eds) *Italy and the West: Comparative Issues in Romanization*. Oxford: Oxford University Press, 2001.

Keevak, M. *The Story of a Stele: China's Nestorian Monument and Its Reception in the West, 1625–1916*. Hong Kong: Hong Kong University Press, 2008.

Kennedy, D. and Riley, D. *Rome's Desert Frontier from the Air*. London: Batsford, 1990.

Kennedy, G. A. *Greek Rhetoric under Christian Emperors*. Princeton: Princeton University Press, 1983.

Kennedy, H. N. 'Gerasa and Scythopolis: Power and Patronage in the Byzantine Cities of Bilad Al-Sham', *Bulletin d'études orientales* 52 (2000), 199–204.

Kennedy, H. N. 'Justinianic Plague in Syria and the Archaeological Evidence', in *Plague and the End of Antiquity: The Pandemic of 541–750*, ed. L. K. Little, 87–96. Cambridge: Cambridge University Press, 2006.

Kennedy, H. N. 'Syria, Palestine and Mesopotamia', in *The Cambridge Ancient History*, Vol. 14, *Late Antiquity: Empire and Successors, A.D. 425–600*, ed. A. Cameron, M. Whitby and B. Ward-Perkins, 425–600. Cambridge: Cambridge University Press, 2000.

Kennet, D. 'The Decline of Eastern Arabia in the Sasanian Period', *Arabian Archaeology and Epigraphy* 18 (2007), 86–122.

Khel, M. N. K. K. 'Political System in pre-Islamic Arabia', *Islamic Studies* 20 (1981), 375–93.

Kim, H. J. *The Huns, Rome and the Birth of Europe*. Cambridge: Cambridge University Press, 2013.

King, G. D. R. 'The Paintings of the pre-Islamic Kaʿba', *Muqarnas* 21 (2004), 219–29.

Kister, M. J. 'The Campaign of Ḥulubān: A New Light on the Expedition of Abraha', *Museum* 78 (1965), 425–36.

Kister, M. J. 'Labbayka, Allāhumma, Labbayka: On a Monotheistic Aspect of a Jāhiliyya Practice', *Jerusalem Studies in Arabic and Islam* 2 (1980), 33–57.

Kradin, N. N. 'Nomadic Empires in Inner Asia', in *Complexity of Interaction* in *Complexity of Interaction along the Eurasian Steppe Zone in the First Millennium CE*, ed. J. Bemmann and M. Schmauder, 11–48. Bonn: Rheinische Friedrich-Wilhems Universität, 2015.

Kraemer, R. S. 'Giving up the Godfearers', in *Crossing Boundaries in Early Judaism and Christianity*, ed. K. B. Stratton and A. Lieber, 169–200. Leiden: Brill, 2016.

Kropp, M. 'Beyond Single Words: Māʾida-Shayṭān-Jibt and Ṭāghūt – Mechanisms of Transmission into the Ethiopic Bible and the Qur'ānic Text', in *The Qur'an in Its Historical Context*, ed. G. S. Reynolds, 204–16. New York: Routledge, 2008.

Kumar, B. *The Early Kusanas*. New Delhi: Sterling Publishers, 1973.

La Spisa, P. 'Martirio e rappresaglia nell'Arabia Meridionale dei secoli V e VI: uno sguardo sinottico tra fonti islamiche e cristiane', *Adamantius* 23 (2017), 318–40.

Lacerenza, G. 'Il dio Dusares a Puteoli', *Puteoli – Studi di storia antica* 12–3 (1988–9), 119–49.

Langfeldt, J. A. 'Recently Discovered Early Christian Monuments in Northeastern Arabia', *Arabian Archaeology and Epigraphy* 5 (1994), 32–60.

Le Maguer, S. 'The Incense Trade during the Islamic Period', *Proceedings of the Seminar for Arabian Studies* 45 (2015), 175–83.

Lecker, M. *'The Constitution of Medina': Muhammad's First Legal Document*. Princeton: Princeton University Press, 2004.

Lecker, M. 'Idol Worship in pre-Islamic Medina (Yathrib)', *Le muséon* 106 (1993), 331–46.

Lemaire, A. 'Solomon & Sheba, Inc. New Inscription Confirms Trade Relations between Towns of Judah and South Arabia', *Biblical Archaeology Review* 36 (2010), 54–9.

Lenski, N. 'Introduction', in *The Cambridge Companion to the Age of Constantine*, ed. N. Lenski, 1–13. Cambridge: Cambridge University Press, 2006.

Letteney, M. and Gross, S. 'Reconsidering the Earliest Synagogue in Yemen', *Studies in Late Antiquity* 6 (2022): 627–50.

Lévi, S. 'Notes sur les Indo-Scythes', *Journal asiatique* 2 (1896), 475–84.

Lewin, A. S. 'Did the Roman Empire Have a Military Strategy and Were the Jafnids Part of It?', in *Les Jafnides: Des rois arabes au service de byzance (vie siècle de l'ère chrétienne)*, ed. D. Genequand and C. J. Robin, 155–92. Paris: Éditions De Boccard, 2015.

Lewin, A. S. 'L'esercito del vicino oriente nel V secolo', in *Governare e riformare l'impero al momento della sua divisione: Oriente, Occidente, Illirico*, ed. U. Roberto and L. Mecella, 225–46. Rome: École française de Rome, 2016.

Lewis, M. E. *The Early Chinese Empires: Qin and Han*. Cambridge, MA: Harvard University Press, 2009.

Lieu, J. *Christian Identity in the Jewish and Graeco-Roman World*. Oxford: Oxford University Press, 2004.

Lieu, S. N. C. *Manichaeism in Mesopotamia and the Roman East*. Leiden: Brill, 1994.

Lieu, S. N. C. and Kim, H. J. '"Nestorian" Christians and Manichaeans as Links between Rome and China', in *Rome and China: Points of Contact*, ed. H. J. Kim, S. N. C. Lieu and R. McLaughlin, 80–107. Abingdon: Routledge, 2021.

Linder, A. *The Jews in Roman Imperial Legislation*. Detroit: Wayne State University Press, 1987.

Luckenbill, D. D. *Ancient Records of Assyria and Babylonia*. Chicago: Chicago University Press, 1926.

Lunn-Rockliffe, S. 'The Invention and Demonisation of an Ascetic Heresiarch: Philoxenus of Mabbug on the "Messalian" Adelphius', *The Journal of Ecclesiastical History* 68 (2017), 455–73.

Luo, X. 'Chinese and Inner Asian Perspectives on the History of the Northern Dynasties (386–589) in Chinese Historiography', in *Empires and Exchanges in Eurasian Late Antiquity: Rome, China, Iran, and the Steppe, ca. 250–750*, ed. N. Di Cosmo and M. Maas, 166–75. Cambridge: Cambridge University Press, 2018.

Luxenberg, C. *Die Syro-Aramäische Lesart des Koran*. Berlin: Das Arabische Buch, 2000.

Maas, M. 'How the Steppes Became Byzantine: Rome and the Eurasian Nomads in Historical Perspective', in *Empires and Exchanges in Eurasian Late Antiquity: Rome, China, Iran, and the Steppe, ca. 250–750*, ed. N. Di Cosmo and M. Maas, 19–34. Cambridge: Cambridge University Press, 2018.

Macdonald, D. 'Dating the Fall of Dura-Europos', *Historia: Zeitschrift für Alte Geschichte* 1 (1986), 45–68.

Macdonald, M. C. A. 'Ancient Arabia and the Written Word', *Proceedings of the Seminar for Arabian Studies* (2010), 5–27.

Macdonald, M. C. A. 'Arabs, Arabias and Arabic before Late Antiquity', *Topoi: Orient-Occident* 16 (2009), 277–332.

Macdonald, M. C. A. 'The Decline of the "Epigraphic Habit" in Late Antique Arabia: Some Questions', in *L'Arabie à la veille de l'Islam*, ed. C. Robin and J. Schiettecatte, 17–27. Paris: De Boccard, 2008.

Macdonald, M. C. A. 'Graffiti and Complexity: Ways-of-Life and Languages in the 343 Hellenistic and Roman Harrah', in *Landscapes of Survival: The Archaeology and Epigraphy of Jordan's North-Eastern Desert and beyond*, ed. P. M. M. G. Akkermans, 343–54. Leiden: Brill, 2020.

Macdonald, M. C. A. *Literacy and Identity in pre-Islamic Arabia*. Farnham: Ashgate, 2009.

Macdonald, M. C. A. 'The Old Arabic Graffito at Jabal Usays: A New Reading of Line 1', in *The Development of Arabic as a Written Language*, ed. M. C. A. Macdonald, 141–3. Oxford: Archaeopress, 2010.

Macdonald, M. C. A. 'Personal Names in the Nabatean Realm: A Review Article', *Journal of Semitic Studies* 44 (1999), 251–89.

Macdonald, M. C. A. 'Reflections on the Linguistic Map of pre-Islamic Arabia', *Arabian Archaeology and Epigraphy* 11 (2000), 28–79.

Macdonald, M. C. A. 'Romans Go Home? Rome and Other "Outsiders" as Viewed from the Syro-Arabian Desert', in *Inside and Out: Interactions between Rome and the Peoples on the Arabian and Egyptian Frontiers in Late Antiquity*, ed. J. H. F. Dijkstra and G. Fisher, 145–64. Leuven: Peeters, 2014.

Macdonald, M. C. A. et al. 'Arabs and Empires before the Sixth Century', in *Arabs and Empires*, ed. G. Fisher, 11–89. Oxford: Oxford University Press, 2015.

Macdonald, M. C. A. et al. 'Provincia Arabia: Nabatea, the Emergence of Arabic as a Written Language, and Graeco-Arabica', in *Arabs and Empires*, ed. G. Fisher, 373–433. Oxford: Oxford University Press, 2015.

MacKenzie, D. N. 'Kerdir's Inscription', in *Iranica diversa*, ed. C. G. Cereti and L. Paul, 217–73. Rome: Istituto italiano per l'Africa e l'Oriente, 1999.

MacMullen, R. *Romanization in the Time of Augustus*. New Haven: Yale University Press, 2000.

Mahamedi, H. 'Wall as a System of Frontier Defence during the Sasanid Period', in *Mēnōg ī Xrad: The Spirit of Wisdom, Essays in Memory of Ahmad Tafazzoli*, ed. T. Daryaee and M. Omidsalar, 145–59. Costa Mesa, CA: Mazda Publishers, 2004.

Mahé, J. 'Les pères syriens et les origines du monachisme géorgien d'après le nouveau manuscrit sinaïtique', in *Monachismes d'Orient – Images, échanges, influences: Hommage à Antoine Guillaumont. Cinquantenaire de la chaire des' christianismes orientaux*, ed. F. Jullien and M.-J. Pierre, 51–64. Turnhout: Brepols, 2011.

Mairs, R. *The Hellenistic Far East: Archaeology, Language, and Identity in Greek Central Asia*. Oakland: University of California Press, 2014.

Manzo, A. 'Skeuomorphism in Aksumite Pottery? Remarks on the Origins and Meanings of Some Ceramic Types', *Aethiopica* 6 (2003), 7–46.

Margoliouth, D. S. 'The Origins of Arabic Poetry', *Journal of the Royal Asiatic Society* 57 (1925), 417–49.

Marr, J. S. et al. 'The Year of the Elephant', *WikiJournal of Medicine* 2 (2015), 1–5.

Marrassini, P. 'Once Again on the Question of Syriac Influences in the Aksumite Period', in *Languages and Cultures of Eastern Christianity: Ethiopian*, ed. A. Bausi, 209–17. Farnham: Routledge, 2012.

Marrassini, P. 'Some Considerations on the Problem of the "Syriac Influences" on Aksumite Ethiopia', *Journal of Ethiopian Studies* 23 (1990), 35–46.

Marrassini, P. *Storia e leggenda dell'Etiopia tardoantica*. Brescia: Paideia, 2014.

Marsham, A. 'The Caliphate and the Inheritance of Late Antiquity, c. AD 610–c. AD 750', in *A Companion to Late Antiquity*, ed. P. Rousseau, 479–92. Chichester: Wiley-Blackwell, 2009.

Marsham, A. *Rituals of Islamic Monarchy: Accession and Succession in the First Muslim Empire*. Edinburgh: Edinburgh University Press, 2009.

Martin-Hisard, B. 'Le roi géorgien Vaxt'ang Gorgasal dans l'histoire et dans la légende', *Actes des congrès de la société des historiens médiévistes de l'enseignement supérieur public* 13 (1982), 205–42.

Martinez, F. J. 'The Apocalyptic Genre in Syriac: The World of Pseudo-Methodius', in *Symposium Syriacum IV: Literary Genres in Syriac Literature*, ed. H. J. W. Drijvers et al., 337–52. Rome: Pont. Institutum Studiorum Orientalium, 1987.

Maspero, H. 'Sur la date et l'authenticite du Foufa tsang yin yuan tchouan', in *Melanges d'Indianisme offerts par ses eleves a M. Sylvain Levi*, 129–49. Paris: Ernest Leroux, 1911.

Mathisen, R. W. 'Catalogues of Barbarians in Late Antiquity', in *Romans, Barbarians, and the Transformation of the Roman World*, ed. R. W. Mathisen and D. Shanzerpp, 17–32. Farnham: Ashgate, 2011.

Matitashvili, S 'The Monasteries Founded by the Thirteen Syrian Fathers in Iberia', *Studies in Late Antiquity* 2 (2018), 4–39.

Mazzarino, S. *Aspetti sociali del IV secolo: ricerche di storia tardo-romana*. Rome: L'Erma di Bretschneider, 1951.

Mazzarino, S. 'La democratizzazione della cultura nel basso impero', *XIe congrès international des sciences historiques, Stockholm 21–8 août* (1960), 35–54.

Mazzarino, S. *Stilicone: La crisi imperial dopo Teodosio*. Rome: A. Signorelli, 1942.

Michel, A. *Les églises d'époque byzantine et ummayyade de la Jordanie – Ve–VIIIe siècle: typologie architecturale et aménagements liturgiques, avec catalogue des monuments*. Turnhout: Brepols, 2001.

McAuliffe, J. D. (ed.), *Encyclopaedia of the Qurʾān*. Leiden: Brill, 2001–6.

McLaughlin, R. and Kim, H. J. 'Sogdian Ambassadors of the Göktürks and the Eastern Roman Empire', in *Rome and China: Points of Contact*, ed. H. J. Kim, S. N. C. Lieu and R. McLaughlin, 43–79. Abingdon: Routledge, 2021.

Milik, J. T. 'Inscriptions grecques et nabatéennes de Rawwafah', *Bulletin of the Institute of Archaeology* 10 (1971), 54–8.

Millar, F. 'Christian Monasticism in Roman Arabia at the Birth of Mahomet', *Semitica et Classica* 2 (2009), 97–115.

Millar, F. *Empire, Church and Society in the Late Roman Near East: Greeks, Jews, Syrians and Saracens*. Leuven: Peeters, 2015.

Millar, F. 'Ethnic Identity in the Roman Near East, 325–450: Language, Religion, and Culture', *Mediterranean Archaeology* 11 (1998), 159–76.

Millar, F. 'Paul of Samosata, Zenobia and Aurelian: The Church, Local Culture and Political Allegiance in Third-Century Syria', *Journal of Roman Studies* 61 (1971), 1–17.

Millar, F. 'Roman Arabia by Glen W. Bowersock', *The Journal of Interdisciplinary History* 16 (1985), 125.

Millar, F. *The Roman Empire and Its Neighbours*. London: Weidenfeld and Nicolson, 1967.

Millar, F. *The Roman Near East, 31 BC–AD 337*. Cambridge, MA: Harvard University Press, 1993.

Millar, F. *Rome, the Greek World, and the East*. Chapel Hill: University of North Carolina Press, 2002–6.

Millar, F. 'Rome's Arab Allies in Late Antiquity: Conceptions and Representations from within the Frontiers of the Empire', in *Commutatio et Contentio: Studies in the Late Roman, Sasanian, and Early Islamic Near East*, 199–226. Düsseldorf: Wellem, 2010.

Millar, F. 'A Syriac Codex from Near Palmyra and the "Ghassanid" Abokarib', *Hugoye* 16 (2013), 15–35.

Miller, B. K. "The Southern Xiongnu in Northern China: Navigating and Negotiating the Middle Ground", in *Complexity of Interaction in Complexity of Interaction along the Eurasian Steppe Zone in the First Millennium* CE, ed. J. Bemmann and M. Schmauder, 127–98. Bonn: Rheinische Friedrich-Wilhems Universität, 2015.

Milnor, K. *Graffiti and the Literary Landscape in Roman Pompeii*. Oxford: Oxford University Press, 2014.

Milwright, M. *Dome of the Rock and Its Umayyad Mosaic Inscriptions*. Edinburgh: Edinburgh University Press, 2016.

Mitchell, S. 'The Cult of Theos Hypsistos between Pagans, Jews, and Christians', in *Pagan Monotheism in Late Antiquity*, ed. P. Athanassiadi and M. Frede, 81–148. Oxford: Oxford University Press, 1999.

Mitchell, S. 'Further Thoughts on the Cult of Theos Hypsistos', in *One God: Pagan Monotheism in the Roman Empire*, ed. S. Mitchell and P. Van Nuffelen, 167–208. Cambridge: Cambridge University Press, 2010.

Mitchell, S. and Van Nuffelen, P. 'Introduction: The Debate about Pagan Monotheism', in *One God: Pagan Monotheism in the Roman Empire*, ed. S. Mitchell and P. Van Nuffelen, 1–15. Cambridge: Cambridge University Press, 2010.

Mokhtarian, J. 'The Boundaries of an Infidel in Zoroastrianism: A Middle Persian Term of Otherness for Jews, Christians, and Muslims', *Iranian Studies* 48 (2015), 99–115.

Monroe, J. T. 'Oral Composition in pre-Islamic Poetry', *Journal of Arabic Literature* 3 (1972), 1–53.

Morley, C. 'The Arabian Frontier: A Keystone of the Sasanian Empire', in *Sasanian Persia: Between Rome and the Steppes of Eurasia*, ed. E. Sauer, 268–83. Edinburgh: Edinburgh University Press, 2017.

Morris, L. 'Central Asian Empires', in *Handbook of Ancient Afro-Eurasian Economies*, Vol. 1, *Contexts*, ed. S. von Reden, 53–94. Berlin: De Gruyter, 2019.

Müller, D. H. 'Arabia', in *Paulys Real-Encyclopädie der Classischen Altertumswissenschaft*, ed. G. Wissowa, 3.344–59. Stuttgart: Metzler, 1895.

Müller-Wiener, M. et al. 'Al-Hira Survey Project: Campaigns 2015–2018', *Sumer* 65 (2019), 84–97.

Munro-Hay, S. C. *Aksum: An African Civilization of Late Antiquity*. Edinburgh: Edinburgh University Press, 1991.

Munro-Hay, S. C. *Excavations at Aksum: An Account of Research at the Ancient Ethiopian Capital Directed in 1972–4 by the Late Dr Neville Chittick*. London: British Institute in Eastern Africa, 1989.

Munro-Hay, S. C. 'Saintly Shadows', in *Languages and Cultures of Eastern Christianity: Ethiopian*, ed. A. Bausi, 221–52. Farnham: Routledge, 2012.

Munt, H. 'Arabic and Persian Sources for pre-Islamic Arabia', in *Arabs and Empires*, ed. G. Fisher, 434–500. Oxford: Oxford University Press, 2015.

Murphy, D. J. *People, Plants and Genes: The Story of Crops and Humanity*. Oxford: Oxford University Press, 2007.

Nallino, C. A. 'Il verso d'Annabigah sul dio Wadd', *Rendiconti accademia nazionale dei Lincei* 29 (1921), 283–90.

Nechaeva, E. 'Patterns of Roman Diplomacy with Iran and the Steppe Peoples', in *Empires and Exchanges in Eurasian Late Antiquity: Rome, China, Iran, and the Steppe, ca. 250–750*, ed. N. Di Cosmo and M. Maas, 357–68. Cambridge: Cambridge University Press, 2018.

Negev, A. 'Nabatean Inscriptions from 'Avdat (Oboda)', *Israel Exploration Journal* 13 (1963), 113–24.

Negev, A. 'The Nabateans and the Provincia Arabia', *Aufstieg und Niedergang der römischen Welt* 2 (1977), 520–686.

Nehmé, L. 'Aramaic or Arabic? The Nabataeo-Arabic Script and the Language of the Inscriptions Written in This Script', in *Arabic in Context*, ed. A. al-Jallad, 75–98. Leiden: Brill, 2017.

Nehmé, L. 'A Glimpse of the Development of the Nabatean Script into Arabic Based on Old and New Epigraphic Material', in *The Development of Arabic as a Written Language*, ed. M. C. A. Macdonald, 47–88. Oxford: Oxford University Press, 2010.

Nehmé, L. 'New Dated Inscriptions (Nabataean and pre-Islamic Arabic) from a Site near al-Jawf, Ancient Dūmah, Saudi Arabia', *Arabian Epigraphic Notes* 3 (2017), 121–64.

Nehmé, L. 'Towards an Understanding of the Urban Space of Madāʾin Ṣāliḥ, Ancient Ḥegrā, through Epigraphic Evidence', *Proceedings of the Seminar for Arabian Studies* 35 (2005), 155–75.

Nehmé, L. et al. 'Mission archéologique de Madain Saleh (Arabie Saoudite): Recherches menées de 2001 à 2003 dans l'ancienne Hijrah des Nabatéens (1)', *Arabian Archaeology and Epigraphy* 17 (2006), 41–124.

Neuwirth, A. *Der Koran als Text der Spätantike: Ein Europäischer Zugang*. Berlin: Verlag der Weltreligionen, 2010.

Neuwirth, A. 'The Qurʾān and Its Biblical Subtext by Gabriel S. Reynolds', *Journal of Qurʾānic Studies* 14 (2012), 131–8.

Neuwirth, A. 'The Qur'ān as a Late Antique Text', in *In the Shadow of Arabic: The Centrality of Language to Arabic Culture*, ed. B. Orfali 495–509. Leiden: Brill, 2011.

Neuwirth, A. 'Qur'ānic Readings of the Psalms', in *The Qur'ān in Context: Historical and Literary Investigations into the Qur'ānic Milieu*, ed. A. Neuwirth, N. Sinai and M. Marx, 733–88. Leiden: Brill, 2010.

Neuwirth, A., Sinai, N. and Marx, M. (eds) *The Qur'ān in Context: Historical and Literary Investigations into the Qur'ānic Milieu*. Leiden: Brill, 2009.

Nevo, Y. D. and Koren, J. *Crossroads to Islam*. New York: Prometheus Books. 2003.

Nicholson, O. (ed.) *The Oxford Dictionary of Late Antiquity*. Oxford: Oxford University Press, 2018.

Nielsen, D. *Die altarabische Mondreligion und die mosaische Ueberlieferung*. Strasbourg: K. J. Trübner, 1904.

Nöldeke, T. 'Arabia, Arabians', in *Encyclopaedia Biblica I*, ed. T. K. Cheyne, 272–5. London: Adam and Charles Black, 1899.

Nöldeke, T. *Beiträge zur Kenntnis der Poesie der Alten Araber*. Hannover: C. Rümpler, 1864.

Nöldeke, T. *Geschichte der Perser und Araber zur Zeit der Sasaniden*. Leiden: Brill, 1879.

Nöldeke, T. *Geschichte des Qorans*. Göttingen: Dieterichschen Buchhandlung, 1860.

Nöldeke, T. *Neue Beiträge zur semitischen Sprachwissenschaft*. Strassburg: Karl J. Trübner, 1910.

Obolensky, D. *The Byzantine Commonwealth: Eastern Europe 500–1453*. New York: Praeger Publishers, 1971.

Okada, Y. 'Early Christian Architecture in the Iraqi South-Western Desert', *Al-Rafidan* 12 (1991), 71–83.Ostrogorsky, G. *History of the Byzantine State*, trans. J. Hussey. New Brunswick: Rutgers, 1969.

Park, H. *Mapping the Chinese and Islamic Worlds: Cross-cultural Exchange in pre-Modern Asia*. Cambridge: Cambridge University Press, 2012.

Parker, G. *The Making of Roman India*. Cambridge: Cambridge University Press, 2008.

Parker, S. T. 'An Empire's New Holy Land: The Byzantine Period', *Near Eastern Archaeology* 62 (1999), 134–80.

Parker, S. T. 'The Nature of Rome's Arabian Frontier', in *Roman Frontier Studies 1989: Proceedings of the XVth International Congress of Roman Frontier Studies*, ed. V. A. Maxfield and M. J. Dobson, 498–504. Exeter: University of Exeter Press, 1991.

Parker, S. T. 'The Roman Frontier in Jordan: An Overview', in *Limes XVIII: Proceedings of the XVIIIth International Congress of Roman Frontier Studies Held in Amman, Jordan*, ed. P. Freeman, J. Bennett, Z. T. Fiema and B. Hoffmann, 77–84. Oxford: Oxford University Press, 2002.

Parry, M. *L'Épithète Traditionnelle dans Homère*. Paris: Les belles lettres, 1928.

Patrich, J. *The Formation of Nabatean Art: Prohibition of Graven Images among the Nabateans*. Jerusalem: Magnes Press, 1990.

Payne, R. E. 'The Making of Turan: The Fall and Transformation of the Iranian East in Late Antiquity', *Journal of Late Antiquity* 9 (2016), 4–41.

Payne, R. E. 'The Silk Road and the Iranian Political Economy in Late Antiquity: Iran, the Silk Road, and the Problem of Aristocratic Empire', *Bulletin of the School of Oriental and African Studies* 81 (2018), 227–50.

Payne, R. E. *A State of Mixture: Christians, Zoroastrians, and Iranian Political Culture in Late Antiquity*. Oakland: University of California Press, 2015.

Peirce, P. 'The Arch of Constantine: Propaganda and Ideology in Late Roman Art', *Art History* 12 (1989), 387–418.

Penkower, L. 'In the Beginning … Guanding 灌顶 (561–632) and the Creation of Early Tiantai', *Journal of the International Association of Buddhist Studies* (2000), 245–96.

Perrogon, R. and Bonnéric, J. 'A Consideration on the Interest of a Pottery Typology Adapted to the Late Sasanian and Early Islamic Monastery at al-Qusur (Kuwait)', *Arabian Archaeology and Epigraphy* 32 (2021), 70–82.

Peter, B. G. *Central Asia in World History*. Oxford: Oxford University Press, 2011.

Peters, F. E. 'The Commerce of Mecca before Islam', in *A Way Prepared: Essays on Islamic Culture in Honor of Richard Bayley Winder*, ed. F. Kazemi and R. D. McChesney, 3–26. New York: New York University Press, 1988.

Phillipson, D. W. *Foundations of an African Civilisation*. Woodbridge: James Currey, 2012.

Piccirillo, M. *L'Arabia Cristiana: dalla Provincia Imperiale al Primo Periodo Islamico*. Milan: Jaca Book, 2002.

Piccirillo, M. 'The Church of Saint Sergius at Nitl: A Centre of the Christian Arabs in the Steppe at the Gates of Madaba', *Liber annuus* 51 (2001), 267–84.

Piccirillo, M. *The Mosaics of Jordan*. Amman: American Center of Oriental Research, 1993.

Piovanelli, P. 'Jewish Christianity in Late Antique Aksum and Ḥimyar? A Reassessment of the Evidence and a New Proposal', *Judaïsme ancien-Ancient Judaism* 6 (2018), 175–202.

Pohl, W. 'Ethnicity and Empire in the Western Eurasian Steppes', in *Empires and Exchanges in Eurasian Late Antiquity: Rome, China, Iran, and the Steppe, ca. 250–750*, ed. N. Di Cosmo and M. Maas, 189–205. Cambridge: Cambridge University Press 2018.

Pohl, W. 'Ethnicity, Theory, and Tradition: A Response', in *On Barbarian Identity: Critical Approaches to Ethnicity in the Early Middle Ages*, ed. A. Gillet, 221–41. Turnhout: Brepols, 2002.

Pohl, W. 'Migrations, Ethnic Groups, and State Building', in *The Cambridge Companion to the Age of Attila*, ed. M. Maas, 247–64. Cambridge: Cambridge University Press, 2014.

Pohl, W. 'Telling the Difference: Signs of Ethnic Identity', in *Strategies of Distinction: The Construction of Ethnic Communities 300–800*, ed. W. Pohl and H. Reimitz, 17–69. Leiden: Brill, 1998.

Power, T. *The Red Sea from Byzantium to the Caliphate:AD 500–1000*. Oxford: Oxford University Press, 2012.

Price, R. 'Politics and Bishops' Lists at the First Council of Ephesus', *Annuarium historiae conciliorum* 44 (2012), 395–420.

Price, R. and Gaddis, M. *The Acts of the Council of Chalcedon*. Liverpool: Liverpool University Press, 2005.

Raffensperger, C. *Reimagining Europe: Kievan Rus' in the Medieval World*. Cambridge, MA: Harvard University Press, 2012.

Raffensperger, C. 'Revisiting the Idea of the Byzantine Commonwealth', *Byzantinische Forschungen* 28 (2004), 159–74.

Raja, R., Bobou, O. and Romanowska, I. 'Three Hundred Years of Palmyrene History: Unlocking Archaeological Data for Studying Past Societal Transformations', *PLoS ONE* 16 (2021), 1–33.

Retsö, J. *The Arabs in Antiquity: Their History from the Assyrians to the Umayyads*. London: Routledge, 2002.

Reynolds, G. S. *The Qurʾān and Its Biblical Subtext*. London: Routledge, 2010.

Reynolds, G. S. 'Variant Readings: The Birmingham Qur'an in the Context of Debate on Islamic Origins', *Times Literary Supplement* (7 August 2015), 14–15.

Rezakhani, K. 'The Road That Never Was: The Silk Road and Trans-Eurasian Exchange', *Comparative Studies of South Asia, Africa, & the Middle East* 30/3 (2010), 420–33.

Rigsby, K. J. *Asylia: Territorial Inviolability in the Hellenistic World*. Berkeley: University of California Press, 1996.

Rippin, A. *The Qurʾān and Its Interpretative Tradition*. Aldershot: Ashgate 2001.

Roberto, U. 'Il Magister Victor e l'opposizione ortodossa all'imperatore Valente nella storiografia ecclesiastica e nell'agiografia', *Mediterraneo Antico* 6 (2003), 61–93.

Robin, C. J. 'Abraha et la reconquête de l'Arabie déserte: Un réexamen de l'inscription Ryckmans 506 = Murayghan 1', *Jerusalem Studies in Arabic and Islam* 39 (2012), 1–93.

Robin, C. J. 'L'Arabie préislamique', in *Le Coran des historiens*, ed. M. A. Amir-Moezzi and G. Dye, 51–154. Paris: Les éditions du Cerf, 2019.

Robin, C. J. 'Before Ḥimyar: Epigraphic Evidence for the Kingdoms of South Arabia', in *Arabs and Empires before Islam*, ed. G. Fisher, 90–127. Oxford: Oxford University Press, 2015.

Robin, C. J. 'Les "filles de Dieu" de Saba' a la Mecque: réflexions sur l'agencement des panthéons dans l'Arabie ancienne', *Semitica* 50 (2000), 113–92.

Robin, C. J. 'Ḥimyar, Aksūm, and Arabia Deserta in Late Antiquity', in *Arabs and Empires before Islam*, ed. G. Fisher, 127–71. Oxford: Oxford University Press, 2015.

Robin, C. J. 'Himyar et Israël', *Comptes-rendus des séances de l'académie des inscriptions et belles-lettres* 2 (2004), 831–908.

Robin, C. J. 'L'institution monarchique en Arabie du Sud antique: les contributions fondatrices d'A.F.L. Beeston réexaminées à la lumière des découvertes les plus récentes', *Proceedings of the Seminar for Arabian Studies* 36 (2006), 43–52.

Robin, C. J. 'The Judaism of an Ancient Kingdom of Ḥimyar in Arabia: A Discreet Conversion', in *Diversity and Rabbinization: Jewish Texts and Societies between 400 and 1000 CE*, ed. G. McDowell, R. Naiweld and D. S. B Ezra, 165–270. Cambridge: Open Book Publishers, 2021.

Robin, C. J. *Le Judaïsme de l'Arabie antique.* Turnhout: Brepols, 2015.

Robin, C. J. 'La pénétration des Arabes nomades au Yémen', *Revue du monde musulman et de la méditerranée* 61 (1991), 71–88.

Robin, C. J. 'The Peoples beyond the Arabian Frontier in Late Antiquity: Recent Epigraphic Discoveries and Latest Advances', in *Inside and Out: Interactions between Rome and the Peoples on the Arabian and Egyptian Frontiers in Late Antiquity*, ed. J. H. F. Dijkstra and G. Fisher, 33–82. Leuven: Peeters, 2014.

Robin, C. J. 'La réforme de l'écriture arabe à l'époque du califat médinois', *Mélanges de l'université Saint-Joseph* 59 (2006), 319–64.

Robin, C. J. 'Les rois de Kinda', in *Arabia, Greece and Byzantium: Cultural Contacts in Ancient and Medieval Times*, ed. A. Al-Helabi, D. Letsios, M. Al-Moraekhi and A. Al-Abduljabbar, 59–129. Riyadh: King Saud University, 2012.

Robin, C. J. 'Les signes de la prophétie en Arabie à l'époque de Muhammad (fin vie siècle et début VIIe siècle de l'ère chrétienne)', in *La raison des signes: présages, rites, destin dans les sociétés de la méditerranée ancienne*, ed. S. Georgoudi, R. K. Piettre and F. Schmidt, 433–76. Leiden: Brill, 2012.

Robin, C. J. 'South Arabia, Ethiopia and Socotra', in *Foreign Sailors on Socotra: The Inscriptions and Drawings from the Cave Hoq*, ed. I. Strauch, 437–46. Bremen: Hempen Verlag, 2012.

Robin, C. J. and Gorea, M. 'Un réexamen de l'inscription Arabe préislamique du Ǧabal Usays (528–529 è. chr.)', *Arabica* 49 (2002), 503–10.

Robin, C. J. and Tayran, S. 'Soixante-dix ans avant l'Islam: l'Arabie toute entière dominée par un roi chrétien', *Comptes rendus de l'académie des inscriptions et belles lettres* 156 (2012), 525–53.

Robin, C. J. et al. 'Inscriptions antiques de la région de Najrān (Arabie Séoudite méridionale): nouveaux jalons pour l'histoire de l'écriture, de la langue et du calendrier arabe', *Comptes rendus de l'académie des inscriptions & belles-lettres* 158 (2014), 1033–128.

Robinson, C. F. *Islamic Historiography.* Cambridge: Cambridge University Press, 2003.

Robinson, M. *Marriage in the Tribe of Muhammad: A Statistical Study of Early Arabic Genealogical Literature.* Berlin: De Gruyter, 2019.

Rodinson, M. 'On the Question of "Jewish Influences" in Ethiopia', in *Languages and Cultures of Eastern Christianity: Ethiopia*, ed. A. Bausi, 179–86. Farnham: Routledge, 2012.

Roggema, B. *The Legend of Sergius Baḥīrā: Eastern Christian Apologetics and Apocalyptic in Response to Islam.* Leiden: Brill, 2009.

Rousseau, P. (ed.) *A Companion to Late Antiquity.* Chichester: John Wiley & Sons, 2012.

Rubin, Z. 'The Sasanid Monarchy', in *The Cambridge Ancient History*, Vol. 14, *Late Antiquity: Empire and Successors, A.D. 425–600*, ed. A. Cameron, M. Whitby and B. Ward-Perkins, 638–61. Cambridge: Cambridge University Press, 2000.

Ryckmans, G. 'Inscriptions sud-arabes (quatrième série)', *Le muséon* 50 (1937), 239–68.

Ryckmans, G. *Les religions arabes préislamiques.* Louvain: Universitaires, 1951.

Ryckmans, J. 'Le panthéon de l'Arabie du Sud préislamique: état des problèmes et brève synthèse', *Revue de l'histoire des religions* (1989), 151–69.
Sarris, P. 'Bubonic Plague in Byzantium', in *Plague and the End of Antiquity: The Pandemic of 541–750*, ed. L. K. Little, 119–32. Cambridge: Cambridge University Press, 2006.
Sarris, P. *Empires of Faith: The Fall of Rome to the Rise of Islam, 500–700*. Oxford: Oxford University Press, 2011.
Sarris, P. 'The Justinianic Plague: Origins and Effects', *Continuity and Change* 17 (2002), 169–82.
Sarris, P. Plague in the Time of COVID-19 (forthcoming).
Sartre, M. 'Deux phylarques arabes dans l'Arabie Byzantine', *Le Muséon* 106 (1993), 145–54.
Sartre, M. *The Middle East under Rome*. Cambridge: Cambridge University Press, 2005.
Sartre, M. 'Namāra du Ṣafā', *Syria* 93 (2016), 45–66.
Sartre, M. *Trois études sur l'Arabie romaine et byzantine*. Bruxelles: Revue d'études latines, 1982.
Sauvaget, J. 'Les Ghassanides et Sergiopolis', *Byzantion* 14 (1939), 115–30.
Schiettecatte, J. and Arbach, M. 'The Political Map of Arabia and the Middle East in the Third Century AD Revealed by a Sabaean Inscription', *Arabian Archaeology and Epigraphy* 27 (2016), 176–96.
Schmauder, M. 'Huns, Avars, Hungarians – Reflections on the Interaction between Steppe Empires in Southeast Europe and the Late Roman to Early Byzantine Empires', in *Complexity of Interaction in Complexity of Interaction along the Eurasian Steppe Zone in the First Millennium CE*, ed. J. Bemmann and M. Schmauder, 671–92. Bonn: Rheinische Friedrich-Wilhelms Universität, 2015.
Schmitt, O. 'Rome and the Bedouins of the Near East from 70 bc to 630 ad: 700 Years of Confrontation and Coexistence', in *Shifts and Drifts in Nomad–Sedentary Relations*, ed. S. Leder and B. Streck, 270–88. Wiesbaden: Dr Ludwig Reichert Verlag, 2005.
Schoeler, G. *The Oral and the Written in Early Islam*. London: Routledge, 2006.
Schulze, R. *Der Koran und die Genealogie des Islam*. Basel: Schwabe Verlag, 2015.
Schwabe, M. and Lifshitz, B. *Beth She'arim*, Vol. 2. Jerusalem: Massada Press, 1974.
Sedov, A. V. 'New Archaeological and Epigraphical Material from Qana (South Arabia)', *Arabian Archaeology and Epigraphy* 3 (1992), 110–37.
Segovia, C. A. 'Abraha's Christological Formula Rḥmnn w-Msıḥ-hw and Its Relevance for the Study of Islam's Origins.', *Oriens Christianus* 98 (2015), 52–63.
Seidensticker, T. 'Sources for the History of pre-Islamic Religion', in *The Qur'ān in Context*, ed. A. Neuwirth, N. Sinai and M. Marx, 293–321. Leiden: Brill, 2010.
Seland, E. H. 'Networks and Social Cohesion in Ancient Indian Ocean Trade: Geography, Ethnicity, Religion', *Journal of Global History* 8 (2013), 373–90.
Seland, E. H. *Ships of the Desert and Ships of the Sea: Palmyra in the World Trade of the First Three Centuries CE*. Wiesbaden: Harrassowitz Verlag, 2016.

Seland, E. H. 'Trade and Christianity in the Indian Ocean during Late Antiquity', *Journal of Late Antiquity* 5 (2012), 72–86.

Sen, A. K. *Identity and Violence: The Illusion of Destiny*. London: Allen Lane, 2006.

Serjeant, R. B. 'Ḥaram and Ḥawṭah, the Sacred Enclave in Arabia', in *The Arabs and Arabia on the Eve of Islam*, ed. F. E. Peters, 167–84. London: Routledge, 1999.

Serjeant, R. B. 'Meccan Trade and the Rise of Islam: Misconceptions and Flawed Polemics', *Journal of the American Oriental Society* 110 (1990), 472–86.

Serjeant, R. B. and Lewcock, R. B. *Ṣan'ā': An Arabian Islamic City*. London: World of Islam Festival Trust, 1983.

Shahbazi, A. S. 'The Achamenid Persian Empire (550–330 BCE)', in *The Oxford Handbook of Iranian History*, ed. T. Daryaee, 120–41. Oxford: Oxford University Press.

Shahid, I. *Byzantium and the Arabs in the Fifth Century*. Washington, DC: Dumbarton Oaks, 1989.

Shahid, I. *Byzantium and the Arabs in the Fourth Century*. Washington, DC: Dumbarton Oaks, 1984.

Shahid, I. *Byzantium and the Arabs in the Sixth Century*. Washington, DC: Dumbarton Oaks, 1995.

Shahid, I. *Martyrs of Najrān: New Documents*. Bruxelles: Soc. des Bollandistes, 1971.

Shahid, I. 'The Roman Near East, 31 BC–AD 337 by Fergus Millar (review)', *The Catholic Historical Review*, 81 (1995), 251–2.

Shahid, I. *Rome and the Arabs: A Prolegomenon to the Study of Byzantium and the Arabs*. Washington, DC: Dumbarton Oaks, 1984.

Shao, R. 'Peter Brown: Inventor of Late Antiquity', *The Daily Princetonian* (20 April 2017).

Sidebotham, S. E. *Berenike and the Ancient Maritime Spice Route*. Berkeley: University of California Press, 2011.

Sigl, M. 'Timing and Climate Forcing of Volcanic Eruptions for the past 2,500 years', *Nature* 523 (2015), 543–9.

Simpson, St J. 'Christians on Iraq's Desert Frontier', *al-Rāfidān* 39 (2018), 2–30.

Southern, P. *The Roman Empire from Severus to Constantine*. London: Routledge, 2001.

Speyer, H. *Die Biblischen Erzaehlungen Im Qoran*. Leipzig: G. Olms, 1931.

Starcky, J. 'Allath, Athèna et la déesse syrienne', in *Mythologie gréco-romaine, mythologies périphériques: Études d'iconographie*, ed. L. Kahil and C. Augé, 119–39. Paris: Editions du Centre national de la recherche scientifique, 1981.

Starcky, J. *Pétra et la Nabatène*. Paris: Letouzey & Ané, 1966.

Stark, S. 'Aspects of Elite Representation among the Sixth- and Seventh-Century Türks', in *Empires and Exchanges in Eurasian Late Antiquity: Rome, China, Iran, and the Steppe, ca. 250–750*, ed. N. Di Cosmo and M. Maas, 333–56. Cambridge: Cambridge University Press, 2018.

Stark, S. 'Luxurious Necessities: Some Observations on Foreign Commodities and Nomadic Polities in Central Asia in the Sixth to Ninth Centuries', in *Complexity of Interaction along the Eurasian Steppe Zone in the First Millennium CE*, ed. J. Bemmann and M. Schmauder, 463–502. Bonn: Rheinische Friedrich-Wilhems Universität, 2015.

Stein, P. 'Montheismus oder religiöse Vielfalt? Du Samawi, die Stammesgottheit derAmir, im 5. Jh. n. Chr.', in *Philologisches und Historisches zwischen Anatolien und Sokotra*, ed. A. Sima, 339–50. Wiesbaden: Harrassowitz, 2009.

Stewart, C. A. 'Churches', in *The Oxford Handbook of Early Christian Archaeology*, ed. W. R. Caraher, T. W. Davis and D. K. Pettegrew, 127–46. Oxford: Oxford University Press, 2019.

Stickler, T. 'The Gupta Empire in the Face of the Hunnic Threat: Parallels to the Late Roman Empire?', in *Complexity of Interaction along the Eurasian Steppe Zone in the First Millennium CE*, ed. J. Bemmann and M. Schmauder, 659–70. Bonn: Rheinische Friedrich-Wilhems Universität, 2015.

Stimpson, C. M. et al. 'Middle Pleistocene Vertebrate Fossils from the Nefud Desert, Saudi Arabia: Implications for Biogeography and Palaeoecology', *Quaternary Science Reviews* 143 (2016), 13–36.

Strauch, I. (ed.) *Foreign Sailors on Socotra: The Inscriptions and Drawings from the Cave Hoq*. Bremen: Hempen Verlag, 2012.

Szylágyi, K. 'Muḥammad and the Monk: The Making of the Christian Baḥīrā Legend', *Jerusalem Studies in Arabic and Islam* 34 (2008), 169–214.

Tang, L. and Winkler, D. W., *Artifact, Text, Context. Studies on Syriac Christianity in China and Central Asia*. Zurich: LIT Verlag, 2020.

Tannous, J. *The Making of the Medieval Middle East: Religion, Society, and Simple Believers*. Princeton: Princeton University Press, 2018.

Teixidor, J. 'Bulletin d'epigraphie semitique', *Syria* 48 (1971), 453–93.

Teixidor, J. *The Pagan God: Popular Religion in the Greco-Roman Near East*. Princeton: Princeton University Press, 1977.

Teixidor, J. *The Pantheon of Palmyra*. Leiden: Brill, 1979.

Tesei, T. 'Heraclius' War Propaganda and the Qur'ān's Promise of Reward for Dying in Battle', *Studia Islamica* 114 (2019), 219–47.

Thompson, D. J. 'Hellenistic Hellenes: The Case of Ptolemaic Egypt', in *Ancient Perceptions of Greek Ethnicity*, ed. I. Malkin, 301–22. Cambridge, MA: Harvard University Press, 2001.

Thomsen, E. 'New Light on the Origin of the Holy Black Stone of the Ka'ba', *Meteoritics* 15 (1980), 87–91.

Tomber, R. 'Bishops and Traders: The Role of Christianity in the Indian Ocean during the Roman Period', in *Red Sea III: Natural Resources and Cultural Connections of the Red Sea*, ed. P. Starkey and J. Starkey, 219–28. Oxford: BAR Publishing, 2007.

Toral-Niehoff, I. *Al-Ḥīra, Eine arabische Kulturmetropole im spätantiken Kontext*. Leiden: Brill, 2014.

Torrey, C. C. *Jewish Foundation of Islam*. New York: KTAV, 1967.

Trimingham, J. S. *Christianity among the Arabs in pre-Islamic Times*. London: Longman, 1979.

Turchin, P. 'A Theory for Formation of Large Empires', *Journal of Global History* 4 (2009), 191–217.

Ulbert, T. *Forschungen in Resafa-Sergiupolis*. Berlin: De Gruyter, 2016.

Ullendorff, E. 'Hebraic-Jewish Elements in Abyssian (Monophysite) Christianity', in *Languages and Cultures of Eastern Christianity: Ethiopia*, ed. A. Bausi, 121–256. Farnham: Routledge, 2012.

Ulrich, B. 'Oman and Bahrain in Late Antiquity: The Sasanians' Arabian Periphery', *Proceedings of the Seminar for Arabian Studies* 41 (2011), 377–85.
Van Nuffelen, P. 'Pagan Monotheism as a Religious Phenomenon in One God', in *One God: Pagan Monotheism in the Roman Empire*, ed. S. Mitchell and P. Van Nuffelen, 16–33. Cambridge: Cambridge University Press, 2010.
Van Rompay, L. 'Society and Community in the Christian East', in *The Cambridge Companion to the Age of Justinian*, ed. M. Maas, 239–66. Cambridge: Cambridge University Press, 2005.
Veccia Vaglieri, L. 'Dūmat al-Dj̲andal', in *The Encyclopaedia of Islam*, ed. P. Bearman, T. Bianquis, C. E. Bosworth, E. van Donzel and W. P. Heinrichs. Leiden: Brill, 2012.
Wallraff, M. 'Constantine's Devotion to the Sun after 324', *Studia Patristica* 34 (2001), 256–69.
Walmsley, A. 'Byzantine Palestine and Arabia: Urban Prosperity in Late Antiquity', in *Towns in Transition: Urban Evolution in Late Antiquity and the Early Middle Ages*, ed. N. J. Christie and S. T. Loseby, 126–58. Aldershot: Ashgate, 1996.
Wansbrough, J. *Qurʾānic Studies: Sources and Methods of Scriptural Interpretation*, Oxford: Oxford University Press, 1977.
Wansbrough, J. 'Reviewed Work – Hagarism: The Making of the Islamic World by Patricia Crone, Michael Cook', *Bulletin of the School of Oriental and African Studies* 41 (1978), 155–6.
Wansbrough, J. *The Sectarian Milieu*. Oxford: Oxford University Press, 1978.
Watson, A. *Aurelian and the Third Century*. London: Routledge, 2003.
Watt, W. M. 'Belief in a "High God" in pre-Islamic Mecca', *Journal of Semitic Studies* 16 (1971), 35–40.
Watt, W. M. *Muḥammad at Mecca*. Oxford: Oxford University Press, 1953.
Watt, W. M. *Muḥammad at Medina*. Oxford: Oxford University Press, 1956.
Watt, W. M. 'The Qurʾān and Belief in a "High God"', in *Proceedings of the Ninth Congress of the Union Européenne ses Arabisants et Islamisants: Amsterdam, 1st to 7th September 1978*, ed. R. Peters, 228–34. Leiden: Brill, 1981.
Webb, P. 'Ethnicity, Power and Umayyad Society: The Rise and Fall of the People of Maʿadd 1', in *The Umayyad World*, ed. A. Marsham, 65–102. Abingdon: Ashgate, 2020.
Webb, P. *Imagining the Arabs: Arab Identity and the Rise of Islam*. Edinburgh: Edinburgh University Press, 2016.
Weerakkody, D. P. M. *Taprobanê: Ancient Sri Lanka as Known to Greeks and Romans*. Turnhout: Brepols, 1997.
Weil, G. *Geschichte der Chalifen*. Mannheim: F. Bassermann, 1846–1862.
Wellhausen, J. *Reste arabischen Heidentums*. Berlin: De Gruyter, 1961.
Whately, C. 'Strategy, Diplomacy and Frontiers: A Bibliographic Essay', in *War and Warfare in Late Antiquity*, ed. A. Sarantis and N. Christie, 101–52. Leiden: Brill, 2013.
Whitehouse, D. and Williamson, A. 'Sasanian Maritime Trade', *Iran* 11 (1973), 29–49.
Whitfield, S. 'Was there a Silk Road?', *Asian Medicine* 3 (2007), 201–13.

Whittow, M. 'Rethinking the Jafnids: New Approaches to Rome's Arab Allies', in *Les Jafnides: Des rois arabes au service de Byzance (vie siècle de l'ère chrétienne)*, ed. D. Genequand and C. J. Robin, 11–36. Paris: Éditions De Boccard, 2015.

Wickham, C. *Framing the Early Middle Ages: Europe and the Mediterranean, 400–800*. Oxford: Oxford University Press, 2005.

Witakowski, W. 'Syrian Influences in Ethiopian Culture', in *Languages and Cultures of Eastern Christianity: Ethiopian*, ed. A. Bausi, 197–208. Farnham: Routledge, 2012.

Wong, D. C. *Chinese Steles: Pre-Buddhist and Buddhist Use of a Symbolic Form*. Honolulu: University of Hawai'i Press, 2004.

Wood, P. 'Christianity and the Arabs in the Sixth Century', in *Inside and Out: Interactions between Rome and the Peoples on the Arabian and Egyptian Frontiers in Late Antiquity*, ed. J. H. F. Dijkstra and G. Fisher, 353–68. Leuven: Peeters, 2014.

Wood, P. '*We Have No King but Christ': Christian Political Thought in Greater Syria on the Eve of the Arab Conquest (c.400–585)*. Oxford: Oxford University Press, 2010.

Woolf, G. *Becoming Roman: The Origins of Provincial Civilization in Gaul*. Cambridge: Cambridge University Press, 1998.

Young, S. H. *Conceiving the Indian Buddhist Patriarchs in China*. Honolulu: University of Hawaii Press, 2015.

Yule, P. 'Zafar: The Capital of the Ancient Himyarite Empire Rediscovered', *Jemen-Report* 36 (2005), 22–9.

Zellentin, H. M. *The Qur'ān's Legal Culture: The Didascalia Apostolorum as a Point of Departure*. Tübingen: Mohr Siebeck, 2013.

Zellentin, H. M. (ed.), *The Qur'an's Reformation of Judaism and Christianity: Return to the Origins*. Abingdon: Ashgate, 2019.

Zwettler, M. J. 'Maʿadd in Late-Ancient Arabian Epigraphy and Other pre-Islamic Sources', *Wiener Zeitschrift für die Kunde des Morgenlandes* 90 (2000), 223–309.

Index

ʿAden, 71
Adulis, 101, 102, 105, 107, 113–15, 117
Aksūm, 74–5, 81–3, 96, 101–19, 122–31, 210–15
Aksūmite rulers
  ʿEzana, 74, 81–3, 113–14
  Kaleb, 107, 111–19, 126, 211
al-Ṭabarī, 61, 64, 94, 105, 118, 120–3, 125, 138–9, 142, 177, 180, 196, 205
Alexandria, 55, 67, 98, 113, 124, 143–5
Ammianus Marcellinus, 26, 45, 46, 57, 153
Antioch, 42, 56–7, 99, 145–7, 168, 212
Arabic, 2–4, 28, 37–8, 51, 61, 95–6, 151–3, 183, 190, 216
Aramaic, 77, 83, 124, 200
Armenia, 43, 68, 98, 112, 134, 217
ʾAsd, 28, 48, 136

Bible, 25, 86, 116, 124, 197, 216
Bowersock, Glen W., 15–16
Brown, Peter, 15
Buddhism, 10, 170, 216
Buṣrā, 41, 44, 46, 49

Caliphate, 37–8, 131, 194, 214
Callinicum, 103, 155
Central Asia, 17, 44, 104, 128
Chalcedonians, 63, 98–9, 109, 116, 125, 133, 141, 144–8, 165
China, 10, 51, 65, 103, 104, 128, 159, 169–70, 215
Chronicle of Zuqnīn, 106–7, 113, 124
Church councils
  Chalcedon, 40, 56–7, 62, 114, 143
  Constantinople, 56–7
  Ephesus, 56–7, 65
  Nicaea, 55–7
Church of the East, 100, 108–9, 124, 146–8
conversion, 51–5, 62, 64, 67, 73, 82–94, 113–16, 126–7, 148–9
Cosmas Indicopleustes, 72, 102, 106, 124
Crone, Patricia, 12, 19, 174

desert, 23–6, 63, 67, 167
Dura-Europos, 42, 43

Edessa, 29, 93, 99, 138, 143, 149
ethnicity, 33–6, 86, 105, 141, 167, 217
Eusebius of Caesarea, 29, 52, 55

Fowden, Garth, 16, 39

Gəʿəz, 75, 81–3, 111, 115, 116, 124, 131
Germans, 27, 50, 159, 163
Goths, 163, 216
Greek, 14, 27, 48, 80–2, 88, 105, 129, 149, 152, 171

ḥadīth, 12, 19, 201
Hatra, 29, 39, 42
Ḥawrān, 2, 150, 152, 155
Hawting, Gerald, 179–80, 202
Hebrew, 76–8, 86, 89
henotheism, 52, 79, 83–4, 177, 208, 211
High God, 74, 80, 84, 187–93, 206
Ḥijāz, 4, 19, 119–20, 172–9, 184, 190–2, 196–8, 200–2, 214–20
Ḥimyar, 30–2, 70–131, 208–15
Himyarite rulers
  Abīkarib Asʿad, 30–1, 102
  Abraha, 31, 117–25, 156
  Maʿdīkarib Yaʿfur, 31, 96
  Malkīkarib Yuhaʾmin, 71, 79, 90
  Shurihbʾīl Yakkuf, 72, 93
  Sumūyafaʿ Ashwaʿ, 103, 111
  Yūsuf, 96–111
Ḥīrah, 61, 138, 147–8, 214
Ḥujrids, 95, 109, 135–7, 147
ḥunafāʾ, 89, 178, 201–2
Huns, 27, 45, 50, 128, 160, 163

Ibn al-Kalbī, 88, 176–80, 184–8, 201
Ibn Isḥāq, 88, 94, 100, 105, 118–21, 125, 178, 184, 196–8, 201

Imru' al-Qays, 28–30, 64
Indian Ocean, 101–6, 110
Iranian rulers
  Ardashīr I, 5, 51
  Bahram V, 107
  Hormizd IV, 134
  Kavādh I, 43, 103
  Khosrow I, 104, 107, 125, 134, 139, 165
  Khosrow II, 134, 138, 146, 165
  Narseh, 5, 47
  Shāpūr I, 5, 41–2, 47, 49, 64
  Shāpūr II, 42–4, 64
  Shāpūr III, 5, 43
  Shirin, 146, 165

Jafnid rulers
  Abū Karīb, 153
  Abū Karīb, 119, 145
  Ḥārith, 136–7, 143–4, 150, 151, 153–6, 162, 181
  Mundhir, 137–8, 145, 150, 151, 154, 156, 158
  Nuʿmān, 138, 145, 154
Jafnids, 132–71, 213–16
Jewish sympathizers, 70, 73, 80–1, 86–91, 210, 219
jinn, 192–5
John Malalas, 72, 106, 113, 118, 136, 151, 155

Kaʿbah, 91, 120–2, 175–8, 189, 201–2
Kaldellis, Anthony, 5, 37, 149
Kindah, 31, 97, 119, 135, 147, 185
Korea, 215–16

Maʿadd, 31, 48, 102, 104, 108, 119, 135
Macdonald, Michael, 2, 29, 35, 51, 183
Manichaeism, 55, 64
Maʾrib, 79, 111, 118, 123–5
Martyrium Sancti Arethae, 97–8, 101, 112, 118
Mavia, 47, 67
Mazzarino, Santo, 15, 217
Mecca, 12, 119–20, 173–7, 188, 196, 198, 201, 207, 216
Medina, 33, 119, 173, 191, 196, 200, 205
Mesopotamia, 30, 60, 134, 146, 161, 214
Miaphysites, 39, 98–100, 109, 116–17, 133, 140–8, 159, 166, 211
miḥrāb, 91
mikrāb, 87
Millar, Fergus, 14–15, 42, 168
Muḥammad, 189–97, 200–7, 218–19
Musaylimah, 205–6
mushrikūn, 179–80, 186, 194, 197, 201, 205, 218

Nabateans, 4, 26–7, 49, 152, 172–3, 176, 182, 217
Najd, 28, 30, 33, 48, 172, 206
Najrān, 72, 92–101, 109–16, 126, 211
Namārah, 28, 30, 47
Nasrid rulers
  Mundhir, 97, 109, 119, 135, 137, 139, 147–8, 153, 155, 181
  Nuʿmān, 138–9, 148, 181
Naṣrids, 28–9, 47–8, 97, 108, 119, 135–41, 147–8, 161–2, 213
Neo-Assyrians, 24–5, 35, 172
Neuwirth, Angelika, 18

Palmyra, 42–4, 48, 54–5
Persian Gulf, 26, 42, 46, 59–61, 69, 110, 138, 169, 213
Petra, 54, 58, 153, 164, 172
Philostorgius, 71–2, 82, 87, 90, 106
pilgrimage, 120, 157, 165, 169, 175–7, 187
plague, 119, 130, 203–4, 213
poetry, 21
Procopius, 14, 89, 103–4, 117, 153–5, 164, 181, 203
Provincia Arabia, 26–9, 41

Qanīʾ, 80, 89, 106
qiblah, 91, 122, 201
Qur'ān, 19, 32, 119, 131, 176–80, 187, 205, 219
Quraysh, 120–1, 174–7, 184, 196, 201, 205, 218

Raḥmān, 189–94, 206, 218
Red Sea, 92, 101, 103–5, 108, 117, 125–31, 211
Robin, Christian, 73, 85, 86, 206
Romanization, 14, 217
Roman rulers
  Anastasius I, 43, 50, 94, 109, 136, 141
  Augustus, 54, 82
  Aurelian, 42–3, 53
  Caracalla, 41
  Constantine, 29, 39, 51, 219
  Constantius I, 53
  Constantius II, 43, 81
  Diocletian, 44, 64
  Heraclius, 138
  Honorius, 72
  Jovian, 43
  Julian, 47, 62
  Justin I, 97, 102, 109, 111, 117, 141
  Justin II, 104, 107, 134, 137, 141
  Justinian, 103–4, 109, 112–13, 134, 136–7, 139, 141–3, 146, 153, 156–8, 164–5, 203
  Leo, 64
  Maurice, 134, 137, 141–2, 145–6, 165
  Philip, 41
  Septimius Severus, 41
  Theodora, 141–3, 146, 165
  Theodosius I, 43, 56
  Tiberius II, 141, 145

Roman rulers (cont.)
  Trajan, 4, 26–7
  Valens, 47
  Valerian, 41
Ruṣāfah, 59, 137, 157–8, 164, 168, 175
Ruwāfa, 27

Sabean, 30–2, 48, 70, 75, 118, 121, 190, 200
Safaitic, 15, 33, 48–51, 50, 74, 91, 177, 183, 190, 200, 217–18
Salīḥids, 46, 90, 135
Ṣanʿāʾ, 13, 120–3
Shahid, Irfan, 13–15, 40, 114, 142, 155, 166, 168
Sogdians, 104–5, 107, 127–30, 160
Sol Invictus, 52–4, 218
Sozomen, 47, 63, 68, 88, 178
steppe, 8, 27, 44, 127, 128, 130, 133, 154, 157, 161, 162, 164
Stylites, 63
Syriac, 26, 61, 95, 99, 116, 124, 205, 216

tafsīr, 12, 13, 19, 33
talbiyāt, 187–8, 190
Tanūkh, 43, 46, 48, 61, 153
Tayma, 25, 172
Thamud, 173, 203–4
Theos Hypsistos, 54, 80
trade, 17, 50, 61, 65, 71, 81, 101–10, 126–30, 157, 168, 174, 176, 213
Trimingham, John, 40, 167
Türks, 107, 127–8, 168, 171

Ummah, 193, 196, 201, 208
Umm al-Jimāl, 40, 44, 46, 59, 153, 184, 190, 212, 217

Xiongnu, 10, 36, 169–71

Zabad, 4, 95, 152
Ẓafār, 71, 111
Zoroastrianism, 9, 68

For EU product safety concerns, contact us at Calle de José Abascal, 56–1°, 28003 Madrid, Spain or eugpsr@cambridge.org.

www.ingramcontent.com/pod-product-compliance
Lightning Source LLC
Chambersburg PA
CBHW060032080425
24757CB00004B/200
* 9 7 8 1 0 0 9 2 5 3 0 0 0 *